International Com
Vocational Education and Training for
Intermediate Skills

International Comparisons of Vocational Education and Training for Intermediate Skills

Edited by

Paul Ryan

 The Falmer Press

(A member of the Taylor & Francis Group)
London · New York · Philadelphia

UK   The Falmer Press, 4 John St., London, WC1N 2ET
USA   The Falmer Press, Taylor & Francis Inc., 1900 Frost Road, 101, Bristol, PA 19007

First published 1991

British Library Cataloguing in Publication Data

A catalogue record for this book is available from the British Library

ISBN 1 85000 899 X cloth
ISBN 1 85000 900 7 paper

Set in 10/12 pt Times by
Graphicraft Typesetters Ltd., Hong Kong

Printed in Great Britain by Burgess Science Press, Basingstoke on paper which has a specified pH value on final paper manufacture of not less than 7.5 and is therefore 'acid free'.

Contents

Notes on Contributors   vii
Preface   viii
Introduction: Comparative Research on Vocational Education and
Training   1

Part 1: Uses and Methods

1 The Grass Looked Greener — Some Thoughts on the Influence
   of Comparative Vocational Training Research on the UK Policy
   Debate
   Ewart Keep   23
2 Scotland v. England: The Place of 'Home Internationals' in
   Comparative Research
   David Raffe   47
3 Prospective Evaluation through Comparative Analysis:
   Youth Training in a Time-Space Perspective
   Richard Rose   68
4 Institutional Incentives and Skill Creation: Preconditions for a
   High-Skill Equilibrium
   David Finegold   93

Part 2: VET, Products and Skill Utilization

5 Productivity and Vocational Skills in Services in Britain and
   Germany: Hotels
   S.J. Prais, Valerie Jarvis and Karin Wagner   119
6 Training Strategies and Microelectronics in the Engineering
   Industries of the UK and Germany
   Adrian Campbell and Malcolm Warner   146
7 Japanese Engineers, Lifetime Employment and In-Company
   Training: Continuity and Change in the Management of
   Engineering Manpower Resources
   Kevin McCormick   159

Contents

Part 3: VET Comparisons in the European Community

8 Interactions in the Markets for Education, Training and Labour:
   A European Perspective on Intermediate Skills
   Robert M. Lindley   185

9 Interventions in Market Financing of Training in the European
   Community
   Keith Drake   207

Part 4: VET and Labour Market Structure

10 Institutional Structures and the Provision of Intermediate Level
   Skills: Lessons from Canada and Hong Kong
   David N. Ashton, Malcolm J. Maguire and Johnny Sung   233

11 Initial Training, Labour Market Structure and Public Policy:
   Intermediate Skills in British and German Industry
   David Marsden and Paul Ryan   251

Index   286

Notes on Contributors

David N. Ashton is Professor of Sociology and Director of Research in the Labour Market Studies Group at the University of Leicester.

Adrian Campbell is lecturer in the School of Public Policy at the University of Birmingham.

Keith Drake is Director of Continuing Education and Training at the University of Manchester.

David Finegold is Research Fellow at the Centre for Education and Industry at the University of Warwick.

Valerie Jarvis was at the time of writing Research Officer at the National Institute of Economic and Social Research, London.

Ewart Keep is Research Fellow in the Industrial Relations Research Unit at the University of Warwick.

Robert M. Lindley is Professor and Director of the Institute for Employment Research at the University of Warwick.

Kevin McCormick is Lecturer in Sociology and Director of the Unit for Comparative Research on Industrial Relations at the University of Sussex.

Malcolm J. Maguire is Research Fellow in the Labour Market Studies Group at the University of Leicester.

David Marsden is Senior Lecturer in the Department of Industrial Relations at the London School of Economics.

S.J. Prais is Senior Research Fellow at the National Institute of Economic and Social Research and Visiting Professor at City University, London.

David Raffe is Reader in Education and co-Director of the Centre for Educational Sociology at the University of Edinburgh.

Richard Rose is Professor and Director of the Centre for the Study of Public Policy at the University of Strathclyde and Guest Professor at the Wissenschaftszentrum, Berlin.

Paul Ryan is Lecturer in the Faculty of Economics and Politics and Fellow of King's College at the University of Cambridge.

Johnny Sung is Research Associate in the Labour Market Studies Group at the University of Leicester.

Karin Wagner is Senior Research Fellow at the Technical University, Berlin.

Malcolm Warner is Fellow of Wolfson College and a member of the Institute of Management Studies at the University of Cambridge.

Preface

The papers in this volume originated in contributions to a seminar of the same title held at the University of Manchester in September 1989. The conference was funded by the Skills Unit of the Training Agency (Employment Department), as it then was, to bring together research and policy constituencies to discuss the recent work of British practitioners of comparative research on vocational preparation, focussing primarily upon intermediate skills.

On behalf of the contributors I thank the sponsors of the seminar for their interest and support. The success of the seminar reflected the commitment shown to it by the staff of both the Skills Unit and the Evaluation and Research branch of the Training Agency, in particular the impetus given by Paul Keen and Eric Galvin, and the organizational diligence of Ken Moody. The views expressed in the volume are, of course, the responsibility of the authors and are not necessarily shared by the seminar's sponsors.

The seminar's *rapporteurs*, David Finegold, Ian Gow, Hilary Steedman and Peter Senker, introduced the papers and initiated discussion. Their efforts, which are reflected only indirectly in this volume, gave the discussions a flying start, not least by providing those of us who contributed papers with a more concise and effective presentation than we might have managed ourselves. Richard Layard and Richard Hillier kindly initiated discussion at the final session, reviewing the issues raised for them by the seminar.

Thanks go also to our publishing editors, Christine Cox and Malcolm Clarkson, for seeing this volume through to publication.

Paul Ryan

Introduction: Comparative Research on Vocational Education and Training

Une nation commerçante est toujours fort alerte sur ses intérêts, et ne néglige rien des connaissances qui peuvent être utiles à son négoce (Voltaire, *Lettres Philosophiques*).[1]

Introduction

The collection of letters in which Voltaire in 1734 conveyed to French readers his impressions of the leading commercial nation of the time belongs to a long tradition of outlining the practices of another country so as to highlight the shortcomings of one's own and promote their reform. Voltaire found the religious tolerance, political freedom and empirical orientation of English life and thought attractive enough in themselves. But he also contrasted them, implicitly and explicitly, to prevailing French attributes as part of his interest in reforming France. His work contributed in its turn to the subsequent recasting of French institutions.

The boot is on the other foot nowadays in terms of vocational education and training — an area to which the interests of commercial nations are increasingly alive and concerning which useful knowledge is plentiful. The defects of English practice have been widely documented by comparative research. The need for reform is even widely accepted. The problem is which route to take and how far to proceed. French and German practice have become increasingly potent sources of both concern and inspiration, reaching recently up to ministerial level in both leading British political parties.

Although comparative assessments of British education and training practice date back to the last century, such research proliferated during the 1980s. Prais (1981) demonstrated the gulf between the extent of qualification in the British and German labour forces. The recently established 'social effect' school of comparative research on work and skills expanded its range to include Britain (Sorge and Warner, 1980).

Much of the subsequent momentum has derived from the research of S.J.

Prais, Hilary Steedman, Karin Wagner and their colleagues at the National Institute for Economic and Social Research (NIESR), published with increasing frequency in the Institute's *Review* as the decade proceded. Studies which compared British productivity in a wide range of sectors — metalworking, woodworking, clothing, hotel and retailing — to that of their German or French counterparts documented large shortfalls in Britain and attributed them largely to the superior vocational preparation of French and German workers.[2]

The effort has been joined by a wide range of academic, consulting, government and business contributions, some of which are represented in this collection. Comparative research has become an industry in its own right, helping to define problems and suggesting lines along which solutions may be sought.

The Problem of Intermediate Skills

A key British deficiency highlighted by the research of the last decade involves intermediate skills — i.e., those above routine skills but below professional ones. Comparative studies of British productivity find the most pronounced underproduction (and even misutilization) of skills in the intermediate category.

The category 'intermediate skills' is heterogeneous in content and imprecise in its boundaries. Its centre of gravity is what in British industry have traditionally been termed craft and technician skills, along with their analogues in the service sector. In the British context the intermediate category must also be construed to include jobs and occupations for which operational and perceived skill requirements may not be high but where an intermediate level of qualification — as opposed to a lower one or none at all — could raise productivity significantly. In other words, employers may use less intermediate skill than they should in their own interests — a possibility raised by more than one contribution to this volume.

The gap between the extent of intermediate skills in the German and French workforces, on the one hand, and the British, on the other, has increased since the mid–1970s, the period for which Prais documented the Anglo-German gap. It will increase further in the medium term, given that French qualification rates are rising rapidly and that British efforts have concentrated thus far on sub-craft skills. Our efforts come late and still aim low.

The importance of intermediate skills for British economic performance reflects three distinctive attributes. Firstly, such skills are costly to develop, which marks them off from routine skills. Secondly, they are — or could readily become — highly transferable across employers, which marks them off from employer-specific skills, however costly. Thirdly, in Britain they have traditionally been developed predominantly through workplace-based training programmes such as apprenticeship, which marks them off from professional skills.

These three attributes not only help to bound the domain of intermediate skills. They also explain why the defects of British vocational preparation have been most marked at intermediate level. Costly transferable skills are the ones for which market failure is liable to be most serious (Ryan, 1984). Employer provision of training is discouraged by a range of informational, contractual and organizational difficulties; employee self-sponsorship, by those of finance, insurance and attitude. Such obstacles are potentially general, but manifestations of the problem differ across countries and different ways of dealing with it have been adopted. The problem is particularly serious in Britain and this country has proved relatively unsuccessful at designing policies to counter it.

The resulting long term economic damage has been indicated at sectoral level by the NIESR research. The short to medium term aggregate consequences have also been serious. Rising shortages of craft and technical skills in industry and construction, reflected in long and increasing job vacancy durations, contributed during the recovery of 1986–9 to the resurgence of wage inflation and the rapid deterioration of the visible trade balance. They thereby helped precipitate yet another 'stop/go' curtailment of growth which, as it slowly curbs inflationary and trade problems, rewidens the productivity gap between Britain and its major trading partners.

There is clearly much more to British economic problems than shortages of intermediate skills. The country would however address its economic difficulties from a much better position could it ensure an adequate supply and an appropriate mix of such skills (Steedman, Mason and Wagner, 1991).

The problem of intermediate skills also touches on issues of equity. Inadequate skill development in Britain itself reflects an education system which has become notorious for, as it has been put, failing more than half of its young participants; and an industrial system still relatively reliant upon 'low trust' and 'low skill' strategies, in which dependence upon shop-floor skills is, as reported in chapter 6 below, often a matter of unease rather than relief to management. The weakness of the country's intermediate skills stock is part of the weakness of opportunities for individuals outside high ability or socially advantaged groups to improve their lot, whether through schooling or through training and promotion within employment.

Scope of Volume

This collection represents the convergence of three factors: the mushrooming of comparative research on vocational preparation, concern about enduring supply side constraints upon British economic performance and long-standing interest in the political economy of intermediate skills. Such interests led to the holding of the 1989 Manchester seminar to discuss recent research in the area.

The seminar was attended in roughly equal numbers by academics and public officials. Financial constraints and a strong response from national academics led to a distinct insularity in the organization of the seminar. Coverage was limited to research involving Britain; contributions and attendance, to persons based primarily or wholly in Britain. The absence of foreign comparative researchers interested in this country — a group less numerous than its British counterpart but one which has already distinguished itself — meant the absence from the proceedings of the perspective from abroad.

The main area of comparative interest amongst Britons, judging by these contributions, is Germany, rather than France; and, more generally, the EC, rather than Sweden or the USA, which are both unrepresented.[3] French practice is notably underrepresented in this volume relative to its place in the comparative research of both the last decade and probably the present one as well. The appeal of German vocational preparation to British research is underlined by its presence in six out of the eight studies in this volume which report on a specific comparative research project. Interest in Germany is motivated partly by its economic and vocational successes and partly by a sense that effective learning may be feasible, given important institutional similarities to Britain — notably in the predominance of the workplace in industrial training.

Although the volume consists for the most part of studies which conform to the rubric contained in the title, three deviations are evident. Firstly, the focus is widened from vocational to all education in the studies which deal with Scotland, Japan and Canada, reflecting the important vocational implications of general education in those countries. Secondly, there is little on vocational secondary education. Comparative assessments of, e.g., the Technical and Vocational Education Initiative or work experience programmes for school students would have been appropriate to this volume but eluded editorial search.[4] Finally, the range of skills represented here extends outside the intermediate category in the case of professional engineers in Germany and Japan. However, in the former case the links to intermediate skills are direct and important; in the latter, indirect only but that seems a small price to pay for coverage of key aspects of Japanese institutions.

Contents of Volume

The first section of the book concerns usage and methods in international comparisons. Ewart Keep reviews in chapter 1 the effects of comparative research on policy towards vocational education and training (VET) in Britain during the last decade. International comparisons have generated an abundance of results relevant to VET policy. They have also had a pivotal role in defining perceptions of the problems to which policy response is required. At the same time, only uneven and disappointing use has been made of their findings. In particular, British policy makers have ignored the social and institutional context of particular VET attributes which they seek to import, thereby jeopardizing the success of the effort.

Three factors are advanced to account for the defective influence on British policy of comparative research. The first is a high-speed, *ad hoc* approach to policy development, in which new VET schemes come and go in successive short life-cycles, and which copies rather than learns from foreign approaches. The second is 'ideological filtering': leaving out the lessons that conflict with political preconception, however integral they may be to VET success abroad. Statutory backing for and social partnership in VET institutions are two notable casualties in this area. The third is 'interest accommodation', particularly the influence upon the government of covert employer resistance to the implications of comparative research.

Keep argues that three desirable attributes of a VET system — transparency, coherence and stability — have consequently been lacking not only in British practice but also in policy response to comparative research. He remains nevertheless optimistic about the role of international comparisons, both in terms of the variety of neglected countries and issues and for their potential influence on policy, presumably under more propitious political conditions.

Comparative research is bedevilled by the difficulty, when assessing the role of a particular VET practice, of standardizing for the host of related factors which differ between the countries in question. David Raffe points in chapter 2 to a comparative source in which standardization can be less problematic: the 'home international', in his case Anglo-Scottish comparisons, but more generally intranational and interregional ones within unitary states. The advantage lies clearly in the similarity of background contexts within most unitary states. Against a common backdrop the effects of divergent VET practices may be traced quasi-experimentally with relative clarity. Raffe notes that economic integration may increasingly move comparative research on EC countries, which dominates this volume, towards the grounds of the 'home international'. The methodological issue is taken up later in this introduction.

Raffe points also to myth as a potent source of both momentum and confusion in comparative research, a point also returned to below. The myth with which he is concerned is that of Scottish education, which is widely perceived in Scotland as 'broad, accessible, democratic, meritocratic and community oriented, particularly compared to England'. Raffe distinguishes the valid from the invalid in the myth of Scottish education. He champions his adopted country to good effect in urging the superiority of several attributes of Scottish VET to those of its English equivalent — not least in the potential of the Scottish Action Plan to test whether a VET system as heterogeneous as the British can be reformed largely intact or whether radical surgery is required.

The importance of considering time as well as place is emphasized by Richard Rose in chapter 3 in comparing the qualifications of the British and

German labour forces now and, prospectively, in the year 2000. Lags between changes in training policy and the attributes of the labour force reflect the small size of the flows relative to the stocks in question. The gap between the extent of qualification in the two countries will consequently increase during the 1990s. The rarity in Britain of qualified workplace trainers akin to the German *Meister*, whose ranks continue to burgeon, is seen as a key constraint on improving British performance.

Rose argues that Britain's future position, assuming the continuance of current trends and policies, should therefore be compared with Germany's situation, particularly its present one, in order both to identify British shortcomings in advance and to promote research which can reduce failure instead of simply documenting its growth.

He also notes the tendency of mainstream economic theory to assume fungibility, or the ready transfer of VET practices from one nation to another, in contrast to the assumption of blockage, or the impossibility of transfer, implicit in much traditional policy discussion. However, as Rose locates VET towards the blockage end of the spectrum, in view of the importance of its social, economic and institutional contexts, he appears implicitly pessimistic about the scope for learning from abroad.

David Finegold considers in chapter 4 the requirements for the 'high-skills equilibrium' which has so rarely been achieved in Britain despite its potential benefits to all parties. He infers three necessary conditions for its realization: a long-term perspective, cooperative structures (within a broadly competitive context) and exposure to competition with foreign VET systems, primarily through internationally traded products.

Defective VET outcomes of the kind often observed in Britain are interpreted in terms of the decisions of rational agents — in particular, individuals, corporate managers and government policy makers — within particular institutional settings, rather than in terms of preordained cultural or social limitations. The second condition for a high-skills outcome — co-operation within competition — evokes game theoretic considerations, with cooperative, skill-favouring solutions promoted both by repetition of the game and by low interest rates, each of which in turn fosters long-term perspectives. The employer's choice between training and poaching as sources of skilled labour provides an outstanding example of strategic interdependence amongst companies and the possibility of skill-promoting as well as skill-denying solutions.

Finegold's approach recognizes the selective presence of high-skill outcomes in contemporary Britain and the need for institutional change to encourage their generalization. The scope for policy is however narrowed by the multiplicity of the institutions which shape agents' choices and the need to operate simultaneously on several fronts. A particular source of difficulty is the need for long-term perspective in public policy, which is impeded in British electoral politics by radical disagreement over education and training policy.

On the other hand, the scope for public policy is enhanced insofar as cultural obstacles are secondary to economic incentives. Moreover, Finegold is optimistic about the potential of VET expansion alone to promote high-skill outcomes by altering the constraints faced by all types of agent.

VET and Product Markets

The second section of the book groups together three papers which examine VET practices in relation to product markets and skill utilization. Two issues come to the fore in all three contributions. The first is the importance of vocational preparation for economic success. The second is the two-way relationship between skill development and utilization in the enterprise, on the one hand, and its product and process strategies on the other.

Chapter 5 reports the National Institute team's study of vocational training and productivity in the hotel sectors of Britain and Germany. S.J. Prais, Valerie Jarvis and Karin Wagner estimate a German advantage in labour productivity of between 50 and 100 per cent higher even than in manufacturing. Differences in inputs of physical capital and technology are too small to account for much of the national differences in productivity. However, that in labour quality is substantial and, through the more flexible work organization and leaner staffing which it both permits and encourages, prospectively the key determinant of Britain's productivity shortfall.

The key difference in labour quality is the extent to which employees possess certified intermediate skills. In the hotels of both countries the lowest jobs are performed overwhelmingly by unqualified workers; differences in the incidence of high level qualifications are also small. However, most reception and supervisory workers in Germany possess intermediate vocational qualifications, in contrast to the small minority of their British counterparts who do so. Hotel managers consequently delegate more work to subordinates in Germany, leaving themselves free to concentrate on more complex tasks, including planning, which tend to be neglected by a British management less able (and perhaps less inclined) to rely on the limited skills possessed by its subordinates. Supplies of intermediate skills, functional flexibility and economic performance thus emerge as no less closely linked in a leading service sector than in industry.

The gap in skill stocks between the two national industries has widened recently at the crucial intermediate level, where German training output has grown at twice the British rate. The British certification effort has concentrated unfortunately on lower level skills, which are too limited to narrow an already large productivity gap.

Intermediate skills are also linked to product markets in Campbell and Warner's comparison in chapter 6 of skills, training and innovation in the metalworking sectors of Britain and Germany. The comparison is by no means uniformly favourable to Germany. German companies, like their British counterparts, suffer from serious shortages of electronics engineers. For intermediate skills, recruitment and training differences between the countries may even have declined as best British corporate practice has improved.

However, a wide gap endures between both the product and process strategies of British and German firms. British companies rely on subcontracting to acquire electronic sub-products, whereas their German competitors normally maintain the necessary expertise in-house. British companies divorce design from production; German ones seek their integration. German firms have responded to new technology by strengthening their intermediate skill base; British ones by reliance on graduate level skills, consistent with widespread managerial aversion to depending on, let alone developing, shopfloor skills.

Campbell and Warner note that British practices may claim to use scarce skills more efficiently by concentrating them in electronics subcontractors. However, such 'allocative' efficiencies are swamped by the 'productive' efficiencies arising from the integration of functions within large German producers. The absence of an adequate intermediate skills base in Britain combines with low managerial appreciation of its importance to weaken product design, manufacturing success and innovation in British companies, impeding necessary increases in the share of electronics in products.

Chapter 7, by Kevin McCormick, considers the Japanese experience, which has provided so powerful a stimulus to the rethinking of VET practice in Western economies. His concern is Japanese employment practice, notably lifetime employment; his context, graduate engineering employment in a group of large industrial companies. He makes selective comparison with personnel practice by large British employers.

McCormick elaborates several attributes of Japanese employment practice: job security, pay progression with seniority and performance, extensive on-the-job training, departmental rotation and group consciousness. Such practices are conventionally interpreted nowadays as the result of a successful business strategy, based on high rates of research, innovation and output growth. McCormick argues that faltering growth prospects, unfavourable demographic trends and changing employee values are already eroding lifetime employment practices, which he even describes as 'yesterday's model'.

At the same time, such practices remain economically functional for the extensive training and employee motivation for which Japanese industry is renowned. McCormick points also to the reverse dependence of successful business strategy on employment practice. Lifetime employment has promoted high growth by Japanese firms through the internal development of managerial skills and attitudes and the linkage of employee career prospects to corporate growth. However, those employment and product strategies could not be adopted without the financial independence of Japanese companies: the absence of take-over threats is central to the heavy weight of managerial and employee interests relative to those of owners.

Similarities between Britain and Japan are noted, particularly in levels of spending on training and the concentration of schooling upon general education. But a long-term perspective less commonly informs employee selection and development in Britain, partly because of the presence of an external labour market for experienced engineers, which alters employee career prospects and employer recruitment policy.

In seeking to match the training and motivational advantages of Japanese firms, inappropriate financial institutions and cultural differences make it impossible for Britain simply to import Japanese practices — which would in any case entail side effects which a liberal society might wish to avoid. McCormick advocates instead functional equivalents to Japanese practice, such as fiscal encouragement of company training, and industrial democracy for increased employee commitment. A further option of increasing importance may be added to his list: to import Japanese ownership and management and observe the employment practices which it finds effective under British conditions.

EC-wide Studies

The third part of the book groups together two papers which cover the European Community. Both synthesize the findings of recent research projects which involved noncomparative national studies, the first project dealing with occupational change, skills and qualifications, the second with the finance of training.

Robert Lindley reports in chapter 8 on research sponsored by the Commission of the European Communities into the links between occupational structures, skills and qualifications in individual member states. He questions the presumption, common in this volume as well as in general discussion, that requirements for intermediate skills are rising inexorably and that training for them must increase if shortages are to be avoided. Dutch evidence suggests that the output of qualifications has increased more rapidly than have the skill requirement of jobs — reviving the threat of overqualification and educational 'crowding out' which caused extensive concern in the 1970s in the context of higher education. Skill polarization is also apparent in Dutch employment, with higher and lower level occupations growing at the expense of intermediate ones. Lindley also urges that skill utilization and product development, rather than training levels, constitute the binding constraints on economic performance and may abort the benefits of any increase in training for intermediate skills in Britain.

However, contradictory tendencies are also apparent. German evidence suggests a shift in the functional division of labour from production towards maintenance and repair skills, associated with electronic technology, to an even greater extent than is suggested by standard statistics. New occupations are created and skill requirements raised in the intermediate area, posing threats of *under*qualification and skill shortages. In this scenario, British VET comes under increased pressure at a vulnerable point, given that workplace-based general training has proved inadequate and school-based preparation has not developed as a substitute.

Lindley notes the variety of non-employer provision and the role of individuals in sponsoring their own training in the US as attributes which Britain might seek to emulate. Finally, he predicts that completion of the European single market will increasingly restrict productivity-relevant public subsidies to the VET category, making British shortcomings in the regulation and finance of VET increasingly damaging.

In chapter 9, Keith Drake surveys recent national research, sponsored mostly by the European Centre for the Promotion of Vocational Training (CEDEFOP), on the financing of post-secondary training in the EC. Noting the variety of financing modes, he urges the importance of financial arrangements for training outcomes. It is encouraging to find that major expansions of training have been associated recently with fairly straightforward financial reforms, involving in each case more public involvement, in both Denmark and the Netherlands.

National financial arrangements are located in practice between two poles: that of unregulated markets, dominated by the decisions of employers and individuals, a situation to which Britain approximates most closely; and that of dominance by public funds, as allocated by government fiat, a situation to which France lies closest. Market and public funding coexist in all economies and neither can claim an unambiguous increase in importance in the last decade. However, Drake holds that market finance would account for the majority of spending in an ideal set of accounts, even if it does not do so in those currently available, particularly in France. (This outcome presumably reflects the exclusion of vocational education from the scope of the research project).

While Drake accepts the importance of market failure, in terms of equity as well as efficiency, as a rationale for the public finance of training, he also recognizes government failure, particularly in tendencies towards control slippage and inflexibility of content. He assesses pragmatically the merits of the two mechanisms, arguing from French and German experience that they may even complement each other, in that employer willingness to fund training may rise in response to that of the state. However, Drake's observation that no EC state relies so much on the market nor shows so little concern about market and managerial failure as does the UK suggests that he would accept more government failure in this country in order to expand finance for training.

VET and Labour Markets

Part Four comprises two studies of VET practices in relation primarily to labour market structure. Both emphasize the distinction between occupational and internal labour markets and the need to align vocational preparation with such features.

David Ashton, Malcolm Maguire and Johnny Sung embark in chapter 10 on a geographically adventurous and original comparison involving Canada and Hong Kong. They distinguish three levels of skill: routinized, applied and conceptual. Intermediate skills, on which they concentrate, are seen as primarily applied — though the importance of their conceptual component may be growing — and it is applied skills which show the greatest variation and fragility of provision.

Preparation for intermediate skills in Canada has increased indirectly by expanding general education, relying on a strong supply of conceptual skills to compensate for both the limited training in applied skills which is provided in employer-based internal labour markets and the low coverage of apprenticeship. Hong Kong has met similar needs by different means: an extension of vocational upper-secondary education and the public and collective funding of occupational training through Industrial Training Boards (ITBs). Both countries have thereby achieved significant advances in preparation for intermediate skills during the last two decades.

Ashton, Maguire and Sung see Britain as in great need of fresh ideas, given the withdrawal of state support for occupational training, the weak achievements of public training schemes and the academic slant and underdeveloped state of upper secondary education. They deny the possibility of simply copying either the Canadian or the Hong Kong route. In particular, class divisions in society and schooling provide a formidable obstacle to any approach along Canadian lines. But they call for the informing of British debate by the kind of approaches developed in countries such as these whose institutions have historical connections with Britain.

(The apparently successful adoption by Hong Kong of Industrial Training Boards, tried earlier but subsequently abandoned in Britain, suggests a new category of international learning — not simply from the successes of other countries but from their ability to make successes out of our failures. The differing fortunes of ITBs in Hong Kong and Britain provide a promising research topic.)

The final contribution, by David Marsden and Paul Ryan (chapter 11), provided the initial stimulus to the holding of the Manchester seminar, which may excuse its exceptional length. Post-war developments in training for intermediate industrial skills in Britain and Germany are compared with a view to elaborating the conditions for a successful system of workplace training for intermediate industrial skills in Britain.

Marsden and Ryan find evidence from changes in trainee pay, training quality and training volumes in the two countries that training costs to employers are a major influence on the number of training places on offer. The lower trainee pay advocated by the British government would indeed stimulate industrial training. However, such a pay differential cannot be achieved by exhortation or deregulation alone but requires attention to labour market structure. It is most readily achieved in occupational markets with jointly-regulated apprenticeship training; least readily, in internal markets with job training determined solely by employers. However, the British labour market has been moving unevenly from occupational to industrial structures, and from apprenticeship to job training, thereby eroding the institutions needed for government training policy to work. In Germany, by contrast, occupational and internal structures fuse more effectively and a 'low pay, high quality, high volume' apprenticeship system has been progressively consolidated.

Low trainee pay is strictly neither necessary nor sufficient for adequate vocational training. But as long as Britain remains wedded to workplace-based training, a system with attributes similar to German ones remains the target and lower trainee pay a desirable component. That requires the revival of externally regulated and collectively funded apprenticeship, either in name or, if they have not already been too widely discredited, through the radical improvement of both the Youth Training Scheme and National Vocational Qualifications.

The Contribution of International Comparisons

The merits of a volume such as this depend on the power of international comparisons as a research technique. The contributors to this volume clearly feel that comparative research has much to offer — why otherwise would so many do so much of it. At the same time, they show a caution concerning the claims to be made from comparative research which invites a fuller discussion of its scientific potential.

International comparisons are used for description and explanation. They have documented differences in vocational preparation between Britain and other countries. They have also been used to explain why those differences have emerged and why they are important. Description faces its own difficulties, such as noncomparability of national categories, e.g., of vocational qualification. However, it is when comparisons become analytical that their contribution becomes particularly fraught.[5] The difficulties affect historical as well as contemporary comparisons (Kindelberger, 1978: Chapter 1; Elbaum and Lazonick, 1986).

There are two important constraints upon the analytical contribution of comparative research: first, myth; second, its intrinsic informational limits.

The Role of Myth

The influence of myth, stereotype and downright wishful thinking is potentially great in international comparisons. The last of these is by no means restricted to comparative work, but the first two are particularly relevant to it.

Raffe points in chapter 2 to the tendency of national VET systems to generate myths, both within the country and without. Myth requires careful handling, as, while it usually contains important elements of truth, its description of reality is liable to oversimplify, stereotype and distort. To complicate things further, myth can be a powerful influence upon reality in its own right. When favourable, it supports the reproduction of the institutions which it describes by inspiring affection and loyalty. When unfavourable, it can promote change, sometimes at the expense of descriptive accuracy.

Raffe illustrates these points in the Anglo-Scottish context but they apply more widely. Two nationally oriented myths may be seen in modern Britain. The first depicts British vocational preparation as a catalogue of failure and that of Germany, Japan, or some other country close to the heart of the comparatist, as one of overwhelming success. The second holds that the policies of the 1980s have catapulted British training and certification to a level of sophistication well beyond that of, eg. an inflexible and old-fashioned German system.

The unfavourable myth has come to dominate public perceptions during the last decade and now widely affects comparative writing, particularly in the media. It contains a substantial component of truth; but it overlooks the areas in which vocational preparation has been successful in Britain: for example, in some large and foreign-owned companies committed to extensive human resource development; in craft training for the electrical contracting industry; and in much professional education.

The favourable myth is a more recent and fragile development, popular mainly amongst the government officials and training practitioners who developed and implemented the policies of the last decade. It has to overlook more truths than has its unfavourable counterpart, in terms of both the failings of British practices and the merits of foreign ones.

It would be rash to hold that the contributors to this volume have remained unaffected by myth. If they have been so affected, it is clearly more by the unfavourable than by the favourable one, but even then mythologizing should be limited. Some reassurance is provided by the sceptical and empirical orientation of many of the contributions. Raffe leads the way in unpicking the various components of the Scottish educational myth. Prais, Jarvis and Wagner focus on closely observed differences between the British and German hotel sectors. Marsden and Ryan, in their account of the merits of German apprenticeship relative to the Youth Training Scheme, point also to the deficiencies of the former and achievements of the latter.

Informational Limits: Degrees of Freedom

The second difficulty facing the analytical use of comparative research can be illustrated in terms of multivariate statistical inference, with each country as a separate observation and each attribute a quantitative variable — as is indeed sometimes the case in comparative research. A small number of observations — usually two — is selected for the study of a relationship between two variables. For example, the effects of funding on the volume of training may be analyzed through an Anglo-German comparison — an issue addressed by Drake, as well as Marsden and Ryan. If German firms offer more training than do British ones and German apprentices bear a higher share of the costs, can it be inferred that the two features are truly associated, in that lower training costs to employers are truly associated with more training in each country?

It cannot, in general, because other influences on the relationship also differ between the two countries and it is usually impossible to control for their effects. Thus the extent of employer organization and aspects of national culture in the two countries may also affect training levels. Does German industry train more young people than its British counterpart because the latter bear more of the costs themselves? Because German employers are under more external pressure to train? Because they have adopted product strategies which require more skilled labour? Because they are German rather than British? Or because of some mixture of such factors?

With only two observations on three or more potentially influential variables, positive 'degrees of freedom' are absent and it is impossible to establish the associations involved. The simple Anglo-German comparison includes too many uncontrolled influences to identify the association between training finance and volume.[6]

Several responses seek to reduce such difficulties. The first increases the number of observations relative to the number of variables. The usual way of doing so is to bring other countries into consideration. Thus the 'corporatism' literature concerning the effects of centralized pay determination upon pay behaviour typically involves a moderately large number of countries and enjoys positive degrees of freedom (Calmfors and Driffill, 1988).[7] None of the studies in this volume uses formal statistical techniques on multicountry samples, though Lindley and Drake draw less formally on the experiences of several EC economies in their studies of skill requirements and training finance.

The second response takes the opposite tack: it selects countries so as to reduce the number of control variables required. If the countries in question are highly similar in other relevant attributes, then any observed relationship is less likely to be caused or distorted by uncontrolled influences. Thus Ashton, Maguire and Sung argue that the historical links to British institutions in Canada and Hong Kong make the latter attractive candidates for comparison. Marsden and Ryan draw comfort, albeit limited, from the historical parallels between craft training in British and German industry in motivating an Anglo-German comparison. Raffe points to the still greater control potential of comparisons within heterogeneous but unitary states such as Britain.

The response is limited by uncertainty about the presence (and importance) of differences in those other influences supposedly controlled implicitly by choice of country. Even if that is no problem, there is the further danger of as low a variability in the influences of interest as in other influences — all are prone to homogenization as part of the common political unit. Even if experimental conditions may be approximated, the experiment may not be performed.

A third response also seeks the implicit controls to be gained by an appropriate choice of country, but without sacrificing identifying variation, by reducing the internationalism of the research — most commonly by seeking out cases of international imitation or diffusion. The national cultural influences which dog comparative research can be avoided when a training practice is observed in a country other than that of origin. For example, the contributions of Japanese organizational techniques and culture to high industrial productivity can be separated more readily from the experience of Japanese owned and managed plants in Britain, which apply some or all of the techniques under British cultural conditions, than they can from that of the same companies' plants in Japan (White and Trevor, 1983; Dunning, 1986; Oliver and Wilkinson, 1988).[8]

Although research on foreign owned plants in Britain (e.g., Buckley and Enderwick, 1985) was not available for inclusion in this volume, the broad research technique still crops up in it. Prais, Jarvis and Wagner note that the one British hotel to employ a large proportion of labour qualified at intermediate levels enjoyed productivity comparable to German levels. Such evidence, were it more widespread, would go a long way towards establishing that higher productivity in German hotels is indeed associated with higher rates of vocational qualification in Germany — as opposed to their both resulting from other uncontrolled influences, such as national culture and institutions. Marsden and Ryan similarly cite the decision of German banks to avoid the Youth Training Scheme in their UK training activities as evidence of the scheme's inadequacy.

The final response develops Rose's advice to use time as well as space for comparative research. If the variables of interest have changed over time in the two countries while other factors have remained constant, then 'taking first differences' — comparing changes over time in the two countries — will remove the influence of factors other than the ones in hand. They are controlled by using the fact that they have not changed.[9]

Marsden and Ryan adopt this approach in linking training volumes to training costs in the Anglo-German context: to the extent that other influences on training levels, such as employer organization and attitudes, have not changed significantly over time, the association between increased trainee payroll costs and decreased training volumes in British relative to German industry cannot be the spurious product of such factors.

Again, results remain tentative. Even if the existence and direction of a relationship can be established, its strength is less readily assessed. Other influences are usually not measured, in which case there is no assurance that they have remained constant. Moreover, if the various influences interact — e.g., if the effects of training costs upon employer training activity depend on employer attitudes and organisation, as is to be expected — considering changes over time will provide an at best partial guide to the underlying relationship.[10]

Finally, even were an association well determined, issues of causality would remain. For example, were a positive association unambiguously established between training and productivity, causality may run in either or both directions. So while it is widely assumed that training causes productivity, the reverse may also be true. Successful companies may spend more of their greater resources on training than do less successful ones simply as part of personnel policy, quite apart from any benefits to productivity (Pratten, 1989). The possibility appears particularly relevant to much of what is conventionally classed as management training. The difficulty of assigning causality, widespread in empirical work, thus complicates further the interpretion of international evidence.

The role of myth and the limits to the informational content of comparative research both contribute to the variety of conclusions drawn from it in the literature. Ewart Keep's charge that the lessons of comparative research have not been absorbed by British policymakers has weight, but it is also true that the ability of comparative research to yield agreed lessons is itself limited — and, as Pratten observes, potentially suspect even when agreement is widespread.

However, while judging the role of international comparisons by the standards of statistical inference indicates their limitations, it hardly does them justice as a research technique. Indeed, going only by the statistical canon, there appears to be little reason to turn to comparative research in the first place. It is time to outline what it has to offer.

The Advantages

In addition to documenting differences between countries, comparative research offers three analytical benefits. The first is its ability to increase identifying variation, i.e., to extend the range of observation on the variables of interest. Training practices and institutions in other countries differ from those at home and the differences may be crucial to finding evidence outside a limited range of variation at home. For example, in the case of training finance, although low trainee payroll costs can be found in Britain both historically and in the Youth Training Scheme, in neither case have they coincided with the effective regulation of training quality, whereas in Germany they have. Consequently, in order to assess the effects on training activity of low trainee pay combined with regulated quality, an Anglo-German comparison is potentially valuable.

The second benefit offered by comparative research is its value to nonstatistical investigation. Like the case-study, it often throws up insights on qualitative factors which cannot be assessed statistically but which may be none the less important for that. Without measurement there may be no science in the strict sense but without qualitative comparative research there would be fewer ideas.

The third contribution of comparative research is perhaps the most important: to throw up new issues and to aid understanding of the network of factors which underlie particular outcomes. The importance of this contribution in the training area was established early by comparative research into 'social effects'. In demonstrating radical differences in the extent of hierarchy and the use of skills in matched French and German companies, research based primarily at LEST[11] threw up a range of new questions for social science. At the same time, it pointed to the interdependence of national systems of education, work organization and industrial relations (Maurice, Sellier and Silvestre, 1986). Such questions and insights might never have emerged without that enterprising comparative exercise.

The influence of the LEST approach can be seen in several attributes of this volume — not least in the widely held view that the interdependence of VET with its socioeconomic institutional context seriously constrains 'policy borrowing' from abroad. Finegold accepts the emphasis on institutional interdependence but questions the importance of the cultural component in national differences. More specifically, the study by Campbell and Warner represents an outgrowth of the same tradition of comparative research (Sorge and Warner, 1980). Similarly, McCormick finds financial institutions and personnel policy as integrally related to the distinctive training practices of Japanese firms.

In the light of these various attributes of comparative research, it is striking — and probably just as well — that the claims made for it by the contributors to this volume tend to the humble. It is widely seen as throwing up interesting questions, defining problems and suggesting a range of possible answers, but it can rarely provide a single one. It is seen as useless for direct copying or 'quick fixes' for policy problems but as useful for outlining alternative approaches to a problem and elaborating the institutional conditions under which a solution may be achievable.

Two Key Issues

Amongst the varied issues raised in this volume two stand out as particularly important. The first is whether or not a substantial increase in training for intermediate skills would by itself benefit Britain. At one extreme, Lindley raises the possibility that it would be of little value without accompanying reforms in the utilization of skill and managerial product strategy, which is where he locates the binding constraints on economic performance.

Campbell and Warner similarly see Britain as lagging behind Germany more in the utilization of skill than in its production. Finegold, McCormick, and Prais, Jarvis and Wagner note the interdependence of corporate decisions about skill development with those about product quality, production process and skill utilization — which raises doubts about the independent contribution to be expected from improved training *per se*. Finally, comparative research has also indicated deficiencies in the training of British management and improvement in that area may be no less essential, particularly for the success of the current 'employer led' training strategy (Handy, 1987).

However, Prais, Jarvis and Wagner also see productivity as dependent upon skill supplies, both directly through improved worker performance in a given job structure and indirectly through job enrichment and increased functional flexibility. Finegold argues that increased skill supplies may have a pump priming effect, prompting employers, individuals and policy-makers to revise their strategies towards high skill development and utilisation. Drake finds evidence of such effects in the response of French employers to increased government commitment to training. Finally, the potential for relaxing the inflation and trade constraints on economic growth in Britain by increasing the supply of intermediate skills to industry was noted earlier in this introduction.

Such considerations suggest therefore that increased supplies of intermediate skills are highly desirable for their direct benefits to industrial performance and macroeconomic management. They would also be welcome for the longer-term indirect pressure which they exert towards more skill intensive and flexible production systems, but they may require complementary changes in managerial training and industrial policy to become fully effective.

If so, the second question arises: how to increase the supply of intermediate skills? Increased development of existing skills may be part of the answer but attention must focus primarily on initial vocational preparation. Two broad alternatives are outlined in the papers by Ashton, Maguire and Sung, and Marsden and Ryan: to revitalize occupational training at the workplace or to let the slide towards job training dominated by individual employer requirements continue, and develop instead upper secondary education, vocational and general, along with encouragement to adults to sponsor their own training. Marsden and Ryan have hopes that the former route remains feasible, though the obstacles are clearly formidable. Lindley inclines towards the latter route. Ashton, Maguire and Sung just want the choice to be made. It is not easily made but it would be better to choose either strategy and pursue it consistently than to dabble with both but to choose neither, as at present.

Notes

1 Paris, Gallimard, 1986, p. 78. ('A commercial nation is always very alive to its interests and neglects none of the knowledge that can be useful in its business'; *Letters on England*, Harmondsworth, Penguin, 1980, p. 54).
2 Research by the National Institute team has also demonstrated the deficiencies of pupil attainment in British schools relative to their German and Japanese

counterparts. Extensive references to the NIESR research are provided in chapters 1 and 11 below.

3 A subsequent conference has been devoted wholly to Anglo-American comparisons (Finegold, McFarland and Richardson, 1991).

4 International comparative research on vocational education proper has been oriented primarily towards LDCs (Lauglo and Lillis, 1988).

5 Of course, without the analytical there is little interest in the descriptive: knowing that there is less VET in Britain is of little interest if it doesn't matter anyway — or if its causes cannot be understood.

6 Comparative research has the advantage over case-studies — and particularly over the grouped sets of single nation studies favoured by some international agencies — of dealing with two or more observations rather than only one. The informational advantage is small, however, as both types of research suffer from inadequate, and normally negative, degrees of freedom. The main advantage of comparisons over case-studies lies elsewhere: the research is pushed from the descriptive towards the analytical. Interesting questions arise even if they were not present at the outset.

7 A major difficulty is that more countries usually means more variables to be controlled as well. In the extreme, as when nationally specific influences (e.g., culture) are important, adding new countries adds nothing to the informational content of the data: Germany has a separate German effect, and so adding it tells us nothing new about the association in question. However, commonly the number of influential variables grows less rapidly than the number of observations — for example, including Scandinavian countries may require controls only for a common Nordic effect; including Benelux countries in the EC, for a small country effect, etc.

8 This assumes that British owned and managed firms have not adopted Japanese organizational techniques themselves. Otherwise, international comparisons are redundant.

9 The econometric formalization of this approach removes 'fixed effects' by taking changes over time. For example, in the analysis of the effects of training on occupational status across individuals, first differences are taken in the hope of eliminating the effect of unmeasured fixed factors such as ability (e.g., Nickell, 1982).

10 Kindleberger (1978:2) suggests a further way of increasing the scientific contribution of comparative research: avoiding 'wide generalisation' and picking limited topics for investigation ('segments, sectors or sections of the economy rather than ... takeoff, decline, backwardness, business cycles, capitalism and the like'), thereby restraining the number of other influences affecting the relationship in question. VET appears to occupy an intermediate position in this regard.

11 Laboratoire d'Economie et de Sociologie du Travail, Aix-en-Provence.

Acknowledgement

I thank S.J. Prais, Cliff Pratten, Mari Sako, Solomos Solomou and Hilary Steedman for comments and suggestions.

References

BUCKLEY, P.J. and ENDERWICK, P. (1985) *The Industrial Relations Practices of Foreign-Owned Firms in Britain*, London, Macmillan.

CALMFORS, L. and DRIFFILL, J. (1988) 'Bargaining structure, corporatism and economic performance', *Economic Policy*, **6**, pp. 14–61.

DUNNING, J. (1986) *Japanese Participation in British Industry*, London, Croom Helm.

ELBAUM, B. and LAZONICK, W. (1986) (eds) *The Decline of the British Economy*, Oxford, Oxford University Press.

FINEGOLD, D., MCFARLAND, L. and Richardson, W. (1991) *Something Borrowed, Something Blue? A Comparison of British and American Education and Training Reforms*, forthcoming, London, Falmer Press.

HANDY, C. (1987) *The Making of Managers: a Report on Management Education, Training and Development in the USA, West Germany France, Japan and the UK*, London, National Economic Development Office.

KINDLEBERGER, C.P. (1978) *Economic Response: Comparative Studies in Trade, Finance and Growth*, Cambridge, Mass., Harvard.

LAUGLO, J. and LILLIS, K. (1988) *Vocationalizing Education: An International Perspective*, Oxford, Pergamon.

MAURICE, M., SELLIER, F. and SILVESTRE, J-J. (1986) *The Social Foundations of Industrial Power*, Cambridge, Mass, MIT Press.

NICKELL, S. (1982) 'The determinants of occupational success in Britain', *Review of Economic Studies*, **49**, pp. 43–53.

OLIVER, N. and WILKINSON, B. (1988) *The Japanisation of British Industry*, Oxford, Blackwell.

PRAIS, S.J. (1981) 'Vocational qualifications of the labour force in Britain and Germany', *National Institute Economic Review*, **98**, pp. 47–59.

PRATTEN, C.F. (1989) 'The importance of training?', mimeo, Department of Applied Economics, University of Cambridge.

RYAN, P. (1984) 'Job training, employment practices and the large enterprise: The case of costly transferable skills', in OSTERMAN, P. (ed.) *Internal Labour Markets*, Cambridge, Mass, MIT.

SORGE, A. and WARNER, M. (1980) 'Manpower training, manufacturing organisation and workplace relations in Great Britain and West Germany', *British Journal of Industrial Relations*, **18**, pp. 318–33.

STEEDMAN, H., MASON, G. and WAGNER, K. (1991) 'Intermediate skills in the workplace: deployment, standards and supply in Britain, France and Germany', *National Institute Economic Review*, 136, pp. 60–76.

WHITE, M. and TREVOR, M. (1983) *Under Japanese Management: The Experience of British Workers*, London, Heinemann.

Part 1

Uses and Methods

1 The Grass Looked Greener — Some Thoughts on the Influence of Comparative Vocational Training Research on the UK Policy Debate

Ewart Keep

Introduction

This chapter reviews the influence which comparative research into vocational training has exercised upon UK policy formulation. The national debate about UK VET (vocational education and training) policy has been marked by a strong inclination to compare and contrast British practice with that of our overseas competitors. Politicians and civil servants have indicated a belief that Britain has much to learn from overseas VET systems, and academics have invested time and effort in order to provide policy makers with data about how such systems operate. This chapter examines the fruits of this investment in terms of its effect upon policy formulation, discusses the problems that have hindered the translation of research findings into policy, and offers some suggestions about the shape of future research efforts in this area.

In order to keep within a reasonable length, the central focus of the chapter is comparative research in vocational training, with only passing reference to the vocational education side of the debate. Also the issue of the influence of comparative research upon discussions about the future of management education and development in the UK has been omitted, in the view that this topic requires separate treatment in order to do it justice.

The chapter begins with a brief overview of the nature and scope of the comparative research that has been available to the British policy-making community, followed by an examination of the degree to which research findings have been instrumental in establishing the agenda for the UK policy debate. The bulk of the chapter then reviews some of the problems that have occurred in attempting to translate the lessons of comparative research into policy. In the light of these difficulties, a final section offers some tentative suggestions as to a future research agenda.

Comparative Research — An Overview

In assessing the influence of comparative research on policy making, a logical starting point is the nature and scope of the comparative research that has been available to the policy-making community. While it would be as difficult as it would be unproductive to attempt here to review the whole field of comparative research, a brief outline of some of the most important sources is necessary.

In terms of the frequency with which they have been cited in public debate, the report *Competence and Competition* (MSC/NEDO, 1984), the work of the National Institute for Economic and Social Research (NIESR; for example, Jarvis and Prais, 1989; Prais, 1981, 1985; Prais and Wagner, 1983, 1985, 1988; Steedman, 1987), and the edited volume *Education and Economic Performance* (Worswick, 1985), have probably figured most prominently. However, there has been much other comparative research produced by UK academics which has offered both information about and a theoretical understanding of, the nature and basis of overseas VET systems (e.g., McCormick, 1988; Clegg, 1986; Daly, 1986; Sako and Dore, 1988; Marsden and Silvestre, 1986; chapter 11, below.

The output of overseas academics should not be forgotten. A wealth of material is available, much of it in English, which throws light on problems that are of direct concern to UK policy makers. Examples would include the study by Maier *et al.* (1986) of the role of small firms in providing vocational training for the young in West Germany, France, Italy and Ireland; Spiers and Watkins' (1987) article on pre-redundancy training in the West German shipbuilding industry; and the work of Windolf on recruitment and selection in Britain and West Germany (1982a) and the use of education as a screening device in France, Britain and West Germany (1982b).

Much of this literature offers valuable theoretical insights into the functioning of national VET systems. In particular, the work of the LEST group at the University of Aix-en-Provence and the French societal approach to the analysis of VET provision has much to offer British academics and policy makers (e.g., Campinos-Dubernet and Grando, 1988; Maurice, Sorge and Warner, 1980; Maurice, Sellier and Silvestre, 1986; Rose, 1985; Sorge and Warner, 1980).

Besides what may be termed an academic output, there has also been some detailed comparative research undertaken by consultants at the behest of bodies such as NEDO (National Economic Development Office). Probably the most impressive example of this was the group of reports prepared, under the banner of *Performance and Competitive Success* (NEDO, 1988; McKinsey and Co., 1988), for the Electronics Industry Sector Group by members of NEDO's Manpower and Education Division and by the consultants McKinsey and Company.

Beyond comparative studies undertaken by academics and consultants, one should acknowledge the influence on policy makers of other sources of comparative information on overseas VET systems. These have included briefings and reports prepared by civil servants (e.g., 'Higher Education Output in Engineering – International Comparisons', 1987) and political advisers, as well as material provided by overseas governments (e.g., Swedish National Labour Market Board, 1987) and by bodies such as the Anglo-German Foundation.

A further source of information for the policy-making community has been the study visit (Lawler, 1985; *CBI Education and Training Bulletin*, June 1986:4; Moore, 1988; Pointing, 1986). The strength of this desire to 'go and see for oneself' should not be underestimated. If press reports are correct (Harper, 1988; *Transition*, May 1988:6), the decision to adopt the USA's PICs (Private Industry Councils) as the model upon which the new British system of TECs (Training and Enterprise Councils) are based, was ultimately taken, not as the result of any detailed academic research or evaluation of PICs, but rather as a consequence of a study tour of a representative sample of two PICs by the then-current Secretary of State for Employment.

One final form of comparative research which, it can be argued, has influenced policy making, albeit at the level of the individual UK company, has been attempts by British training managers to undertake their own analysis of training provision in overseas concerns. One of the best known examples of this was the work undertaken by personnel specialists from Lucas (Brown and Read, 1984; see also Garnett, 1989), but there has been other, unpublished, work by several large companies.

Even from this necessarily extremely brief and partial survey of the field, it is apparent that there has been no lack of information and analysis available about overseas VET systems. However, it must be recognized that the ready availability of data and analysis does not always guarantee its automatic use in policy deliberations.

Setting the Agenda

In one sense, there can be little doubt that researchers have been able to influence the course of the current debate about a national VET strategy. Concern about VET in Britain has seen the use of comparative research, both by academics and the MSC and NEDO, to instil a sense of urgency into the national debate. By seeking to quantify the degree to which the UK trails its overseas competitors, the need for action and for new policies has been emphasized, both to government and to other actors within the policy-making community, such as employers and trade unions. In so doing, researchers have helped to establish the basic parameters of the national policy debate in terms of comparative economic failure (Sheldrake and Vickerstaff, 1987:1).

This perspective is nothing new. A strong comparative dimension to discussions about levels of VET and its relationship with economic performance in Britain has been traditional for over a century (Perry, 1976; Sheldrake and Vickerstaff, 1987). Reoccurring UK policy debates have normally been framed by our perceived long-term economic decline and the apparent superiority of the national VET systems possessed by our overseas competitors.

The continuing dominance of the comparative definition of the UK's 'VET problem' is reflected in official reports and pronouncements. For example, *A New Training Initiative — A Consultative Document* (MSC, 1981a), in opening discussion about the future of vocational training in Britain made it clear, in a section entitled 'What the Problem Is', that 'our methods and attitudes contrast markedly with those of our competitors' (MSC, 1981a:3). The *Youth Task Group Report* (MSC, 1982), in making the case for the proposed Youth Training Scheme (YTS) again juxtaposed the poor state of vocational training for the young in Britain with the training opportunities available to the same age group in France and West Germany.

To bring the story up to date, the Government's latest White Paper on training, *Employment for the 1990s*, having surveyed the evidence of long-standing dissatisfaction with Britain's relative performance in the provision of VET, states that:

> in recent years, a series of studies including those of the National Institute of Economic and Social Research makes clear that, though the best of British firms may stand comparison with the best in the world, the breadth and depth of our training, its quality and its standards still show up badly by comparison with our competitors on the Continent, in North America and in the Far East. (DE, 1988:29)

Similar expressions of concern have come from trade union leaders and employers. A statement by Ken Gill and Clive Jenkins, the joint general secretaries of the MSF trade union, suggested that 'a new national consensus is emerging on the importance of training. Government, employers and trade unions all now recognise that Britain is lagging behind its major competitors' (MSF, 1988:4). The TUC, in *Skills for Success — A TUC Statement on Training* (1988), echoes this sentiment.

Individual employers, such as Jaguar Cars, British Steel, and Lucas have acknowledged that an awareness of higher levels of training by overseas competitors has acted as a stimulus to their own efforts to improve the provision of training and development. As Sir John Egan, the chairman of Jaguar, commented, 'the pressure is on our Training Department to educate our employees to keep up with ... international rivals' (MSC *Focus on Adult Training*, No. 12, 1987:6). Collectively, the CBI (Confederation of British Industry) has gone to considerable lengths to promote the need for improvement in the levels of training and development provided by British employers (MSC *Focus on Training*, May/June 1988:9; Transition, October 1988:8).

While it would be unwise to attribute this awareness in its entirety simply to the effects of well-disseminated comparative research, there can be little doubt that this has played a pivotal role in concentrating attention on Britain's shortcomings. The number of times which NIESR and other studies are actually cited in statements made by policy bodies and actors in the policy community indicates that comparative research has defined the scale and scope of the problem that needs to be addressed.

This apparently broad consensus has, however, masked a number of problems in translating the findings and lessons of comparative research into actual policy formulation. The following section reviews these difficulties and discusses their causes.

The Policy Process

The process by which research findings influence policy formulation is extremely complex, being mediated by a host of fluctuating ideological and practical considerations. Moreover, the very phrase 'policy formulation' carries with it connotations of a rational, deliberative and orderly process. Such associations arguably hark back to a past, and possibly an idealized, model of governmental activity. For Britain has never possessed the sort of coordinated policy-making mechanisms needed to address the broad sweep of societal factors that affect VET provision — a fact which may go some way to explaining the longevity of the UK's problems over VET. Inter-departmental rivalries, lack of any real industrial strategy, and weak (at least by European standards) employer interest groups, have all made the evolution of coherent national policy problematic.

During the last decade Government strategy has, if anything, further weakened the ability of the UK's policy-making machinery to deliver coherence. It has moved away from more traditional modes of evolving policy, such as the use of royal commissions, which carried with them a commitment to the use of detailed research and analysis as a basis for identifying future avenues for policy formulation. This reflective model of policy making has, in the area of VET policy at least, largely been superceded by a more action-orientated approach. While tripartite bodies, such as the MSC and NEDO, may have wished to utilize research as a precursor to considered development of national training strategies, the Government has apparently not viewed detailed academic research as an essential precondition for the successful formulation of policy options. Indeed, in recent years the Government has made clear its belief that tripartite decision-making machinery is inappropriate and has abolished the MSC.

The resulting policy focus has been essentially *ad hoc* in nature. Despite the considerable volume of change and innovation referred to below, there has been no real attempt to design a national VET system from first principles (Kushner, 1985). To some extent the reason for this failure, particularly during the period in the early 1980s when youth unemployment was a major issue for training policy, has been the political necessity for the government to be seen to act swiftly and decisively to tackle problems. The time needed to undertake detailed prior research and analysis before designing new policy initiatives was simply not deemed to be available. An example of these pressures at work can be seen in the planning process which led up to the introduction of YTS (Youth Training Scheme; Keep, 1986). More broadly, the last ten years have witnessed a period of unparalleled change and innovation in British vocational training, with the institutional landscape undergoing sweeping changes, in terms of both the provision of new VET courses and the institutional mechanisms available to deliver them. Thus the change that has taken place in the style and mode of policy formulation is partly a reflection of the pace of reform that the government has sought to promote.

The significance of the policy-making style and focus that has been associated with this pace of change is that the integration of the results of comparative research into it has proved extremely problematic. Academics are only one of a number of sources of information competing in a crowded market for the attention of policy makers, and they are handicapped by the fact that the analytical perspective they adopt is often complex. They argue that national systems of VET provision are influenced by a variety of structural and societal factors that go well beyond the relatively narrow confines of the shape of training institutions and schemes. By contrast, the great value to policy makers of other, more superficial forms of information gathering is that their results are swiftly digestible and less likely to call into question the effectiveness of simple remedies. This is particularly important when policy formulation is taking place against tight time constraints. Thus the difficulties that comparative research has posed for those operating within a short-term policy-making context have been considerable.

In essence, these difficulties are bound up with the attitudes and actions of two groups within the policy-making community. For while trade unions have usually proved happy to assimilate the messages coming from comparative research, employers and government have on occasion proved less willing to do so.

Employer Resistance

The first area where problems have emerged has been a tendency by some employers to baulk at research findings that have indicated that their efforts lag behind those of their counterparts overseas. The example of this difficulty that has received the greatest public attention centred on the comments made by a group of large engineering employers, led by the Ford Motor Company, concerning what they saw as the use by the MSC of misleading international comparisons of training expenditure (Wilson, 1987:4). Ford also advanced the view that the record of British employers on adult training was not seriously worse than that of their overseas rivals. They suggested that, 'the main distinction between ourselves, West Germany and Japan is not our general failure to train our adult workforce but in the long duration and better quality of education and initial training of their young workforce' (Shepherd, 1987:3).

The influence wielded by this group of companies should not be under-estimated. They collectively employ half-a-million people, or one-third of all those covered by the EITB (Engineering Industry Training Board), and their opposition to the continuance of a statutory ITB in the engineering sector after 1981 has arguably greatly constrained and weakened the board (*Transition*, May 1988:4). Moreover, the group's calls for a reform of British training provision based on 'national standards, local delivery' (Wilson, 1987:4) have been reflected in the policies announced in the latest white paper on training.

At a wider level, the CBI has, in its public input to national training policy, tried to acknowledge the need for British employers to undertake more training and accepted the existence of a causal linkage between investment in VET and international competitiveness. However, the CBI as a representative body has to take into account the wide spectrum of views that exist among its scattered and heterogeneous membership. Those managers who follow the line taken by Ford, but who have been less public in their protestations of dissent from current orthodoxy, have at times extracted some accommodation from the CBI. The result is that the Confederation has found itself facing in two directions at once on the importance of comparative VET research findings.

This ambivalence is neatly captured in *Training and Vocational Education*, which was prepared in early 1985 by the CBI's Education and Training Division as a response to the publication of *Competence and Competition* (MSC/NEDO, 1984). The document makes the comment that:

> The validity of some findings and recommendations in the Report [*Competence and Competition*] can and should be questioned and there are doubts about the extent to which lessons for the UK can or should be drawn from international comparisons in which like is not always compared with like.... It is by no means easy — and it could be as dangerous as it is difficult — to draw comparisons between levels of training and educational activity and a country's economic and industrial performance and then say with any proven accuracy that the former has an overriding influence on the latter. (CBI, 1985:2)

In the same document, the CBI claims to 'accept the broad message that more and better training and vocational education in the UK is needed' (1985:2), but simultaneously rejects the grounds on which the case for such improvements are constructed by taking the view that 'training requirements and provision will and should respond to economic change but cannot of themselves be the cause of that change' (1985:7). The CBI advances no arguments in support of this rejection of any active role for VET as an agent of economic change. Arguably this stance reflects the degree to which some employers have felt themselves swept along by the general rhetoric of the

VET debate and its acceptance of an *a priori* link between training and economic success, while at the same time maintaining a private, but deeply-felt belief that training is at best peripheral to mainstream business activity.

Training and Vocational Education also illustrates the resentment which many employers have evidently experienced at the inference that can be drawn from much of the comparative research that it is with British employers, rather than other actors within the policy making community, that the blame for the UK's poor performance largely rests. The final section of the document is devoted to a strongly-worded attack upon what some firms plainly saw as the central message of *Competence and Competition*:

> To many employers, efforts which can at best offer only partial solution to the problem of making Britain economically and commercially competitive are being advocated as cure-alls — and even more disturbing there is an implication in all this that employers should carry much of that effort because they are responsible in the first place for deficiencies in vocational education and training which more truly are the result of long-standing social and cultural attitudes ... employers recognise more may need to be done. Many are willing to do more and to encourage others to do likewise — but they object to any suggestion that willingness to accept responsibility is tied to an acceptance of blame.... They are ... resentful of blanket suggestions that industry should spend more. They do not object to the debate being opened but they do not believe that the contributions made so far have helped to carry the debate to a workable conclusion. (CBI, 1985:8)

The unwillingness of at least some employers to accept either the validity of international comparisons or the existence of a causal relationship between levels of training and development and competitiveness is unfortunate. It is unfortunate not least because, the example of Ford notwithstanding, employers have on the whole been unwilling to debate their reservations in public or to challenge openly the general direction of national policy. As a result, the debate has proceeded with an air of unanimity that has masked quite deep-seated differences of opinion about the direction and pace of change that is required. Employers, through the CBI, may have endorsed the three strategic objectives for the reform of vocational training which were established by the 1981 New Training Initiative, but it is questionable whether this endorsement carries with it an active commitment on the part of the majority to take the practical steps needed to make these objectives a lasting reality.

The danger inherent in this situation is that VET initiatives, such as YTS, have achieved superficial acceptance by some employers, who have felt themselves obliged to participate for a variety of reasons, many of which have had little to do with an acknowledgment of the need for more and better vocational training (Keep, 1986). At the same time, the underlying change in attitudes towards the value of training that is needed to sustain such reforms has not been as wide or as uniform as might have been hoped. The result, in the long-term, may be that when the immediate pressures that triggered the initiative have vanished, such as high levels of youth unemployment in the case of YTS, so too will the measures taken to tackle the problem.

A second set of difficulties with employer attitudes towards the findings of comparative research have centred on the issue of quality in training. Comparative research has indicated a gap between the UK and its competitors in terms of both the quantity and quality of the vocational training being provided by employers. Unfortunately, while some progress has undoubtedly been made in increasing the volume of training provided, the goal of persuading the majority of employers to upgrade skill levels has proved more elusive.

One reason for this has been that many of the policy initiatives taken to improve training concentrated, particularly in their early stages, on the volume of training being delivered, often at the expense of the quality of training being provided. YTS and ET (Employment Training) would seem to be examples of this problem. As NIESR's 1986 study of clerical training in the UK and France indicated, clerical schemes on YTS often aimed to produce trainees qualified at a level which the French were then planning to eliminate 'as being too low ... to be useful to industry' (Steedman, 1986:22).

It is to be hoped that the work of the NCVQ (National Council for Vocational Qualifications) will aid attempts to match the general quality of training provided overseas, but evidence from a recent NIESR study of the clothing industry in Germany and the UK indicates that even when industries produce a YTS scheme that meets NCVQ standards, the result still falls significantly short of what is expected of comparable trainees in West Germany (Steedman and Wagner, 1989). Much the same proved to be true when comparing the level of vocational qualifications in the French, West German and British retail sectors (Jarvis and Prais, 1989). A related point is the concern that has been expressed (Steedman and Wagner, 1989:48–9; Jarvis and Prais, 1989:62–70) that British employers appear, in contrast to their French and German counterparts, to want vocational training that focuses only on a narrow range of job-specific skills, rather than upon courses and qualifications that offer a mix of job specific training and additional general education.

Reconstructing UK employers' conceptions of likely future levels of skill requirement has proved exceptionally difficult. Despite the evidence of studies of the West German 'dual system', and of the higher levels of vocational training provided in most developed countries, British concepts of what constitutes quality training continue to lag behind. While individual companies have chosen to try to match the best that their overseas rivals provided, progress in changing attitudes at the aggregate level has been slow (DE, 1988:29).

Government Attitudes towards the Design of an Effective UK VET System

The difficulty of persuading employers to accept the validity of comparative research findings has been overshadowed by an even more important problem, that posed by the attitudes of the government and its supporters towards attempts to translate such research into the design of an effective VET system for the UK. That the process of producing such a system would not be an altogether straightforward one has been emphasized by a number of commentators. As John Cassels, the director-general of NEDO, and Geoffrey Holland, the then-director of the MSC, put it in their foreword to *Competence and Competition*, 'there is no one model and wholesale adoption of the practices of another country is not the way forward'. The authors of the report made the same point, emphasizing what they saw as 'the danger of copying separate elements of someone else's system in the hope that they will produce the same result in the UK' (MSC/NEDO 1984:iv).

Unfortunately, some of those involved in the policy-making process, particularly within government, have not paid as much heed to these warnings as perhaps should have been the case. The result has been a failure to appreciate the essential difference between learning from, and trying to copy, overseas VET systems. Put simply, British policy makers have preferred to attempt to copy isolated institutional elements from overseas systems, rather than try to draw any wider lessons about the social and economic contexts in which these systems operate, or about the general forces and principles that underpin their success.

This focus is partly bound up with the changes in the style of policy formulation outlined above. The development of a less reflective, more *ad hoc* approach, which has short planning horizons and is more action-oriented, has been coupled with the adoption of a distinctive ideological approach to VET policy. This ideological stance rejects corporatist arrangements and a strong, active role for trade unions, and instead is heavily convinced of the efficacy of market forces operating within a voluntaristic, employer-led training system.

Societal factors.   It is difficult to escape the conclusion that the result of this dominant focus has been to blind the Government and other senior policy makers to many of the messages coming out of comparative research. Indeed the Government has frequently chosen to make only selective use of this research. Interest has gone from a general perception that 'foreigners do it better', to a narrow focus on the individual institutional structures within overseas VET systems, without any apparent intervening appreciation of the broader social, economic, technological and organizational contexts within which these institutions operate (Ford, 1986:206). As Sorge and Warner have argued (1980), there is a need to allow for the unique effects of each individual national society in its historical context on the functioning of national institutions. A grasp of these broader forces which shape choice and actions within national institutional structures appears to have eluded many British policy makers. Nor is there much evidence that the Government have sufficiently appreciated that VET systems function 'as groups of interrelated institutions and mutually supportive economic and social relationships' (Keep *et al.*, 1988:4), and therefore the examination of these complex interactions is vital to understanding a system's successful operation.

The range of interacting elements that require integration into any policy analysis is considerable. Marsden and Silvestre (1986) indicate that investigation of the structure of training provision needs to occur within the context of the organization and functioning of the particular labour markets which it serves. Thus factors such as the degree to which companies operate internal labour markets rather than rely upon external occupational labour markets are of crucial importance in structuring the shape and nature of training provision. Marsden and Ryan (chapter 11, below) suggest further factors, such as payment and reward systems; the structure and conduct of industrial relations, including the degree to which training is the subject of collective bargaining or co-determination; and the shape of work organization. To these might be added the historical circumstances and processes of industrialization, and the relationship that exists between qualification and employment.

NIESR's matched plant comparisons (Daly, Hitchens and Wagner, 1985; Steedman and Wagner, 1987, 1989) certainly suggest that a full understanding of the dichotomy in company training provision that exists between companies operating in the same industry in Britain and West Germany can only be arrived at if factors such as differing product market strategies are taken into account. What these studies indicate is that consideration of the institutions that deliver training, on its own, does little to illuminate the key issue of why companies in different countries adopt such dissimilar approaches to the provision of training and re-training.

Even at the institutional level, there is a need to appreciate how the various elements within the overall matrix of a national VET system interact. Concentrating on and copying a single element from another national VET system is unlikely to lead to a successful reproduction of that system's results. For example, the White Paper *Employment for the 1990s* singles out West Germany and the USA as possessing 'more locally-based training systems with the close and continuous involvement of employers and employer institutions. Such systems are much more likely to be attuned to the shifting pattern of employer needs, and to individuals' requirements, than the more inflexible arrangements at national and industry levels' (DE 1988:29).

This represents something of an over-simplification. In reality, the West German system operates as a series of inter-locking and complex relationships between four system levels: national, sectoral, regional, and workplace (Streeck *et al.*, 1987). While the delivery of training is controlled at local level through the chambers of commerce, the coordination, planning and design of training schemes have a genuine national and sectoral dimension. Moreover, training occurs within a manpower planning system that is coordinated nationally, but which also involves company level plans arrived at through co-determination. A fuller understanding than is revealed in the White Paper, of the interplay between the functions of these different levels in West Germany has an obvious relevance in the British context of current debate about the possible shape of the relationship (or lack of it) between the local TECs (Training and Enterprise Councils) and existing national sectoral training bodies, such as the NSTOs (Non-Statutory Training Organizations).

Attempts by British policy makers to try to copy isolated institutional elements of overseas VET systems without any wider understanding of how these systems function also ignore the possible existence of a causal cycle that determines the levels of training provided by a national system. As Clegg (1986) has argued, in order to learn anything of lasting value from a study of Japanese VET, it is necessary to examine the synergy between the different elements within the overall system of human resource management in Japanese industry. As Clegg puts it:

> The problem is not to identify the individual characteristics which pre-
> dict success but rather to examine the ways in which certain national
> and company factors are designed and managed to combine together
> consistently and effectively. (1986:39)

In the European context, Streeck (1985) takes this argument further, suggesting that the willingness of West German and Swedish employers to train their workforces is bound up with a number of economic, legal and social pressures that force employers in this direction. To take just one example of these external pressures, German and Swedish companies, in marked contrast to their British counterparts, are not able to turn easily to the external labour market to resolve fluctuations in demand for skills and labour. Legal and social pressures ensure that the shedding of labour through redundancy is far less easy and more expensive than in Britain. At the same time, the recruitment of skilled workers into the firm is made difficult by co-determination laws, which offer trade unions legal rights to insist upon long-term manpower planning, and which strengthen their ability to force employers to re-train existing workers before any recourse to external sources of skill supply can be contemplated.

Streeck goes on to build the case for the existence of a series of strong, mutually-interlocking external rigidities which push motor manufacturers in Sweden and West Germany towards investing in 'a product range that is quality rather than price competitive' (1985:14). This strategy in turn carries with it a requirement for high levels of skill in the workforce.

This 'virtuous circle' argument finds its counterpart in the UK with Finegold and Soskice (1988), who make the case for the existence in Britain of what they term a 'low skills equilibrium'. This is made up of 'a self-reinforcing network of societal and state institutions which interact to stifle demand for improvements in skill levels' (1988:22). The elements which Finegold and

Soskice suggest form this network include industrial organization, the design of the work process, the industrial relations system, and the structure of finance capital. Because these individual elements are closely linked in a mutually-reinforcing cycle, Finegold and Soskice argue that any alteration to a single factor in isolation will have little effect upon the overall result.

If this analysis is correct, and the longevity of the UK's training problem suggests that the underlying causes are deep-seated and structural, then policy makers' attempts merely to adjust the structures through which VET is delivered may have marginal effects upon the overall long-term volume of what is provided. Indeed, comparative research indicates the futility of such a course of action. If there is a causal cycle which can either take the form of a virtuous or vicious circle, then strategies formulated to create change in the supply of VET will need to address a wide range of policy issues, with the aim of re-structuring societal forces in order to create a positive synergy.

A further difficulty, even at the level of attempting to import institutional elements, has been confusion among policy makers as to which country we are seeking to copy. Thus, for example, there is insufficient appreciation that the much-vaunted system of industrial training provided by Japanese employers is built upon the foundations of a lengthy period of broad-based, general education which contains little in the way of vocational elements (McCormick, 1988; Sako and Dore, 1988). The result is that we find British enthusiasm for the Japanese system of industrial training going hand in hand with attempts to increase the importance of vocational elements within the education system, somewhat along the lines of the French or Swedish VET systems, while at the same time YTS is developed as our equivalent of the West German 'dual system'.

This 'pick 'n mix' style of policy making indicates that, somewhere along the way, the fact has been lost that these different systems embody mutually exclusive choices. Those engaged in the design of our national VET system do not yet appreciate sufficiently the point referred to above, that each national system functions as a distinctive group of interrelated and mutually-supportive institutions and relationships, rather than as a disconnected agglomeration of isolated structures that can be plucked at random from the national contexts from which they draw their form and identity.

Ideological filtering. It seems not unreasonable to deduce that the wider perspectives revealed by comparative research have been afforded little attention by policy makers because they have often failed to accord with the dominant ideological perspective of the Government. Two examples would be the significant roles which research indicates are often played in Western European and Scandinavian countries by legislative backing for VET provision and by active trade union participation in VET decision making.

To take the issue of statutory backing for VET first, in France, successive Governments have erected an elaborate system of legislative underpinning for VET provision. Besides an apprenticeship tax, and the existence for workers of individual legal rights to paid educational leave, there is also a national training tax levied upon employers' payrolls (Oeschslin, 1987). Rather than leave training provision to market forces and the choice of the individual employer, the French rely on a statutory-based series of universal rights and obligations, which collectively act to define vocational training as 'a national duty' (Oeschslin, 1987:660).

In Germany, federal legislative backing for training is less direct, but, for example, imposes a statutory duty on employers to belong to their local chamber of commerce, and provides for the legal enforcement of training agreements between employer and apprentice. In the individual federal states, half now have legislation covering workers' rights to varying forms of paid educational leave (*European Industrial Relations Review*, 169, February 1988:22–3). Moreover, at a broader level, legislation creates the context of management/worker co-determination which plays a central role in helping to define company manpower planning and training provision.

The part played by some form of statutory backing for training in many European countries has not been lost on senior MSC officials, and at times they have sought to place the issue on the policy agenda. In the 1981 document *A New Training Initiative: An Agenda for Action*, the MSC noted that:

> Most of our major European competitors have found it necessary to give statutory underpinning to their industrial training arrangements. There are a number of areas in which legislation could conceivably play a part in securing better training provision here

and promised 'further consideration of all the options' (MSC, 1981b:7).

Brian Nicholson, the chairman of the MSC, in an interview given just before his retirement from the post, made the comment that:

> The individual training allowance or a variation on the French system is worth consideration. Without something like that, which enables everyone to suffer equal advantage and equal pain, large numbers of people won't take part. (Pickard, 1987:11)

This acceptance of the potential for 'market failure' in training by the upper echelons of the MSC and the belief that Britain might have something to learn from overseas experience in the area, has not been shared by recent governments. Comparative research findings notwithstanding, market forces and the efforts of individual employers, untrammelled by state interference, are seen as the most effective ways of ensuring the delivery of an adequate level of training and development. This refusal to contemplate legislative backing thus marks Britain out as distinctive in Europe (Mansell, 1985).

The second area where British policy makers might be said to have ignored, for ideological reasons, the lessons of Western European experience, relates to the concept of social partnership. The active involvement of the social partners in the governance of training and manpower policies, is one that helps underpin the West German (Lawler, 1985; Fisher, 1988; Streeck *et al.*, 1987) and Swedish (Swedish Institute, 1987; Swedish Labour Market Policy, 1988; Swedish National Labour Market Board, 1987) vocational training systems, and, to a lesser extent, the French system (Oeschslin, 1987). In each case the role ascribed to the trade unions and/or worker representatives as social partners varies, as do the institutional mechanisms through which they exert influence. Nevertheless, there is a clear underlying belief in these countries that the direct and active participation of trade unions is an important element within the design of a successful national system of VET. This belief would appear to spring in part from a widespread acceptance that worker representatives can provide information about training that is not available from employers. It also reflects the view that union involvement in tripartite structures helps provide their decisions with greater legitimacy.

It is difficult to believe that the Government can be unaware of this. Research has certainly drawn attention to this feature of European VET systems. For example, surveys of the operation of the West German 'dual system' have made plain the integral role assigned within it to active trade union participation (Lawler, 1985; Maclure, 1985; Streeck, 1985; Streeck *et al.*, 1987). Indeed, Fisher (1988) quotes an official of the West German Federal Institute for Occupational Training who suggests that it is impossible for other countries to copy the West German training system precisely because 'it can only work in a particular labour-employer constellation'. Nor can anyone casting even a cursory glance at Sweden's training and labour market policies fail to be aware that these are formulated within the broader context of a distinctive industrial relations system.

Nevertheless, despite the availability of such information, British policy makers have filtered out any real appreciation of the role afforded to the social partners when enthusing about the merits of European VET systems. This has been particularly so in the case of West Germany, where British admiration of the output of the 'dual system' has either masked ignorance of, or a refusal to accept, the integral role allotted at all levels within this system to the trade unions. Thus, when senior policy makers, like Brian Nicholson, the ex-chairman of the MSC, seek to typify the West German system as being employer-led (Pickard, 1987:11), they are describing it in terms that would arguably not be accepted by the majority of those who operate this system.

The Government's decision in 1988 to abolish the tripartite MSC, and effectively exclude the TUC from national policy making marks the degree to which the UK has pursued a policy of employer-led vocational training. The role of trade unions is to be minimized, and future participation in VET decision making is to be by employer invitation to individual unions. The notion of social partnership figures nowhere in the Government's policies.

Three Unlearned Lessons

Besides the problems referred to above, the senior echelons of the UK policy-making community have also avoided acting upon other quite fundamental messages about the strategic preconditions for the design of effective VET systems that emerge from comparative analysis. It is possible to suggest at least three such general lessons that might have been drawn from an overview of the operation of successful overseas vocational training arrangements, but which in the event have almost entirely failed to inform UK policy deliberations.

Information Flows about VET

The first of these preconditions is the need for adequate flows of information between the various actors in the national VET system. As Hayes and Fonda point out, all three of the countries which they studied maintained VET systems that possessed a high degree of 'transparency', in that they:

> share the view that ET can most effectively be pursued if information is available to all parties. In all three competitor countries, extensive data collection efforts seek to discover how the ET system is working. Not only is this information collected; it is also disseminated among all those who have an interest in the system's performance — employers, trade unions, the public, Government, educational bodies. (MSC/NEDO, 1984:88)

By contrast, the UK's information gathering about VET activity was judged to be relatively patchy and poorly coordinated.

Examination of much of the comparative literature on overseas training systems reinforces this message. The amount and quality of the information available in the UK is simply not as high as is the case in many of our European competitors. For example, French academics can quote national statistics on the levels of retraining undertaken in companies (Mehaut, 1988). Comparable information is simply not available here.

One of the reasons for this situation is that, since the abolition of the majority of the ITBs (Industrial Training Boards) in 1981, mechanisms for gathering information on current training activity have not been available. Reliance has thus had to be placed on snapshot views of employer activity gathered through surveys. These have in themselves revealed the paucity of British employers' attempts to create and maintain detailed records of levels of training activity and expenditure (Pell, 1989).

Only in the last few years has the MSC tried to tackle this problem through the development of systems such as the LENS (Local Employer Networks) and the CALLMI skills database. There still remains much to be done before Britain achieves the quality and volume of information flows that are common within overseas VET systems, and it is open to question whether employers have yet accorded this issue the importance that it deserves (Pell, 1989:12–3). Without such transparency within the UK's VET system, it appears difficult either properly to monitor the effectiveness of current initiatives or to plan for future requirements.

The Problem of Coherence

The second general lesson from study of overseas VET provision is that a basic level of coherence within any national system appears to be associated with success. Effective national structures of VET provision operate as a system, with the different institutions within it, and the various elements and courses of VET which it offers, together forming a relatively cohesive and easily understandable whole. Britain has not yet evolved a coherent system of provision (Kushner, 1985), and the competing departmental responsibilities that exist between the various government agencies involved in VET policy formulation have done little to facilitate the creation of such a system (Keep, 1987). To take just one example, British VET provision for the crucial 14–19 age group remains confused, with a jumble of competing and overlapping schemes and operational responsibilities (Evans and Watts, 1985:3; Bolton, 1985).

The Need for Stability

A final, and closely related, lesson that comes from analysis of overseas VET systems, is a requirement for stability. This is not to say that change is not taking place overseas, but continual and wholesale restructuring of the basic institutional mechanisms and content of provision has not normally occurred with the frequency or speed of British institutional developments. Where alterations have occurred, they have tended to build upon the foundations of the existing system. In marked contrast, in the last decade the UK has witnessed a situation of what might be termed 'permanent revolution', with the established training system being progressively dismantled, and with VET courses and institutions in many cases having a product life cycle of only a few years. The latest White Paper (DE, 1988) ushers in yet another set of sweeping changes in the way in which vocational training is planned, organized and delivered. It is hard to bring to mind any other national VET system that has undergone change of such sustained pace and profundity.

In many senses the above-mentioned White Paper, *Employment for the 1990s*, could act as a summary of these problems. It reaffirms the Government's commitment to deregulation and increasing labour market flexibility, to the continued reduction of trade union power, and to pursuing voluntary moves by companies towards financial participation and employee communication as an alternative to any notion of social partnership.

Furthermore, while carrying a disclaimer that 'there is no one simple model which could be borrowed from any of our competitors to help us solve our own problems' (DE 1988:29), the White Paper then proceeds to adopt a narrowly institutional focus and propounds the adoption of a locally-based training system which is modelled (though not acknowledged to be so) upon the USA's system of PICs. Its authors offer a brief review of the features which they believe mark out successful national VET systems:

> At the outset of life, they teach and expect high standards across a broad range of subjects. They value practical competences as well as theoretical knowledge. They have a belief in continuing education and training through life. Above all, training and vocational education are treated as an essential commercial investment on a par with research and development. (DE, 1988:29)

The White Paper has nothing, however, to say about what broader factors might underpin and sustain these beliefs and attitudes. While it is undoubtedly true that many of our overseas competitors do see training as an investment rather than a cost, the problem comes in understanding why this should be the case.

If nothing else, *Employment for the 1990s* serves to underline the difficulties of integrating detailed analysis into policy formulation. A summary of the influence of comparative research on the UK policy debate must record what is, at best, a mixed set of results. It would seem fair to state that whereas comparative research has been extremely successful in defining the problem, it has not achieved comparable influence over the policy solutions to the problem. Comparative research has undoubtedly influenced a number of leading British companies, and there is evidence that it has helped shape the perceptions of senior MSC officials, but it has not, in general terms, had any very apparent effect upon Government thinking.

That this should be the case is not entirely suprising. As has been suggested above, the narrowly-focused, *ad hoc* style of policy making and the time constraints under which it has frequently operated have all militated against the ability and/or willingness of many of the dominant actors in the British VET policy community to take on board the lessons that have so far emerged from comparative research. Furthermore, a number of the messages that have emerged from European comparative research have clashed with the dominant ideological stance of the Government.

A Possible Future Research Agenda

The problems discussed above have a number of implications for the formulation of a possible future research agenda. Most researchers would probably wish the data and theoretical insights which their work produces to help inform policy making. Nevertheless, academic research is undertaken for a variety of reasons, only one of which is its possible use in governmental or quasi-governmental processes of policy formulation. If this is the case, then a number of avenues for future investigation suggest themselves.

One starting point is to fill in the geographical gaps in the current research portfolio. Inspection reveals that, while the majority of comparative research in Britain has focused on Western Europe, Scandinavia and Japan, the government is increasingly interested in the United States as a source of inspiration and of institutional models worthy of replication in the UK. That this should be so is hardly suprising. To a government ostensibly committed to free market economics, deregulation, and the disengagement of central government from interference in economic decision making, the United States has obvious attractions compared to Europe, with its traditions of heavier state intervention and legislation.

There are, however, some fairly obvious reasons why British researchers have chosen to centre their efforts within a European, rather than North American context. Historically, the USA has arguably not been seen as a country in which economic success could be strongly linked to an emphasis on VET. Only in recent times, as the USA has tried to grapple with the threat posed by foreign competition and comparative economic failure, have attempts to reform its VET system attracted attention. At a practical level, the cost of undertaking representative comparative research in America tends to be greater, a fact not unassociated with the physical scale and diversity of VET provision in the USA. Europe is nearer at hand, and made up of countries closer in size to the UK. Furthermore, the structure of existing research contacts and European research networks, such as the European Centre for the Development of Vocational Training (CEDEFOP), and the existence and activities of the EC, have all contributed towards making research in Europe a more practical option than the USA. This discongruence between academic and governmental focuses of interest raises problems about the ability of research to influence policy. One message would appear to be that, despite the difficulties and costs, academics in future need to concentrate more attention on US VET policy debates and institutions.

There are also lacunae in terms of the other countries that have not been used as a focus for research by British academics. Little UK comparative work has examined those countries that share a common linguistic and cultural heritage with the UK, such as Canada, New Zealand, and Australia. While these are not countries with international reputations for operating highly successful VET systems, they do offer opportunities to pursue issues, such as the influence of specific cultural and industrial relations heritages upon VET, that are of particular importance in the context of UK debates. Because of their shared language and the extensive linkages between their higher education institutions and our own, they are also countries in which comparative research may easily be undertaken.

Elsewhere within the Commonwealth there are other, even more intriguing under-explored possibilities. One example, is the colony of Hong

Kong, whose record on VET draws a passing but favourable mention in *Employment for the 1990s* (DE 1988:10). Perhaps the failure of the British government to draw greater public attention to the apparent success of VET policies in one of its colonies may relate to the sharply contrasting division of responsibility between state and employer that occurs between Hong Kong and the 'mother country' (Sek-Hong, 1987). Since the early 1980s Hong Kong has been moving in the opposite direction to Britain, as the colony's government has intervened to make good deficiencies caused by a failure on the part of employers to invest sufficiently in training. This contrast suggests that Hong Kong may represent a pertinent subject for comparative research (chapter 10, below).

In suggesting new parts of the world to research, it is important not to ignore the distinct possibility that increased European competition after 1992 and EC legislation on the social dimension of the single market may yet concentrate the British government's attention back towards a European focus. Therefore, nothing above should be taken as suggesting that comparative research within Europe should be abandoned — far from it. There remain considerable opportunities here, not least in probing issues such as the relationships that exist between the different institutional levels in the VET systems of France and West Germany. The role of employers' organizations in France in organizing the provision of training through various regional, inter-industry, and occupational training associations could be contrasted with the UK's NSTOs and TECs. A further possibility are studies of the varying roles played by legislative frameworks in the delivery of VET in Europe.

Another potential area, given the government's stress on the primary role of the individual employer in designing and delivering training, would be a comparative investigation of the factors that influence and shape managerial attitudes towards investment in training. For example, building on the work of Dore (1985) on Japan, there is a need for more attention to the varying structure of the relationship between finance and industrial capital and its effects upon the propensity to train. A comparative analysis of the effects of differing internal financial control systems within firms might also repay attention. Finally, more work probing the links between VET and economic success, whether at company, sectoral, or national and international level would be helpful.

Overall, the thrust of the arguments presented above suggests that, whatever the specific individual research focus, a societal approach to the comparative analysis of VET systems is valuable in promoting greater understanding of the factors that underpin our competitors' relatively superior performance. If nothing else, such a perspective is a valuable antidote to the worrying tendency of British policy makers simply to attempt to copy bits at random of other countries' VET systems.

At the end of the day, British researchers are aware that high quality research does not ensure the construction of rational or sophisticated policies. It is perfectly possible to design and manage a process of policy formulation so that, despite its being informed by the provision of accurate, relevant and thought-provoking data and theories, it will still produce policies that are tactical rather than strategic in nature, and incoherent rather than coherent. Given the multiplicity of intervening variables, time constraints, ideological filtering, the requirements of interest accommodation, and the range of competing sources of information and advice available to policy makers, the best that academics can realistically hope is that they will be able to inform, rather than dictate, the shape of policy formulation.

Nevertheless, given the complexity of the inter-related problems which VET presents to policy makers (Keep and Mayhew, 1988), high quality research must ultimately form an essential prerequisite for the design of policies that stand any reasonable chance of long-term success. Researchers have a vital role in alerting the various actors and interest groups in the policy-making process to the alternatives that are available to them.

Streeck (1985:10) has commented that cross-national differences concerned with social interpretations of aspects of the employment relationship form 'a complex pattern that is difficult and challenging to disentangle'. Nowhere is this more true than in the area of the arrangements different nations make for the provision of vocational education and training. Difficult and challenging though it may be, the disentanglement of these factors is arguably a necessary, if not sufficient, condition for sound policy formulation.

Acknowledgment

The author would like to thank David Finegold, Dr Helen Rainbird, and Professor Keith Sisson, for their helpful comments and suggestions about this piece. As ever, any errors, omissions, or weaknesses of argument remain the sole responsibility of the author.

References

Bolton, E. (1985) 'An HMI perspective', in Watts, A.G. (ed.) *Education and Training 14–18: Policy and Practice,* Cambridge, Careers Research and Advisory Centre.

Brown, G.F. and Read, A.R. (1984) 'Personnel and training policies — Some lessons for western companies', *Long Range Planning,* **17**, 2, pp. 48–57.

Campinos-Dubernet, M. and Grando Cereq, J-M. (1988) *Vocational Education and Training for Workers: Three European Models,* Coventry, University of Warwick, Warwick VET Forum (mimeo).

Clegg, C. (1986) 'Trip to Japan — A synergistic approach to managing human resources', *Personnel Management,* August, pp. 35–39.

Confederation of British Industry (1985) *Training and Vocational Education,* London, CBI, Education and Training Division (mimeo).

Daly, A. (1986) 'Education and Productivity: A Comparison of Great Britain and the United States', *British Journal of Industrial Relations,* **24**, 2, pp. 251–67.

Daly, A., Hitchens, D.M.W.N. and Wagner, K. (1985) 'Productivity, machinery and skills in a sample of British and German manufacturing plants', *National Institute Economic Review*, 111, pp. 48–61.

DEPARTMENT OF EMPLOYMENT (DE) (1988) *Employment for the 1990s*, Cm 540, London, HMSO.

DORE, R.P. (1985) 'Financial structures and the long-term view', *Policy Studies*, 6, 1, pp. 10–29.

EVANS, K. and WATTS, A.G. (1985) 'Introduction', in WATTS, A.G. (ed.) *Education and Training 14–18: Policy and Practice*, Cambridge, Careers Research and Advisory Centre.

FINEGOLD, D. and SOSKICE, D. (1988) 'The failure of training in Britain: analysis and prescription', *Oxford Review of Economic Policy*, 4, 3, pp. 21–53.

FISHER, A. (1988) 'A success story called training', *Financial Times*, 25 August.

FORD, B. (1986) 'The transfer of culturally specific technologies to Australia', in FORD, B. and TILLEY, L. (eds), *Diversity, Change and Tradition*, Canberra, Australian Government Publishing Service.

GARNETT, N. (1989) 'Learning the lesson of low-cost production', *Financial Times*, 12 April.

HARPER, K. (1988) 'Frontiers', *The Guardian*, 23 September.

'Higher education output in engineering — International comparisons', *Employment Gazette*, December 1987, pp. 603–10.

JARVIS, V. and PRAIS, S.J. (1989) 'Two nations of shopkeepers: Training for retailing in France and Britain', *National Institute Economic Review*, 128, pp. 58–73.

KEEP, E. (1986) *Designing the Stable Door: A Study of How the Youth Training Scheme was Planned*, Warwick Papers in Industrial Relations, No. 8, University of Warwick.

KEEP, E. (1987) *Britain's Attempts to Create a National Vocational Education and Training System: A Review of Progress*, Warwick Papers in Industrial Relations No. 16, University of Warwick.

KEEP, E. and MAYHEW, K. (1988) 'The assessment: education, training and economic performance', *Oxford Review of Economic Policy*, 4, 3, pp. i–xv.

KEEP, E., RAINBIRD, H., RICHARDSON, W. and SCHULLER, T. (1988) *The French School of Formation/Emploi — A New Approach to the Problem of Vocational Education and Training*, paper presented to First National VET Forum Conference, University of Warwick, December 1988 (mimeo).

KUSHNER, S. (1985) 'Vocational 'chic': An historical and curriculum context to the field of transition in England', in FIDDY, R. (ed.), *Youth Unemployment and Training: A Collection of National Perspectives*, London, Falmer Press.

LAWLER, G. (1985) 'Land of youth opportunity', *Times Higher Education Supplement*, 14 January.

MACLURE, S. (1985) 'An industrial education lesson for UK?', *Times Educational Supplement*, 1 February.

MAIER, H.E., CORSI, M., JOHN, G. and MOELLER, F. (1986) *The Role of Small Firms and Craft Businesses in the Professional Integration of Youth: A Comparison of the Federal Republic of Germany, France, Italy and Ireland*, Berlin, Federal Republic of Germany, International Institute of Management, IIM/LMP 86–18.

MANPOWER SERVICES COMMISSION (1981a) *A New Training Initiative — A Consultative Document*, MSC, London.

MANPOWER SERVICES COMMISSION (1981b) *A New Training Initiative — An Agenda for Action*, MSC, London.

MANPOWER SERVICES COMMISSION (1982) *Youth Task Group Report*, MSC, London.

MANSELL, J. (1985) 'Competence for all in UK Ltd', *Times Educational Supplement*, 25 January.

MANUFACTURING SCIENCE FINANCE UNION (1988) *Training for a future: Can Britain compete?*, London, MSF.

MARSDEN, D. and SILVESTRE, J-J. (1986) *The economic crisis and labour market regulation in France and Great Britain. Is there convergence to a new pattern of regulation?*, paper presented to the Conference of the International Working Party on Labour Market Segmentation, Cambridge, July 1986 (mimeo).

MAURICE, M., SELLIER, F. and SILVESTRE, J-J. (1986) *The Social Foundations of Industrial Power*, London, MIT Press.

MAURICE, M., SORGE, A. and WARNER, M. (1980) 'Societal differences in organizing manufacturing units: A comparision of France, West Germany and Britain', *Organisation Studies*, **1**, 1, pp. 59–86.

MCCORMICK, K. (1988) 'Vocationalism and the Japanese education system', *Comparative Education*, **24**, 1, pp. 37–51.

MCKINSEY and COMPANY INCORPORATED (1988) *Performance and Competitive Success — Strengthening Competitiveness in UK Electronics*, London, National Economic Development Office.

MEHAUT, P. (1988) 'New firms' training policies and changes in the wage-earning relationship', *Labour and Society*, **13**, 4, pp. 443–56.

MOORE, A. (1988) 'Training in industry — Are the criticisms justified?', *Youth Training News*, **50**, November.

MSC/NEDO (1984) *Competence and Competition*, London, NEDO.

NATIONAL ECONOMIC DEVELOPMENT OFFICE (Manpower and Education Division). (1988) *Performance and Competitive Success — Comparative Education and Training Strategies*, London, NEDO.

OECHSLIN, J.J. (1987) 'Training and the business world: The French experience', *International Labour Review*, **126**, 6, pp. 653–67.

PELL, C. (1989) 'Forward planning is a way through the funding jungle', *Transition*, January, pp. 10–13.

PERRY, P.J.C. (1976) *The Evolution of British Manpower Policy,* London, British Association of Commercial and Industrial Education.

PICKARD, J. (1987) 'Ironing out quibbles in a quango', *Transition*, October, pp. 10–11.

POINTING, D. (1986) 'Retail training in West Germany', *MSC Youth Training News*, April, pp. 2–3.

PRAIS, S.J. (1981) 'Some practical aspects of human capital investment: Training standards in five occupations in Britain and Germany', *National Institute Economic Review*, **98**, pp. 47–59.

PRAIS, S.J. (1985) 'What can we learn from the German system of education and vocational training?' in WORSWICK, G.D.N. (ed.)

PRAIS, S.J. and WAGNER, K. (1983) 'Some Practical Aspects of Human Capital Investment: Training Standards in Five Occupations in Britain and Germany', *National Institute Economic Review*, **105**, pp. 46–65.

PRAIS, S.J. and WAGNER, K. (1985) 'Schooling standards in England and Germany: Some summary comparisons bearing on economic performance', *National Institute Economic Review,* **112**, pp. 53–76.

PRAIS, S.J. and WAGNER, K. (1988) 'Productivity and management: The training of foremen in Britain and Germany', *National Institute Economic Review*, **23**, pp. 34–45.

Ewart Keep

Rose, M. (1985) 'Universalism, culturalism and the Aix group: Promise and problems of a societal approach to economic institutions', *European Sociological Review*, **1**, 1, pp. 65–83.

Sako, M. and Dore, R. (1988) 'Teaching or testing: The role of the state in Japan', *Oxford Review of Economic Policy*, **4**, 3, pp. 72–81.

Sek-Hong, N.G. (1987) 'Training problems and challenges in a newly-industrialised economy: The case of Hong Kong', *International Labour Review*, **126**, 4, pp. 467–78.

Sheldrake, J. and Vickerstaff, S. (1987) *The History of Industrial Training in Britain*, Aldershot, Gower Publishing Co.

Shepherd, R. (1987) 'Why indiscriminate adult training is not the answer', *Transition*, March, p. 3.

Sorge, A. and Warner, M. (1980) 'Manpower training, manufacturing organisation and workplace relations in Great Britain and West Germany', *British Journal of Industrial Relations*, **18**, 3, pp. 318–33.

Spiers, B-G. and Watkins, G. (1987) 'Hamburg's answer to shipyard redundancies', *Transition*, September, pp. 15–17.

Steedman, H. (1987) 'Vocational training in France and Britain: Office work', *National Institute Economic Review*, **120**, pp. 58–70.

Steedman, H. and Wagner, K. (1987) 'A second look at productivity, machinery and skills in Britain and Germany', *National Institute Economic Review*, **122**, pp. 84–95.

Steedman, H. and Wagner, K. (1989) 'Productivity, Machinery and Sills: Clothing Manufacture in Britain and Germany', *National Institute Economic Review*, **128**, pp, 40–57.

Streeck, W. (1985) *Industrial Relations and Industrial Change in the Motor Industry — An International View*, Coventry, University of Warwick, Industrial Relations Research Unit.

Streeck, W., Hilbert, J., Van Kevelaer, F., Maier, F. and Weber, H. (1987) *The Role of the Social Partners in Vocational Training and Further Training in the Federal Republic of Germany*, Berlin, Federal Republic of Germany, European Centre for the Promotion of Vocational Training.

Swedish Institute (1987) *Fact Sheets on Sweden*, Stockholm, The Swedish Institute.

Swedish Labour Market Policy (1988) London, Campaign for Work.

Swedish National Labour Market Board (1987) *Employment Training*, Solna, Sweden, National Labour Market Board Information Division.

Trades Union Congress (1988) *Skills for Success — A TUC Statement on Training*, London, TUC.

Wilson, T. (1987) 'Opinion', *Transition*, May, pp. 3–4.

Windolf, P. (1982a) *Recruitment and Selection in Enterprises — A comparative view on Britain and Germany*, Berlin, Federal Republic of Germany, International Institute of Management, IIM/LMP 82–17.

Windolf, P. (1982b) *Education as a Screening Device — Patterns of Qualified Manpower Utilization in France, Germany and Great Britain*, Berlin, Federal Republic of Germany, International Institute of Management, IIM/LMP 82–21.

Worswick, G.D.N. (ed.). (1985) *Education and Economic Performance*, London, Gower Publishing Co.

2   Scotland v. England: The Place of 'Home Internationals' in Comparative Research

David Raffe

Introduction

In a government office in London a notice on the wall exhorts the statisticians who work there to 'Remember Scotland!' (Underneath a further message has been added: 'Forget Wales').[1] The reminder (for Scotland, that is) is probably needed. Scotland is a long way north of Watford; from the south-east of England the differences between England, Great Britain and the United Kingdom may seem unimportant. But the exhortation should perhaps also be addressed to students of comparative education and training (ET). Scotland is largely missing from their comparative maps. Frequently it is simply absent, like other small countries, from studies which pick on the larger and better known ET systems for comparison. At other times, and more regrettably, 'England' is treated as synonymous with Britain or the UK.

The purpose of many of these comparative studies is, at least ultimately, practical and inward-looking. They are driven by the question, 'what can we learn from other systems?' or even, 'what can we borrow from other systems?' Yet it is recognized that any practical conclusions from these comparisons are indirect and difficult to draw. Other things are not equal. Other countries' ET systems are too different for piecemeal borrowing of institutions or practices to be effective or even possible. And the different political, cultural, economic and industrial contexts further confound attempts to draw practical lessons. For such comparisons 'societal analysis', or at least a recognition of the interdependence of ET with other economic and social structures, is necessary (Maurice *et al.*, 1986; Finegold and Soskice, 1988). By comparison, the Scottish and English systems are, at least in an international context, much more alike. And politics, culture, economic organization and industrial relations in the two countries are, if not identical, at least much closer to each other than to any overseas country. Where Scottish and English institutional arrangements do differ, therefore, there may be more scope for learning practical lessons from their comparison: the other things are more nearly equal.

This chapter aims to put Scotland on the comparative map of ET systems. After a discussion of problems of evidence posed by the 'myth' of Scottish education, the main institutions of Scottish ET, particularly for 14–18 year olds, are outlined and analyzed, highlighting the key differences from England. The chapter continues with a discussion of the extent to which Scotland has a separate ET system. Does common statehood mean that Anglo-Scottish differences are more appropriately made the dependent rather than the independent variable of any comparative analysis? Does Scotland have the right to field a full international team? Finally, the place of 'home internationals' against other UK nations, particularly England, is discussed. What, and how, can England learn from Scotland?

One caveat — or perhaps apology — is needed. To take England as the comparator, and to ask 'is Scotland different?', is probably to get the question the wrong way round. By most international standards England not Scotland is the deviant case. Scottish educationists rightly object to comparisons which treat England as the yardstick: among other things, this encourages a complacency about Scottish ET which comparisons with other systems might challenge (Grant *et al*., 1989). Because this chapter was originally written mainly for a UK audience, it focuses on the role of 'home international' comparisons within the UK. But comparisons between Scotland and overseas countries would be equally valid and valuable.

The Myth of Scottish ET

The task of portraying the differences between Scottish and English ET is made more difficult by two factors. First, both systems, and particularly their more 'vocational' elements, are in a process of rapid and continuing change. This raises the question of whether it is meaningful or useful to compare two systems that are both changing, particularly when some of the changes share common political sources, and I return to this point later in the chapter. At a more practical level, it means that most standard sources on the Scottish system, and on Scottish-English differences, are already very out of date.

The second factor is more profound. In an earlier study colleagues and I identified a 'myth' of Scottish education as broad, accessible, democratic, meritocratic and communally oriented, particularly compared to England (Gray *et al*., 1983; see also McPherson and Raab, 1988). In calling it a myth we did not mean that it was necessarily false. Rather we suggested (following Durkheim, 1915) that to the extent that myths guided people's actions they might help to reproduce the very social structures that they professed to describe. However the myth has multiple functions: to describe, to celebrate and to prescribe. In reading any account that is influenced by the Scottish myth, the reader must disentangle these elements.

Myths play an important part in many international comparisons of ET, not only those between Scotland and England. For example *Competence and Competition* (MSC/NEDO, 1984), one of the most influential comparative studies of recent years, drew substantially on the mythology of the three systems it described, as communicated by key informants. To the extent that a myth provides a significant motive force for a country's ET system, this may be a valid approach. However, it is important to distinguish the myth by which a country describes itself, and which is therefore a constitutive part of the system it refers to, from the stereotyped perceptions of outsiders.

One danger inherent in myths is that they may encourage a selectiveness of treatment, focusing attention on parts of the system that conform to the myth, and ignoring those that do not. But there are several reasons why the Scottish myth should be particularly problematic for international comparisons. Scotland is a small country, and consequently less researched than England. There is less systematic evidence available with which to test empirical propositions arising from the myth. Moreover, the Scottish myth is capable of different interpretations. There are several different 'Scottish traditions' in ET (McPherson and Raab, 1988). Commentators can be selective in the features of current Scottish practice that they attribute to the Scottish tradition; the features they dislike can always be blamed on English inter-ference. Different commentators select differently: TVEI, for example, has variously been held up as an unacceptable Anglicizing influence or as the means through which the best of the Scottish vocational tradition could be realized.[2]

Since 1987 the identity and tradition of Scottish education have assumed particular political significance. Up to the 1987 election the Government pur-sued a broadly consensual educational policy in Scotland. The consensus was severely damaged by an industrial dispute involving school teachers from 1984–87 (longer and more bitter than in England: see Ross, 1987); but at least those parts of educational policy that were not made in the Treasury were broadly in line with much educational opinion in Scotland. Following the 1987 election, and the appointment of a right-wing Scottish education minister (Michael Forsyth) from 1987–89 this consensus was openly challenged. The Government began to introduce changes — notably national testing, 'opting-out' arrangements and 'technology academies' — which had not been mentioned in the Conservatives' Scottish manifesto, but resembled current policy changes in England and Wales. The government was consequently accused of Anglicizing the Scottish system, replying in turn that its policies were the true interpreters of the Scottish tradition. The accusation is a serious one: church, law and education have been symbols of Scottish identity ever since the Union of 1707, and as church and law have become less prominent in public life so has the symbolic role of education become more powerful.

The Scottish myth and the Scottish tradition now lie at the intersection of educational, political and constitutional debates. In such circumstances disinterested and objective analysis may be hard to find.

David Raffe

The Institutions and Character of Scottish ET

Institutions

Most of Scottish education is within the purview of the Scottish Education Department (SED), a Department of the Scottish Office. The main exception is the university sector, which came (until the 1991 proposals at least) under the Department of Education and Science (DES). Schools and further education colleges are administered by the local education authorities. Public sector higher education is the direct responsibility of the Scottish Office.

The responsibilities of the Training Agency (TA) — formerly the Manpower Services Commission (MSC) — cover Scotland as well as England and Wales. After 1977 the MSC reported to the Secretary of State for Scotland with respect to its activities in Scotland, and a separate Committee for Scotland was set up, serviced by an Office for Scotland and a Scottish director, but most policies remained British in scope. In 1991 most of the powers of the TA in Scotland will be transferred to two new bodies, Scottish Enterprise and Highlands and Islands Enterprise.

Scottish children start primary school at 5 and attend for seven years. They transfer to secondary school at 12. The vast majority attend secondary schools that are public, comprehensive, co-educational and offer courses to 18 years. The private sector is smaller in Scotland than in England (but see Walford, 1987). The comprehensive system is more firmly established and school organization is more uniform.

Because of the later transfer, the third and fourth years of secondary school in Scotland correspond roughly to the fourth and fifth years in England. Courses taken over these two years lead to O grade or Standard grade examinations, which correspond to English O levels and GCSE respectively. Since 1984–86 the Standard grade has been phased in, to replace the O grade, on a subject-by-subject basis. The process is still not complete. Like their English equivalents both O and S grade are mainly subject-based, and a pupil might attempt up to seven or eight subjects.

Formally 16 year olds in Scotland face the same options as in England: school, college, the Youth Training Scheme (YTS) and (un)employment. But the meaning of these options, particularly the first two, is significantly different.[3]

More Scottish than English 16 year olds continue in full-time education at 16, and most do so at school. Most stayers study for Highers, the principal qualification for higher education. In contrast to the A level the Higher is normally attempted after a one-year course taken in the fifth (first post-compulsory) year, and most higher education entrants have passes in at least five subjects. The Higher serves a much broader client group than the A level. Whereas the A level caters mainly for the most 'academic' stayers who plan to enter higher education, a much larger proportion of Scottish 16 year olds embark on at least one Higher, and many take only one or two subjects. The

50

rest of their time may be devoted to new or repeated subjects at O or S grade, or to vocational modules for the National Certificate (NC) of the Scottish Vocational Education Council (Scotvec). Half of the voluntary stayers leave at the end of the fifth year. The age of 17 is therefore a key transition point in Scottish education, linked with the four-year honours degree course and the tradition of early entry to university (now largely restricted to the west: McPherson, 1984). For those who stay on, the sixth year may be spent taking more Highers, O/S grades or NC modules, re-sitting subjects, or studying for the Certificate of Sixth Year Studies — a course designed to provide scope for individual and in-depth study for those who have passed through the one-year and rather pressured Highers course (McPherson and Neave, 1976).

College courses for young people are more exclusively 'vocational' than in England, and usually occupationally specific. In contrast to England, where full-time non-advanced further education (NAFE) typically runs parallel to post-compulsory schooling as an alternative 'stream', in Scotland it more often lies end-on to it; most school-leaver entrants to full-time NAFE are 17 or 18 rather than 16. The other major difference affecting NAFE is described later in this section: most Scottish NAFE students, full-and part-time, study Scotvec NC modules.

A slightly larger proportion of Scottish than English youngsters enters YTS, probably reflecting the generally weaker labour market in Scotland, although as in England the scale and character of the scheme vary locally. Scotland made faster progress than England towards providing trainees with opportunities for certification, largely due to the availability of NC modules. More off-the-job training in Scotland is provided by further education colleges, partly because of the NC and partly because more YTS providers are small employers or organizations unable to provide their own off-the-job training.

The fourth option for 16 year olds — if less available at 16 now than two decades ago — is a job. The occupational composition of youth employment differs only slightly between Scotland and England (Raffe and Courtenay 1988). One implication of this is that differences in the level and character of training are not primarily the result of different occupational structures. Average employment rates (particularly for young men) are lower in Scotland than in England, but average differences are dwarfed by the enormous variation across local labour markets. The English north-south divide is mirrored by a west-east divide in Scotland.

Comparisons of survey data on 17–18 year olds in full-time jobs in 1986 suggest that more Scots than English and Welsh were receiving training in their present jobs: 63 per cent compared with 51 per cent. The difference may partly reflect different question wordings in the respective surveys, but this does not easily explain the much larger proportion of boys who reported receiving training covering three years or more: 33 per cent in Scotland compared with 19 per cent in England and Wales. Further analysis suggests that Scotland had about twice the proportion of long-term trainees among young male workers in each of the following sectors: metal goods, engineering and vehicles; construction; distribution, hotels, catering and repairs; and 'other services'.[4] These data must be treated with considerable caution but they suggest that apprenticeship or similar training arrangements for boys may have withstood recent shocks to the labour market more effectively in Scotland than in England. In neither country do many girls enter apprenticeships or long-term traineeships, except in hairdressing.

Systematic evidence on the organization and content of industrial training is harder to come by. Published studies (e.g., Fairley, 1982) date quickly. The formal structures of apprenticeship are much the same as in England, although its scale has traditionally been greater in Scotland. The ITBs and most non-statutory training organizations (NSTOs) cover all of Britain, but some NSTOs are Scottish in scope (Varlaam, 1989). In areas such as construction, plumbing, distribution and agriculture, distinct Scottish organizations help to shape arrangements for training. In general there tends to be a greater educational (college) input into training in Scotland, and a smaller role for the private sector.

I have mentioned the modular National Certificate, introduced following the SED's (1983) Action Plan. This deserves a fuller discussion, partly because it is probably the feature of Scottish VET that is best known internationally, and partly because the modular system has, or aspires to, an integrating, co-ordinating and rationalizing role with respect to most of the institutions and practices I have just described.

The Action Plan was published in January 1983, and implemented from August 1984. It has replaced nearly all non-advanced vocational courses with a system of modules, each of notional forty hours' duration, available in schools, colleges and some private centres. Each module conforms to a standard design framework, and is specified by a module descriptor which includes a list of learning outcomes. To complete a module, a student must achieve all the learning outcomes to a level specified by performance criteria. Passes are not graded; a module is either completed or not completed. Completed modules are accredited by a single National Certificate, awarded by Scotvec. There are no general levels of modules, although there may be recognized lines of progression within a subject area. Modules vary widely in 'difficulty' and are designed for all ability levels. On paper at least the modular system increases flexibility and choice with respect to the content, place and pacing of study, with multiple entry and exit points.

I have discussed the background and strategy of the Action Plan elsewhere (Raffe, 1985, 1988a; Raffe and Tomes, 1987). It is important to stress that the reform was about more than merely modularization. Modules 'are contributory to solutions, they are not solutions in themselves' (Mack, 1989:27). The reform covered pedagogy and assessment and the content as well as the structure of the curriculum. Moreover, as an example of 'modularization' the Scottish framework is distinctive by virtue of its comprehensive national scope, its strategy of 'institutional versatility',[5] the full-hearted application of the principle of criterion-referencing, and the absence of general levels or grading of modules. Perhaps most important is the uniform specification of modules, and the scope for curricular rationalization, coherence and progression made possible by a single qualifying body, Scotvec.

Modularization and related reforms of curriculum, pedagogy and assessment are now being extended to advanced courses. The group certificates (HNC and HND) are being retained.

Initially there was no formal grouping of NC modules, except as implied in 'equivalences' negotiated with the CGLI. However Scotvec is now introducing 'National Awards' for specified groups of modules[6] although it will still be possible to take any other combination. National Awards that match industry-defined standards for specific occupations will be recognized as Scottish Vocational Qualifications (SVQs), equivalent to National Vocational Qualifications (NVQs) in England and Wales.

Partly as a consequence of its separate and earlier reforms of vocational qualifications, Scotland has never been covered by the National Council for Vocational Qualifications (NCVQ). A consultative paper (SED, 1988) raised the question of NCVQ membership, but most responses opposed the move. In December 1988, the Secretary of State announced that Scotland would remain outside NCVQ for the time being.

Part of the reason for this decision was the progress in 1988 of the 'Hughes initiative' (by the current chairman of the Scottish CBI) which was to lead to the reorganization of training in Scotland. Proposals were outlined in a December 1988 White Paper (IDS, 1988a) and a Commons statement of July 1989. The Training Agency in Scotland will be replaced by two bodies. Scottish Enterprise (SE) will be formed from a merger with the Scottish Development Agency (SDA), and Highlands and Islands Enterprise (HIE) will be formed from a merger with the Highlands and Islands Development Board (HIDB). Most of the Scottish population will be covered by SE. SE and HIE will contract various tasks, including the training functions formerly delivered by TA area offices, to Local Enterprise Companies (LECs): twelve in the SE area and eight in the HIE area. Two-thirds of the board of each LEC will be drawn from the private sector.

The most obvious difference between these proposals and the parallel creation of TECs in England is that the new Scottish bodies will have broader responsibilities, encompassing the former SDA and HIDB functions as well as those of the TA. Other possible differences between the emerging Scottish and English systems concern the definition of areas and performance targets for the LECs. As proposed in July 1989 the LEC areas will largely coincide with local education authorities. And the White Paper listed possible performance targets for LECs, for example relating to equal opportunities, which hinted at a more socially responsive role than that played by TECs in England.

One other key difference between the Scottish and English developments lies in the role of SE and HIE themselves. However, the training policy framework will continue to be determined at a British level, and it is likely that the strategic role of SE and HIE with respect to training will be limited. (I discuss this further in the section headed 'A Full International Team?') The July 1989 statement also announced that responsibility for TVEI in Scotland would move to the Industry Department for Scotland.

Character

The preceding discussion has, I hope, provided a reasonably uncontroversial guide to the institutions of Scottish ET. Adopting now a more analytical approach, review the problem of evidence arising from the multiplex nature of the Scottish myth, discussed above, and from current political sensitivities. I discuss three aspects of Scottish ET: structure, curriculum and government.

Structure. Commentators on the Scottish system have described it as being closer to Turner's (1961) model of 'contest' mobility through education than England, which was Turner's example of a 'sponsored' system (McPherson, 1973; Raffe and Courtenay, 1988). In contest systems selection decisions are postponed and the bases for selection less clearly prescribed; in systems of sponsored mobility future members of the elite are identified at an early stage and given separate educational preparation for their future roles.

The structure of Scottish ET encourages higher participation, weaker streaming between academic and vocational tracks, and more flexibility than in England and Wales. More young people continue full-time education beyond 16; and many more take at least one subject for Highers than take A levels in England and Wales. Consequently young people in Scotland keep their options open for longer, and those entering vocational training in Scotland tend to do so from a higher educational base. The one-year Highers course, and the modular structure of vocational certificates, make it much easier to combine academic and vocational study during the post-compulsory stage, either simultaneously or serially (with significant transitions from school to full-time NAFE at 17 and 18). The boundary between academic and vocational tracks is further weakened by the 'education-led' character of the latter, discussed below, and by the smaller role of the private sector in training in Scotland. This contrasts with the situation in England and Wales, where the 'industry-led' NCVQ with its emphasis on work-based competences and on 'output' rather than 'input' controls, is perceived to accentuate the gap between academic and vocational provision (Spours, 1988:8–10). In the Scottish system integration and progression are (at least on paper) further facilitated by the existence of a single body issuing vocational awards, and by the standard design framework for NC modules which promotes consistency in pedagogy and assessment and coherence in content. A further consequence is that the distinction between vocational and pre-vocational, never as clear as in England, has been abolished in educational terms, even if the institutional and labour-market differences associated with this distinction still matter (Raffe, 1988a). The weaker boundaries, broader curriculum and shorter course units of the Scottish system create more flexibility for the individual as well as for the system as a whole.[7]

These advantages are not without cost: in particular, the one-year, five-subject Highers course encourages a more restricted pedagogy and shallower curricular coverage than the two-year, three-subject A-level course. The government is considering proposals to extend the Higher to two years (but not to reduce the curricular range to three subjects). This would bring benefits, but at the possible cost of reduced participation beyond 16 and (more significantly) of increased 'streaming' from 16 to 18.

Curriculum. Commentators have laid claim to a Scottish 'tradition' of VET that emphasizes its integration with general education. The Education for the Industrial Society Project, the Scottish equivalent of the Schools Council Industry Project, gave voice to this view:

> *Vocational education* refers to those aspects of schooling which have relevance to the world of work, are economically useful to pupils in later life, and provide a vocational impulse now.... In summary, what is required is a broad, general education fully in keeping with the Scottish tradition. (CCC, 1983:30)

The most cogent recent statement of this view of Scottish VET is by Weir (1988). As it has evolved in Scotland, vocational education (according to Weir) is part of general education and for all students: part of the common course of the comprehensive school. It is not occupationally specific, but prepares young people for a range of occupations and for adult life more broadly. It is learner-centred, and process rather than content based.

Parts of Weir's account of the Scottish tradition, and of current practice, may seem dewy- (and Dewey-) eyed. His book exemplifies the multiple functions of myth — to describe, to prescribe and to celebrate — and these strands must be disentangled in his account, Nevertheless, the descriptive case for the Scottish tradition is well argued, and it is not difficult to find current examples. Perhaps the most important is the Scottish National Certificate. In contrast with the NCVQ framework south of the border, the NC tends to be education-led rather than industry-led (although this may be changing under the influence of lead industry bodies); standards are maintained through controls over 'inputs' as well as 'outputs'; the content is broader and less 'occupationally' focused (see Spours, 1988). One of the architects of the Scottish framework has expressed the difference thus:

> The integration of 'education' and 'training' in VET (rather than 'vocational training' and 'education') is a point of Scottish distinctiveness, as is the tendency to stress the importance of general educational elements (language, number, problem solving, and so on) in vocational programmes: such elements were 'designed in' to many Action Plan modules (rather than 'analysed out' afterwards).[8]

The integration of vocational with general education is favoured by the structure of post-compulsory education, with its weak streaming and potential for combining academic and vocational subjects. (It may, therefore, be put at risk by a two-year Higher.) I have usually referred to ET rather than VET in this paper, to reflect the fact that Scottish VET can only be described in the context of the broader ET system.

Government. At least three features of the government of Scottish ET are frequently noted by commentators. The first is rationalization. Thus the national NC framework, under a single qualifying body (Scotvec), contrasts with the English system where 'the competitiveness and entrepreneurism of all the validating bodies have resulted in complete failure to produce a more rational framework of certification' (Spours, 1988:7). NCVQ offers at most a second-best solution to this problem (Spours, 1989). What is significant is that rationalization was judged politically possible in Scotland, but not in England.

Second, 'industry-leadership' is not much in evidence north of the border. Industry has been involved in Scottish developments through consultation, but it has rarely led. There are some practical reasons for this: to have industry-leadership you must first have some industry, and the leaders of that industry must be closer than south-east England or North America. There are fewer organizations capable of leading on behalf of industry at a Scottish level than at a UK (or English) level. Of course, generalizations about industry-leadership can be difficult to confirm or refute. The true picture is likely to be patchy, across sectors and across areas (Bennett *et al.*, 1989). At a Scottish level the Hughes initiative provides a recent, if very debatable, example of industry-leadership. And one may question the extent to which there has been true industry-leadership of VET anywhere in the UK. The way in which British industry has had leadership thrust upon it by both the MSC/TA and the government could be seen as powerful evidence of its lack of leadership potential. But even these attempts to stimulate industry-leadership have fitted less well in the Scottish scene. Lead industry bodies (LIBs), for example, were introduced several years too late from Scotland's point of view, and proved awkward to accommodate to Scotvec's existing consultative arrangements.

The corollary of the lack of industry-leadership is strong education-leadership, especially from the SED and in particular the inspectorate. Once again the contrast between the Action Plan and the NCVQ is instructive. The SED produced the Plan, led the writing of the new modules and then set up a new body (Scotvec) to run the system it had created. The main stage of the process — from publication of the Plan to delivery of the first modules — took just nineteen months. It is hard to imagine the DES ever behaving in this way, especially in its more passive mood of the early 1980s.

The greater 'centralization' of Scottish education is the third feature of the governance of Scottish ET, and a powerful component of the Scottish myth. It tends to be attributed less to the institutions of Scottish education (many of which offer no more scope for central control than in England and

Wales) than to the degree of consensus in Scottish education and its tradition of 'looking to the centre for a lead' (McPherson and Raab, 1988, chapter 2). The consensual basis of Scottish central control has been contested by critics such as Humes (1986), and McPherson and Raab (1988) discuss at length the SED's active role in constructing and managing the consensus, at the cost of limiting its own freedom of manœuvre. The next section will discuss how the SED performed this role in respect of the Action Plan.

But in discussing the management of consensus, and the limits to the SED's freedom of manœuvre, we must examine the Scottish myth's suggestion that not only is ET centralized, but that 'the centre lies only in Scotland' (McPherson and Raab, 1988:481). To a remarkable extent debates about the 'centralization' of Scottish ET have shut the rest of the UK out of explicit consideration. But for the present discussion the UK dimension is obviously important. Differences between Scotland and England — or the absence of such differences — may themselves be an explicit object of policy. Before we can place Scotland on a comparative map of ET systems we must determine the extent to which Scotland is indeed a 'system'.

The Role of Home Internationals

Anglo-Scottish comparisons raise two salient issues. The first involves viability. Are differences between the two countries sufficiently great to be of interest? The second issue involves content. Given that there is scope for Anglo-Scottish comparisons, what are the lessons to be drawn, particularly for English ET?

A Full International Team? The Semi-dependent Status of Scottish ET

At least three factors restrict not only the SED's control, but more broadly the capacity of Scottish ET to develop in a different direction from England.

First, the labour market and its institutions exert a strong pressure towards uniformity. All the ITBs and most trades unions and employers' organizations are British in scope, as are most LIBs. There is 'virtual national uniformity in the conditions and forms of labour market regulation' (Ashton, 1988:14). The structure of the youth labour market and the processes within it differ little between Scotland and England — particularly once the effects of educational differences are discounted (Raffe and Courtenay, 1988). Both labour markets provide similar 'contexts' for the ET system, and transmit similar market signals, typically encouraging early leaving and the pursuit of academic rather than vocational qualifications. It is no coincidence that neither system has developed a full-time 'technical' sector of standing comparable to many school-based continental systems (Raffe and Tomes, 1987; Raffe, 1988b).

Second, common political control has encouraged uniformity. Public funding for VET in Scotland is kept in line with the rest of the UK. Although the formula which governed Scotland's share of exchequer spending for much of this century was relatively generous to Scotland, it prevented a radical departure between the two systems (McPherson and Raab, 1988:178–9). Most of the political milestones in ET over the last quarter century have affected Scotland as well as England: the rise and fall of the ITBs, comprehensive re-organization, the raising of the short-leaving age (ROSLA), TVEI, YTS, 'opting out', city technology colleges, TECs, and so on.

From a Scottish viewpoint the issue is not just the British-wide application of political initiatives but that the problems to which they respond, and the solutions they offer, tend to be English rather than Scottish ones. TVEI, LIBs and CTCs are just three examples of initiatives which responded to English problems and were designed for English circumstances, but have nevertheless been imposed on Scotland. Of the three, TVEI has adapted most successfully to Scotland but the process of adaptation was slow and costly.[9] A Scottish-designed initiative might have achieved much more.

This brings me to the third constraint on the development of the Scottish system — the MSC, now absorbed into the Department of Employment. The MSC was always British in scope, notwithstanding its formal accountability, after 1977, to the Secretary of State for Scotland with respect to its Scottish activities.

There is a parallel with the evolution of the European Community (EC). The Treaty of Rome specified vocational training as a matter of Community competence but left education policy to the member states. However this division of responsibilities came under pressure as the interdependence of education and training were increasingly recognized (Neave, 1988). How could the Community promote the harmonization of training when its complement, education, remained subject to the divergent policies of member states? The same tension can be seen within the UK. The MSC's own policies for young people helped to turn the spotlight on the deficiencies of the education system (Keep, 1986) and were increasingly premised on the interdependence of education and training. Given this premise, and given the different education systems of Scotland and England, the logical course for the MSC would have been to differentiate its policies to articulate with these different education systems. To a large extent this never happened. The MSC did not adopt a single major policy initiative that was Scottish in scope. The best that Scotland could hope for was either exemption from the English policy (e.g., MSC control over work-related NAFE) or local modifications to the imported product (e.g., TVEI). Possibly the dynamic organizational style of the MSC relied upon tight central control: too much devolution of initiative might have released uncontrollable centrifugal forces.[10] Possibly the MSC anticipated resistance from the SED to a more active Scottish role. Whatever the explanation, the MSC's failure to assume a distinctive Scottish role was the dog that didn't bark in Scottish ET.

As a consequence of these three factors it has been difficult for Scottish ET to plan itself as a system. The problems of policy making in Scottish ET resemble those of a man who wishes to build a house in the style of Robert

Adam, but has to incorporate design features to match the mock-Tudor villa that his neighbour is planning. To make matters worse the neighbour keeps changing his mind about the style he wishes to follow, and tends to build with the cheapest available materials.

But Scotland's semi-dependent status has had three further and more subtle consequences. First, given the MSC's failure to develop a distinctive Scottish policy, and the relative weakness of Scottish industrial leadership, the only major source of Scottish-wide initiative in ET has been the SED itself. This has powerfully reinforced the Scottish 'tradition' of ET — and VET — as education-led. It may now be under threat if the current reforms allow a significant strategic role for Scottish Enterprise.

Second, Scotland's semi-dependent status has helped the SED to construct a consensus around its ET policies. The Action Plan was widely perceived as the SED's attempt to pre-empt or control MSC incursions into Scotland, and this helped it to attract a level of support matched by few other ET policies of the Thatcher government (Raffe, 1985). The honeymoon has since ended, but there remains wider support for the National Certificate than seems to exist in England for the NCVQ.[11]

Third, the SED's incomplete control of Scottish ET has influenced the nature of its policies. It is as though the builder described above chose a style that could accommodate design features from any style that his neighbour decided to introduce. The Action Plan strategy of 'institutional versatility' was chosen to maximize rationalization and influence in a system over which the SED's control was incomplete. Rather than an expression of Scottish centralization, the Action Plan strategy can also be seen as a response to the limits of central, and especially SED, power.[12]

Two current developments raise questions concerning the future of the Scottish dimension in ET. The first is the grouping of NC modules and other units into SVQs, in order to 'allow a closer alignment of vocational qualifications within the UK'.[13] Like NVQs, SVQs must be based on industry-defined national standards; not only are they industry-led, but most are led by industry bodies that are British or UK in scope. But unlike NVQs, SVQs must first be recognized as 'National Awards', the criteria for which include breadth of application, range of activities and relevance beyond immediate technological and market conditions. It remains to be seen how actively Scotvec will use these additional criteria to avoid becoming a rubber-stamp for NVQs north of the border.

The second development is the establishment of SE and HIE to replace the Training Agency in Scotland. When the idea of SE was first mooted in 1988 it was billed as offering 'Scottish solutions to Scottish needs'. But the strategic role of SE and HIE, in relation to LECs on the one hand and to London and Sheffield on the other, remains unclear, at least as far as ET is concerned. The Department of Employment retains lead responsibility for training and the remit of the National Training Task Force covers the whole of Great Britain. The July 1989 statement implied that the strategic role of SE and HIE would relate largely to enterprise and development, the former responsibilities of the SDA and the HIDB. With respect to training, it merely said that SE and HIE should 'ensure that the Government's Great Britain-wide training policies and priorities are pursued and Government guarantees fully satisfied'. The fact that there will be two Scottish bodies at this level may further inhibit SE and HIE from developing a major strategic role in respect of training. So may the organizational dynamics (and inertia) arising from the transfer of staff and responsibilities from the SDA, the HIDB and the TA.

Were SE and HIE to develop a strategic training role, against the odds, this might have two seemingly contradictory consequences. On the one hand it might increase the differences between Scotland and England by allowing greater policy differentiation at the Scottish level. On the other hand, by pro-viding alternative sources of initiative and leadership to the SED, it might result in the Scottish system becoming less 'education-led' and thereby bring it closer to that of England.

What and How can England Learn from Scotland?

To some extent Scotland's semi-dependent status sets a limit on the practical lessons we are likely to learn from comparisons with England. Many of the failings of British ET, especially training, can be attributed to a long-term lack of political will. This has resulted in public and private under-funding, in the need for reforms of ET to piggy-back on other political debates such as youth unemployment, in the subordination of ET policy to other ideological and pol-itical concerns, in frequent shifts of policy, and so on.[14] Whatever the internal politics of Scotland, it is part of the same political system as England, and affected by the political priorities of the UK as a whole. This limits the scope for separate development of Scottish ET, and consequently limits the scope for other UK nations to learn or borrow from Scottish experience.

A further consequence of Scotland's semi-dependent status is that many distinctive features of Scottish ET are a consequence of, or an accommodation to, its lack of autonomy. This may make these features harder, or less appro-priate, to replicate elsewhere. Indeed many of these features may have succeeded precisely because of Scotland's peculiar status. For example, one reason why central leadership has been more widely accepted in Scotland is that it has been seen as an alternative to leadership from the other centre south of the border. Scottish-style 'centralization' would have a very different reception if replicated in England. Once again, Scotland's semi-dependent status inhibits the easy replicability of its ET institutions. However, Scottish-UK relations may themselves offer interesting insights into the future develop-ment of UK-EC relations. 'Home internationals', perhaps, belong at one end of a spectrum of types of international ET comparisons. Further along this spectrum are comparisons between members of supra-national organizations, like the EC, with active policies for the harmonization of education, training or qualifications. At the other end of the spectrum are comparisons between countries with no such links. Some of the factors which currently make Anglo-Scottish comparisons different from other international comparisons may, increasingly during the 1990s, make intra-EC comparisons different from comparisons with non-EC countries.

So can England learn from Scotland? Yes, but the question must be re-formulated to ask how, rather than what, England can learn; and the answers must be based on a view not only of the differences, but also of the similarities, between Scotland and England. I suggest that most of the *processes* of ET are common to both countries: the processes of learning, people's orientations to ET, students' propensities to respond to different incentives, and the patterns of social differentiation in ET, are all similar in the two countries. So to a large extent are the cultural, social, economic and labour-market *contexts* of ET. The principal differences lie in some of the *institutions* of ET, such as the length and structure of courses, the formal curriculum and assessment procedures, the organizations in or through which ET is delivered, and the mechanisms for coordinating provision. These institutional differences tend to be greater on the 'education' side of ET. The important task in any comparison of Scotland and England is to respect these different levels of analysis. Together with the foregoing discussion this points to at least four ways in which England might learn from Scotland.

The first is simply by (England) *learning from study of Scotland's own experience*. For example Scottish evidence suggests, among other things: that comprehensive education has increased average attainments and reduced class inequalities in attainment (McPherson and Willms, 1987); that rising levels of parental education have boosted children's attainments in secondary edu-cation (Burnhill *et al*., 1988); that employers tend not to use broad-based vocational qualifications as criteria in selecting young people (Bell and Howieson, 1988; Raffe, 1988a); that YTS has consolidated its status by 'going with the grain' of the youth labour market (Raffe, 1988b); that YTS has helped non-employed young people to find employment (Main and Shelly, 1988); and so on. All these conclusions can, I believe, be generalized to the rest of Britain with only modest qualification. But why should England bother to look to Scotland to learn these lessons? One reason is that many policy changes in Scotland have been introduced more swiftly and more uniformly than in England, and their effects are more easily studied (for example comprehensive education and the reform of vocational qualifications). Another reason, I believe, is that only Scotland has had adequate research data to study many of these issues: but here I must declare an interest.

Second, there is scope for learning from *systematic comparisons between England and Scotland*. Such comparisons would focus on specific institutional differences between England and Scotland — such as the different length and structure of post-compulsory courses — and assess their effects on variables of interest such as participation rates, curriculum balance and so on. The design of such studies would be at best quasi-experimental, and at their simplest they would allow only one 'degree of freedom' for inference. But the scope for inference could be increased by comparing national differences across different subgroups and categories of theoretical interest, by comparing national trends over time, or by contrasting the processes involved.[15] The potential for learning from such comparisons is largely untapped. I have mentioned possible comparisons of post-compulsory course structures. Other examples include TVEI, where the availability of a nationally certificated modular framework in Scotland potentially overcomes one of the main obstacles to curriculum development in England and Wales. As far as I am aware, there has been no systematic cross-border comparison of TVEI. Similar comparisons in respect of YTS would be useful. Comparisons of the two systems over time, for example their responses to the current demographic downturn, could be of immense value. Will the greater 'flexibility' of the Scottish system really help it to overcome the anticipated skill shortages, or will the 'rigidities' associated with social, educational and labour-market demarcations prove more powerful? The introduction of separate systems of Scottish LECs (and perhaps Welsh TECs) may provide further possibilities for learning from 'home international' comparisons.

An advantage of comparisons between Scotland and England is that they may illuminate not only the possible consequences of institutional changes, but also their limits. A possible example of this might be a comparison of progression patterns in ET in England and Scotland. This could look not only at the proportions of students or trainees progressing from comparable courses to further education or training, but also at more qualitative aspects of progression. Do Scottish students experience more coherence and continuity in curriculum, pedagogy and assessment? Is progression in Scotland more flexible across occupational or subject areas? Is it more flexibly paced, with modules accumulated more at students' convenience? Such comparisons might show how far progression is restricted by the internal barriers within the NVQ system (Spours, 1988) or, conversely, whether social, economic and labour-market factors, which tend to be common to England and Scotland, are the major impediments to progression (Raffe, 1988a).

Third, Scotland can serve as a *testbed for policy innovations* which are then adopted in the south. At one level this can simply mean either country saving time by taking over policy blueprints developed in the other. For example, the GCSE has much in common with the Scottish Standard grade, and at least the building blocks of the NVQ system are similar to the Scottish National Certificate. I do not know how much either GCSE or NVQs consciously borrowed from the Scottish experience, but the similarities seem too close for coincidence. More interesting examples of 'testbed' developments are where the learning could only take place in Scotland because of its distinctive institutional arrangements. For example, Scotland's early possession of a nationally certificated modular framework made it a convenient testing ground for potential new developments in assessment and work-based learning.

More strategically, one can view the Scottish Action Plan as an experiment to see whether the 'mixed' model of post-compulsory ET in the UK can ever be adapted to modern requirements. While other countries may have institutionally diverse systems, one mode of ET, such as full-time education or an apprenticeship system, is usually dominant (OECD, 1985). In the UK no single mode of ET dominates; there is a mixed system whose constituent parts tend to undermine each other. The products of this system include barriers to progression, a fragmented and unsatisfactory curriculum, and low participation. The Scottish Action Plan represents the best current attempt in the UK to reverse these effects and to impose consistency and coherence. If it fails, the argument for more radical restructuring of post-compulsory ET in the UK may become unanswerable.

Finally, there is scope for Scotland to exercise an *intellectual influence* on England (Spours, 1989:7). Commentators who bemoan the failings of 'British' ET should at least be aware of the plurality of systems within Britain and of the potential leverage that this provides for change from within. And those who believe that the Scottish research results listed above are not applicable to England should be invited to ponder the implications of their belief. How has the centralized British state been able to nurture two such different systems? The intellectual influence of Scotland on English ET is diffuse and in the past has rarely been strong. When Scotland has been most influential it has often been the 'Scottish myth', rather than rigorous observation of Scottish practice, that has been invoked. But this is not wholly inappropriate: to the extent that myths inspire practice they may be, to an extent, self-fulfilling. Perhaps the most important point is simply that there are, within Britain, other respected traditions of ET than the English one. Scotland has something to contribute to debates on ET that are, at least in name, British.

Acknowledgments

Work on this paper was supported by the UK Economic and Social Research Council, of which the CES is a Designated Research Centre. For comments and help in the preparation of this paper I am grateful to John Fairley, David Finegold, Cathy Howieson, Donald Mack, Andrew McPherson, Lindsay Paterson, Charles Raab, Richard Rose, Paul Ryan, Graham Senior, Bert Whiteside and participants at the Manchester Seminar. Responsibility for errors and for the opinions and judgments expressed in this chapter is mine alone.

Notes

1 I am grateful to Peter Burnhill for divulging this Official Secret.
2 On Scottish reactions to TVEI, see Bell *et al*. (1989) and Howieson (1990).
3 The following paragraphs draw on Raffe and Courtenay (1988).
4 Based on unpublished comparisons of data from the Youth Cohort Study (England and Wales) and the Scottish Young People's Survey.

5 Institutional versatility refers to 'the ability to cover a diverse range of institutions (using the term in its broadest sense, to embrace not just school and college but also education and training that is full- and part-time, pre-employment and in-service, education-based and work-based, and MSC and local initiatives) with a single, integrated and coordinated framework' (Raffe, 1988a:163). The same chapter discusses the strategy of institutional versatility, and its limits, in more detail.

6 National Awards may be awarded for combinations of NC modules and/or Higher National units and/or workplace-assessment units awarded by Scotvec, but must meet specified criteria (see section headed 'A Full International Team?').

7 Because of the wider participation and broader curriculum, many more Scottish school leavers have maths or physics at Highers than have maths or physics at A level in England. This is seen to give greater flexibility in increasing the entry to science-based courses, of whose graduates there is a growing shortage (IDS, 1988b).

8 Address by Donald Mack to an Anglo-Dutch conference on VET, April 1988.

9 When TVEI was first announced it was immediately rejected by the SED, as well as local authorities, as unnecessary in Scotland: Standard grade and the Action Plan were already achieving the same ends. But Scotland joined TVEI a year later when the preferred alternative, of rejecting the policy but accepting the money, proved not to be available. The principle was established, however, that TVEI should be compatible with, and support, Standard grade and Action Plan developments. TVEI was fiercely resisted by many people in Scottish education, especially within the EIS, the largest teachers' union. There were major difficulties in implementing the policy, particularly at the 16–18 stage (Bell *et al.*, 1988, 1989). In the event it has generally integrated well with Scottish education, had a positive influence in many areas, and even been claimed as a significant contributor to the Scottish tradition of vocational education (Weir, 1988). But it might have been much more effective had it been designed, from the start, to suit Scottish conditions.

10 The MSC had an advisory Committee for Scotland and a Scottish Director, serviced by an Office for Scotland, but these were not empowered to initiate policy or programmes: see Moore and Booth (1986). Indeed, the Office for Scotland was almost wholly by-passed in the chain of command for TVEI, arguably the initiative where separate Scottish decision-making was most needed because of its educational focus. The activities of the MSC in Scotland are described in Brown and Fairley (1990).

11 At first the Hughes initiative which launched the idea of Scottish Enterprise seemed to attract consensual support similar to that which had greeted the Action Plan. But the Hughes initiative and the ensuing policy proposals were more overtly 'political' and the consensus has since foundered.

12 See note 5 and Raffe (1988a:167–168). The Action Plan strategy can be seen as an alternative to institutional reorganization, and it allowed SED to retain influence over TVEI, YTS and other likely initiatives of the unpredictable MSC.

13 Speech by Ian Lang, Scottish education minister, introducing the new SVQs in October 1989.

14 See, for example, Anderson and Fairley (1983), Raffe (1984), Keep (1986) and Lee *et al.* (1990).

15 This is analogous to Campbell's (1979:59) discussion of case studies where the

social scientist 'test(s) the theory with the degrees of freedom coming from the multiple implications of any one theory'.

References

ANDERSON, M. and FAIRLEY, J. (1983) 'The politics of industrial training in the United Kingdom', *Journal of Public Policy*, **3**, pp. 191–208.

ASHTON, D.N. (1988) 'Sources of variation in labour market segmentation: A comparison of youth labour markets in Canada and Britain', *Work Employment and Society*, **2**, 1, pp. 1–24.

BELL, C. and HOWIESON, C. (1988) 'The view from the hutch: Educational guinea pigs speak about TVEI', in RAFFE, D. (ed.) *Education and the Youth Labour Market: Schooling and Scheming*, London, Falmer Press.

BELL, C., HOWIESON, C., KING, K. and RAFFE, D. (1988) *Liaisons Dangereuses? Education-Industry Relationships in the First Scottish TVEI Pilot Projects: An Evaluation Report*, Sheffield, Training Agency.

BELL, C., HOWIESON, C., KING, K. and RAFFE, D. (1989) 'The Scottish dimension of TVEI'. In BROWN, A. and McCRONE, D. (eds) *Scottish Government Yearbook 1989*, University of Edinburgh, Unit for the Study of Government in Scotland.

BENNETT, R., McCOSHAN, A. and SELLGREN, J. (1989) *TECs and VET: The Practical Requirements: Organisation, Geography and International Comparison with the USA and Germany* Research Paper, London School of Economics, Department of Geography.

BROWN, A. and FAIRLEY, J. (eds) (1990) *The MSC in Scotland 1974–1988*, Edinburgh, Edinburgh University Press.

BURNHILL, P., GARNER, C.L. and McPHERSON, A.F. (1988) 'Social change, school attainment and entry to higher education 1976–1986', in RAFFE, D. (ed.) *Education and the Youth Labour Market: Schooling and Scheming*, London, Falmer Press.

CAMPBELL, T.D. (1979) '"Degrees of freedom" and the case study', in COOK, T.D. and REICHARDT, C.S. (eds) *Qualitative and Quantitative Methods in Evaluation Research*, Beverley Hills, Sage.

CONSULTATIVE COMMITTEE FOR THE CURRICULUM (1983) *An Education for Life and Work: Final Report of the Project Planning Committee of the Education for the Industrial Society Project*, Glasgow, Jordanhill College.

DURKHEIM, E. (1915) *The Elementary Forms of the Religious Life*, London, George Allen and Unwin (5th impression, 1964).

FAIRLEY, J. (1982) 'Industrial Training in Scotland', in DRUCKER, H.M. and DRUCKER, N.L. (eds) *Scottish Government Yearbook 1982*, Edinburgh, Paul Harris.

FINEGOLD, D. and SOSKICE, D. (1988) 'The failure of training in Britain: Analysis and prescription', *Oxford Review of Economic Policy*, **4**, pp. 21–53.

GRANT, N. *et al.* (1989) *Scottish Education: A Declaration of Principles*, Edinburgh, Scottish Centre for Economic and Social Research.

GRAY, J., McPHERSON, A.F. and RAFFE, D. (1983) *Reconstructions of Secondary Education: Theory Myth and Practice since the War*, Henley, Routledge and Kegan Paul.

HOWIESON, C. (1990) 'The impact of the MSC on secondary education', in BROWN, A.

and FAIRLEY, J. (eds) *The MSC in Scotland 1974–1988*, Edinburgh, Edinburgh University Press.

HUMES, W. (1986) *The Leadership Class in Scottish Education*, Edinburgh, John Donald.

INDUSTRY DEPARTMENT FOR SCOTLAND (1988a) *Scottish Enterprise*, Cm 534, Edinburgh, HMSO.

INDUSTRY DEPARTMENT FOR SCOTLAND (1988b) *New Entrants to the Labour Market in Scotland in the 1990s*, ESU Discussion Paper No. 19, Edinburgh, IDS.

MSC/NEDO (1984) Manpower Services Commission/National Economic Development Office, *Competence and Competition*, London, NEDO and MSC.

KEEP, E. (1986) *Designing the Stable Door: A Study of How the Youth Training Scheme was Planned*, Warwick Papers in Industrial Relations No. 18, University of Warwick.

LEE, D., MARSDEN, D., RICKMAN, P. and DUNCOMBE, J. (1990) *Scheming for Youth: A Study of YTS in the Enterprise Culture*, Milton Keynes, Open University Press.

MACK, D. (1989) 'The Scottish Action Plan', in SPOURS, K. *et al. Modularisation and Progression: Issues in the 14–19 Curriculum*, Working Paper No. 6, University of London Institute of Education, Post-16 Education Centre.

MAIN, B. and SHELLY, M. (1988) 'Does it pay young people to go on YTS?', in RAFFE, D. (ed.) *Education and the Youth Labour Market: Schooling and Scheming*, London, Falmer Press.

MAURICE, M., SELLIER, F. and SILVESTRE, J.J. (1986) *The Social Foundations of Industrial Power*, London, MIT Press.

MCPHERSON, A.F. (1973) 'Selection and survivals: A sociology of the ancient Scottish universities', in BROWN, R. (ed.) *Knowledge Education and Cultural Change*, London, Tavistock.

MCPHERSON, A.F. (1984) 'The sixth year', in RAFFE, D. (ed.) *Fourteen to Eighteen: The Changing Pattern of Schooling in Scotland*, Aberdeen, Aberdeen University Press.

MCPHERSON, A.F. and NEAVE, G.R. (1976) *The Scottish Sixth*, Slough, NFER.

MCPHERSON, A.F. and RAAB, C.D. (1988) *Governing Education: A Sociology of Policy since 1945*, Edinburgh, Edinburgh University Press.

MCPHERSON, A.F. and WILLMS, D. (1987) 'Equalisation and improvement: Some effects of comprehensive reorganisation in Scotland', *Sociology*, **21**, 4, pp. 509–39.

MOORE, C. and BOOTH, S. (1986) 'Hunting the Quarc: An Institution without a Role?', mimeo, Strathclyde Business School, Department of Administration.

NEAVE, G. (1988) 'Policy and response: Changing perceptions and priorities in the vocational training policy of the EEC Commission', in LAUGLO, J. and LILLIS, K. (eds) *Vocationalizing Education: An International Perspective*, Oxford, Pergamon.

ORGANISATION FOR ECONOMIC COOPERATION AND DEVELOPMENT (1985) *Education and Training after Basic Schooling*, Paris, OECD.

RAFFE, D. (1984) 'Youth Unemployment and the MSC: 1977–1983', in MCCRONE, D. (ed.) *Scottish Government Yearbook 1984*, Edinburgh, Unit for the Study of Government in Scotland.

RAFFE, D. (1985) 'The extendable ladder: Scotland's 16-plus Action Plan', *Youth and Policy*, **12**, pp. 27–33.

RAFFE, D. (1988a) 'Modules and the strategy of institutional versatility: The first two years of the 16 plus Action Plan in Scotland', in RAFFE, D. (ed.) *Education and the Youth Labour Market: Schooling and Scheming*, London, Falmer Press.

RAFFE, D. (1988b) 'Going with the grain: Youth training in transition', in BROWN, S. and WAKE, R. (eds) *Education in Transition*, Edinburgh, Scottish Council for Research in Education.

RAFFE, D. and COURTENAY, G. (1988) '16–18 on both sides of the border', in RAFFE, D. (ed.) *Education and the Youth Labour Market: Schooling and Scheming*, London, Falmer Press.

RAFFE, D. and TOMES, N. (1987) *The Organisation and Content of Studies at the Post Compulsory Level: Country Study: Scotland*, OECD Educational Monograph, Paris, OECD.

ROSS, D. (1987) *An Unlikely Anger: Scottish Teachers in Action*, Edinburgh, Mainstream.

SCOTTISH EDUCATION DEPARTMENT (1983) *16–18s in Scotland: An Action Plan*, Edinburgh, SED.

SCOTTISH EDUCATION DEPARTMENT (1988) *Relationship between Scotland and the National Council for Vocational Qualifications: A Consultation Paper Issued by the Secretary of State for Scotland*, Edinburgh, SED.

SPOURS, K. (1988) *The Politics of Progression*, Working Paper No. 2, University of London Institute of Education, Post-16 Education Centre.

SPOURS, K. (1989) 'Promoting progression: Prospects for a post 16 modular framework', mimeo, University of London Institute of Education, Post-16 Education Centre.

TURNER, R. (1961) 'Modes of social ascent through education: Sponsored and contest mobility', in HALSEY, A.H., FLOUD, J. and ANDERSON, C.A. (eds) *Education, Economy and Society*, New York, Free Press.

VARLAAM, C. (1989) 'Non-statutory training organisations', in HARRISON, A. and GRETTON, J. (eds) *Education and Training UK 1989*, Newbury, Policy Journals.

WALFORD, G. (1987) 'How important is the independent sector in Scotland? *Scottish Educational Review*, **19**, 2, pp. 108–21.

WEIR, A.D. (1988) *Education and Vocation 14–18*, Edinburgh, Scottish Academic Press.

3   Prospective Evaluation through Comparative Analysis: Youth Training in a Time-Space Perspective

Richard Rose

The real world in fact is perhaps the most fertile of all sources of good research questions calling for basic scientific inquiry.

Herbert A. Simon, Nobel laureate lecture

Introduction

Just as Molière's Monsieur Jourdain was always talking prose without realizing it, so policymakers are always making comparisons across time and space. The simplest form of comparison is that between a government's present performance and its past performance, in order to see what changes, if any have occurred. A second alternative involves comparative statics; the present performance of one country is compared with another in order to see how each stands in an international league table of performance. Third, present performance can be compared with an ideal state that is meant to be attained at some speculative future date (Rose, 1988).

Evaluation necessarily involves comparison; current performance is compared with a pre-specified criterion. For example, information about the quantity of unemployment in Britain can only be evaluated by comparison with an external reference point, such as the level of unemployment at an earlier point in time, unemployment rates in other countries, or a more or less vague goal of full employment or of a non-accelerating inflation rate of unemployment (cf. Solow, 1986:30ff).

Prospective evaluation compares one country's present with the future of another. The question is: under what circumstances and to what extent *could* a programme in effect in country X today work if it were introduced in country Y tomorrow? Comparison across time and space is an exercise in comparative dynamics. It differs from historical comparisons of past rates of change in two or more countries, such as studies of economic growth rates. Prospective evaluation is forward looking; it requires speculation about the future. Yet it puts bounds on speculation by basing speculation upon what Simon (1979) describes as the most fertile of all sources of stimulation, the real world.

Prospective evaluation is instrumentally oriented; it uses comparison to test the likely success of actions that government might take to improve policies. It differs from social science comparisons that simply test hypotheses by reference to past events. To give reasons why Sweden has a lower unemployment rate or Germany has a lower inflation rate than Britain or the United States does not tell British and American policymakers what to do. An explanation of Germany's low inflation as a reaction against the hyper-inflation of early Weimar and of four-power military occupation after 1945 is hardly a course of action that another country could or would follow willingly. The benign explanations offered for Sweden's low unemployment are attractive to social democrats, and Japan's export success may also be explained by attractive measures.

It does not follow that just because a particular policy works in one country it will work in another. Historical, institutional and cultural analyses often assume total blockage: nothing can be learned from what works elsewhere that can be of use in one's own country, because of national differences in history, institutions and culture. By contrast, policy prescriptions based upon 'stylized facts' usually omit obstacles to transferring policies across national boundaries, and prescriptions deduced from abstract models of an economic system assume perfect fungibility, in which anything that works in the world of theory is equally applicable everywhere. In an imperfect world, most programmes are unlikely to be either totally fungible or totally blocked.

Although the education and employment of young people is a common problem of advanced industrialized societies, nations respond in different ways. Notwithstanding the presence of two dozen nations in the Organization for Economic Cooperation and Development (OECD), there are not two dozen totally different systems of vocational education and training (VET). There are many similarities in the policy instruments which different governments use in their efforts to help youths leaving schools become skilled adult members of the labour force.

The immediate stimulus to prospective evaluation comes from the British government's proclaimed intention to introduce a dual system of VET that combines training at work with vocationally relevant off-site education.[1] There are many different ways in which a dual system can be organized; to say that Germany has a dual system of VET and Britain is seeking to introduce such a system does not mean the two are (or ought to be) identical, but only that they share a restricted number of attributes which also differentiate them from systems in place in Sweden, France, the United States or Japan.

The object of prospective evaluation is to consider *under what circumstances or to what extent* Britain can develop in the foreseeable future a dual system of VET as effective as that in effect in Germany today. The introduction of a dual system takes more than a decade to accomplish, for it involves major changes in employers, employees, and educational and vocational institutions. We cannot evaluate empirically until the latter half of the 1990s the success or failure of what is still an incipient system. By the time that retrospective evaluation studies can be published, some four million more youths will have entered the world of work. As Judith Marquand (1989:191) of the Training Agency cautions: 'Many of the programmes are far too recent for effects to be seen'. Yet because Germany has had a dual system of VET for generations, it is possible to undertake empirical analysis of the German dual system today.

To determine whether a VET policy working in one country could work in another we must first understand how the dual system of VET works in Germany, and compare it with the transitional state of British VET today. Next we must make a forecast or judgment, based upon past accomplishments and present alterations, about how British VET can change in the decade ahead. Prospective evaluation then compares the likely state of British vocational education and training in the late 1990s with that of Germany in 1990.

Prospective evaluation leaves open whether the new British system will be a success or failure. If one evaluated VET solely across time within Britain, one might conclude that improvement had occurred. Combining cross-national with cross-time comparisons can produce a different answer, finding that Britain's training practices have improved from an inferior past, but are likely to remain inferior to other nations for years ahead. Insofar as prospective evaluation identifies major shortcomings in a proposal, it then becomes possible to take action here and now to remedy the faults thus identified.

The logic of treating time and space as complementary perspectives, is set out in the first section of this chapter. The second section considers contrasting assumptions about learning from abroad. A conceptual framework is necessary to organize the collection and interpretation of data drawn from countries with different languages and practices; a generic model of the VET process is outlined in the third section; step-by-step comparison identifies major gaps between the achievement of the present German system and the proposed British system. The conclusion puts bounds to speculation about greatly changing the qualification level of the British labour force before the year 2000. The obstacles to success are not so much a function of space, that is, national differences, as they are a function of the time it takes to replace an unsatisfactory inheritance from the past with something better.

Using Time and Space to Evaluate Public Policies

The scope of a particular comparison is determined by the problem at hand. In dealing with everyday problems of budgeting, the government of the day is likely to compare next year's level of public expenditure with last year's, whereas social scientists concerned with the growth of government will focus

Figure 3.1   Comparisons across time and space

Across space	Across time	
	No	Yes
No	Satisfactory routine	Incremental trends, speculation
Yes	Comparative statics: OECD league tables	Comparative dynamics: Prospective evaluation

on a much longer time span and arrive at very different pictures, (cf. Wildavsky, 1988; Peacock and Wiseman, 1961). A variety of methods may be used to explore the transition from time present to the future. The distance to travel in making comparisons across space is least in comparing local government units within a nation, thus holding many institutional variables constant. This strategy is used by the Local Government Audit Commission, and it can also be used within a federal system or a multi-national United Kingdom (Raffe, chapter 3 above; Rose, 1982:chapters 5, 6). Comparisons are more likely to identify contrasts as the boundaries of sovereign countries are crossed. Yet the idea of sovereignty is rejected by the European Community, which assumes harmony or commonality in labour market policies after 1992.

When we say that a programme is working, this can mean that it is doing better than previously, a comparison across time. Or it could mean that it is working better than in other countries, a comparison across space. International comparisons of the growth rates of national economies involve comparisons across both time and space. The simplest form of evaluation expresses satisfaction without making any comparison at all (Figure 3.1).

No comparison: routine satisfaction.   The simplest method of evaluation is to compare present conditions with present aspirations. As long as a routine glance at monthly labour market figures indicates that achievement matches aspiration, then there is satisfaction. No further knowledge is necessary. If everything is deemed satisfactory, or at least 'not unsatisfactory', policymakers can ignore both national trends and what is happening in other countries. This can continue as long as changes in the environment do not destabilize programmes and create a gap between aspirations and achievements.

In an unprecedented period of full employment in postwar Britain, demand for vocational education and training stabilized at a low level. Both employers and employees were satisfied with the performance of the economy, even though it was run on a 'low skills equilibrium'. Reports were published comparing British performance in VET unfavourably with other countries, but in a world of shortages and few competitors they did not create dissatisfaction (Keep and Mayhew, 1988; Finegold and Soskice, 1988).

When unemployment began to rise in Britain during the 1970s and 1980s, the resulting gap between current conditions and aspirations based upon past achievement did create dissatisfaction. Policymakers found that they could no longer be satisfied by assuming a continuation of last month's figures for another month, especially when rising unemployment promised further increases in the months ahead. As dissatisfaction became strong and persisted, policymakers were under pressure to search for 'satisficing' measures that could remove the cause of dissatisfaction (March and Simon, 1958:169; Rose and Page, 1990). However, evidence of dissatisfaction can provoke dissent among both politicians and economists about the need to act (e.g., before or after inflation is under control) or what ought to be done next (e.g., stimulate demand or concentrate on supply-side problems; Rose, 1987).

Compare present with past national trends, or speculate about the future. When policymakers find that present conditions are moving in a negative direction, then the quickest response is to search the past and do more of what has already been done. Incremental adjustments in established programmes can be made, spending more money on labour market programmes on the assumption that increased spending inputs will produce an increase in the output of benefits. Incremental increases in programmes already in place face few difficulties in implementation and additional money can be spent quickly. Incrementalism depends upon 'after the fact' evaluation. Measures that appear to work can receive more money, and those that do not can be abandoned or replaced by revised or new measures (Braybrooke and Lindblom, 1963). Counter-cyclical policies are a second familiar example of searching the past. In response to the recurrence of unemployment, Keynesians may once again prescribe the re-introduction of policies stimulating demand. But this assumes that the past inevitably repeats itself, and that the lessons of a nation's past are unambiguous (cf. Neustadt and May, 1986).

When there is a structural change in the economy, doing what worked last time will not dispel dissatisfaction, and policymakers will want to search further afield. In response to structural change, policymakers are under pressure to seek new programmes. By definition, a new programme is speculative. It implies a set of what-if hypotheses: if we do A, then X will follow. Such hypotheses are problematic and, to paraphrase Simon, can easily enter the realm of 'unbounded' rationality. Politicians can use rhetoric or the authority of office to leave out inconvenient but palpable facts, and opposition criticisms are often motivated by a desire to blame the government for its alleged failings. Mathematical simulations of the presumed effects of a new programme can be faulted because the bounds imposed in very stylized models often exclude influences that are critical for successful implementation.

Comparative statics: look elsewhere. Dissatisfaction with youth unemployment has shattered routines and made policymakers reject the idea that past practices can successfully be projected into the future. Policymakers want to break with the British tradition of neglecting youth training. The idea that the British government could do nothing because it was British would strike

Parliament as a lame excuse for inaction. An Employment White Paper thus proclaims:

> Comparisons with where we were a few years ago are irrelevant, as are comparisons with what other British companies and organisations are doing. The comparison which counts is that with our overseas competitors, and that is to our disadvantage. (DE/DES, 1986:2)

Unlike social scientists engaging in comparison for its own sake, policymakers can seek lessons from other nations. The fact that they may do it badly or with ulterior political motives (cf. Keep, chapter 1, above) is not an argument against seeking to learn from other nations. The hope, and *ex ante* it can be no more than that, is that something can be learned from foreign experience to help cope with present difficulties; for example, a country that ranks below-average in an OECD league table assumes that it has the capacity to regress toward the mean, that is, to become more like other countries.

If a programme being considered for adoption in one country is already in effect elsewhere, then policymakers can examine it to inform their thinking about how such a programme works. To do so does not presume an identity between countries; it simply avoids the opposite fallacy, the assumption that because two countries are not identical, they have nothing in common and nothing can be learned from comparison. A working system can be a template and a source of inspiration for individuals; the experience of seeing what *is* done in another country can encourage thinking about what *could* be done in one's own country. The OECD and the European Commission support visits between local leaders in economic development activities, assuming that a town in a rural area of Italy may have more in common with a similar community in Ireland than with an industrialized city in its own country (Pellegrin, 1989).

Comparing the operation of public policies across national boundaries is more difficult than comparing the output of policies. Output analysis involves familiar problems of statistical comparability, whereas programme analysis involves differences between political institutions and context. The importance attributed to contextual variables in comparative public policy is disputed; at one extreme, attributes of national style are said to colour every major policy area, thus inhibiting transference. However, insofar as programmes matter, then the nature of specific problems creates commonalities regardless of national cultures or styles (Rose, 1985; Freeman, 1985).

The greater the contextual differences between countries, the greater the tendency to prefer introverted speculation. But ignoring what happens abroad assumes that Britain is a closed society. Although there are non-tradeable sectors of the economy relatively immune to foreign competition, there are also 'extroverted' sectors that require an increasingly well-trained workforce to compete internationally. The median enterprise is probably producing goods and services similar to those found in other OECD nations even if operating largely within the national economy. Pressures from foreign competition are likely to grow as the Single Europe Act takes effect in the 1990s.

Comparative dynamics: their present, our future. If a government decides to introduce a policy similar to that already in effect elsewhere, it can then combine cross-time and cross-national comparison, evaluating the experience of another country today in order to learn how to be better off tomorrow. Any reference to 'catching up' or 'following' assumes that where country X is today, country Y could be tomorrow. When a country seeks to introduce a new national policy, the experience of other nations provides the only empirical evidence available to put bounds on speculation.

Conventional evaluation research is *ex post facto*; it can only analyse what has already happened several years previously. Because of time lags between data collection and publication, the Training Agency report about YTS issued in January, 1989 reports data about those completing the programme in 1986/87. The opening words of this current status report are: 'Looking back ...' (TA, 1989b:3; see also Dutton, 1987:221). As long as a scheme has been implemented and the eventual evaluation is satisfactory, the time lags involved in retrospective evaluation are of limited concern. But if an evaluation is not positive, then time, money and opportunities are lost.

Prospective evaluation focuses upon shortcomings in advance of the implementation of a programme; the purpose is to *reduce rather than document failure*. The implementation of a new set of measures intended to develop a dual system of VET is bound to take years, and in the course of that time many shortcomings are likely to appear. If one looks at the experience of another country that has already overcome the problems of introducing a dual system of vocational education and training, shortcomings arising from the introduction of an untested set of measures may be identified sooner rather than later.

Alternative Assumptions about Transferability

Abstract theories of social science, and particularly economics, assume that programmes, that is the specific institutional, administrative and financial mechanisms for achieving a policy objective, are perfectly fungible. A programme that works in one place is expected to work in another. Policy instruments for achieving a given objective such as youth employment are assumed to be transferable between countries in the same way that parts for a Ford automobile are expected to transfer from a factory in Barcelona to repair a broken-down Ford in Dundee. By contrast, historical and institutional analyses often presuppose total blockage. Nothing that works in one context can be expected to work in another. The critical features of Swedish and British labour market policies are not generic attributes, but reflect the fact that one programme is Swedish and the other is British.

Both perfect fungibility and total blockage are familiar ideas; they are also contradictory. If policy instruments are as fungible in reality as in analytic models, then blockages are of no consequence. However, insofar as differences of time and place are obstacles, then policy instruments are not transferable.

Perfect fungibility. Social scientists concerned with models for their own sake concentrate upon abstractions. Analysis involves reasoning by deduction within a closed system. Fungibility is assumed rather than demonstrated empirically. In striving for clarity and logical coherence, abstract models omit many phenomena, including differences between nations. Although models do allow for variability, this is usually not the contextual variability in institutions and historical circumstances that typically constrain policymakers.

Many aspects of contemporary economic theory achieve perfect fungibility at an excessively high price. Although clear in the abstract, they are applicable nowhere in particular. The omissions are particularly significant in labour market policy and particularly vocational education and training, for its starting point is the situation of young people and not that of the economic system. A model that does not allow for the variability of family, youth psychology, politics and culture is doomed to omit much that is relevant to the actual practice of VET (Jones, 1988). As Marquand (1989:xii) emphasizes, there is a big difference between a social scientific analysis of all the elements that make youth unemployment a problem in the economy, and a reductionist analysis that excludes these considerations in order to analyze the problem in a closed model of an abstract economic system.

Raffe's (1988:111) wish about Britain — 'Ideally, the campaign to reform the quantity and quality of youth training in Britain would have started from somewhere else' — is realized in the idealized world of the economic system. Britain is made exogenous, that is, many of the problems that characterize the British labour market are excluded *a priori*. Any reference is to stylized facts that are forced to fit the assumptions of the model world — albeit at a price. Within this framework it is not possible to consider institutional, social and historical influences that are important in differentiating VET systems across national boundaries (Schmid and Reissert, 1988; Finegold and Soskice, 1988:25). As Bruno and Sachs (1985:274) comment:

> It would seem only natural that a theory for a country's, or several countries', response can only be formulated if one takes its specific institutional or structural features into consideration. However, macro-theory, whether Keynesian or monetarist, has for a long time tended to consider one and the same basic model as applicable to all economies.

Perfect blockage. While economic theorists may be willing to sacrifice verisimilitude for clarity, policymakers cannot. Public officials who formulate policies are always aware of many details that may not have theoretical import but are of immediate practical significance: the problems of established programmes, the interests supporting different programmes, current relations between government departments and agencies, the standing of a minister in Cabinet, and so forth. When the cooperation of non-governmental institutions is a condition of success — and vocational education and training is such an example — then striking a bargain or sealing a deal with all affected interests can become the object, rather than a logically coherent plan.

Insofar as an historical explanation of a problem states a particular sequence of events occurring within a specific configuration of institutions, laws, and values treated as unique in time and place, this implicitly endorses total blockage. External influences are ignored, as are parallel developments in similar countries. The approach proclaims as a virtue what Raffe ruefully acknowledges: 'we cannot start from somewhere else. The difficulty in learning from such ideographic description is that there is no way in which what is said about one country can be applied to any other' (*ibid.*).

Studies that describe themselves as empirical (that is, descriptive) or practical often imply total blockage. Most writing about vocational education and training in Britain is highly context-specific. A representative study is likely to draw upon British government documents, press reports written in London, and British articles and books. The framework is chronological or evolutionary: present British problems are seen as an outgrowth of past events within Britain.

Knowing the national context is a necessity for policymakers, and important for prospective evaluation too. No one would expect policymakers consciously to adopt impractical modes of thinking. Yet descriptive empiricism is faulty for, as Oakeshott (1951:11) notes, 'Purely empirical politics are not something difficult to achieve, they are merely impossible'. In addition to descriptive facts, policymaking involves what Oakeshott calls 'something corresponding with specific hypotheses in science'. Every analysis, no matter how detailed the description, is based upon an implicit set of assumptions that may be all the more powerful because they are inarticulate.

Under what circumstances? To what extent? In practice most policy areas involve both nation-specific and fungible elements. Time rather than space may be the primary obstacle to transferring a policy. For example, Margaret Thatcher, as Prime Minister, was a great obstacle to transferring Swedish labour market programmes to Britain, however favourable their estimated consequences. However, the critical variable — the British Prime Minister of the day — can change with the swing of political fortunes, thus overcoming resistances often attributed to national culture. What first appears as a permanent block to lesson-drawing can thus be seen as a contingent obstacle of limited duration.

The potential for transferability varies from policy area to policy area. It is likely to be greatest for programmes that depend upon 'hard' technology, such as an air force using jet planes. Interdependence between nations also gives grounds for transferring policies, for example monetary policy is increasingly internationalized because of interactions of central banks. The importance of national context rises when a programme depends upon many social, economic and institutional factors specific to place, and this would appear to be true of vocational education and training.

Given that there is something that *might* be learned from some foreign nations' ways of dealing with a subject, the problem then becomes: which countries to examine? Policymakers have a bias towards drawing illustrations from countries near at hand; for Canada, this would be the United States. It is not clear what country is nearest Britain. In a geographical sense France and Ireland are the two countries closest to Britain in distance. But little or no attention is paid to their public policies. The United States is often treated as the country closest at hand, yet many social, economic and political conditions differ between the United States and Europe.

The starting point of this prospective evaluation is the way in which the German dual system of vocational education and training works today, awarding more than 600,000 vocational qualifications to young people who have been examined after a two- to three-year apprenticeship based upon on-the-job training and work and off-site training. While the system can be criticized (e.g., Williamson, 1983:161; Dehnbostel and Rau, 1986; Schoenfeldt, 1986), critics agree with proponents about its chief features, and the thrust of criticism is to fine-tune the system. The German *Berufsbildung* system is long established (Taylor, 1981) and, notwithstanding unemployment rising from 220,000 in 1973 to more than 2,200,000 today, the system has not been threatened with collapse. Given the high degree of stability in the programmes of the past decade — critics would even argue, inflexibility in the face of the need for more active policies — the German VET system can be expected to work in the 1990s much as it does today.

The reason for examining German VET comes from Britain, not Germany. The British Government is now in the process of adopting a system of VET that *appears* to resemble the German system more closely than that of any other OECD nation. This does not mean that the German system is the best in any absolute sense — or that the British system can become similar to the German system, or as successful as it is meant to be. It simply means that insofar as Britain is capable of learning lessons from abroad about how to operate the new British dual system, then Germany provides a better source of prospective evaluation than the French or Swedish systems, which put much more emphasis upon vocational education in schools, or the Japanese system of sophisticated in-firm training for lifetime employees.

Putting Bounds to Speculation

Prospective evaluation is not so much a method of prediction as it is a means of accident prevention; it imposes discipline upon otherwise unbounded

Figure 3.2   The framework of a dual system of VET

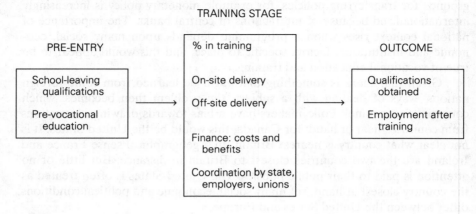

TRAINING STAGE

PRE-ENTRY

| School-leaving qualifications |
| Pre-vocational education |

$\longrightarrow$

| % in training |
| On-site delivery |
| Off-site delivery |
| Finance: costs and benefits |
| Coordination by state, employers, unions |

$\longrightarrow$

OUTCOME

| Qualifications obtained |
| Employment after training |

speculation. By contrast, politicians asked to evaluate the future course of a programme need recognize no bounds to what is possible or reasonable. They can assert the occurrence of desirable effects without any idea of causation, or argue from one implausible premise to another, or simply appeal for 'confidence' in what the government is doing, and in its good intentions.

Identifying the steps in a step-by-step process.   To make comparisons between vocational education and training systems we need generic concepts that are not restricted to time or place. To read up studies in German of its *Berufsbildung* system may improve one's linguistic abilities but does not of itself provide the basis for comparison with, let alone prospective evaluation of, Britain. Activities in different nations can only be compared if we have a model that describes in generic terms the anatomy of a dual system. The use of functional concepts does not mean that both countries are the same; comparison may highlight 'incomparable' features of each system.

The progress of a young school leaver through the dual system of vocational education and training involves three stages: pre-entry schooling; the training stage; and post-training entry to the adult labour force (Figure 3.2). This simple model provides a check-list of questions that must be asked in the process of a step-by-step comparison of VET in Britain and Germany. In order to make a comparison we first need to know: what standard of school-leaving qualifications are obtained by youths in Britain and Germany? What provision for training on and off the job is made in the two countries? What vocational examinations do youths have at the end of their training, and how does this relate to their employment prospects as adults?

Although all the elements in Figure 3.2 are necessary, they are not sufficient. The output of trained youths is also influenced by social conditions and by macro-economic conditions. Policymaking structures differentiate themselves according to particular economic and social responsibilities. The Department of Employment takes the lead in promoting vocational education and training, whereas the Treasury takes the lead in macro-economic policies, and the Department of Education and Science is concerned with general education. Although macro-economic conditions affect employment opportunities, that does not create a pool of trained labour or necessarily guarantee full employment. As Rist (1986:3) notes, if growth is the 'bottom line', then the 'bottom bottom line' is that 'economic growth is a necessary but not sufficient condition for ensuring employment'.

Vocational education and training concentrate upon the majority of youths leaving school for work without the academic qualification necessary to enter university. This group of 16 and 17 year olds constitutes three-quarters of the labour force in Britain and in Germany. Generalization about groups this large inevitably blurs considerable differences in training within each nation, arising from contrasting occupations, industries, skills and gender of youths in VET.

The object of evaluation is the outcome of vocational education and training; this is indicated by the quantity and quality of occupational qualifications that youths obtain, and by their prospects for adult employment, since skilled workers are less likely to experience unemployment. The economy benefits too, for the higher pay that more skilled workers earn is a reflection of greater value to employers, and a more skilled labour force can produce a higher rate of economic growth.

The gap today: qualified Germans, unqualified Britons. The first step in prospective evaluation is to take stock of the present. In the dual system a youth moves through three stages: pre-entry schooling; the training stage; and qualification and entry to the adult labour force. To cover the details of a point-by-point comparison of VET in Britain and Germany would require a book-length study and is best done elsewhere (Rose and Wiganek, 1990). Here, attention can be focused upon points that illustrate the use of prospective evaluation.

At the pre-entry level the greatest difference is in the educational foundations of the middle third of the youth population. In both countries more than a quarter of youths give evidence of an academic education, obtaining a good set of O or A levels or better, or in Germany the *Abitur*, the university entrance qualification. In addition, more than a third of Germans pass a set of examinations (the *Mittlere Reife*) that including German, mathematics, a foreign language and at least two other subjects, set at a higher standard than the handful of poor O levels or CSE passes secured by the middle third in Britain (Prais and Wagner, 1985).

The definition of training that is offered youths differs fundamentally. In Germany, occupational qualifications are defined nationally for more than 400 different occupations, and the German VET (*Berufsbildung*) system defines training as preparing for a theoretical and practical examination that confers one of these occupational qualifications over a period of two to three years of work experience and training on-the-job and at vocational colleges. The number of youths actually in training at any given time is about 1,800,000, and more than 600,000 youths sign an apprenticeship contract to train for a specific occupation on leaving school. Only a low percentage of youths leaving school before the age of 18 or 19 do not enter an apprenticeship.

By contrast, in Britain there is confusion about the nature of training. The major five-volume empirical study sponsored by the Training Agency defined training as an activity, 'the process of acquiring the range of future knowledge and skills that are related to current or future working requirements by formal or structured or guided means' (i.e., excluding pure experience; Rigg, 1989:17). Training is then measured by *exposure*, the number of days a year in which a youth or adult is exposed to work-relevant knowledge and skills. The Training Agency (1989a:53) reports that this measure is very unreliable, showing a

> disparity between the results of the individuals' survey (which supports an estimate that around 20 per cent of employees received training during 1986/87) and the results of the employers' survey (which found that 48 per cent of employees had been trained in that year).

By any measure, the proportion of British youths currently exposed to training is far lower than that of German youths, and their exposure is far less. For example, most of the hundreds of thousands of youths who enter the Youth Training Scheme, the principal British programme, drop out before the end of the first year and only one in seven leaves with any kind of a vocational qualification (Roberts *et al.*, 1987; TA, 1989b). YTS is not a means by which a youth gains training that leads to a vocational qualification; it is a parking place in which a youth gains some exposure to work and to knowledge and skills while waiting for a 'real' job (that is, a job paid at a market wage above the YTS rate) to come along.

In the training stage, the most immediately important difference is in who does the training. In Germany, training is the responsibility of an expert, skilled member of a firm's production process (normally an *Industriemeister* or a *Handwerk* (craft) *Meister*). A *Meister* is a big step above the skilled worker. After earning a vocational qualification and acquiring several years of experience working at the relevant trade, a skilled worker must undertake a part-time course of study extending over several years to qualify as a *Meister*. The examination for this qualification covers theoretical knowledge; *Technik* (that is, evidence of knowing what to do on the job and how to make things); management or business skills relevant to securing further promotion or starting a small business; and pedagogical instruction and practice in training young apprentices (see e.g., Lawrence, 1980:156ff). Upwards of two million German workers have earned this qualification or its equivalent.

A *Meister* normally has status, authority and higher pay *vis-à-vis* fellow workers, and is able to deal with both management and the shop floor. The adult front-line supervisor of a youth in training is not segregated from normal production workers and categorized (or stigmatized) as an instructor, as is often the case in Britain. On average, the time of a *Meister* is allocated thus (IDW, 1988:7):

	%
• Organization of activities of the work unit	28
• Checking, inspecting, quality control	23
• Meetings, planning for new activities of the unit	18
• Training	12
• Planning, construction, health and environmental protection, transportation	11
• Technical knowledge, preparing reports	8

Since a trainer is personally responsible for the behaviour of trainees on the site and for their success in the final external examinations, there is a social psychological motivation to see that youths in their charge succeed, and that other adults in the firm assist in the training process. An adolescent thus has, on-site, an adult who can be a role model for a youth, having the same occupation as the youth may expect to achieve later in life, and earning a good wage, the esteem of others at the work place, and authority (Dickenson and Erben, 1985; Hamilton, 1987).

By contrast, the current and prospective British system appears as one of training without trainers, in default of a large *cadre* of master workmen with the expert skills, status and authority to supervise youths on the job. There can be unofficial assignment of responsibility for youth supervision within a particular firm, but no system of training can operate if it depends solely upon *ad hoc* and informal arrangements — and if the actual delivery of training, as distinct from the planning or finance of training, is not recognized as of primary importance (Varlaam and Pole, 1988). British firms can have training departments that run training courses, but classes remain classes, whether they are taught within the firm or off-site, and money spent in buying off-site training may complement but cannot substitute for direct supervision by expert adult workers on a daily basis.[2]

Given differences in the definition and practice of training, outcomes differ too. Young adults in both Britain and Germany face the same question from a prospective employer: what can you do? A German at 19 or 20 will be able to produce a vocational qualification obtained by an external examination; an employer's recommendation based upon three years of regular employment; and a majority will also have passed academic examinations at the level of five good O levels. By contrast, a British youth will have no vocational qualification, a poor O level or CSE record, and often lack a steady work history as well.

Table 3.1 Qualifications of British and German labour force today

	Britain %	Germany %	Difference %
Academic	(33)	(13)	(20)
Degree, including teachers	10	10	0
Only A,O level, *Abitur*	23	3	20
Vocational*	(20)	(66)	(−46)
Technician, *Meister*	4	7	−3
Trade, craft	16	59	−43
None**	47	21	26

Notes: *British technicians: HNC/HND; HND/OND; BEC or TEC. Trade, craft: Apprenticeship, City and Guilds or nursing.
  **Includes CSE below grade 1 and other.
Source: 1987 Labour Force Survey as reported in *Employment Gazette*, 1988: Table 1; Tessaring (1988, Table 4).

In Germany vocational qualifications are meant to be occupation-specific and additional to school examination achievements. In Britain, by contrast, qualifications are normally described, even in Training Agency documents, in academic terms. Neither youths nor employers consider number of days exposed to training as a qualification. Work experience is the primary vocational qualification and, in a decade when youth unemployment has reached as high as 25 per cent on annual average even after allowing for major government job-creation schemes, most youths will not have steady work experience by the time they become adults.

When we compare the qualifications of the British and German labour forces today, the first striking difference is that far more Britons are *qualified only in academic terms* (Table 3.1). A good academic education is desirable in itself, but it is not a vocational qualification *per se*. Insofar as the cult of the amateur still prevails, it may be cited as a claim for exemption from vocational training on the grounds that a well-educated person can pick up vocational knowledge on the job. Although the number of Germans with a good academic record is also substantial, it appears small in Table 3.1 because many Germans with a good general education *add* to this a vocational qualification.

A second contrast follows: more than three times as many Germans have a vocational qualification that is secured through an apprenticeship involving practical work experience, on-site and off-site training, and assessment by external examinations that cover both theory (e.g., principles of electricity, bookkeeping or, for a retail clerk, properties of materials commonly used in clothes) and also practice (e.g., proof that a youth can repair a faulty engine or plaster a room). In Britain, only 23 per cent have a trade or technical qualification, such as a completed apprenticeship, or appropriate City and Guilds qualifications.[3] Thus, half the British labour force has either a practically oriented vocational qualification or an academic qualification; in Germany half the labour force has both.

A third difference follows: the German VET system succeeds in developing skills in the bottom half of the labour force as well as the top half. Four-fifths of Germans have a vocational or an academic qualification or both, and the great majority of workers in routine or nominally semi-skilled jobs are trained in the work that they are doing. The job of vocational counsellors is to see that youths with limited ability do make the most of whatever their potential is, and among the 400 qualifications there are some suited for low achievers at school as well as others suited for high achievers. By contrast, nearly half the British labour force has neither a vocational nor an academic qualification, and more than three-quarters is without any vocational qualification.

Although millions of Britons are as well qualified for their work as are their German counterparts, Germany still has millions more qualified workers today. If one compares the proportion of the labour force with either a vocational or educational qualification, then, even after controlling for small differences in national populations, Germany has at least six million more qualified workers in its labour force than does Britain. If qualifications are defined in terms of vocational qualifications, then Germany has at least ten million more qualified workers than Britain.

What Prospect for Change?

Britain and Germany do not differ in prospective goals: both countries want a well-trained labour force. Immediately, the difference is in inheritance of the past. The German *Berufsbildung* system is more than twice as old as the Federal Republic itself; the Bonn regime was founded in 1949, whereas the systematisation of VET in Germany dates back to the Kaiser's time. The British inheritance also shows a consistent pattern, but it is that of a low-skills equilibrium. Differences in past achievements thus account for the present gap.

A shift in goals from producing jobs to producing training defines what is new, but leaves open when — or whether — the shift will be complete. Changing goals is not enough; innovation also requires the implementation of new programmes, and implementation is contingent (Pressman and Wildavsky, 1973; Alexander, 1989). Even though the aspiration for a dual system can be announced in a one-day debate in Parliament, the behaviour of young people, employers, and others involved in VET cannot be changed in the span of a single Parliament. The 1988 White Paper (DE, 1988) summarizing Government intentions was entitled *Employment for the 1990s*; thus, it not only heralded change but also implied that it can take a decade to achieve change.

Importance of inheritance. Policymakers are heirs before they are choosers. A newly-elected government inherits a legacy of an accumulation of commitments made in several previous decades and generations (Rose, 1990).

The labour force that the Thatcher Government inherited in 1979 reflected the cumulative consequences of youth training or non-training going back to 1929. The legacy that a Government leaves to its successors also has long-term significance. Policies affecting youths in the 1980s can continue to have some influence until these youths retire from the labour force after the year 2030.

To answer the question — when does a new policy take effect? — we must look backwards and forwards in time. The adoption of a new goal does not mean that past influences upon training have disappeared; they are carried forward by the force of inertia. Consider the problems facing the National Council on Vocational Qualifications, established in 1986. A Council without an inheritance might have decided, for example, to adopt standards laid down by CEDEFOP, the European Community institution for cross-national comparison of VET, on the grounds that this would ensure that youth training matched the standards of European competitors. What the NCVQ has faced is a plethora of qualifications that had been issued by a variety of examining bodies for up to a century. In addition, schools have started to introduce 'sub-academic' certificates that are intended to have more or less vocational significance. The basic issue facing the NCVQ is not that of deciding what standards it would like to have, but what to do about standards already in place.

When a new programme is introduced where none has previously existed, it must overcome the inertia of institutions that are immobile in its area. The Technical and Vocational Education Initiative (TVEI) illustrates the time needed to develop a programme in the absence of any tradition of pre-vocational teaching in British secondary schools. It was introduced on a pilot basis in 1983. Five years later all local education authorities had a pilot scheme in place, but only 2 per cent of the relevant age group was participating. The Department of Employment forecasts that a decade after launching nine-tenths of all schools and colleges will be participating in the programme (HMT, 1989:9), a phrase that leaves open how large or small a proportion of youths in these schools will actually be involved. It will take even longer before the post-school effects of TVEI programmes can be fully observed and evaluated retrospectively.

The desire of policymakers to take credit for good intentions encourages unbounded speculation. Sir Bryan Nicholson's (1990) desire to break the low skills equilibrium leads him to herald CBI recommendations for Exchequer-funded grants to youths for vocational training as if they had already been approved by the Treasury and were in the process of bringing youths up to what he describes as 'the vocational equivalent of two A levels'. The next step is to treat the consequences of adopting a hypothetical proposal as if they were certain, e.g., claiming that a proposed reform 'will rapidly drive up the qualifications level'. From this it is but one more bound to conclude that by 1995 Britain is likely to have achieved 'a quantum leap from where we are now with youth training schemes and general workforce training' (*ibid.*).

The logic of changing an inheritance.   Continuity with the past does not rule out change; it simply places bounds upon the speed with which goals can be introduced. The less the gap between present conditions and future aspirations, the quicker a goal can be obtained. The slower the rate at which conditions change, the longer it will take to achieve a goal. Changes in vocational education and training can take many years to accomplish.

We can represent the relationship between the labour force today and at a future date through a very simple identity. The present stock consists of skills and qualifications achieved by everyone in the labour force today from age 16 to age 65. In the course of time this stock is reduced by older workers retiring. It is augmented by younger people entering the labour force. If young people entering the labour force have a higher level of training than older people, then the number of qualified persons will gradually rise. If they do not, then the overall level will remain the same, or fall.

The logic of inheritance is that little change can occur overnight, or in five years — whatever policymakers would like to happen, or like others to believe. Yet the inexorable logic of demographic change means that it is possible for big changes to occur gradually, as seemingly small annual changes can cumulatively become large. Insofar as Germany has a mature (or even a decaying) vocational education and training system, then Britain is trying to catch up with a target that is not moving ahead. Insofar as more than a decade of changes in Britain have had positive effects, then the momentum of change should substantially reduce the gap by the year 2000.

Prospective evaluation: the gap remains.   The larger the number of young people in training by comparison with older people, the faster a stock of trained workers will accumulate in the labour force. In fact, the proportion of British youths in formally denominated vocational training today is similar to the proportion of trained persons in the total adult work force, for those in Youth Training Schemes and apprenticeships are less than one-quarter of the youth cohort in 1988 (TA, 1989a, Table 2.7). The change from the past is very limited because in the 1930s and 1940s there were more apprenticeships than today, and because YTS schemes are not commitments to training but transitional placements for youths between school and what they perceive as a real job.

The big difference between British youths and older members of the labour force is in the proportion of youths with an academic qualification; 44 per cent of youths age 20 to 24 in 1987 had attained five O levels or better in school examinations, compared to 18 per cent of those still at work above the age of 50. However, there was only a 2 per cent difference between the oldest and youngest group in the attainment of vocational qualifications. Thus, nearly the whole of the fall in the number of totally unqualified workers has been a result of increased academic education, with vocational education and training attracting well under half of young school-leavers today as in the past (calculated from *Employment Gazette*, 1988, Table 2).

In Germany projections assume that the proportion of workers with no qualification will continue to fall and the proportion of youths with a degree or a good academic education will continue to increase. But this will not alter the proportion of vocationally qualified people in the labour force, for many young people with a good academic background will continue to earn a vocational qualification as well. Insofar as an increase in the number of academically qualified increases competition for jobs, then the need for a double qualification will increase.

A comparison of Germans at age 25 to 30 with Germans over the age of 50 shows that 65 per cent of younger Germans today have earned a vocational qualification. This is not an indicator of rapid change in the 1990s, for 53 per cent of German workers over the age of 50 in 1985 had also earned a vocational qualification. The forecast for the 1990s is a persistence in the present distribution of German youths between school-leavers gaining a vocational qualification directly, and youths continuing in advanced education, with upwards of half taking a vocational qualification too (Tessaring, 1988).

If all one did were to concentrate upon trends within Britain, then it would be possible to regard present achievements as encouraging, for the number of unqualified persons is falling rapidly; whereas 63 per cent of older British workers have neither an academic nor a vocational qualification, only 35 per cent of younger Britons are without either qualification.

Comparison, however, shows a very different picture. *The vocational qualification gap between younger Germans and younger Britons is greater than in the older generation.* In the older generation, 53 per cent of Germans and 20 per cent of Britons have a vocational qualification, a difference of 33 per cent. In the younger generation, 65 per cent of Germans as against 22 per cent of Britons have a vocational qualification, a difference of 43 per cent.[4]

If one only projected the consequences of the demographic turnover in the British labour market up to the year 2000, then the overall picture is positive, showing an increase in number of academically and vocationally qualified workers, and a decrease of 8 to 11 per cent in the proportion of those without any qualifications (Table 3.2). Assumption (a) in Table 3.2 assumes that the higher level of achievement of younger Britons today is maintained throughout the 1990s, thus raising the total stock of qualifications as older and less qualified workers leave the labour force.

An optimistic assumption is that there is a substantial growth in the proportion of young people taking academic and vocational qualifications. Column (b) in Table 3.2 assumes that among those entering the labour force between 1987 and the year 2000 there will be an increase of one-fifth in the proportion of graduates over the final achievement of those 20 to 24, and a similar increase in the proportion of entrants who are vocationally qualified. An increase of one-fifth is actually an ambitious target. Any increase would take some years to reach this level and, in order to compensate for lesser increases in the first year of a gradual build up the increase between 1987 and the year 2000 would have to be a third or better.

Table 3.2   Forecast of qualifications in labour force in the year 2000

	Germany	Britain (a)	(b)	Minimum difference
Academic	19	36	38	19
Degree	15	13	15	0
A,O level, only *Abitur*	4	23	23	+19
Vocational	67	25	26	−41
None	14	39	36	+22

Notes: (a) Cohort replacing those retiring age 52−64 has same distribution of qualifications as adjusted cohort age 20−24 in 1987.

  (b) Cohort replacing those retiring has one-fifth more graduates, and vocationally qualified than adjusted cohort age 20−24 in 1987.

Sources: Germany: Tessaring (1988: Ubersicht 7); Britain: Projected from 1987 Labour Force Survey data reported in *Employment Gazette*, 1988: Table 2; Qualifications defined as in Table 3.1.

A substantial increase in educated or vocationally qualified youths would not produce a great alteration in the labour force overall. Youths entering the labour force between 1987 and 2000 constitute only one-sixth of the labour force; the proportion of these vocationally qualified would thus constitute only 4 or 5 per cent of the total labour force, whatever the likely rate of increase in its size. Even if one assumed that *every* youth entering the labour force in the next decade secured either an academic or vocational qualification, this would raise the estimated stock of qualifications in the British labour force in the year 2000 by only an additional 5 or 6 per cent.[5] Britain will only retain its lead over Germany in the proportion of youths with the academic potential to take a vocational qualification but who have not realized that potential.

While the assumptions of forecast can be challenged, it is important to realize that a change in assumptions could *widen rather than narrow* the gap between the two countries. A critical assumption of this prospective evaluation is that the training received by British youths in a craft apprenticeship or an ONC or BTEC course is equivalent in value to that received by young Germans who qualify through the *Berufsbildung* system. Given evidence previously cited, a case could be made that this understates the skills difference between the two countries. The presence of expert *Meisters* should raise the informal level of on-the-job training well above that available in the average British factory, shop or office.

Because so large a proportion of adult German workers have both a sound academic education and a solid foundation of vocational training, they are better able to benefit from further training as adults. For a British worker, a vocational qualification taken in youth is likely to be the only systematic long-term training received. By contrast, for a German, it is the first step in what adult workers and their employers often see as the first in a series of steps in a process of continuous training of adaptation to the opportunities and demands of technological change.

It could be argued that since more than a quarter of youths entering the British labour force have a good academic training, it should be possible for such persons to learn quickly without being required to take formal vocational qualifications. Yet even if this were to some extent the case, the gap between vocational training in Britain and Germany is so great that it would not alter the fundamental conclusion of prospective evaluation. Moreover, it would also imply that the gap between the unqualified half of the labour force and the top fraction is even greater than that depicted in the tables, since those without a good mind or vocational training would be defined as incapable of learning much from experience on the job. From a comparative perspective, this would mean that while German adults are upgrading their skills, the skills of a large proportion of British adults are deteriorating in relation to current demands and technology.[6]

Time can erode obstacles.   Prospective evaluation is not so much about understanding what went wrong as it is about taking action to improve conditions in future. But to recommend that Britain take steps to increase the supply of and demand for skilled manpower assumes the inheritance of the past is *not* totally deterministic, and there is no permanent blockage preventing Britons from being like Germans or Swedes, French or Japanese, to whom it appears obvious that training in youth will lead to a better job as an adult for themselves or for their children.

Since effective demand for training is not found in Britain, this is sometimes treated as evidence that British employers and workers have a fixed cultural preference for high current wages and profits rather than seeking the long-term advantages of investment in training. To say that Britons appear to have different time preferences from Germans may be accurate as a description, but it is not accurate as a diagnosis, for it confuses cause and effect. Moreover, it treats a disinclination to train as a fixed and immutable characteristic of all parts of British society.[7]

A striking feature of British training is its *variability*. The English Channel or the North Sea is not the dividing line between workers who are trained and those who are not. The dividing line runs *within* Britain, differentiating industries and occupations from each other, and in some cases differentiating firms within an industry, and even workers within a firm. A minority of British firms *do* invest in training and a minority of British youths *do* secure good vocational qualifications. Just as the best educated British university graduates are fully comparable to the best German university graduates, so the best trained British school-leavers can be a match for their German counterparts. We say that Britain and Germany differ because Germany has a much larger number of well-trained workers. Differences within Britain reject the argument that there is something inherent in the British condition that makes every youth subject to a 'British' disease that inhibits learning vocational skills.

The shortage of skilled labour today cannot be the fault of a dual system that has yet to come into full operation. It reflects the cumulative inheritance of a low supply of training by employers, and low demand by workers. The dual system today is best considered an embryo, capable, with careful nurture of developing into something worthwhile in future. The fact that changes cannot occur as quickly as the government of the day claims or as anxious citizens would like is not an argument for inaction. Instead, it is an argument for making more use of prospective evaluation, so that the efforts of the 1990s will not be wasted on false starts but will accelerate the slow and steady changes required to bring the British labour force up to international standards after the year 2000.[8]

Acknowledgments

The research reported herein has been supported by the Anglo-German Foundation for Research in Industrial Societies. In thinking through this paper, I have benefited from being a Guest Professor at the Wissenschaftszentrum Berlin. Dr Edward Page of the University of Hull and Guenter Wignanek of the Free University, Berlin have helped in collecting materials on vocational education and training. David Finegold made constructive comments on an earlier draft of this paper.

Notes

1 The goal of the Government of the day is here taken as a given. Others challenge the direction of policy or accept training at work and off-site as desirable, but argue that the British government is taking inadequate steps to achieve this goal.

2 Finance is not discussed here because differences in financial arrangements do not appear to account for differences in what is actually defined as training and how youths are actually trained. In both countries, large sums of money are spent, and in both countries most of the numbers involved in reported expenditure are 'soft', that is, imputed costs and benefits (Noll *et al*., 1983; Noll, 1986; Deloitte, 1989). Training Agency studies have found differences in magnitude between their researchers' estimates of employer spending on training, £8.6bn, and that entered in the accounts of firms, £2.5bn (Deloitte, 1989:46). Moreover, four-fifths of firms reported that they made no analysis of benefits of training, and only 3 per cent reported making a cost-benefit analysis of training (Deloitte, 1989, Figure 6.14). For further details, see the review in Rose (1990, chapter 6).

3 Detailed cross-national comparisons of examinations in different occupations show that German standards are at least as high as British standards.

4 For full details of these calculations and notes on sources, see Rose (1990, chapter 8).

5 If Britain in the year 2000 were evaluated by the standard of Germany in 1985, in keeping with the idea of prospective evaluation as 'their present, our future', the

overall conclusions would remain the same, so great is the present gap between the two countries.

6 British employers appear to believe that their better-educated employees do need training, for this group of the labour force receives much more training than do less skilled workers (TA, 1989a, Table 6.5), underscoring the point about the possible deterioration of unqualified and uneducated British workers by comparison with German adults.

7 Finegold and Soskice (1988:22) give a footnote disclaimer that not all British firms and workers neglect training, but unlike Antal (1989) do not consider the implications of this fact.

8 For specific proposals, see Rose (forthcoming, chapter 9), which offers a supply-side prescription, namely, the need to increase the pool of expert adult workers analogous to a German *Meister*, not only for their intrinsic value but also as a *precondition* of a major increase in the demand for youth training. To stimulate demand without improving the supply of expert front-line workers who can ensure the delivery of quality training at the work place risks a dilution of effort and if exposure to diluted training is treated as a vocational qualification, this would maintain, or cause, a deterioration in the present skills gap between Britain and Germany.

References

ALEXANDER, E.R. (1989) 'Improbable implementation: The Pressman-Wildavsky paradox revisited', *Journal of Public Policy*, 9, pp. 451–65.

ANTAL, A.B. (1989) *Making Ends Meet: Corporate Responses to Youth Unemployment in Great Britain and the Federal Republic of Germany*, Berlin, Wissenschaftszentrum Berlin.

BRAYBROOKE, D. and LINDBLOM, C.E. (1963) *A Strategy of Decisions*, New York, Free Press.

BRUNO, M. and SACHS, J. (1985) *Economics of Worldwide Stagflation*, Oxford, Oxford University Press.

DEHNBOSTEL, P. and RAU, E. (1986) 'Youth unemployment in the Federal Republic of Germany: Are the West Germans better off?', in RIST, R. (ed.) *Finding Work*, London, Falmer Press.

DELOITTE (1989) Deloitte, Haskins and Sells with IFF Research Ltd, *Employers' Activities*, London, HMSO, for the Training Agency.

DEPARTMENT OF EMPLOYMENT (DE) (1988) Cm. 540 *Employment for the 1990s*, London, HMSO.

DEPARTMENT OF EMPLOYMENT/DEPARTMENT OF EDUCATION AND SCIENCE (DE/DES) (1986) *Working Together — Education and Training*, Cmnd. 9823 London, HMSO.

DICKENSON, H. and ERBEN, M. (1985) 'An aspect of industrial training in the Federal Republic of Germany: Sociological considerations on the role of the *Meister*', *Journal of Further and Higher Education*, 9, pp. 69–76.

DUTTON, P. (1987) 'YTS: Training or a placebo?' in JUNANKAR, P.N. (ed.) *From School to Unemployment? The Labour Market for Young People*, London, Macmillan.

Employment Gazette (1988b) 'Economic activity and qualifications', 96, pp. 548–65.

FINEGOLD, D. and SOSKICE, D. (1988) 'The failure of training in Britain: Analysis and prescription', *Oxford Review of Economic Policy*, 4, pp. 21–53.

FREEMAN, G.P. (1985) 'National styles and policy sectors: Explaining structured variation', *Journal of Public Policy*, 5, pp. 467–96.

HAMILTON, S.F. (1987) 'Work and maturity: Occupational socialization of non-college youth in the United States and West Germany', in CORWIN, R.G. (ed.) *Research in the Sociology of Education and Socialization*, Greenwich, CT, JAI Press.

HER MAJESTY'S TREASURY (HMT) (1989) *The Government's Expenditure Plans: 1989–90 to 1991–92*: Cm. 607 London, HMSO.

INSTITUTE DER DEUTSCHEN WIRTSCHAFT (IDW) (1988) 'Industriemeister: Neues Anforderungsprofil', *Informationsdienst des Instituts der deutschen Wirtschaft*, 14, 17 March, pp. 6–7.

JONES, I.S. (1988) 'An Evaluation of YTS', *Oxford Review of Economic Policy*, 4, pp. 54–71.

KEEP, E. and MAYHEW, K. (1988) 'Education, training and economic performance', *Oxford Review of Economic Policy*, 4, pp. i–xv.

LAWRENCE, P. (1980) *Managers and Management in West Germany*, London, Croom Helm.

MARCH, J.G. and SIMON, H.A. (1958) *Organizations*, New York, John Wiley.

MARQUAND, J. (1989) *Autonomy and Change: the Sources of Economic Growth*, London, Harvester Wheatsheaf.

NEUSTADT, R.E. and MAY, E.R. (1986) *Thinking in Time*, New York, Free Press.

NICHOLSON, SIR BRYAN, (1990) 'Radical reform of vocational training has begun', *Financial Times*, Letters, 2 January.

NOLL, I. (1986) *Methodenbericht: Darstellung und Begruendung der bei der Nettokostenerhebung 1980 eingesetzten Methoden*, Berlin, Bundesinstitut für Berufsbildung Heft 80.

NOLL, I., BEICHT, U., BOELL, G., MALCHER, W. and WIEDERHOLD-FRITZ, S. (1983) *Nettokosten der betrieblichen Berufsausbildung*, Berlin, Beuth.

OAKESHOTT, M. (1951) *Political Education*, Cambridge, Bowes and Bowes.

PEACOCK, A.T. and WISEMAN, J. (1961) *The Growth of Public Expenditure in the United Kingdom*, Princeton, Princeton University Press.

PELLEGRIN, J. (1989) 'Local initiatives for enterprise', *OECD Observer*, 158, pp. 8–11.

PRAIS, S.J. and WAGNER, K. (1985) 'Schooling standards in England and Germany', *National Institute Economic Review*, 112, pp. 53–76.

PRESSMAN, J. and WILDAVSKY, A. (1973) *Implementation*, Berkeley, University of California Press.

RAFFE, D. (1988) 'Going with the grain: Youth training in transition', in BROWN, S. and WAKE, R. (eds) *Education in Transition: What Role for Research?*, Edinburgh, Scottish Council for Research in Education.

RIGG, M. (1989) *Individuals' Perspectives*, London, HMSO, for the Training Agency.

RIST, R.C. (1986) 'Economic growth and job creation', in Rist. (ed.) *Finding Work*, London, Falmer Press.

ROBERTS, K., DENCH, S. and RICHARDSON, D. (1987) *The Changing Structure of Youth Labour Markets*, Research Paper No. 59, London, Department of Employment.

ROSE, R. (1982) *Understanding the United Kingdom: the Territorial Dimension in Government*, London, Longman.

ROSE, R. (1985) 'The programme approach to the growth of government', *British Journal of Political Science*, 15, pp. 1–28.

ROSE, R. (1987) 'The political appraisal of employment policies', *Journal of Public Policy*, 7, pp. 285–305.

ROSE, R. (1988) 'Comparative policy analysis: The program approach'. In DOGAN, M. (ed.) *Comparing Pluralist Democracies*, Boulder, Col., Westview Press.

ROSE, R. (1990) 'Inheritance before choice in public policy', *Journal of Theoretical Politics*, **2**, pp. 263–91.

ROSE, R. (forthcoming) *Prospective Evaluation of Youth Training: Lessons for Britain about the Year 2000*.

ROSE, R. and PAGE, E.C. (1990) 'Acting in adversity: Responses to unemployment in Britain and Germany', *West European Politics*, **13**, 4, pp. 66–84.

ROSE, R. and WIGANEK, G. (1990) *Training without Trainers? How Germany Avoids Britain's Supply-Side Bottleneck*, London, Anglo-German Foundation.

SCHMID, G. and REISSERT, B. (1988) 'Do institutions make a difference? Finance systems of labour market policy', *Journal of Public Policy*, **8**, pp. 125–50.

SCHOENFELDT, E. (1986) *The Dual System of Vocational Education*, Mannheim, Deutsche Stiftung für internationale Entwicklung.

SIMON, H.A. (1979) 'Rational decision making in business organizations', *American Economic Review*, **69**, pp. 493–513.

SOLOW, R. (1986) 'Unemployment: Getting the questions right', *Economica*, **53**, pp. 23–34.

TAYLOR, M.E. (1981) *Education and Work in the Federal Republic of Germany*, London, Anglo-German Foundation.

TESSARING, M. (1988) 'Arbeitslosigkeit, Beschaeftigung und Qualifikation: en Rueck- und Ausblick'. *Mitteilung AB*, **2**, pp. 177–205.

TA (Training Agency) (1989a) *Training in Britain: the Main Report*, London, HMSO for the Training Agency.

TA (Training Agency) (1989b) *YTS Progress Report 1986/87*, Sheffield, Training Agency.

VARLAAM, C. and POLE, C. (1988) *The Training Needs of Trainers in Industry and Commerce: a Feasibility Study*, Sheffield, Trainer Development Section of the Training Agency.

WILDAVSKY, A. (1988) *The New Politics of the Budgetary Process*, Glenview and Boston, Scott Foresman Little Brown.

WILLIAMSON, B. (1983) 'The peripheralisation of youth in the labour market'. in J. AHIER and M. FLUDE, (eds) *Contemporary Education Policy*, London, Croom Helm.

4   Institutional Incentives and Skill Creation: Preconditions for a High-Skill Equilibrium

David Finegold

Introduction

Why are some economic actors, whether firms, regions or countries, able to pursue innovation-oriented, high-skill strategies while others are not? In this chapter I will sketch the outlines of a new methodological approach to comparisons of advanced industrial economies that can be used to answer this question. The analysis is built around a simple model, based loosely on game theory, that explores the logic underlying decisions that can lead to a low- or high-skill equilibrium (LSE or HSE).[1]

The game consists of three players, representing the three main investors in education and training (ET): individuals who have completed compulsory schooling, company managers and government policymakers. Each player is seeking to maximize his well-being while making decisions based on rules and incentives created by the institutional setting in which he is placed. This game, of course, is a radical over-simplification of reality. Many actors are left out and those who are included are aggregates of myriad different types of individuals — from unskilled workers to professionals — each with a set of motivations that goes well beyond economic self-interest.[2] The model, then, is intended solely as an analytical tool that is useful for revealing the combination of conditions that may need to exist if an economy is to reach a high-skill equilibrium. It is important to note at the outset that the term 'equilibrium' is not meant to suggest a static condition — exogenous shocks will cause frequent readjustments in corporate and individual strategies — but rather to emphasize the self-reinforcing nature of the institutional factors in the model; a change in one variable, without corresponding shifts in the other elements, is unlikely to lead to a long-term shift from the original position.

The 'rational actor' perspective offers an alternative to explanations of economic decline that place the blame on education and training or cultural factors (e.g., Wiener, 1981; Barnett, 1986). This is not to deny that there are real differences across countries or classes in individuals' attitudes toward skill acquisition, but rather to demonstrate that many of these attitudes can be seen as rational responses to the institutional structures in which the players operate and the incentives which these institutions create.

Far more promising than conventional cultural explanations is the 'societal analysis' approach developed by a group of French sociologists and economists (Maurice *et al.*, 1986). They explain each nation's distinctive salary hierarchies by reference to the interaction of the ET system, business organization and industrial relations environment. By adding an element of game theory, I hope to overcome some of the problems which 'societal analysis' shares with cultural approaches: notably, the inability to account for variations within countries or across historical periods (Marry, 1988). Using this model, it should be possible to demonstrate how within a general low-skills equilibrium, individual companies or regions may successfully pursue a high-skill strategy if they can create, or are subject to, the necessary structures and incentives.

The model is also an attempt to highlight common elements in recent research from a number of different disciplines on the factors necessary to survive and prosper in the turbulent economic environment of the 1990s. At the micro-level, management consultants and business school professors have conducted case studies of thriving companies' organizations and strategies to unlock the secrets of their success (Magaziner and Patinkin, 1989; Walton, Allen and Gaffrey, 1987; Fonda and Hayes, 1988). Likewise, the study of high growth regions or industrial districts — such as Italy's Emilia Romagna or the Silicon Valley in the US — has become an industry in itself, with economists, geographers and sociologists all contributing to the literature on 'flexible specialization' (Hirst and Zeitlin, 1989; Piore and Sabel, 1984; *Society and Space*, 1988). And at the macro-level, many political economists have focused their attention on isolating the factors that have enabled certain countries to adjust more rapidly than others to the new competitive conditions (Soskice, 1990; Katzenstein, 1985; Dore, 1986; Zysman, 1983).

The Advantages of an HSE

The first stage in the game is determining if it is in the interests of each player to strive for a high-skill equilibrium (Figure 4.1). Let us start with the motivations of the *individual* who is nearing the end of compulsory schooling and is faced with a crucial set of choices: should s/he stay on in full-time education, and if so, what type of course (academic or vocational) should s/he pursue? Or will s/he be better off leaving school to search for a job that may or may not offer training? When making these decisions s/he will weigh the costs of additional education and training, both direct (course fees) and indirect (foregone earnings), versus the increased future rewards s/he is likely to receive in return for acquiring higher levels of qualification. S/He will, of course, have to factor in a number of non-monetary considerations, such as

Figure 4.1   *Motivations of ET investors*

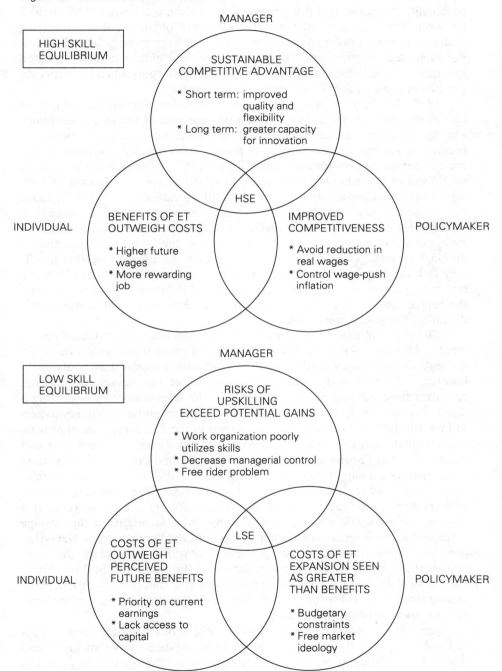

her/his likelihood of success in obtaining additional qualifications and the probability that these qualifications will gain her/him entry into her/his desired vocation. The greater satisfaction that s/he may obtain from a career that offers more varied tasks and responsibilities will have to be balanced against the increased pressure and hours this work may entail. In the simplified model, then, the individual will opt for a higher-skill route when the expected benefits of continuing ET are greater than its costs.[3]

While studies attempting to quantify the benefits of investment in ET are notoriously difficult, most have found a positive rate of return to individuals who opt for further education and training. There are, however, a number of reasons why people, if left alone, will tend to underinvest in training from a societal perspective (Marquand, 1989; Thurow, 1970). Teenagers, for example, may discount the value of future earnings relative to present income at a far higher rate than society as a whole. In addition, individuals tend to be more risk averse than the government when making investment decisions, since they usually have less information available on future manpower requirements and their calculations are based on a single case — their own — rather than a national average. Those who are willing to take the risk of investing in ET, may lack the financial means to do so; often students, or their families, are not in a position to sacrifice current earnings for future gains from ET and the capital markets may be reluctant to advance them the funds due to the difficulty of assessing credit risk.

The player in a position to ensure that the sum total of individuals' investment in their own skills does not add up to a societally suboptimal level of ET is the *government policymaker*. Although substantial expense is associated with boosting education and training provision, all of the advanced industrial countries have acknowledged the merits of this expenditure by allocating a significant percentage of their budgets to ET. The incentives for policymakers to invest in higher level skills have increased in the last decade, as improving international competitiveness has become a major target of economic and industrial policy (Bruno and Sardoni, 1989). To gain a productivity edge over its competitors, a nation must lower the relative cost of its labour and/or raise output per worker faster than its industrial rivals. The advantage to the policymaker of the latter course is that it does not entail a reduction in real incomes, which would mean a decline in the living standards of the average voter and a shrinking tax base to support government programmes. Nevertheless, not all governments or the policymakers within them place the same emphasis on raising industrial competitiveness (Finegold and Soskice, 1988). As I shall show later, the extent to which this is a state priority, particularly among those responsible for ET, will help determine the policymaker's willingness to push for a high-skill strategy.

Another advantage to the government official of raising the level of skills in the country is that it can help control inflation. As an economy grows and demand for labour increases, skill shortages can develop in key industrial sectors, leading to an upward spiral in wage negotiations. While improving the supply of skills in the most sought after occupational categories will not by itself solve this problem — particularly in areas of full employment — it can help delay or lessen the severity of the pressure facing the government by removing a principal driver of wage-push inflation.

The most critical player in the game, however, is the *company manager*, who faces a difficult choice between high- and low-skill routes. Not only are there significant costs associated with upskilling — e.g., investment in training, reorganization of work, etc. — but the strategy, even if successful, also entails major risks, as skilled workers will have improved bargaining power and greater potential to disrupt the work process. It is only by exploring how a company in a developed country is able to achieve sustainable competitive advantage in the international marketplace that we can understand why some managers are willing to assume these costs and risks.

In order for a competitive advantage — in price and/or quality — to be sustainable it must, by definition, be one that is difficult for rivals to replicate. The source of this competitive advantage will vary depending on the nature of the business.[4] In mining or oil exploration, for instance, the pivotal success factor will be access to plentiful supplies of natural resources; even the most sophisticated technology and training could not make the Swedish coal industry competitive with the rich Australian fields (Magaziner and Patinkin, 1989). In other fields, a patented research breakthrough — such as the discovery of a drug for AIDS — may be the basis of comparative advantage. Marketing and brand name recognition are often the route to long-term prosperity for consumer goods companies, such as Coca-Cola or Proctor and Gamble.

In the manufacturing sector, which is a central driver of international competitiveness and, hence, the main focus of this chapter, the key to building comparative advantage often lies in the production process. Through the example of a manager contemplating the introduction of a new computer-integrated work system, it is possible to analyze the merits of upskilling versus deskilling. Initially, the deskilling option may be very appealing. It will allow her/him to cut labour costs, minimize the risks of strikes and increase managerial control over the work process by separating manual from cognitive functions. Ultimately, however, the relative superiority of the high-skill strategy becomes apparent in two distinct ways: its greater efficiency in the current competitive situation and the greater likelihood that it will enable a company to maintain or increase its source of advantage.

There are several characteristics of the economic environment in the 1990s that favour high- over low-skill strategies. First, the rapid fluctuations in product demand and declining length of product life cycles mean that companies must adapt quickly in order to survive (Piore and Sabel, 1984). The corporate capacity to anticipate and respond to change is directly related to the skills of the work force (Fonda and Hayes, 1988). Production workers who are trained to reprogramme their machines and to shift easily between jobs and managers who have a knowledge of the whole organization rather than a functional specialty, will give a company greater flexibility in responding to external shocks. Another advantage to the high-skill production system is that it is cheaper to build quality into the product from its inception than to monitor for it after production is completed (Sayer, 1986). This advantage is becoming more pronounced as companies move into the next stage of automation, shifting from isolated, computer-based work stations to integrated computer management systems, thereby multiplying the costs of any error or downtime in production (Walton, 1985).

The key to the success of the high-skill enterprise, however, lies in its ability to sustain its comparative advantage through an emphasis on continual innovation — in both the product and the work process — at all levels of the organization.[5] When a company uses a machine to deskill a particular job, the task at hand may be performed more efficiently, but the firm has lost a small part of its capacity for innovation, since the machine is not able (at least with the current state of artificial intelligence research) to come up with ways of improving upon the job it performs. A worker, on the other hand, particularly one who has been trained to understand the theory underlying the tasks s/he performs and the relation of her/his job to the success of the enterprise, will have numerous opportunities to suggest ways of increasing productivity. The cumulative effect of such small improvements enables high-skill firms both to respond more efficiently to external shifts and, more importantly, to take an active role in shaping the markets where they compete.

Corning Glass, for example, was the leader in the development of fibre optic cable, a product which dramatically increased the capacity of telecommunications systems. In 1979, it built the first factory capable of mass producing the glass cable; rather than rest on this initial advantage, Corning continued to invest in innovation, using the lessons learned from the production process to design new factories. In their study of the firm, Magaziner and Patinkin (1989:294–5) observed that 'even the most aggressive companies revamp their machinery no more than every four or five years. As of late 1987, Corning was revamping on average once every eighteen months — five times in eight years.'

The final reason for adopting a high-skill strategy lies in the underlying logic of international competition. A company based in an advanced industrial country will inevitably suffer from a relative labour cost disadvantage when compared to firms in developing countries. It may attempt to overcome this handicap by installing a highly automated production system which minimizes labour costs. If at the same time, however, it removes the skill content from the work process it will make it easier for the entire technological system to be shifted to the Third World where the wage rates will be a fraction of those prevailing in the industrial powers. If these countries are to retain their manufacturing base, therefore, they must concentrate on those areas that will support high-skill production.

The Institutional Requirements for an HSE

Given the benefits to all the relevant players of a high-skill strategy, why haven't more companies in the real world adopted this approach? A few years ago, the explanation might plausibly have been argued to be lack of information — the players not being aware of the high-skill option or how to achieve it; but recently a number of management consultants have publicized the success of companies that concentrate on building the capabilities of their organizations and the people within them. The fact that many corporations and whole economies follow the low-skill path can no longer be attributed to ignorance; rather, the rationale for this choice lies in three institutionally-based factors that constitute necessary preconditions for an HSE. When these three factors are not present, the incentives confronting the players will lead them toward a low-skill strategy. The following sections will describe each of these elements in turn, specifying the precise way in which the factors interact to maintain the equilibrium.

A Long-Term Outlook

An investment in training, like money spent on research and development, has a long payback period. The outlay of expenditure begins as soon as the training commences, but it is only after the trainee has acquired and mastered a new area of expertise — which may take years in the case of higher level skills with strong theoretical content — that the individual or firm can realize the full return on this investment through greater productivity. Whether the players elect to go ahead with an investment in upgrading skills will depend on the timeframe that they use to evaluate this decision. A manager who is searching for ways to maximize quarterly profits, for instance, is unlikely to channel resources into raising skill levels, since this would raise costs without improving performance in the short term; indeed, if her/his firm is under pressure to raise short-term profitability, as often occurs when demand for its products falls in a recession, a manager may be tempted to cut training expenditure in order to make the current balance sheet more palatable. The deferred nature of returns to training investment, thus means that players are far more likely to pursue a high-skill strategy if they have a long-run, strategic perspective.

A player's capacity to adopt a long-term time horizon toward investment decisions and to think strategically about how each decision relates to her/his future, might at first appear to be more a matter of attitudes and individual abilities than institutions. But it is organizational structures and the signals which these send to the participants that shape their attitudes over time and determine the timescale they use when taking decisions on training. If interest rates are high, for example, the players will apply greater discounts to future earnings and be less likely to make long-term investments.

In the case of the company *manager*, the critical institutional variable is the relationship between financial and industrial capital: what are the primary sources of investment for her/his company? What returns do these sources expect on their investment and over what period of time? What forms of control do they exercise? To see how particular structures of ownership and control can affect managerial decision-making regarding training, assume first that the manager is part of a publicly-held corporation listed on a stock exchange, where investors are free to buy and sell shares at will. In this type of capital market, an insider-outsider problem can arise, as numerous investors seek ways to value a company; when they see a fall in earnings, for example, they may be unable to determine if it signals the start of a decline in performance or is the result of long-term investments that have reduced short-term profitability.

Managers, for their part, will be reluctant to release information that will adversely effect the value of their stock. Financial experts, in turn, will discount company pronouncements regarding future performance, focusing their research on those factors that can most easily be forecast — notably fluctuations in current levels of profitability. As a consequence, investors will tend to display little loyalty to a given corporation, concerned more with what the share price will be in three days rather than three years time (Soskice, 1990).

Senior managers can discount this speculative battle for short-term return on investment the more ownership of shares is separated from control of the corporation. This gap is narrowed, however, if the market places few restrictions on hostile takeovers. In that case, managers who make long-term investments — such as training and R&D (research and development) needed for a high-skill strategy — that depress short-term profits face the risk of an outside interest seizing control over the company and raising the share price by slashing investment or selling off the assets of the corporation that are undervalued by the market.[6] Even if management is successful in fighting off a takeover bid, it may leave the company so saddled with debt that it cannot afford long-term investments.

All of the companies located in a country where the operation of the financial institutions approximates this capital-market model will not necessarily be subject to this short-term pressure. Privately-held firms may have owners who are concerned with the long-term appreciation of their investment, thereby encouraging managers to think strategically. Managers in state-owned enterprises may also have a different timescale and set of priorities than publicly-traded companies, as they receive government backing to restructure their operations or preserve employment levels. Furthermore, some corporations may be too large to be threatened by a hostile takeover, although the advent of new financing mechanisms — such as leveraged buyouts — has made size far less of an obstacle to corporate raiders.

Competitive capital markets, which have played a critical role in shaping the industrial development of Britain and the US (Moorhouse, 1989), are not the only potential configuration of a financial system; alternative, credit-based financial systems, such as those that have evolved in Japan and West Germany, may be more conducive to a high-skill strategy, as Zysman (1983) observes in his comprehensive study of the effects financial institutions have on the capacity of governments to formulate and implement economic policy and promote sustained growth. A regulatory framework that mitigates against hostile takeovers, furnishes the state with instruments to influence the price and availability of funds for firms and allows banks or other financial institutions to take ownership positions in industrial companies can create incentives for shareholders to take a greater long-term interest in the strategic planning of the enterprise. A bargain may result that is to the mutual benefit of financial and industrial capital.

In a credit-based system like Germany's, for example, a bank provides the manager with a stable source of investment and expert advice acquired from its involvement with other major economic actors and in return gains intimate knowledge of the firm's operations and input into long-term planning that enables it to safeguard both its equity stake and the loans that it has made to the corporation. If restructuring or a shift to a high-skill strategy is called for, the players can agree to forego current dividends in the expectation of greater future earnings.

As long as the game remains simplified, with a single manager representing the interests of the company, there is no need to discuss the intermediary institutional structures that transmit the signals from financial markets to front-line workers. Running a real corporation, however, requires numerous layers of managers, each taking decisions that will affect whether the firm reaches its targets for profits and growth. Decisions on training, for example, are often taken by managers several steps removed from those setting corporate strategy. If the firm is to meet its financial targets, therefore, it must adopt a corporate structure that brings the decisions taken in each operating unit or cost centre in line with the aggregate targets. This will involve institutional mechanisms such as cost accounting systems, managerial reward and promotion structures and financial targets set by head office.

The ability of lower-level managers to adopt a long-term timeframe toward investment in skills will depend on the nature of the institutional incentives they face. Each organizational structure may or may not contain a component that encourages a high-skill strategy — e.g., is the building of subordinates' capacities a part of managerial assessment? Even if these systems encourage investment in skills and new technologies, however, the cost centre approach may discourage middle managers from making the leap to an innovation strategy because of the risks involved; rather, they may focus their investment on incremental changes in the work process that yield small, but measurable improvements.[7]

Training is particularly likely to suffer in the design of internal company systems, since its benefits are so difficult to quantify. Training expenditure does not, like R&D, lead directly to products that generate revenue for the corporation; rather, raising the skills of employees can improve productivity

David Finegold

only if it occurs simultaneously with other changes — e.g., new technology, reorganization of work — within the firm and it will often be impossible to isolate the training factor from the other elements, as in Japan, where much of the training occurs in the workplace through a systematic process of job rotation. Research by Campbell and Warner on the British microelectronics industry (chapter 8b, below) illustrates the problems cost monitoring systems can pose for high-skill strategies; they found some middle managers were forced to conceal the training they did because there was no allocation for it in their budgets.[8]

While financial institutions and corporate structures will exercise a dominant influence on the time horizon of managers in large, publicly-owned corporations, there are a host of small- and medium-sized firms for whom the relationship with customers and suppliers will be more important than the capital markets in shaping management's evaluation of investment decisions. Take the case of a manager who runs a company that is a subcontractor for several multi-national manufacturing companies. S/He is trying to decide whether to purchase a new generation of CNC machine tools and upgrade the skills of her/his workforceso that they can handle the new technology. Her/his assessment of this investment in physical and human capital will depend on the length and nature of her/his relationship with the main purchasers of her/his products. If s/he has a contract that guarantees a minimum order for the next three years, for example, s/he will be more secure in financing a high-skill approach than if her/his customers are liable to cut off purchases without warning. Similarly, if the corporations that subcontract out production set demanding quality specifications and, at the same time, offer her/him assistance in training her/his employees and introducing the new technology, than s/he will have greater incentives to opt for a high-skill strategy.[9]

The capacity of the *individual* to view her/his own ET decisions from a long-term perspective is also a crucial element in a high-skill equilibrium. As shown earlier, the greater the chance that additional ET will lead to significant future rewards, the more likely an individual will be to continue in some form of education or training after compulsory schooling. The probability that skills will be rewarded is itself determined by the structure of both internal and external labour markets. On the internal labour market, institutionalized forms of employment security, coupled with a promotion structure based on competence rather than strict seniority, can encourage individuals to view training as an investment for the future by providing them a guarantee that their job will be safe while they train and offering the prospect of advancement within the company once they have acquired new skills.

Where employment guarantees are not common, an external labour market that features a well-defined, high status structure of qualifications will encourage individuals to contribute towards the costs of their own training, since it increases the likelihood that they will find a desirable job at the end of a course. A student working to become a plumber or chemical engineer, for example, is unlikely to know where s/he will end up working, but can be fairly certain s/he will find employment. Clear routes of progression between the various levels of qualification will further strengthen individuals' long-term outlook by relating current investments in training to future career paths.

The *government policymaker* who is able to view ET programmes from a long-term perspective will also make a major contribution to the creation of an HSE. Policies to foster higher-level skills that are attuned to the changing demands of industry and new technologies are both expensive and time-consuming to create. Whether ET decision-makers have the resources — both human and financial — to design programmes to meet such objectives and the patience needed to wait for the initiatives to develop will depend on a number of institutional factors: notably, the structure and powers of the relevant parts of the government bureaucracy and the degree to which they are distanced from immediate political imperatives. Policymakers will, for example, depend on a continuous flow of ET research and labour market statistics if they are to keep initiatives from becoming obsolete.

Often, however, policymakers lack the institutional support or time required to concentrate on high-skill ET policies. Training can serve a number of purposes besides fostering an HSE, such as reducing the number of people counted as unemployed or alleviating pressing, but low-level, skill shortages. Programmes designed to accomplish these latter objectives may be more common than their high-skill counterparts not only because they are cheaper and easier to monitor, but also because of the disjuncture between the timescales of politicians and career bureaucrats. Politicians naturally place greater emphasis on responding to immediate electoral concerns than civil servants, and thus may be more tempted to go for the low-cost training option, particularly in times of high unemployment. The extent to which those responsible for ET policy are insulated from short-term political pressures will, therefore, be one critical factor in determining a government's capacity to adopt a high-skill strategy. The autonomy of ET policy makers will in turn be determined by such institutional factors as: the nature of recruitment for the civil service, the structure of policy networks, the relationship between the executive, legislature and bureaucracy and the type of electoral and political systems (Zysman, 1980:300–2; Atkinson and Coleman, 1989).

Cooperation within a Competitive Environment

A long-term perspective is a necessary component of an HSE, but it is not sufficient. Players may each see the potential future benefits of increasing training but still fail to invest in skills because of collective action problems. These can arise in two ways: first, a problem of coordination may exist among the different types of players, where all would be better off if they invest in training, but if one acts on her/his own, s/he may be worse off than if s/he had not invested any funds. For example, an individual who acquires a particular type of higher-level skill, but then finds no companies pursuing strategies that will

Figure 4.2   Poaching as a prisoners' dilemma

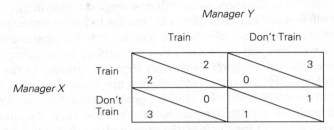

Note: Higher numbers equal more preferred options; lower portion of each box is the outcome for Manager X, upper portion is the outcome for Y.

Rules:
1. Training costs the company money
2. Skills are transferable
3. Trained workers will choose company that offers highest wage

make full use of her/his competencies, may be unable to realize and adequate return on her/his investment. Instruments for improving information flow among the players, such as careers guidance or business-education partnerships, can help avoid this difficulty. Sweden has addressed this concern by making it compulsory for all employers to report job vacancies to local labour market centres, which in turn are responsible for training programmes.

The second form of collective action problem occurs when many of the same type of player (e.g., company managers) operate in a free market, leading to the risk that workers trained by one company will be 'poached' by competitors. 'Poaching' is a classic prisoner's dilemma or free rider problem which can be illustrated using a simple game theory diagram (see Figure 4.2). Imagine two players (Managers X and Y), who each have the option of either training or not training. There are three assumptions or rules in the game: 1) it costs the firm money to train; 2) the skills provided are transferable; and 3) once trained, workers will move to the company that offers the highest salary. In this game, no matter what Player X chooses, it will always be in the interests of Player Y to avoid training, since if X trains, Y can use the savings from not training to poach the skilled worker and if X does not train, Y will be outbid for the services of any skilled worker he produces (the same, of course, holds true in reverse). Thus, if the game is played only once, the most likely outcome is an absence of training (lower right box), even though the players would both be better off if they provided training (upper left box).

Each of the assumptions in the game suggests strategies that companies in the real world may use to overcome the poaching problem. Firms can pass on part of the costs of training to individuals, by offering lower wages during the training period to reflect the reduced productivity of the worker. While this may solve the firm's dilemma, individuals who have a short-term time horizon may opt for jobs without training that offer greater immediate returns. Second, companies can emphasize firm-specific skills over general skills in the training, thereby decreasing the value of the worker to competitors. This solution, however, will reduce the total supply of transferable skills in the labour market. Finally, firms may adopt policies that ensure their investment in training will pay off before workers can leave, such as the Army's insistence that enlistees stay for a certain number of years or the old, time-served British apprenticeship system. Alternatively, firms can offer inducements (such as further training or employment security) that will encourage trainees to stay on, though competitors may offer the same rewards.

In reality, of course, the game is not so simple, with play recurring over and over again and numerous companies taking part in any sector. When the game is repeated (called a 'supergame'), the chances of players reaching a cooperative agreement to train are improved, because each participant knows that if s/he poaches in the first round, others are likely to respond by cutting training in subsequent rounds. Research on prisonner dilemma supergames has shown that the optimum strategy for players to adopt in this situation is 'tit for tat' — to cooperate in the first round and then copy the previous move of the other player in ensuing rounds (Axelrod, 1984). The willingness of players to adopt this strategy, however, will depend on their personal discount rate (McLean, 1987:135). If they do not have a *long-term perspective*, placing a high value on immediate gains over future returns, then it may pay them to poach rather than use a tit for tat training strategy. The likelihood of free riders electing not to train also increases as more companies are added to the game, since it becomes more difficult to identify the players who are poaching.

One institutional vehicle for surmounting the anonymity problem is employer associations, organized on either a geographical or sectoral basis. They bring managers together to discuss a range of issues, including training, that are of common interest. The extent to which this avenue for communication can be translated into an effective tool for discouraging free riders will depend upon such variables as: how encompassing are the institutions (what per cent of relevant employers belong)? Do they have a legislative basis (i.e., is membership compulsory)? What sanctions and resources do they have at their disposal? Can they impose a penalty — perhaps only one that affects a firm's reputation in the community — if a company fails to train to a certain standard?

The difficulties posed by collective action problems for establishing an HSE are compounded by the fact that training is simply one of many components in a successful, innovation-oriented strategy. A high-skill strategy requires a number of investments that may be beyond the means of any one player to finance, but to their mutual benefit if they share the costs and the risks involved. For example, one critical element needed to secure a niche for high quality goods and services in the international marketplace is export marketing. There are, however, large economies of scale involved in setting up an effective international sales and promotion network. A small- or medium-sized company may develop a product for which it believes there is a market overseas, but lack the money or expertise required to sell it. Similarly, a critical mass may be required to support investment in research and development that is essential to the innovation process. Particularly in areas that are on the cutting edge of scientific research — e.g., superconductors, biotechnology — the uncertainty and expenditure may be too great for a single company to bear.

The key to overcoming these obstacles to a high-skill strategy is developing institutional mechanisms that allow the players to cooperate and share information. In some cases, the institutional arrangement may be formal, like the introduction of a training levy that is used to discourage free riders and increase expenditure on transferable skills or the creation of a consortium among several companies to provide services — such as the accumulation and diffusion of information on new production technologies — that they could not afford individually. In other cases, the cooperative relationship or sanctions may be more informal, based on familial or cultural bonds (Piore and Sabel, 1984). The players involved will also vary, with government policymakers sometimes playing a leading role and at other times leaving companies to fend for themselves.

While companies may be able to devise cooperative arrangements and joint planning for their industry, they are not in a position to look at occupational needs that cross sectors. Nor has centralized state manpower planning proved effective. What can help a national economy respond rapidly to changing competitive conditions and guide individuals and companies in a high-skill direction are macro-institutional forums for negotiation between the main economic actors and government officials. These corporatist institutions not only improve information flow, but also can ease the process of restructuring, by forging a consensus among key decision-makers on those measures needed to shift investment and skills from declining to high growth sectors (Streeck and Schmitter, 1985). If corporatist arrangements are to be more than just talking shops, however, it is essential that the actors — such as trade unions and employer associations — have the power to ensure the compliance of those they represent in national negotiations.

Establishing cooperative links, however, does not entail abandoning competition. Partners in such organizations may continue to fight aggressively for market share, while working together in those areas of their operations that are to their mutual advantage. A good illustration of how these cooperative relationships work in practice is provided by the much-publicized 'industrial district' of small engineering firms in the Emilia Romagna region of Italy (Hirst and Zeitlin, 1989; Leborgne and Lipietz, 1988). With the help of the local government, these autonomous companies set up an Industrial Service Centre that supplies them with expert advice on export marketing and coordinates vocational training provision for the area. While the firms continue to complete, their cooperative relationship has facilitated specialization, with enterprises concentrating on those products where they have a competitive edge.

On a much larger scale, no single European company could have justified the billions of dollars in investment required to challenge US supremacy in commercial airline manufacturing. By joining together in a government-backed Airbus consortia, however, they were able to spread the investment burden among a number of partners and pool their existing capabilities, eventually building a strong competitive position in arguably the most technically sophisticated of all manufacturing industries (Magaziner and Patinkin, 1989). The explosion in the number of joint ventures among the large corporations of all the major developed countries provides additional evidence for the importance of cooperation in the current economic environment (Cooke, 1988).

Even if an external infrastructure can be constructed that alleviates collective action problems, thus making all of the ingredients of a high-skill strategy affordable to individual players, the success of this strategy remains contingent on the outcome of a second game taking place within firms. While the key players in the former game are managers and government policy-makers, the major participants in the internal company game are managers and individual employees, or their representatives: the trade unions. The stakes over which they are bargaining are: who controls the work process? How is it organized? What qualifications will each job require? How will each job be rewarded and what skill differentials will result?

The outcome of these negotiations will have a major impact on whether management can pursue a high-skill strategy. To make the investment in training and the other components of an HSE pay off, a company must be able to organize the work process in a way that encourages continual innovation. It makes no sense, for example, to raise the competencies and expectations of a production worker if s/he is then given a narrowly defined job that consists of a series of repetitive tasks. Some of the organizational features common in innovative enterprises include: a reduction in job demarcations, allowing workers to move easily between tasks, often as part of work teams; a flattened managerial hierarchy, devolving decisions down to line workers, thereby improving response times; and the creation of groups (such as quality circles) and incentives to encourage input from all employees on ways of improving performance (Walton, 1985; Hyman and Streeck, 1988; Sayer, 1986).

Moving from the traditional, Fordist assembly line to such new work practices, however, can pose a threat to the individual — not only to the production worker, who may be reluctant to suggest ways of raising productivity that could lead to redundancies, but also to line managers, who may be forced to relinquish or share some of their powers with work teams. Companies may be able to use the threat of increased international competition and plant closures to force employees to go along with changes in the organization of work, but they cannot compel individuals to innovate. Innovation requires active cooperation, not acquiescence. Thus, for a high-skill strategy to succeed, a firm must develop cooperative internal relationships analogous to the external relationships discussed in the previous section.

The capacity of a given firm to create a cooperative internal environment will generally be dependent on the broader industrial relations structure: what percentage of the work force is unionized? Is it single or multi-union? Are white- and blue-collar workers in separate organizations? At what level does collective bargaining normally take place and which issues are included in the negotiations? What legislative powers or restrictions are placed on unions? What input, if any, do they have into the company's strategic decision-making and the introduction of new technologies? These factors will determine the relative strength of the given players and whether they see a reorganization of the work process as in their own interests.

As Rainbird (1988) has observed, the rewards attached to a particular skill are often contingent on it being exclusionary. Broadening the competencies of the entire work force may undermine the power of the small cadre, who previously benefited by restricting access to their specialized skills. Whether the new, more flexibly trained workers are treated as 'skilled' will in turn depend on bargaining over the revised job definitions.

The way in which the industrial relations structure can affect the outcome of the internal company game can be illustrated by imagining two identical firms seeking to move towards a high-skill strategy, one where each craft occupation is represented by a different union, the other where the vast majority of the work force, including lower-level management, is under the auspices of a single union. In the former case, the individual worker and his union may be in a no-win situation: if they accept the change, they face a potential loss of membership and reduction in status, while if they oppose it, the firm may be forced into more severe redundancies or bankruptcy. In contrast, the encompassing union may be in a position to exchange the flexible work practices management desires for a greater say in the operation of the enterprise and a share in the improved performance that can be divided among its members.

As is the case with external cooperative arrangements, however, new forms of industrial relations do not entail abandoning competition. Critical issues — such as wages, benefits and the length of the work week — will continue to be subject to legitimate disagreement and conflictual bargaining between management and workers, while in other areas — such as initial training and retraining — they may perceive the benefits of working in tandem.

Exposure to International Competition/Export Orientation

While the first two elements of the HSE deal with the capacity of the players to adopt an innovation-centred strategy, the third — a focus on exports — refers to the players' motivations. Even if the players have the institutional means to pursue a high-skill strategy, they may not feel the urge to do so if they are producing a non-traded good or service (Rose, 1989). In those businesses that are not subject to international competition — which may range from the very large (e.g., national railroads or utilities) to the very small (e.g., corner shop or hair stylist) — there will be less pressure to invest in upgrading skill content and product quality, since the customer cannot look abroad for an alternative and all the companies in the sector are drawing on the same ET system for their labour. If, however, companies are seeking high value-added niches in world markets, then they must meet the quality and ET standards of the top corporations in other countries if they are to survive.

There are four caveats to the importance of export orientation for a business. First, exposure to international competition, without a long-run perspective and cooperative institutions, cannot ensure that companies in developed countries will focus on high-skill market niches; in the short-term, firms may still prefer the lower value-added end of the market, despite the fact that they are likely to lose share over time to lower-wage nations. This point has been well documented in the British case where, despite a relatively exposed economy since the Second World War, the majority of companies have been concentrated in the low-quality, low-skill end of product markets (Finegold and Soskice, 1988). Second, if a country or company is attempting to catch up in the race for high-skill products, then full exposure to world competition, before it has had the chance to attain sufficient scale and develop cooperative relationships, may cripple a promising enterprise. Third, the decline in transportation costs and spread of global telecommunications has steadily increased the range of industries open to international competition, with sectors — such as retailing and restaurants — that were previously dominated by domestic companies now being contested by multinational corporations. And fourth, even if an industry is immune from foreign competition, there may be a sufficient number of firms within a single country to propel some companies to move toward a high-skill strategy.

Nevertheless, an export orientation can act as a strong impetus to a high-skill strategy for all the relevant players. In the case of *companies*, there is a real danger that if managers are not subject to short-term stock market pressures and cooperate with others in their sector, that stagnation, not innovation will result. It is the constant threat posed by rivals in other nations, particularly the newly industrialized economies such as South Korea and Singapore, that will force managers to keep their competitive edge and push them toward skill upgrading if they are to prosper.[10] As a company concentrates on more specialized, higher quality products and services, however, the size of its domestic customer base is likely to contract, making exports essential to maintain growth and profitability.

An additional advantage to an export focus for managers is that it may facilitate cooperative ventures with other companies in the same industrial sector. When a relatively closed national market is seen as the natural limit to sales, then a manager will inevitably see other domestic firms in her/his sector as her/his primary competitors; if s/he aims for worldwide distribution, however, these same competitors may be transformed into potential allies, as they realize the necessity of joining forces if they are to attain sufficient scale in the battle for international markets.

For the *government policymaker*, the significance of the link between export orientation and the development of an HSE has been well demonstrated by Katzenstein (1985). In his study of the success of small countries in international markets, he showed how the openness of an economy was positively correlated with the development of institutional structures (such as those outlined in earlier sections of this chapter) designed to attract high-skill companies. The logic holds equally true for the major industrial powers, where policymakers realize that the only way to ensure long-term improvement in the relative wealth of their country is to maintain a positive balance of payments. But while all of the industrialized countries have adopted measures to encourage exports, those which have been the most successful — namely, Japan and former West Germany — have concentrated their industrial policies on encouraging investment and building infrastructure in high value-added businesses.

In the case of the *individual*, the benefits of an export focus for a high-skill strategy were alluded to in the discussion on industrial relations. Employees will be more likely to accept the need for new technologies and the reorganization of work if they understand how their jobs and incomes are dependent upon the competitive position of their company in world markets. Volkswagen took this factor into account when designing a new apprenticeship programme for its clerical workers in conjunction with the local college. The entire three-year training package is built around a computer simulation of an automated factory so that workers are able to see how their jobs will relate to the overall performance of the firm and how the firm's cost structure compares to its major international rivals (Diepold, 1988).

Altering the Incentives: First Steps Towards an HSE

To this point, I have focused on developing a theoretical approach that reveals some of the institutional incentives which can lead key decision-makers to either a low or high-skill equilibrium (Figure 4.3). I will now turn briefly to the implications of this analysis for policymakers in areas where high-skill companies are not already present, but who are seeking to foster their development. As the game framework has attempted to show, no single initiative will, by itself, lead to an HSE, since there are several factors which need to be present if innovation-oriented companies are to prosper. The chapter, however, has identified a number of institutional factors that could, if altered in a coordinated manner, increase the likelihood of an HSE developing: strengthening employer and union organizations, improving the clarity and progression of routes through the structure of qualifications, decreasing the dominance of capital market financing, etc.

Figure 4.3   Institutional preconditions for a high skill equilibrium

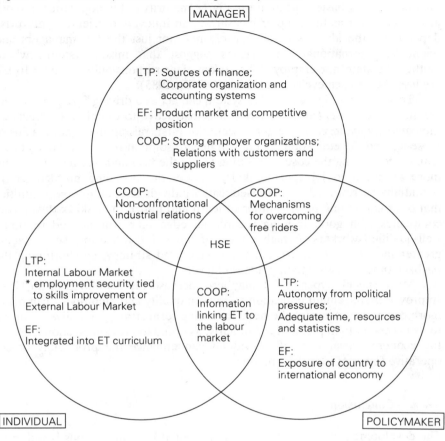

MANAGER

LTP: Sources of finance;
    Corporate organization and
    accounting systems

EF: Product market and competitive
    position

COOP: Strong employer organizations;
    Relations with customers and
    suppliers

COOP:
Non-confrontational
industrial relations

COOP:
Mechanisms
for overcoming
free riders

HSE

LTP:
Internal Labour Market
* employment security tied
  to skills improvement or
External Labour Market

EF:
Integrated into ET curriculum

COOP:
Information
linking ET to
the labour
market

LTP:
Autonomy from political
pressures;
Adequate time, resources
and statistics

EF:
Exposure of country to
international economy

INDIVIDUAL

POLICYMAKER

Legend:
Long Term Perspective (LTP)
Export Focus (EF)
Cooperation within a Competitive Environment (COOP)

An additional way forward is to improve the ET system. The precise form which an efficient ET system should take in the rapidly changing economic environment of the 1990s is far from clear: some nations achieve high ET standards by retaining the vast majority of young people in state institutions until the age of 18 or beyond (e.g., Japan, Sweden), while others rely on a dual system, where most individuals leave school at 15 or 16 to enter an apprenticeship, alternating between school or college and work-based training for an additional three years (Germany, Switzerland). Likewise, some state-centred systems place a large emphasis on vocational and technical courses, while others stress an academic curriculum, leaving it to companies to provide work-related skills. What is important, however, is that the ET system should provide a strong basic education for a large majority of the population and not just an elite, for as the chapter has shown, an innovation-oriented enterprise depends on the abilities of all participants, not just the top managers and scientists. International comparisons suggest that mixed systems, where neither the state nor employers has taken clear responsibility for post-16 ET are less likely to achieve this objective (OECD, 1985).

To see how a high quality ET system can act as a driving force behind the creation of an HSE (Streeck, 1989), it is instructive to examine its effects on the *company manager* in the game scenario. First, raising the general skills of those leaving the education system will negate some of the public goods problem, by decreasing the costs of training facing the firm and freeing it to devote more attention to job-specific skills; indeed, the poaching problem could potentially be reversed, as better-educated individuals seek job opportunities that offer continuing opportunities to learn and utilize their skills, thus giving companies with good training records an edge in recruiting and retaining well-qualified workers. A higher level of initial ET will also give managers greater incentives to invest in an innovation-led strategy, by shortening the payback time necessary to upgrade skill levels.

More specific types of ET may also increase the likelihood of an HSE. Improved management education — in both quality and quantity — can make more companies aware of the need for a long-term strategy and give them the tools necessary to implement it. Similarly, as noted in previous sections, raising the economic awareness of individuals can enhance the probability of co-operative forms of industrial relations.

Conclusion

The development of this model for international ET comparisons is still in its early stages, leaving open a number of possible routes for future research. Let me end by highlighting four potential ways forward: 1) additional players, such as ET deliverers or trade unionists, could be added to the three principal ET investors currently featuring in the game; 2) additional factors that may influence whether actors reach a high- or low-skill equilibrium could be added to the framework; 3) the game theory elements of the model could be formalized, using mathematical equations to specify the strategies and payoffs for each player; and, perhaps most important, 4) empirical work could explore the motivations underlying the actions of managers, policymakers and individuals in various countries — such as the factors that lead students to stay on or leave full-time education. The hope is that by viewing the choice between low- and high-skill strategies as the product of rational decisions taken in response to a set of institutional incentives, it will be possible to improve our understanding of the relationship between ET and the economy in different national settings.

Acknowledgments

The author would like to thank David Soskice, David Raffe, Len Schoppa, Peter Senker, Paul Ryan and William Richardson for their comments on earlier drafts of this chapter, and the University of Warwick's Centre for Education and Industry for providing the time necessary to prepare the article for publication.

Notes

1 In a previous article (Finegold and Soskice, 1988), I argued that Britain has been trapped in a 'low-skills equilibrium', where the majority of companies produce low quality goods or services using workers and managers whose education and training is relatively poor by the standards of the advanced industrial countries. This chapter is intended to complement that empirical and historical analysis of the reasons for Britain's ET and economic failure by providing a theoretical account of the institutional prerequisites for a high-skill equilibrium.

2 Other players — notably ET practitioners (e.g., teachers and *Meisters*) and trade unionists — play an important part in determining the success of high-skill strategies and thus could be included in an expanded version of the model; they have been omitted for simplicity and due to space constraints.

3 There are a number of factors that will affect a person's propensity to invest in education, such as parental influence, religion, class, and national culture, that are beyond the scope of this rational actor model. For a more detailed discussion of individuals' motivations for continuing in ET and ways of improving incentives see White (1989).

4 When searching for a source of competitive advantage it is crucial to distinguish between a 'business' and an 'industry'; in an industry such as steel, for example, some businesses, like making steel beams that are relatively cheap and bulky, will depend to a large extent on transport costs, while in others — such as high quality stainless steel flatware — transportation will be a relatively minor cost factor (Magaziner and Reich, 1982).

5 This broad version of 'innovation' is intended to avoid the common mistake of viewing innovation as an activity confined to the research and development department.

6 A hostile takeover need not always engender a short-term outlook. If the buyer is not seeking a quick profit, but rather spots an under-valued company that can be revitalized by good management, then a leveraged buyout can have a similar effect to the ownership arrangements in Japan and Germany: the active investor may bring added knowledge and resources to the company's board and by taking it private, remove the firm from the short-term pressures of the stock exchange, while the debtholders will take a major interest in the long-run success of the enterprise to safeguard their investment. The major drawback to the LBO as far as training is concerned, however, is that it makes cash flow rather than growth the firm's number one priority in order to meet debt payments (Jensen, 1989).

7 Magaziner and Reich (1982) cite the example of the US steel industry, which invested heavily in the 1960s and 1970s, but spent unwisely on modifications to

outdated production lines that could yield quick returns, rather than building entirely new mills, as their competitors did in Japan and South Korea.

8　The tendency of internal corporate structures when designed to satisfy pressure from financial markets to maximize quarterly profits to promote short-term managerial decision-making can be illustrated by the example of a diversified publishing company, taken from my work as a management consultant. (It is described in terms which are sufficiently abstract to maintain the client's anonymity.) The firm was divided into a number of divisions, each treated as a financial cost centre with specific targets for expanding sales and profits. The divisional chief executive knew that he had to meet these targets if he was to keep his job and advance in the company. He was in a quandry because these targets did not leave room for what he saw as the investment requirements of his business. For instance, one section of his operation was suffering from overburdened computer programmers. The addition of six more programmers would, he believed, improve efficiency by removing costly bottlenecks and allowing the programmers time away from their immediate tasks to redesign systems that were wasting a great deal of their time. He could not afford to hire and train these additional workers, however, because the upfront costs would have caused him to miss his quarterly profit target.

Similarly, his division had designed two new products that seemed capable of claiming the market share from a key competitor. The test marketing results were very positive and the division head was eager to launch them before his rivals had time to respond. He decided to delay them both for a year, however, because, while the development costs could be carried on the budget under capital investment, as soon as he began full-scale production the costs would have been transferred to the main balance sheet. As with any new product, the start-up costs entailed in manufacturing, advertising and retraining the salesforce make it very difficult to break even in the first year, and thus would likely have depressed his division's earnings. Had the manager not been under the short-term pressure imposed by the corporate accounting system, he might have reached different decisions which would have expanded the market share and created a more profitable enterprise in the future.

9　For a good example of how subcontracting relationships can effect decisions regarding skills and work organisation see Lorenz (1989).

10　Magaziner and Patinkin (1989) give a very readable account of how South Korea and Singapore have succeeded in moving from low- to high-skill markets, with literacy and education participation rates that now surpass all but a few of their richest rivals.

References

ATKINSON, M. and COLEMAN, W. (1989) 'Strong states and weak states: Sectoral policy networks in advanced capitalist economies', *British Journal of Political Science*, **19**, 1, pp. 47–67.

AXELROD, R. (1984) *The Evolution of Cooperation*, New York, Basic Books.

BARNETT, C. (1986) *The Audit of War*, London, Macmillan.

BRUNO, S. and SARDONI, C. (1989) 'Productivity competitiveness among non-cooperating integrated economies: A negative-sum game', *Labour*, **3**, 1, pp. 73–94.

COOKE, P. (1988) 'Flexible integration, scope economies and strategic alliances: social and spatial mediations', *Society and Space*, **6**, 3, pp. 281–300.

DIEPOLD, P. (1988) 'A New Concept of Vocational Education and Training', presented at 'Strategic Occupational Training: German Experience of a Systems Approach', London, The Prospect Centre, November.

DORE, R. (1986) *Flexible Rigidities*, Palo Alto, Stanford University Press.

FINEGOLD, D. and SOSKICE, D. (1988) 'The failure of British training: Analysis and prescription', *Oxford Review of Economic Policy*, **4**, Autumn, pp. 21–53.

FONDA, N. and HAYES, C. (1988) 'Education, training and business performance', *Oxford Review of Economic Policy*, **4**, 3, Autumn, pp. 108–19.

GERSCHENKRON, A. (1962) *Economic Backwardness in Historical Perspective*, Cambridge, MA, Harvard University Press.

HIRST, P. and ZEITLIN, J. (eds) (1989) *Reversing Industrial Decline?*, Oxford, Berg.

HYMAN, R. and STREECK, W. (eds) (1988) *New Technology and Industrial Relations*, Oxford, Basil Blackwell.

JENSEN, M. (1989) 'Eclipse of the public corporation', *Harvard Business Review*, September–October, **68**, 5, pp. 61–74.

KATZENSTEIN, P. (1985) *Small States in World Markets*, Ithaca, NY, Cornell University Press.

LEBORGNE, D. and LIPIETZ, A. (1988) 'New technologies, new modes of regulation: Some spatial implications', *Society and Space*, **6**, pp. 263–80.

LORENZ, E. (1989) 'The search for flexibility: Subcontracting networks in British and French engineering', in HIRST P. and ZEITLIN, J. (eds) (1989) *Reversing Industrial Decline?*, Oxford, Berg, pp. 122–32.

MAGAZINER, I. and PATINKIN, M. (1989) *The Silent War*, New York, Random House.

MAGAZINER, I. and REICH, R. (1982) *Minding America's Business*, New York, Harcourt Brace Jovanovich.

MARQUAND, J. (1989) *Autonomy and Change: The Sources of Economic Growth*, London, Harvester Wheatsheaf.

MARRY, C. (1988) 'Societal analysis by LEST', paper presented to the VET Forum, Warwick University, December.

MAURICE, M., SELLIER, F. and SILVESTRE, J.J. (1986) *The Social Foundations of Industrial Power*, Cambridge, MA, MIT Press.

McLEAN, I. (1987) *Public Choice: An Introduction*, Oxford, Basil Blackwell.

MOORHOUSE, H.F. (1989) 'No mean City? The financial sector and the decline of manufacturing in Britain — Review Article', *Work, Employment and Society*, **3**, pp. 105–18.

OECD (1985) *Education and Training After Basic Schooling*, Paris, OECD.

PIORE, M. and SABEL, C. (1984) *The Second Industrial Divide*, New York, Basic Books.

RAINBIRD, H. (1988) 'New technology, training and union strategies', in HYMAN, R. and STREECK, W. (eds) *New Technology and Industrial Relations*, Oxford, Basil Blackwell, pp. 174–88.

ROSE, R. (1989) 'What's New in Youth Unemployment? From Producing Jobs to Producing Training', Studies in Public Policy, University of Strathclyde, No. 177.

SAYER, A. (1986) 'New Developments in Manufacturing: the Just-in-Time System', *Capital and Class*, **30**, pp. 43–72.

Society and Space (1988) Environment and planning D, Vol. **6** (3) Sept.

SOSKICE, D. (forthcoming) 'Reinterpreting corporatism and explaining unemployment: Coordinated and non-coordinated market economies', in BRUNETTA, R. and

DELL'ARINGA, C. (eds) *Markets, Institutions and Cooperation: Labour Relations and Economic Performance*, London, Macmillan.

STREECK, W. (1989) 'Skills and the limits of neo-liberalism: The enterprise of the future as a place of learning', *Work, Employment and Society*, 3, pp. 89–104.

STREECK, W. and SCHMITTER, P. (1985) *Private Interest Government: Beyond Market and State*, Beverly Hills, Sage.

THUROW, L. (1970) *Investment in Human Capital*, CA, Wadsworth Publishing Co.

WALTON, R. (1985) 'From control to commitment in the workplace', *Harvard Business Review*, 63, pp. 76–84.

WALTON, R., ALLEN, C. and GAFFNEY, M. (1988) *Innovating to Compete: Lessons for Diffusing and Managing Change in the Workplace*, San Francisco, Jossey-Bass.

WHITE, M. (1989) 'Motivating education and training,' *Policy Studies*, 10, pp. 29–40.

WIENER, M. (1981) *English Culture and the Decline of the Industrial Spirit*, Cambridge, Cambridge University Press.

ZYSMAN, J. (1983) *Governments, Markets and Growth*, Ithaca, NY, Cornell University Press.

Part 2

VET, Products and Skill Utilization

5   Productivity and Vocational Skills in Services in Britain and Germany: Hotels*

S.J. Prais, Valerie Jarvis and Karin Wagner

Introduction

This is the fourth, and final, in the National Institute's present programme of comparisons of matched firms in Britain and Germany to elucidate the effects of better training and better equipment on productivity. Our previous comparisons with Germany were based on three branches of manufacturing: metal working, woodworking, and clothing.[1] The present study is our first attempt to examine in the same way a branch of the 'services sector', namely, hotel-keeping. Our principal interest lies in the wider issues of human capital formation which are, perhaps, adequately summarized in the following two questions.

First, are there in fact international differences in productivity in a service sector such as hotels of an importance similar to that observed in manufacturing? In manufacturing, substantial international differences in productivity are not entirely surprising and can be understood in terms, for example, of varying rates of adoption of advanced technologies, varying scope for large-scale operation and varying scope for specialization; but in a sector such as hotels, so much depends on person-to-person service that large international differences in labour productivity seem less likely. Attempts to measure productivity differences in hotels and catering on the basis of aggregate statistics for the sector as a whole have so far not yielded firm results;[2] a first objective of the present study is to provide estimates of productivity differences in hotel-keeping based on our direct observations of matched samples of hotels in Britain and Germany.

Secondly, having found evidence — as we shall see — of very important international differences in productivity, we have to ask whether differences in education and training in the apparently straightforward activities involved in

---

*   A fuller version of the study reported in this chapter was published in the *National Institute Economic Review*, November 1989; fuller technical references and appendices that may be of interest to researchers will be found in that version.

hotel-keeping can contribute significantly to higher productivity. This touches on a very broad issue: those who question the relevance of the wide-ranging German system of obligatory vocational training (which applies, with modifications, also in adjacent countries — Switzerland, the Netherlands, Austria and Denmark) usually concede that their three-year vocational courses are justified for technical occupations characteristic of manufacturing and construction. However, they doubt whether the system is justified for occupations of the simpler kind characteristic of hotel-keeping or, say, retailing. We therefore need to examine in which specific activities German hotels have found it useful to employ a greater proportion of personnel who have passed qualifying examinations at the end of two to three year vocational courses; and we must trace in practical detail, as far as possible, how more training has contributed to greater productivity.

The hotel industry is undoubtedly a substantial employer, and thus a worthwhile sector for investigation in relation to training policies. Official figures indicate that the industry was fairly similar in importance as an employer in Britain and Germany: about 250,000 full-time equivalent persons were engaged in hotels in Britain in 1987, and about 190,000 in Germany in 1985. In both countries about two-thirds of all employment in hotels is female; part-timers are more important in Britain, accounting for 41 per cent of all employment compared with 19 per cent in Germany; self-employed and family members are more important in Germany, accounting for 14 per cent of all engaged in the industry in Britain and 24 per cent in Germany.[3]

The hotel industry is of interest not only because it is a substantial employer, but also because it is an expanding employer — as a result of falling travel costs, rising real incomes, the spread of car ownership, and the consequent growth of business and holiday travel. In the decade 1977–87 employment by hotels has grown in both Britain and Germany by 12–13 per cent; this contrasts with a sharp fall in manufacturing employment in Britain of 29 per cent, and a slight fall in Germany of 3 per cent. It is the less skilled kind of employee who has been released from, or is no longer recruited by, manufacturing industry; and it might be thought that this kind of person who, because of family commitments or other reasons is less inclined to take up technically complex work, might be employed in an expanding service sector such as hotels.[4]

Hotels vary from magnificent palaces of a thousand and one beds, to modest establishments taking in a few overnight guests for bed and breakfast; there is consequently considerable variety in organizational styles, in the number of levels of responsibility, and in the mix of skills required at each level. In a study of this kind, limited as it must be by resources, we thought it best to concentrate our comparisons on the central range of hotel sizes, and to hotels in large towns. The distribution of hotel sizes is very similar: in both countries half of all bedspaces are in hotels of over twenty-seven bedrooms, and a half below. For our main comparisons of productivity we aimed to approach hotels in the common size range of ten to one hundred rooms which account for 54 and 67 per cent of hotel rooms in Britain and Germany respectively.

Of hotels initially approached by telephone, fourteen agreed to visits in Britain, accounting for about a third of those approached; in Germany we visited twenty-four hotels, accounting for about a half of those approached. The arithmetic average size of the sample hotels was very similar: in Britain fifty-eight rooms, and in Germany fifty-seven rooms. At the pilot phase we also visited hotels with international affiliates and other very large hotels to obtain a broader view of the industry's current concerns; in both countries together we visited a total of some fifty hotels. We also visited four vocational colleges and had phone discussions with a dozen more vocational colleges on specific issues. Discussions were also held with industry-wide bodies and unions in both countries. At each hotel we conducted a number of interviews — usually with the acting manager, and often with a receptionist, a housekeeper, and sometimes also with the head of catering. To save travelling costs, we conducted half the British interviews in London and the remainder in three major towns in England and Wales; in Germany, just over half were in Berlin, and just under half in Frankfurt and three other large towns in Western Germany. The visits were carried out mainly between mid-1988 and mid-1989.

The remainder of this chapter proceeds as follows. The matching of the quality of hotels in our samples was a major consideration: this is described in the next section, together with our estimates of productivity differences between the two countries. Differences in buildings and in equipment that might improve productivity are then outlined, followed by an account of differences in the proportion of personnel with vocational qualifications, and a description of how vocational training in our sample-hotels affected working practices. The main features of the vocational courses and qualifications available in the two countries are then described, followed by a discussion of current developments in training policies and a summary of the argument.

Product Quality and Productivity

When undertaking international comparisons of industrial efficiency it is important — as seen in our previous comparisons of manufactured products — that the product is adequately similar in the establishments under comparison; this is particularly so for a 'service' industry where the *quantity* of labour input — and the mere availability of personnel to carry out a customer's bidding without delay — is to a certain degree an indicator of *quality*.

Our aim in the present comparisons of hotels was to eliminate three particular uncertainties that would be attached to comparisons based simply on aggregate statistics for the hotel sector as a whole: (a) British and German hotels on average might offer substantially different standards of service; (b) numbers employed in hotel-keeping need to be related to precisely the same group of establishments as those for which guest-nights are recorded (which is not the case for the national statistics in either country); (c) the restaurant side of hotels might be of different average importance in the two countries, and hence require different numbers of employees. Further, the quality of restaurant services is so very variable — from snacks in a cafeteria to *haute cuisine* in splendid dining rooms — that a very much larger study would be needed if the restaurant side of hotels were to be included. Accordingly, we chose our samples of hotels from similar quality bands; and our productivity calculations took into account only those employees engaged on the bed-and-breakfast side of the business, and excluded those engaged in the restaurant for other meals and in the bar (where necessary, employees' time was apportioned between activities).

Rather than rely simply on our own scale of values, we decided to follow the quality grading of the well-established *Michelin* guides. These are based on inspectors' confidential reports on a hotel's services judged as a whole; the guides have been published annually for Britain and Germany since 1974 and 1964 respectively. Hotels in both countries are classified into six classes, ranging from 'luxury in the traditional style' to 'simple comfort'; the British guide has an additional lower grade of 'other recommended accommodation at moderate prices'. The same principles are used internationally in classifying hotels in these guides.[5]

For our samples we chose hotels classified into two medium-quality grades — those designated by Michelin as 'good average' and 'fairly comfortable'; half the hotels in our samples in each country came from each of these two grades. These two hotel grades were fourth and fifth from the top of the Michelin grading; bearing in mind that the guides do not cover the simplest grades, they are probably fairly close to the national averages. We were not surprised to find some variability in our samples within each of the two grades we examined; nothing on our visits however led us to doubt the broad international comparability of the grading.

For our samples of hotels matched in this way, the average number of guest-nights per employee, taking all full-time-equivalent employees (reckoned on the basis of actual hours worked by each employee, including those working on breakfasts in the restaurant but not on other meals), was 2.06 in the British sample and 4.01 in the German sample. To put it conversely, German hotels in our sample employed 0.25 persons per guest-night, and the British 0.49; thus, German hotels apparently require only about half the labour per guest-night as do British hotels of the same quality-grading — a much greater difference than we had expected.

Average bed-occupancy rates in our samples were similar, at 54 and 57 per cent in Britain and Germany respectively: these were very close to occupancy rates of 56 per cent for both England as a whole and for Berlin, based on large samples collected for official statistics in the two countries.[6]

In an attempt to trace the sources of the overall gap in productivity, we distinguished two sub-categories of employees: (a) those engaged mainly in

Table 5.1   Output per employee in British and German hotels

	Britain	Germany	Labour requirements in Germany as percentage of Britain
Average number of guest-nights per housekeeping employee	6.05	10.33	59
Average number of occupied rooms per receptionist	5.83	9.26	63

Table 5.2   Labour requirements in Germany as percentage of Britain

	Sample averages	After adjustment London	Provinces
Guest-nights per employee, in total	51	68	46
Guest-nights per housekeeping employee	59	— 56	—
Room-nights per reception employee	63	72	58

the more physical work of *housekeeping*, including housemaids, linen porters and housekeeping supervisors — a group for whom systematic courses of vocational training might seem of less obvious value; and (b) those engaged in the organizational work associated with *reception* — including preparation of bills, accepting payments, bookkeeping, assisting guests in their various requirements — for whom vocational courses might more obviously seem important. We then calculated two sub-measures of output per employee — but found very similar results (Table 5.1).[7]

We adjusted these estimates of comparative labour productivity to control for several ancillary influences. (1) A greater proportion of German hotels were of the *hotel garni* type, not providing a restaurant service apart from breakfast, which may lead to greater efficiency. (2) Efficiency might vary with size of hotel; as the distribution of hotel sizes was not exactly matched between samples for the two countries, the measured average might thus be distorted. (3) As we thought, the quality-gradings of two hotels in our samples were borderline, we examined the effects of grading on efficiency and made a separate allowance for those two hotels. (4) London's higher room-occupancy rates, and its higher labour turnover, may have affected our comparisons; we therefore examined the differential effect of a hotel being in London, rather than elsewhere in Britain. Frankfurt and Berlin were similarly examined in the regression analysis.

The net effect of allowing for these factors was to reduce the estimated gaps in labour requirements for London hotels, and to increase them slightly for English provincial hotels (Table 5.2).[8]

German hotels function with, say, only some 60 per cent of the labour force of British hotels; equivalently, labour productivity in German hotels is about 65 per cent higher than in British ones. The German productivity advantage in this branch of the service sector is thus not lower — and, if anything, is slightly higher — than in manufacturing, where it was estimated at around 40 per cent in the early 1980s.[9] It is in any event clear from our comparisons that the opportunities in British hotels for economies in labour usage are considerable, and certainly greater than all but a few experts had hitherto thought possible.[10]

While many factors affect the price of hotel rooms, it is worth noting that despite higher wage costs in Germany, prices of hotel rooms in major towns in Germany were 20 per cent lower (at official exchange rates) than in Britain in the quality grades that we have focused on here; their greater efficiency in the use of labour presumably has played an important part in this. This appears from the room rates we compared from the Michelin guides for 1986 based mainly on 1985 quotations. That year was chosen for comparison because of the availability of a larger inquiry comparing prices for international purchasing-power-parity (PPP) calculations; those showed that goods and services in general were 16 per cent dearer in Germany than in Britain: the relative costs of staying in a German hotel were thus about a third lower than in Britain — comparable to the differences in labour requirements estimated from our matched samples.[11]

Differences in Physical Capital

This section outlines the main differences between the countries found in our samples of hotels in relation to the capital stock — buildings, their maintenance, fixtures and equipment — which might be expected to affect working efficiency. From an economist's point of view we need to distinguish whether the *value* of the available capital stock per hotel room is significantly higher in Germany or whether the *quality* of the capital equipment is more suited to its tasks, without significantly greater costs being incurred.

Buildings

There was considerable similarity in the range of buildings. Close to half the sample hotels in each country had been purpose-built, and half had been converted from private residences. In Britain the conversions were usually from large Georgian or Victorian residences with narrow frontages, and often involved connecting a few such houses; in Germany more of the conversions had been from single apartment blocks (of three to six storeys) originally divided into large residential flats of about ten rooms each, and had been easier to convert. About two-thirds of the sample hotels in each country were equipped with a lift; these were, of course, usually the larger hotels. Nearly all the hotel rooms in both our samples had a private bath or shower.

Refurbishment

Refurbishment of rooms took place equally frequently in both countries, usually at intervals of three to five years, and provided opportunities for incorporating labour-saving improvements. Examples observed were: tiling of bathrooms; fittings suspended from walls to ease cleaning; bed-bases down to the floor to reduce dust collecting underneath. Improvements of this sort had been introduced in the great majority of bedrooms we saw in the German sample as part of a concerted approach in the reduction of running costs. Refurbishment of rooms in the British sample occurred as frequently as in Germany; but labour-saving improvements of the kinds mentioned were observed in only a minority of British hotels.[12]

Computers

The past decade has seen the progressive adoption of computers at the hotel reception and 'front desk'. The capital cost of a computer (including software) suitable for most hotel work is now equivalent to roughly one year's salary of a receptionist, or a little less. For the very largest hotels — mainly outside the range of our sample — computers have assisted in a remarkable variety of tasks: reservations; updating of room-occupancy; credit control; lists of departing guests for room-cleaning staff and the cashier; preparation of guests' bills on a continuous basis; recording regular guests' preferences on room locations; management summaries of receipts and budgeted gross operating surplus; forecasts of occupancy rates to be used as a tool for marketing initiatives to fill spare capacity; and writing 'marketing' letters to previous guests.

For medium-sized hotels the benefits of computers do not as yet appear to outweigh the initial investment; the general opinion in both countries is that a good manager in a small hotel should see 'at a glance' the state of bookings, and keep other relevant details in his head. We found half our sample hotels were without a computer, and half had purchased a computer; the dividing line was determined by much the same size boundary in both countries, at about fifty rooms.

Among the larger hotels in our sample in which computers had been installed, we were told that there was no immediate apparent saving in staff (though we formed the view that in the longer term there would be marginal manpower savings). In Germany, management was usually satisfied that a computer enabled receptionists to carry out their functions more promptly, to look ahead on the basis of better information, and to give more attention to guests' requests; in Britain it was more often said that a computer enabled staff with lower qualifications to be employed, and they would be able to carry out their functions with fewer errors.

There were, however, significant differences between the countries in the scope of the computer programmes used in our sample hotels. In the German hotels, programmes were usually 'packages' specifically designed for the needs of hotels; they incorporated credit control, costing and forecasting facilities, and sometimes automatically logged guests' telephone calls and restaurant bills. The British programmes were generally simpler — often merely book-keeping programmes. Specialized packages for hotels were available in Britain at the time of our interviews, but had not yet been adopted in hotels in our sample.

Cleaning Adjuncts

Without going into detailed housekeeping matters, it is important to note here a difference affecting cleaning procedures generally, namely, the provision of special-purpose chambermaids' trolleys loaded with linen, towels, soaps, guest supplies (hotel guides, information leaflets), cleaning tools and materials. Their cost amounts to hardly more than one or two week's wages of a chambermaid. These trolleys were used in almost all the German hotels we visited, but only exceptionally in the British hotels we visited. Suppliers of hotel trolleys in Britain told us that they were more frequent in larger hotels than in our size range. These trolleys facilitate the transporting of supplies to and from the room, thus eliminating the employment of specialized 'linen porters' (invariably male, who do heavier work including bringing sheets and towels to each floor as required, and taking away soiled linen); and they elim-inate the maid's waiting time while the porter is on his way. They promote more systematic, and therefore more reliable, working as the chambermaid 'works through her trolley' (less chance of the maid running out of some item, and forgetting to come back to that room). Rough estimates we received put the saving in labour at about a quarter.

The way many British hotels had been designed and reconstructed, did not facilitate the use of such trolleys. For example, because rents in London are high, corridors are narrow; older adjoining residences had sometimes been joined to form a hotel, leading to half-floors, many stairs, or small lifts — all of which make trolleys difficult to use. No doubt these factors played their part. Our impression, however, was that there was a lower degree of cost-consciousness in the hotels we visited in Britain, and less pressure on the use of chambermaid's time; this was more evident in the provinces where chambermaid's wages were about a quarter lower than in London.

In short, our impression was that German hotels had probably spent more on equipment and refurbishing, but the additional investment was small both in relation to the total capital cost of the building (which was of the order of £30,000 per room and upwards), and in relation to the considerably more efficient usage of labour in Germany. We were more impressed by the expertise in German hotels that had gone into the detailed choice of fittings, furniture and equipment with a view to saving maintenance labour.

Table 5.3   Estimated number of persons qualifying for hotel occupations in Britain and Germany, 1987[a]

Britain		Germany	
Management level			
University degree (BA, BSc)	100	University degree	350
Polytechnic degree (CNAA)	350	*Fachschule* Diploma	400
BTEC Higher National		*Hotelmeister*	70
Certificate and Diploma	1,200		
Post-graduate certificates	150		
HCIMA part B	150		
	1,950		820
Supervisory/Craft level			
BTEC National Diploma in		Hotel administrator	800
Hotel, Catering &			
Institutional Operations	(1,400)	Hotel craftsman	6,200
BTEC National Certificate in			
Hotel, Catering &			
Institutional Operations,		Domestic management	
and in Housekeeping and		of public institutions	(500)
Catering	(700)		
HCIMA part A	100	Housekeeping and catering	(800)
	2,200		8,300
Hotel assistants			
Receptionist (C&G 709)	450	Hotel assistant	1,800
Accomodation services			
(C&G 708)	500		
C&G 708/709 combined	400		
	1,350		1,800
TOTAL	5,500		10,900

Numbers in brackets are very approximate
Note: [a]Categories defined in *NIER*, Nov. 1989.

Differences in Human Capital

There has long been a general legal obligation in Germany for all under the age of 18 — who are not undergoing full-time education — to attend part-time vocational courses, mostly extending over three years and associated with standardized schemes of on-the-job training.[13] Vocational studies in Britain, on the other hand, are voluntary and — when undertaken — tend to extend for shorter periods. A greater proportion of the workforce is consequently vocationally qualified in Germany than in Britain, the excess varying from one occupation to another.[14]

The numbers qualifying in hotel occupations at comparable levels in the two countries in a recent year (1987) are shown in Table 5.3, distinguishing those who have completed longer or higher-level courses leading to positions of responsibility, and those on shorter courses which require at least one year of day-release, and lead primarily to 'operative' positions. Some definitional points must first be noted. (1) Very short introductory courses such as are available in Britain for those on the Youth Training Scheme (and through the industry's Caterbase scheme), are not included here; they cover only a small fraction of the subject matter required for the lowest German qualification and will be discussed below together with other current developments. (2) To remain within the occupational scope of this study, the numbers in the table relate as far as possible only to lodging activities, and exclude specialist qualifications in restaurant work (cooks, waiters). (3) Some courses are intended both for those wishing to work in hotels and for those wishing to work on the domestic side of hospitals, residential colleges and similar public institutions; our numbers are confined to estimates of those going into hotel work. (4) As far as possible the numbers shown relate to the number of *persons* passing at the highest qualification they attain, rather than to the total number of *courses* passed; the elimination of double-counting in the published figures of courses passed relies on estimates by college teachers of the proportions involved. The main features of the courses are described in the next section: at this stage we need only note that British courses tend to be narrower in scope than German courses; and that the matching of courses between the countries, and of the numbers qualifying, should be treated as approximate.

Despite these reservations the difference between the countries in total numbers qualifying at all levels is indisputably significant, with some 11,000 a year qualifying in Germany and 5,500 in Britain. The twofold advantage of Germany in hotel occupations is close to the ratio found for qualified mechanics and electricians in our previous comparisons between Britain and Germany, and distinctly lower than the tenfold and higher factors found for office occupations and retailing. Confining ourselves to main craft level, the gap between the countries in hotel-related occupations is nearer fourfold, with 8,000 passing in Germany compared with 2,000 in Britain. The greater excess at the craft level reflects the German requirement, mentioned above, for vocational courses lasting two to three years till the end of compulsory part-time vocational instruction at age 18.

Some 2,000 qualified at the top management level in Britain (degrees or Higher National qualifications) compared with 800 in Germany, and this offsets slightly the main quantitative deficiency at the craft level. However, one of the German courses grouped here at craft level — that of 'hotel administrator' with 800 qualifying a year — is of a higher standard, and might be grouped with the management level.[15] The real difference at the top level is thus not as great as appears from our table. In any event, the German view is that the number qualifying for the top level in Germany is 'more than is really needed by the industry', and further expansion in training should be at craft level.[16] At the 'hotel assistant' level the table shows much the same number qualified in each country (about 1,500).

Turning to our hotel samples, we found that 30 per cent of all employed in our German sample had attained vocational qualifications in hotel work; a further 5 per cent had qualified in office work, maintenance and other hotel-related occupations, making a total of 35 per cent. Of those employed in our British sample of hotels, 12 per cent had vocational qualifications in hotel-related occupations, and a further 2 per cent were qualified in maintenance-related work. The two-and-a-half fold difference between the countries in our samples is similar to the difference in the current annual output of all vocationally qualified persons, and corresponds more or less with differences that may be deduced from other sample surveys of manpower qualifications in this industry.[17]

The difference in the number of trainees currently on the books of our sample hotels was remarkable: some 9 per cent of the full-time equivalent workforce in the German hotels we visited were on approved apprentice courses, compared with under 2 per cent of the workforce in our British sample who were trainees of various types, including those on the Youth Training Scheme.

We must next examine how these differences in the proportion of trained personnel affect operating efficiency. We considered in detail two important functions of hotel-keeping: first, the familiar activity of housekeeping; secondly, the organizationally more demanding work of the receptionist. Finally, some comments are offered on differences in management.

Housekeeping

The difference between the countries in training for housekeeping occurred virtually entirely at the supervisory level, known as the housekeeper (*Hausdame*). Three-quarters of all housekeepers in our German sample of hotels had attained vocational qualifications following three-year apprenticeships and had worked in other hotels before promotion to their present position. In the British sample virtually no housekeeper (only one exception) had attained any vocational qualifications, nor had attended any systematic external courses in hotel work.

Each housekeeper was responsible for a very similar number of chambermaids in both countries: an average of 5.1 in Britain (5.7 if we include linen porters) and 6.2 in Germany. And in both countries hardly any of the chambermaids had acquired vocational qualifications in hotel or other work. The greater efficiency in Germany in this department of hotel-keeping is thus to be attributed to better qualification at the supervisory level and to the provision of labour-saving fittings and equipment.

Labour turnover was low amongst housekeepers and very high amongst chambermaids in both countries (between 50 and 100 per cent a year was mentioned for chambermaids, corresponding to a new recruit every two to three months in a fifty-room hotel); consequently one of the prime duties of housekeepers in both countries is to recruit new chambermaids and introduce them to their work.

German housekeepers spent more of their time on organizational tasks such work-scheduling, stock control, purchasing, and organizing external laundry-work. In the British hotels we visited such tasks tended to be undertaken at a higher level (by the manager; in larger hotels, by the 'executive housekeeper'). The qualified status of the German housekeeper brought her/his closer in standing to the managerial level: s/he exercised greater responsibility in selecting labour-saving equipment, and seemed more successful in demanding more efficient working-practices and high quality standards from her/his staff. Work-scheduling was carried out more precisely. It involved giving each chambermaid a list of rooms, calculated to allow for guests staying and leaving (the latter requiring more time), and allocating any budgeted 'left-over' time to a thorough 'spring cleaning' — shampooing of carpets, washing down of woodwork, vacuum cleaning of curtains, and so on.

The British housekeeper spent much of her/his time on detailed checking of cleaning, and would often finish off imperfect work her/himself. The German housekeeper relied more on sample 'spot checks': her/his instructions to maids were based on a clear understanding of what standards should be achieved, and with what efficiency they should be achieved. The hotel rooms we visited could be described as 'clean' in both countries, but the Germans seemed to place more emphasis on this aspect. A hotelier who had been active in the hotel trade in both countries for many years stated that the same standard of cleanliness can be found in both countries, but in Britain it is necessary to go to a hotel one grade higher to find the same level of cleanliness as in Germany.

There is undoubtedly much variability arising from the individual capabilities and preferences of the operative, and from the varying mix of tasks in each hotel; but without having carried out a time-and-motion study (which would probably be a worthwhile exercise), the following differences — in brief — seemed important to us. A chambermaid in Germany goes about her task in a more systematic and independent way, having tools and supplies to hand in her trolley; she completes all cleaning activities in one room before proceeding to the next. In Britain work is less routine; sometimes the chambermaid waits while supplies of linen are brought by a 'linen porter', at other times she rushes to bring supplies of smaller items herself; work is carried out in a varying order, to deal with jobs omitted in previous rooms while waiting for supplies; a single cleaning operation — linen changing or vacuum cleaning — is more often applied to a group of rooms simultaneously, resulting in an impression of greater activity (but greater disorder, with soiled linen lying about the corridors instead of packed away in the special bag at the back of a cleaning trolley as each room is completed).

Reception

Greater economy in manning at the reception desk was usually immediately apparent on entering a hotel in Germany in the lower number of visible staff — without apparently any lower quality of attention to guests' needs. Adjusted in proportion to the same hotel size of say, fifty bedrooms, our sample hotels in Germany had on their books an average of 4.0 equivalent full-time persons in the reception area, compared with 6.6 in Britain; allowing for multiple shift-working and week-ends. This corresponds to there being an average of 1.6 persons in attendance at the front desk of a German hotel, compared with an average of 2.6 persons in Britain.[18]

Of those employed in our sample hotels in the reception area, 55 per cent in Germany had gained a qualification following a three-year apprenticeship. Those not qualified who were working at the reception desk were mostly taking an apprenticeship course, or were on night duty when lower standards seemed acceptable; during normal daytime working hours, some 70 per cent at the reception desk were vocationally qualified or in the process of qualifying. In the British sample, only 17 per cent had hotel-relevant qualifications or were in training (22 per cent, if porters are omitted).

The benefits of the broad scope of receptionists' training courses in Germany were apparent from the way those at reception carried out a variety of tasks that were often in separate hands in Britain: reservations, room allocation, information for guests, carrying luggage to guests' rooms, switchboard operation, supervision of room cleaning, guest accounts, payments and, often, breakfast preparation — all were carried out by the 'receptionist' in German hotels as part of her/his normal duties, together with the operation of the central computer where available. If two guests arrive simultaneously at a German hotel, and two staff-members are working primarily as cashier and receptionist respectively, then both staff-members turn to work on 'checking in'; in Britain, narrower training and narrower job-definitions would more often rule this out.

There were no specialist luggage porters or *concierges* ('uniformed services') in our German sample; whereas in our British sample porters accounted for nearly one in four of all front-office staff. They usually did not have very precisely defined duties: they added a certain *je ne sais quoi* of dignity, they carried luggage, made tea for the front office staff, gave a hand in 'keeping the place tidy' and 'helped out generally'.

Management

The degree of responsibility assumed by housekeepers and receptionists in German hotels, as will be clear from the foregoing, is considerably higher than in British hotels; this has important consequences for the duties of the general manager. The British manager spends much of her/his time dealing with day-to-day duties and, sometimes in the famous style of Basil Fawlty in *Faulty Towers*, grappling with minute-to-minute problems ('fire-fighting' as it is usually termed in industry). For example, in some British hotels the manager dealt with advance room allocations for group bookings, leaving only immediate bookings to the receptionist; s/he also dealt with problems resulting from over-booking; s/he re-ordered cleaning materials, and arranged for laundry collection; and chased late deliveries. In the German hotels, on the other hand, the chief receptionist often acted as 'duty manager' and dealt with routine problems of this type.

The British manager thus allows her/himself to be preoccupied with routine duties, and feels s/he needs 'to be there' in case of problems. Most had not had sufficient time for longer-term issues. In relation to computers, for example, British managers in these medium-sized hotels had not familiarized themselves with the appropriateness of alternative computer systems; having recently installed a computer, there sometimes appeared to be an unnecessary delay in eliminating the previous paper record system.

In these respects we found managers of German hotels better informed, and with more time to plan their longer-term marketing strategies. Hotel business today often requires close working with travel agents, and with hotel wholesalers who take large block-bookings in advance at discounted rates; this requires careful commercial calculation, sales campaigns, and advertising. Much more of this was in the forefront of the German manager's thinking.

Nearly all managers in our sample of German hotels had vocational qualifications, compared with just under half in Britain. The type of qualifications also differed between the countries, with the British managers' qualifications generally being based on attendance at full-time courses not requiring an apprenticeship, whereas most German managers had qualified by starting with an apprenticeship requiring practical experience in the full range of hotel work.[19] A better grasp of the practical realities of working, and better working relations with staff in Germany, seemed to be the consequence. However, in our final judgment the real difference in management between the two countries rested not simply on differences in their *own* qualifications, but rather on differences in the competences of those immediately below them; the German manager was able to delegate many routine duties which the British manager — perhaps rightly, in the circumstances — had to retain to her/himself.[20]

Quality of Training

The greater numbers gaining vocational qualifications in Germany might seem to provide sufficient explanation of much of the higher productivity in their hotels, but are there also differences in the quality of training that are relevant? We here consider this question in terms of five dichotomies in course attributes: (a) full-time versus part-time; (b) breadth versus depth; (c) the needs of large versus small hotels; (d) national versus local syllabuses; (e) qualification based on internal assessment versus testing by external examiners and written examinations. The needs of the two countries' hotel industries as a whole seem sufficiently similar for there to be no black and white differences in these respects; we shall, however, see that there are differences in the *mix* of alternatives under each of these heads, and these carry certain lessons.

Full-time or Part-time Courses

In both countries qualifications for hotel occupations can be acquired either by attending full-time courses, usually for two years at ages 16–18; or by attending part-time day-release classes for two to three years, usually in the age-range 16–19, combined with a traineeship or apprenticeship with an employer. Even the so-called full-time courses are not wholly spent in college, since spells of work-experience are usually specified for qualification. The ratio of work to college is reversed from, say, 4:1 on the part-time route to 1:4 on the full-time route.

In Britain there is a greater reliance on full-time courses: of the total numbers qualifying (Table 5.3) about 65 per cent followed a full-time course in Britain, compared with only 15 per cent in Germany. Colleges can obviously give more attention to theoretical elements, while apprenticeship gives more attention to the practical side. Facilities at colleges for practice in cooking are usually adequate, but space and equipment for accommodation work are more difficult to provide in a college setting; thus HM Inspectors, in reporting on colleges in England, noted particularly 'insufficient practical work in accomodation studies, mainly because of poor facilities'.[21] The difference between the countries thus comes down to a difference in judgment on the optimum mix required in hotel trades of those following preponderantly theoretical, or preponderantly practical, instruction. Of the lower total numbers qualifying in Britain, a greater proportion have set their sights on managerial positions; and this might be thought to justify the greater role of full-time courses in Britain.

The German view, however, is, different. Those seeking managerial positions in Germany tend to begin by taking a three-year apprenticeship course, and only after some years of work experience do they proceed to high-level courses. While theoretical instruction is unquestionably an essential component, the German view is that in hotel occupations greater weight needs to be given to learning by experience. This judgment was in effect accepted by a visiting expert team of British hoteliers and educationists who examined German training in 1982; they concluded that the German 'insistence that every apprentice must have a good grounding in practical skills before continuing his education and becoming a manager is extremely important. In the UK ... the full-time [BTEC] programmes have a weakness in this respect'.[22]

Breadth and Depth of Courses

The breadth of German part-time hotel courses is well illustrated by their nationally-specified scheme of rotation for apprentices amongst the six main departments of a hotel: reception, administration and accounts, housekeeping, stores, kitchen, restaurant. The national scheme sets down in some detail what is to be covered in each department. For example, for the housekeeping department; detergents for different stains and materials; methods and timing of room-cleaning; construction of daily and weekly cleaning rotas.

For Britain, we need to distinguish full-time and part-time courses, and the type of student entering them. The full-time BTEC Diploma courses are intended for those who are roughly in the top third of the ability-range, having obtained school-leaving certificates including four O-level passes or better. The scope of the BTEC Diploma is similarly broad to that just outlined for Germany. To give some examples of test questions: the student is expected to be able to specify 'five of the areas under the control of the Uniform department'; select a 'food theme', devise a sample menu, and cost it; and discuss the 'importance of nutritional considerations in menu planning with the continued growth in public interest in healthy eating.'[23] The German pupil on the part-time *Hotelfachmann* course is expected to answer rather more specific, and slightly more technical, questions on the same range; for example, which activities belong to the front desk (ordering supplies, room reservations, receiving goods, staff holiday rotas)? At what temperature should tea-cloths be laundered? What storage defects give potatoes green spots? What is meant by Sauce Mornay, and what main course does it accompany?[24]

The part-time BTEC Certificate is intended for pupils with attainment levels close to, but on the whole a shade lower than, those taking the Diploma just described; and the part-time City and Guilds courses are intended mostly for those with school-leaving attainments another step lower (passes in two subjects at O level or CSE grade 1), but still above the average school-leaver. The important difference from the German approach is that both these types of British part-time courses are much narrower when it comes to specific technical skills. The BTEC Certificate includes general courses on administration, the nature of the hotel industry, staff placement, purchasing and costing; but on specific skills it requires a choice to be made, usually from either reception or housekeeping. The City and Guilds courses similarly relate to either reception or housekeeping; a candidate may take both — but it would be a rarity to take restaurant and kitchen work also. Even the lower-level German course for hotel assistants, which requires only two years of part-time attendance at college, is broader in requiring nearly half a year in each of four departments: reception, housekeeping, kitchen, restaurant (with short periods in other departments).

Differences between the two countries must also be noticed in general educational subjects, taken as a component of vocational courses. In Germany, instruction in applied mathematics, the native language, social studies and usually also a foreign languages all form distinct parts of the curriculum for vocational qualifications: they are separately examined, and contribute towards the total mark required for qualification. In Britain ostensibly corresponding 'general studies' — incorporating literacy and numeracy — were a compulsory discrete component of BTEC courses until 1988. Since then, as part of fashionable moves towards 'integrated' learning, separate classes in 'general studies' have been abandoned; any requisite elements of mathematics or language are now to be imparted together with vocational instruction.

It is important to notice the portion of the ability range in the two countries from which trainees taking these courses are recruited. The German part-time hotel courses recruit pupils mostly from the middle and lower portions of the ability ranges[25] and they expect a level of mathematical competence between that of our City and Guilds and our BTEC courses which recruits from the top half or top third. This conforms with our previous findings on higher German schooling standards in mathematics for middle and lower-range pupils.[26] It helps to explain why a considerably greater proportion of German youngsters are able to qualify on vocational courses than here.

In short, it seems clear that German vocational courses are taken by a broader cross-section of pupils, and the courses are significantly broader in scope than the Britain courses. This greater breadth has clearly not required any reduction in depth.

Hotel Size

In large hotels there is scope for an efficient division of labour amongst switchboard operators, cashiers, porters, etc.; one of the virtues of the German training system is that it provides for the needs of middle-size hotels, of the kind surveyed in our sample, where an over-division of labour is uneconomical. This seems to be the basis for the insistence in Germany that those who train, for example, as a receptionist should become proficient in the full range of tasks that can efficiently be carried out by a single individual in hotels of that size.

As noted earlier, over half of all hotel rooms in both countries are in hotels of thirty bedrooms or less. Someone who had gained one of the specialized British qualifications may find it difficult to use the knowledge gained on her/his course for more than a fraction of her/his working-time in a hotel of that size; and s/he might do well to seek employment in a larger establishment. It is thus not entirely surprising that hotels of medium size in Britain are often characterized by a fair degree of amateurism.

National or Local Syllabuses

In both countries steps have been taken to promote nationwide similarity in the content of courses so as to achieve wider acceptability of the resulting qualification. The extent to which this is achieved in practice depends on the detail in which common syllabuses and work-programmes are laid down, and on whether qualifying examinations are set locally or nationally.

In Germany each of the eleven provinces (*Länder*) has the right to prescribe college syllabuses; but five authorities have combined, and 54 per cent of all German apprentices in hotel work now take the same written tests; the remainder take tests set by each of the *Länder*. The detail of the prescribed syllabuses in Germany is considerable. Practical tests are more variable, and are determined by the local examining panel within a national list of topics to be tested.

In Britain the written examinations of City and Guilds are set centrally, and have virtually nationwide currency for the receptionist and housekeeping courses mentioned above. But qualifications validated by BTEC — which account for the majority of qualifications in hotel work — are based on what has been taught in each college and on assessment by each college; these may vary even between colleges in the same town. The lack of a common final examination for BTEC qualifications has led to great variability (criticized by HM Inspectors of Education in their 1985 report). While BTEC has published specifications of course contents and 'sample learning activities', the final detailed choice of what is included remains with each college.

Excessive variability amongst colleges in scope of subject-matter covered in BTEC courses, and in standards, appeared to us to remain a serious problem for employers. On the whole, Germany seems much closer to having achieved nationwide acceptance for its hotel qualifications; on present policies, the tendencies in the two countries are likely to continue to diverge.

Assessment or Examination

The final difference between the countries relates to the reliability (objectivity) of the qualifications. In Germany qualifications are awarded on the basis of final written and practical examinations set and marked by external examiners; in Britain there are no final qualifying examinations for BTEC awards, and the general tendency — which has also affected City and Guilds qualifications — is to rely increasingly on internal continuous assessment, by the pupil's teacher or supervisor at work, of tasks which 'the candidate should participate in designing', carried out at various stages in the middle of the course (rather than at its end) and when the candidate 'feels confident to do so'.[28]

It is perhaps worth adding here some details on the way the German final examinations for the main *Hotelfachmann* course are conducted. The examination is conducted in a hotel — but not the one in which the candidate served her/his apprenticeship — in front of three examiners who do not know the candidate (the examiners are appointed, respectively, by employers, the education authorities, and the relevant trade union). The examination usually takes four to five hours and typically includes the following activities. *Front office*: answer the usual daily letters for advance bookings etc., including 20 minutes for typing letters in the accepted commercial form at a minimum speed of 25 words per minute (corresponding to our RSA level 1). *Housekeeping*: work out next week's rota for chambermaids, check laundry, or clean a set of rooms. *Kitchen and restaurant*: cook a set menu (1½ hours), lay table, demonstrate 'silver service waiting' (¾ hour). About a dozen candidates can be given the practical examination by an examining panel in the course of a day.

Of course, similar practical activities feature in perhaps most British courses; but there is no final comprehensive, externally-marked test as in Germany. We found German employers much clearer on the reliability and content of qualifications, and they felt able to engage prospective employees on that basis; in Britain this confidence was not so apparent, but City and Guilds' qualifications were given greater credence than those of BTEC.

Recent Developments

The numbers attaining vocational qualifications in hotel work have increased substantially in both Britain and Germany in recent years, reflecting the growth in demand for hotel services and consequent increased employment; but it is important to understand at which vocational levels the growth has taken place. We focus here mainly on changes in the past five years during which the heavy subsidies to training provided in Britain under the Youth Training Scheme may be expected to have had an impact.

The changes in Germany are easier to describe and may be summarized first. At the main craft and assistant levels, the numbers qualifying have risen between 1982 and 1987 from 6,700 a year to 10,100, that is by some 10 per cent a year. Three-quarters of the increase has been in the three-year course at craft level, and one-quarter in the two-year course at assistant level. There are no national courses at lower levels than this in Germany. The courses have been broadened since 1980 by requiring all trainees in hotel and restaurant work who until then had taken specialized courses, to take the same courses for the first two years in order to improve flexibility; specialization is now confined to the third year of the course. Those aspiring only to 'assistant' positions take the shorter two-year course and cover the same range of subject matter in that period as those who follow the longer courses.

Numbers qualifying in Britain at the corresponding craft and assistant levels rose in 1983–88 from 2,500 to 3,200, that is by some 5 per cent a year. But the major growth in Britain has taken place in the certification of shorter courses for specific, narrowly-circumscribed, skills. That for 'Room Attendant' (chambermaid in Oldspeak), developed by City and Guilds, may serve as an example: 'all training and assessment must be completed within three months'; practical assessment based on cleaning ten hotel rooms in one day, and one 'departure room' in twenty-five minutes; and an oral test of fifteen questions on room cleaning, to be administered and marked by a supervisor at work. Off-the-job training totalling two hours per week for six to eight weeks is recommended, but no college attendance is required.[29] Numbers receiving certificates for this particular skill varied from a peak of 700 in 1984 to 150 in 1988.

Other skill-certificates at this 'modular', basic, level have been developed by the industry's Training Board under its 'Caterbase' scheme; about a hundred modules have so far been defined — such as 'bedmaking', 'answering the telephone' and 'handling linen' — each of which is assessed in the workplace by the trainee's immediate supervisor, and entered into the trainee's 'Caterbase Passbook'. Broad impressions suggest that the great majority of completed modules have related to restaurant work; in hotel reception and accommodation work only about 3–5,000 modules a year have recently been completed. Allowing for (say) three modules per trainee, this suggests that some 1–2,000 trainees have completed a modest range of basic training each year in hotel work. Taken together with awards by City and Guilds at the basic level just described, a total of perhaps 4,000 a year entering hotel work now attain some basic qualifications; this compares with just under 1,000 five years ago.

These elementary qualifications were introduced largely in response to two financial stimuli, namely, the catering industry's levy and rebate scheme, and the Youth Training Scheme's subsidies. The catering industry's levy scheme, which applied until 1988, remitted virtually the whole (97 per cent) of the levy of 1 per cent of the payroll if adequate training was carried out by the firm. Since 1986, YTS required trainees to be given the opportunity to gain a vocational qualification, as a condition for the government's subsidy averaging some £35 a week per trainee. It was one thing to provide the *opportunity*, and quite another actually to qualify, and to do so at a level corresponding to European standards. Of the 8,000 trainees registered as starting YTS each year in hotel and catering since 1985, information from a postal survey is available for 2,700 a year who left in 1986–8; of these, only 23 per cent gained *any* qualification, including Caterbase modules and general school-leaving certificates. Another sample survey (response rate, 60 per cent) based on those who joined YTS in April–September 1986 (and probably more reliable since it excludes those who joined later, and might not have had sufficient time to complete the course) showed 34 per cent had gained *some* qualification. Very few of those qualifications were of a standard equal to or above that of the intermediate examination taken by German trainees at the end of the first year of their course; possibly a sample consisting predominantly of those who had joined the more recent two-year YTS will show better results. However that may be, it seems clear that so far the Youth Training Scheme had made only a modest contribution to raising the number of persons qualifying in hotel work at levels corresponding to those recognized in Germany.

As part of the UK government's efforts to provide greater coherence to the framework of vocational qualifications, the National Council for Vocational Qualifications was established in 1986. In hotel work and catering, under the advice of the industry's Training Board, the Council has so far approved seven basic qualifications relating to hotel work in reception and housekeeping. The basic qualification at their newly-defined NVQ Level 1 in 'Accommodation Services' consists of following the City and Guilds programme for Room Attendants described above (no college attendance required) and completing experience of six prescribed Caterbase modules ('bedmaking', 'handling linen', etc.). No written test has so far been required, but this may change following questioning of NCVQ's approach. The award has been accredited entirely on the basis of assessment by the workplace supervisor, with all the limitations of that method.[30]

To put this into the perspective of our present comparisons, we need only remind ourselves that these NVQ awards at Level 1 can be obtained usually within six to eight weeks of beginning work. The main German qualifications with which we have been concerned in this study correspond more or less to the proposed NVQ Level 3, and require two to three years of training and study. The scope of subject matter covered in the NVQ qualification for a Room Attendant, for example, could be covered in Germany in the first four to six weeks of the basic German traineeship.

In short, there has undoubtedly been much concern and much activity in Britain in the past five years in order to increase Britain's vocational skills in hotel work; and a degree of success has crowned these efforts at all levels (while in engineering, for example, despite great efforts, the numbers attaining craft qualifications has declined). By German standards, however, the numbers qualifying remain low; and the level of skills certificated under the new arrangements attests more to the trainee's experience than to his knowledge, and is significantly lower in scope and depth than would be required in Germany for the award of their lowest level of vocational qualification.

Summary

As part of a wider investigation of international differences in productivity, a sample of fourteen hotels in Britain was compared with twenty-four in Germany; the hotels were matched for size and quality standards. Average labour requirements, reckoned on a full-time-equivalent basis, were found to be about 50 per cent greater per guest-night in the London hotels than in the German hotels, and about twice as great in the hotels in large English provincial towns as in Germany.

Only minor differences between the countries were observed in total spending on capital equipment. The main difference in resources used by hotels was in qualified manpower. In our sample of German hotels 35 per cent of all employed had attained craft-level qualifications in hotel and catering occupations, compared with 14 per cent of employees in our sample of British hotels with qualifications at more or less comparable levels. This difference in our samples closely reflected the national totals attaining vocational qualifications in the two countries in recent years in hotel-related occupations. In both countries those working as chambermaids were unqualified; the differences were marked elsewhere. Almost all who were working in German hotels — even in small family-run hotels — in management, reception, and at the supervisory level in housekeeping, had attained broad-based vocational qualifications in hotel work; in Britain qualified personnel were less usual in management, rare at the reception desk, and were hardly ever to be found in the supervision of housework.

The standards and content of the two to three year courses leading to the main craft-level qualifications in the two countries had much in common, but certain differences are worth noting:

(i)   German courses covered all departments of hotel work, in contrast to specialized departmental qualifications which were more usual in Britain. This led to greater flexibility of German personnel between departments.

(ii) German courses had a greater practical foundation (more part-time than full-time courses), leading to a better integration of technical knowledge and operational realities.

(iii) The award of qualifications in Germany depended to a much greater extent on externally-set, and externally-marked, final written and practical examinations (rather than the various forms of internal assessment now preferred in Britain). This contributed to a greater nationwide acceptability of their qualifications and the higher status attached to them. British BTEC qualifications vary in content and standard between colleges; policy on this needs to be reconsidered.

(iv) In contrast to British vocational courses, those in Germany are required to include explicit instruction in general educational subjects (e.g., mathematics and languages); this contributes to progression to higher-level courses, and indirectly adds status to vocational qualifications.

Because of the greater breadth and greater practical content of German qualifications, they were better suited to the needs of the middle range of hotel sizes, where flexibility is an essential part of daily work for all personnel. With the current transfer of responsibilities for UK training to local Training and Enterprise Councils, it will be important to ensure that the latter do not become dominated by large firms with their greater scope for personnel trained in narrow specializations, and that the needs of smaller establishments for broadly-trained personnel are adequately represented.

Schooling standards in Germany are such that, in general, a much broader cross-section of school-leavers than in Britain acquire the mathematical and other learning tools, and the interest in their working application, that are needed to embark on craft-level vocational courses. This was also evident in recruitment for courses on hotel work. Until schooling standards in Britain are similarly raised for the broad cross-section of school-leavers, the task of raising workforce skills to German levels is bound to remain difficult in Britain.

In the past five years considerable activity in Britain's hotel industry has been directed to the improvement of training, encouraged by the Youth Training Scheme's subsidies which reinforced the existing training levy (and rebate) system to the hotel industry. Numbers attaining craft-level qualifications have risen in Britain by some 5 per cent a year; in Germany they rose by 10 per cent a year. The main growth in Britain has been at lower levels: a new series of certificates has been developed attesting to experience in the constituent atomistic operations of hotel work (for example, bedmaking, telephone answering). The National Council for Vocational Qualifications has now validated several combinations of such constituents as 'Level 1' vocational qualifications; nothing correponding to such elementary certificates exists in the German (nor the French) system of vocational qualifications. Substantial as these new initiatives may seem in Britain, they have not as yet led to any great follow-through into the craft-level broad-based qualifications on which German hotels depend for their efficiency. The current system of training subsidies seems to focus in an undifferentiated way too much on certificating elementary skills, rather than promoting higher levels of vocational qualification which would increase flexibility and adaptability.

Acknowledgments

We are grateful to the many hotels in Britain and Germany which kindly gave their time to help with this study; without them this article could not have been written. In addition we received much helpful information and comment from those connected with the hotel industry, and should like particularly to thank the following people.

In Britain: M. Aivaliotis, D. Battersby and M. Teare, Hotel and Catering Training Board; D. Billam and C. Wilkin, BTEC; W. Blacklock and S. Issler, City and Guilds London Institute; D. Brown, Michelin Maps and Guides; G. Craven, Ealing College Higher Education; I. Fairlie, Hotel and Catering Committee, TUC; K. Johnson, Huddersfield Polytechnic; J. Lawrence and S. Parker, Westminster College; S. Medlik, Visiting Professor, University of Surrey; S. Painter, Weston-super-Mare FE College; Dr D. Parsons, Leisure Industries EDC, NEDO; and Mrs P.A. Wood, Polytechnic of North London.

In Germany: J. Armbrechtung, Stiftung Warentest; J. Busch, Aufgabenstelle für Kaufmännischen Abschluss und Zwischenprüfungen, IHK,

Nuremburg; N. Holst, Ausbildungszentrum für das Hotel und Gaststättengewerbe, Berlin; H. Leyer, Hote und Gaststätteninnung, Berlin; R. Knoop, C. Lentz, Fachoberschule für Ernährung und Hauswirtschaft (Berufsschule, Berlin); G. Ludwig, Fachschule für Hotel- und Gaststättengewerbe, Berlin; R. Schone, Industrie- und Handelskammer, Berlin; M. Thamm, Lette-Verein, Hauwirtschaftliche Berusfachschule, Berlin.

Financial support was provided by the Economic and Social Research Council, the Training Agency and the Department of Employment. Many helpful comments were provided by officials of these departments, by HMI, and by our colleagues at the National Institute; but they are not responsible in any way for the views expressed in this chapter.

Notes

1 Daly, Hitchens and Wagner (1985); Steedman and Wagner (1987; 1989).
2 See the recent examination of the problems of measuring the real output of the service sector, and the apparent decline in productivity in British hotels of 1.2 per cent a year in 1971–86, by our colleague A.D. Smith (1989, especially p. 87). The main problem seems to be lack of adequate adjustment for changes in the quality of hotel services, a matter discussed below.
3 We have here treated the self-employed as full-time, and a part-time employee as equivalent to half a full-time employee.
4 Reality is of course more complex: it is male full-time employees that have been released from manufacturing in Britain, while female part-time employees have gone into hotel work.
5 So we were assured by the publisher, though an explicit list of criteria was not made available. Independent experts have confirmed to us the international comparability of this classification, making due allowances for climate and other circumstances.
6 English Tourist Board, *English Hotel Occupancy Survey*, results for 1987; *Statistisches Jahrbuch*, 1988, p. 240, taking an average of the winter and summer periods shown there for 1986–87.
7 For housekeeping employees we took the number of *guests* — or 'bed occupancy' — as the relevant measure of output, since it takes longer to clean a room if occupied by two persons than by one; for receptionists we took the number of *rooms* occupied as the relevant measure of output, since it hardly takes longer to book a double room than a single. It makes no great difference to the ratios of labour requirement if the denominators are interchanged; for the sake of brevity, we quote only our preferred alternatives.
8 See Appendix A of the version of this article in NIER, November 1989.
9 Smith, Hitchens and Davies (1982), p. 5.
10 A firm of industrial consultants which studied five British hotels twenty years ago concluded that labour-saving of about a third was possible (NEDO, 1968).
11 Our calculations of hotel prices were based on half a dozen large towns in each country, excluding London and Frankfurt in which very high ground rentals unduly affected hotel costs. We calculated separate averages, for each of our two quality-

grades, for the minimum price of a single room and for the maximum price of a double room; we then took a simple average of the resulting four ratios. The general PPP is taken from OECD, 1987.

12   In a *Fawlty Towers* event, a hotel manager demonstrated a recently installed folding wall-bed (which looked like a cupboard); the handle, he said, was carefully chosen to be 'guest-proof' and would not come off. It immediately came off in his hand.

13   Two-year part-time vocational courses are often taken in Germany by those who have repeated a year at school, and continued in full-time schooling to 16 rather than the usual age of 15; these lead to 'assistant' qualifications. Those unable to obtain apprenticeship or trainee positions on leaving school were previously required to attend non-specific part-time courses at vocational schools; more recently, this has been replaced by an additional full-time year in a vocational school. Only a minority of school-leavers follow that path; the general statement in the text above thus continues to represent the essence of the contrast between British and German 15–18 year-olds.

14   See, for example, Prais (1981).

15   On entry, the majority of the trainees have *Abitur*, corresponding to our A-levels; the final examination includes much bookkeeping, and the questions on hotel administration are of a significantly greater difficulty than the other German craft-level tests.

16   HCITB (1983) pp. 19 and 22.

17   From the German Labour Force Survey (*Microzensus*, unpublished tables) for 1985 it appears that a considerably higher proportion, 49 per cent, of all employed in hotels and catering (industry group 66) had vocational qualifications; but some persons with vocational qualifications in non-related occupations (e.g., retailing, seamstresses) were excluded from our count. A survey of 302 British hotels and restaurants in 1979–80 showed only 9 per cent of the workforce had qualifications in hotel and catering subjects (compared with the 12 per cent in our sample); a further 12 per cent had qualifications in other subjects — but these were widely defined and included CSEs (the lowest school-leaving examination). See HCITB (1983), p. 12.

18   Hotels run over-lapping shifts during the day to cope as far as possible with peak-periods; an average of 2.6 persons thus means, for example, that there might be three persons in attendance during peak periods of the day, two persons during off-peak periods, and only one on the night-shift.

19   Some had proceeded from apprenticeship to a *Fachschule* Diploma (roughly equivalent to our HND). Most graduates of courses in hotel management in both countries aspire to larger hotels than included in our sample; most who attend such courses in Germany do so only after completing a three-year apprenticeship in the trade.

20   A 'exception which proves the rule' may be footnoted. After we had completed our statistical summaries we found that one very pleasant hotel in our British sample was exceptionally efficient in terms of staff-ratios; we suspected errors in our recording. A second interview confirmed our original figures, but also revealed the following: the manager had substantial Continental experience and had decided, as a matter of policy, to appoint only qualified or highly-experienced staff in the same way as on the Continent. His pay-scales were accordingly higher; but

because of his lower manning levels — which corresponded to our German averages — his total costs per guest were lower.

21 HMI (1985) pp. 3 and 7.
22 Ripper and Russell (1983) p. 32. Lecturers to whom we spoke in British FE colleges took the same view of the importance of the practical route for most trainees: it is simpler to teach the details of hotel-keeping on a day-release basis since it is then not necessary to explain the many day-to-day occurrences with which the trainee will have become familar at work. Further, having become accustomed to work-place pressures, young people on day-release courses apply themselves in a more motivated fashion while at college.
23 BTEC National Diploma, *Front Office Operations*, Ealing College of Higher Education, Year 2, End of Unit Phase Test, March 1988, question 3. *Hotel Catering and Institutional Operations*, Integrated Project Level III, Summer 1987, Weston-super-Mare College of FE, question II. *Food Production*, Level II, (College) Phase Test 1, question 2 (ii).
24 From the final examinations of the Nuremberg Chamber of Commerce body for hotel examinations taken by over half of all apprentices in Germany, set in the Winter of 1988.
25 See *Bildung und Kultur*, series 11.3, German Federal Statistical Office, 1985, p. 69.
26 Prais and Wagner (1985).
27 HMI (1985) p. 5.
28 The quotations are from the City and Guild's publications on courses 708 *Accommodation Services* (1987, p. 37) and 720 *Diploma in Hotel Reception and Front Office Practice* (1987, p. 40).
29 City and Guilds, *Specific Skill Schemes: 700/2 Room Attendants* (1983, p. 12), revd. *Scheme Pamphlet: 7002 Room Attendants* (1989), p. 3.
30 There is no requirement in NCVQ's ideology for external marking — quite contrary to the German and French approach (Prais, 1989). There has been some recognition by NCVQ that the 'validity and credibility [of work-based assessment] have still to be firmly established', NCVQ (1987) p. 14; but so far the Council has been content to tread its own path.

References

DALY, A., HITCHENS, D. and WAGNER, K. (1985) 'Productivity, machinery and skills in a sample of British and German manufacturing plants', *National Institute Economic Review*, **111**, pp. 48–61.
HCITB (1983) *Manpower Changes in the Hotel and Catering Industry*, London, Hotel and Catering Industry Training Board.
HER MAJESTRY'S INSPECTORATE (HMI) (1985) *Survey of Programmes for Higher National Diploma Awards of BTEC in Hotel, Catering and Institutional Studies*, London, HMSO.
NCVQ (1987) *The National Vocational Qualification Framework*, London, National Council for Vocational Qualifications.
NEDO (1968) *Service in Hotels*, London, National Economic Development Office.
OECD (1987) *Purchasing Power Parities and Real Expenditures*, Paris, OECD.
PRAIS, S.J. (1981) 'Vocational qualifications of the labour force in Britain and

Germany', *National Institute Economic Review*, **98**, pp. 47–59.

PRAIS, S.J. (1989) 'How Europe would see the new British initiative for standardising vocational qualifications', *National Institute Economic Review*, **129**, pp. 52–4.

PRAIS, S.J. and WAGNER, K. (1985) 'Schooling standards in England and Germany: Some summary comparisons bearing on economic performance', *National Institute Economic Review*, **112**, pp. 53–76.

RIPPER, C. and RUSSELL, R. (eds) (1983) *Education and Training for the Hotel and Catering Industry*, Studies in Vocational Education and Training in the Federal Republic of Germany, number 8, Blagdon, Further Education Staff College.

SMITH, A.D. (1989) 'New measures of British service output', *National Institute Economic Review*, **128**, pp. 84–95.

SMITH, A.D., HITCHENS, D. and DAVIES, S. (1982) *International Industrial Productivity*, Cambridge, Cambridge University Press.

STEEDMAN, H. and WAGNER, K. (1987) 'A second look at productivity, machinery and skills in Britain and Germany', *National Institute Economic Review*, **122**, pp. 84–95.

STEEDMAN, H. and WAGNER, K. (1989) 'Productivity, machinery and skills: clothing manufacture in Britain and Germany', *National Institute Economic Review*, **128**, pp. 40–57.

6 Training Strategies and Microelectronics in the Engineering Industries of the UK and Germany

Adrian Campbell and Malcolm Warner

Introduction

This chapter is derived from an Anglo-German research project (Campbell, Sorge and Warner, 1989) focusing on the responses to microelectronics-related technical changes in products by the personnel and training functions of companies in the engineering industries of the UK and, what was at the time, West Germany. Data was gathered from twenty-seven cases in each country. Data-collection involved:

(a) questions concerning the numbers of personnel in each function and, where possible, skill category, and the directions in which such numbers were moving;

(b) questions on the overall strategy being followed by the enterprises concerned, in particular the role of microelectronics in the company's products, and the kinds of microelectronics-related work being carried out in-house;

(c) questions on the strategies adopted with respect to meeting the skill requirements generated by the trends referred to above (including the definition of such requirements), numbers recruited/trained, kinds of persons trained, institutional involvement in training and types of courses.

Access focused on personnel and/or training managers, with interviews extending to managers from engineering, production and other functions wherever possible.

Main Findings 1: Recruitment and Training

The overall findings may be divided into two types for the purposes of this chapter. On the one hand, there are findings related to the types of training and recruitment carried out by the companies in the two samples. On the other, there are the more fundamental differences in product and manufacturing strategy which provide the context for the personnel practices involved. It is argued that differences in the second area may have a greater long-term significance than those in the former category where, albeit slowly, some convergence was beginning to appear (that is, if one allows for the most significant difference of all, the lack of a coherent national system of vocational training in Britain).

Regarding training practices, there was some confirmation of the Anglo-German differences already familiar from the work of Prais and Wagner (1983) and Sorge and Warner (1986) among others, although confirmation was at least partly mitigated by a degree of convergence in some key areas of difference. British companies, like German companies, had been developing closer links with public education, there had been a degree of internal 'training up', although not on a scale comparable for the mid-career technical training of craft workers in Germany, and there had also been an expansion of training (technical and attitudinal) for employees in supervisory positions.

These tentative signs of convergence in individual companies should not mask the most significant difference, that is, the reliance in Britain on a voluntarist, or individualist, system of vocational training as opposed to the more collectivist dual system of the Germans (Keep, 1989). Thus any convergence from the British side tended to be the result of individual initiatives in particular firms which, although impressive in themselves, did not appear to present an adequate solution to problems at sectoral or national level.

If the main differences remain, albeit in a partially mitigated form, there was a clear convergence in terms of the problems perceived by respondents in the two countries. In both the UK and West Germany, skill shortages in terms of electronics hardware and software graduates (shortages regarding both quality and quantity) were seen as the most pressing human resources problem in a majority of the firms, and in large firms in particular. There was little to distinguish between the individual responses of companies in the two countries to this problem; in both there were attempts at conversion training for graduates from other disciplines, and in both there was a variety of methods (more selective recruitment, some extra training) applied to reduce the problems caused by hardware and software specialist recruits not being acquainted with the needs and disciplines of the industrial sector in which they were now employed.

Main Findings 2: Strategic and Structural Differences

A survey by Northcott (1986) found that the gap between the rates of diffusion of microelectronics product applications within British electrical/electronics engineering sectors was wider than that occurring between comparable companies in West Germany. German mechanical engineering firms were seemingly more able to incorporate technical shifts in the product than their British counterparts.

This finding was echoed in our own study. In our sample, all the firms covered had, by definition, incorporated microelectronics into at least some of their products. It was found, however, that the British mechanical engineering firms which had incorporated microelectronics were more dependent on outside suppliers for microelectronics-related development and production, than their German counterparts, who had for the most part successfully vertically integrated regarding microelectronics. This is described in more detail below. Cases from the two countries were classified according to whether microelectronics affected a primary or secondary product function, i.e., whether or not information-processing was what the product was primarily used for. Where information-processing was a primary function (as in the electronics industry generally) such companies were placed in category 'A'. Where information-processing was a secondary function (as in mechanical engineering or aeronautics), such companies were placed in category 'B'. 'A' and 'B' type companies were then compared to see how far they had vertically integrated microelectronics-related development and production.

This aspect of the findings was important in that the greater the vertical integration, the greater the demand for microelectronics-related skills. Conversely, the fewer the skills available, the less a strategy of vertical integration would be practicable.

It was to be expected that in both countries, 'A' type companies would have vertically integrated microelectronics to a greater extent than 'B' type companies, since in the latter cases information processing (and therefore microelectronics) was not the main focus of the products. What was less expected was the relatively clear-cut pattern of national difference that emerged from the sample. A large majority of the German companies appeared to have vertically integrated microelectronics with many companies in both 'A' and 'B' categories being involved in the development and assembly of microelectronics sections of the product down to component level. Although 'A' companies in the German sample went further than 'B' companies on the whole, the separation between the two was not as wide as had been expected.

In the British sample, by contrast, not only was there less vertical integration overall, but also a much more marked polarization between 'A' and 'B' companies. Almost all the non-information processing companies were wholly dependent on outside suppliers for development and assembly of microelectronics-related sections of the product, whilst the larger 'A' type companies were, on the whole, attempting to move away from direct involvement, component-level development and assembly, and towards a more systems-related approach to the product, where value-added lay more in the arrangement and linking of modules rather than in the design and complexity of modules themselves. These findings regarding manufacturing strategy are presented in detail in Campbell, Currie and Warner, (1989).

Implications of Product Strategy Findings

A benign view.   On the surface, the findings for the British sample in terms of product and manufacturing strategy give no cause for alarm. They could, on the contrary, be taken as suggesting a plausible trajectory of successful industrial adjustment. According to this view, expertise associated with microelectronics hardware and software would be concentrated in larger electronics-based firms (who in turn could draw on software houses and consultancies). As both hardware components, sub-assemblies and software became increasingly standardized into off-the-shelf packages, and application-specific chips removed the need for more sophisticated hardware design (and there is evidence to support this part of the logic), these firms would sharpen their make/buy decision-making. They would pull out of direct intervention below module level, concentrate on what they did best, and therefore avoid 'reinventing the wheel' (an almost unanimously expressed fear in the British sample). The main thrust of training and recruitment policy would then be to ensure an adequate supply of cross-disciplinary systems engineers, capable of operating across the different modules of the electronic system and its links to the other sections of the product. This approach would form part of the trend towards multi-firm projects, with the specialist inputs of different firms co-ordinated by generalist project managers who had an awareness of the product as a whole.

There would thus be a complementary relationship between electronics/ information processing and mechanical/non-information processing firms. The first type of firms would hold the design authority for the microelectronics-related sections of the products produced by non-electronics-based engineering firms, who would therefore have little need to develop their skill base in relation to microelectronics. In return, the non-information processing firm would keep the electronics/software supplier aware of the needs of the product so that the information processing aspects served its function (and customers) appropriately.

The plausibility of the above is such that the relative absence of evidence for it in the German sample comes as something of a surprise. One explanation offered is that the strengths of the German system in the post-war period — high status for production, emphasis on quality, delivery and detail, and therefore also on practical, intermediate skills (Lawrence, 1980) — may ultimately become its weaknesses. A stolid German thoroughness would, in an age of low-cost, standardized hardware and software, become obsolete. Attention would be shifted towards the more 'noble' aspects of manufacturing — ironically the term was cited by German aerospace managers — namely the cerebral orchestration of the ready-made parts into systems. This would then justify the 'flight of skills from the factory floor' in British manufacturing (Sorge, Warner, Hartmann and Nicholas, 1983; Senker and Beesley, 1986) after all.

Although there are elements of truth in the scenario outlined above, it masks serious problems in the British case, just as the 'post-industrial society' paradigm, very popular in the early 1980s, and which suggested a shift towards information skills, helped to camouflage and justify what was in fact a simple case of British manufacturing failure (Hampden-Turner, 1984).

A less benign view. It was stated earlier that British and German firms suffer from similar shortages of electronics graduate skills. The shortages operate in different industrial contexts, however. Although it would be an exaggeration to state that the shortages in the one were a function of sectoral weakness, and in the other, a function of strength, it was found that German mechanical engineering firms have microelectronics-related skill shortages because they have incorporated microelectronics-related development and assembly into their in-house activities, whereas large British mechanical engineering firms have shortages because they have not been able to do so, and the shortage continues to prevent them from doing so. In one British case, for example, shortages of electronics hardware and software engineers occurred because the job assigned to them, that of quality assurance of work done by suppliers (who have full design authority over the electronics side of the product) is insufficiently interesting to retain people who are in demand elsewhere. Such findings are not necessarily an indication of the weakness of the firms themselves, but rather of the relative weakness of engineering firms as recruiters in the British economy. The high status of the financial and retailing sectors in the economy has meant that engineering firms have difficulty in attracting and retaining people qualified in disciplines which are also in demand in those sectors (as has been the case with electronics hardware and software over the last ten years).

The Role of the Competence Shift

The main point here is that the West German mechanical engineering firms appear to have coped better with the competence shift occurring in the sector. In doing this they have been hindered by skill shortages at graduate level, but have been able to fall back on the relative strength of their broadly-trained (and retrained) intermediate skill base. The previous 'benign' scenario suggested that mechanical firms could rely on electronics firms to provide those parts of the product which now involve microelectronics. In practice, not only is it difficult to fulfil this liaison effectively without having a critical mass of the relevant skill in-house (so that the output of the different disciplines can be tailored to the needs of the product as a whole), but the disciplinary shift is not a one-off occurrence, but a continuing trend. Thus in one complex mechanically-based product, the proportion of total value accounted for by microelectronics-based controls had over five years increased from 15 per cent to 25 per cent, while in aircraft manufacture, it was said that the value of electronic control systems would surpass that of all other components within a few years. If and when this occurred it was not certain that the airframe manufacturers would remain the prime contractors, but could instead become the sub-contractors of electronics/information processing companies.

Although this shift had been under way in the days of electro-mechanical controls, miniaturization of circuitry had accelerated it considerably. With each stage of miniaturization, existing functions would be compressed into a smaller space within the product, and provided at a lower price. Customer pressure (which in most firms represented a more consistent influence on product development than before) would then demand more functions to be added in to 'fill out the space'. In some relatively simple products a 'ceiling' is soon reached whereby no further additions of microelectronics-based functions are required. In more sophisticated products, however, this 'ceiling' continually recedes; more and more microelectronics-based functions are added in, their total value increasing even as their unit cost falls. (Campbell and Warner, 1987, discuss this 'simplicity-complexity cycle' in product development.) In terms of the core competence changes outlined above, therefore, a significant Anglo-German difference emerges in the way industrial change is perceived. The picture suggested by the British sample is that of the subordination of mechanical engineering firms to electronics firms, or, worse, a 'shake-out' of mechanical firms and a complementary growth (as yet not as significant as expected) in the electronics sector. From the German sample, the picture is that of industrial transition within the enterprise itself, whereby new disciplines are incorporated into the core competences of the firm, this shift being accomplished through retraining.

Design and Production

Differences still appear even where British companies have managed to make this transition. Several British companies in the medium-sized bracket had achieved a dramatic shift in the weighting of disciplines from being wholly mechanical, to being between one and two-thirds electronics-based. Where this has occurred, however, it has frequently been accompanied by the intensification of another characteristic of British industry which is relatively under-represented in Germany, namely the separation of design from production. In one case a mechanically-based firm had built up an electronics

design and development facility which had gradually become relatively independent, increasingly taking on its own contracts from outside, without any
involvement from the overwhelmingly semi-skilled mechanical workforce. In
other firms design and production took place on wholly separate sites, with a
minimization of skill not only at the production end, but also in the prototype
building stage of design, so that 'our too many clever people down there'
would not improve on the designs once the latter left the CAD drawing office.
(Such improvements would not be recorded officially and would therefore
interfere with inter-site communications.)

Considerations such as these may underlie the relative lack of a skilled
electronics workforce (or a hybrid mechanical/electronics workforce for that
matter) in the British sample. The assumption was that technical change
meant a shift from blue collar to white collar, from production to design and
from mechanical to electronic.

One large firm which had begun the competence shift at an earlier stage
(most of its management were former mechanical engineers, while most of
its engineers were in electronics hardware) was accelerating it through transferring apprenticeships — and individual apprentices — from mechanical craft
apprenticeships to technical electronics apprenticeships. This reflected the
established British tradition of 'early extraction of elites' (Sorge and Warner,
1986), in effect an attempt to relieve skill shortages at higher levels by draining
the lower levels of the more talented workers. This would set a vicious circle
in motion whereby the pool of intermediate skills would be dried up, and
no remaining craft workers would be of sufficient standard for retraining
or cross-training at a later stage, thus increasing the already existing over-
emphasis on recruiting already-qualified staff at technician or graduate level.

This ties in with a tendency in large British engineering firms, when
implementing process innovations such as CAD/CAM (computer-aided design
and manufacturing), to see that the discretion threshold, the level in the skills
hierarchy where active intervention in the process can occur, is kept as high as
possible (Campbell, Currie and Warner, 1989). Such interpretations of new
technology by management reflect management's impatience with shop-floor
demarcations, through which have been preserved the narrow conceptions
of training and skill that have characterized British industry (Keep, 1989).
Managements in Britain (despite much rhetoric in recent years) have found
it more convenient to undercut workforce skills than to develop them
towards flexibility. This contrasts with the position in West Germany where, at
least in core industries, German management 'is primarily concerned to obtain
functional flexibility and is not motivated by attempts to achieve a downward
adjustment of terms of employment' (Lane, 1988).

'Information Society' and the Pitfalls of Elitism

Lack of awareness regarding the strategic importance of training, endemic in
Britain at senior management level, has been the subject of much criticism,

especially since the Coopers and Lybrand report (1985). Equally responsible, however, are the policymakers closer to government who have, in the earlier part of the decade, popularized the idea of de-industrialization as if it were a form of progress (Pollard, 1982, Williams, Williams, Haslam and Wardlow, 1989).

At the level of smaller companies, or operational levels of larger companies, there has been an increasing disillusion with what might be termed the 'information society' approach to technological change and skills (Sorge *et al.*, 1983). This view suggested a strategy of vertical disintegration, with the core of the firm becoming the preserve of 'information workers'. In practice, managers in both the UK and West Germany spoke of their increasing disinclination to recruit graduates or technicians with purely software-based qualifications. These were seen as not only causing problems through upsetting pay differentials as a result of their market scarcity, but also being generally unaware of the nature of the product. However, moving away from pure software qualifications — to qualifications of mixed hardware and software, or software in relation to a particular industrial sector — appeared to be an easier option in Germany where electronics degrees were said to involve both hardware and software in most cases. This contrasted with Britain, where the prevailing enthusiasm for 'information' skills in the early 1980s had led to a disproportionate increase in the availability of purely software engineers — although, paradoxically there were still too few to meet the cross-sectoral demand.

In more complex products, the need for hybrid skills, and for a broader view of the product as a whole had become critical. In many cases the boundaries between the contributions of different disciplines had blurred, so that the whole became considerably more complex than the sum of its parts. For at least one respondent in the British sample, the difficulty engineering firms had in coping with these developments had been heightened by the tradition of over-specialization, not only at shop-floor level, but at the level of graduate designers. In this training manager's view there had been a reversal of the skill requirements trend· of recent years; rather than there being a need for more highly-qualified specialists, there was in fact a need for more broadly practical staff qualified at intermediate level ('such as a good ONC'), who, in his view, would be better placed to grasp how systems were linked together.

With the drastic cut-back in apprenticeships, such people were often more difficult to recruit than graduates, although less difficult to retain. This finding was confirmed in interviews with managers in employment agencies. The agencies, who were transferring skilled personnel around the country on temporary contracts, were aware that their services were being used as a substitute for training and were beginning to campaign for their clients to train more. The agencies knew that, with the decline in engineering training in recent years, the same people (ONCs in particular) remained on their books year after year, with no new additions. 'They just get older and older, there's no one being trained. You try and find an ONC with two years experience, anywhere. In the end there'll be no one left to send out to clients … and it'll be their fault' (Campbell and Currie, 1988).

This shortage of intermediate skills may be placed in the context of the disintegration strategies referred to earlier. A number of companies seemed to approach this strategy as if it was synonymous with a university-trained specialist core, and a periphery of sub-contractors and occasional agency staff. In fact, it could be argued, the strategy stood more chance of being successful if it was founded on a base of generalist skills at the craft/technical level. British companies in the larger category tended to hold an elitist view of skill requirements, assuming that graduate-level qualifications were needed for jobs which could, in fact have been carried out by technicians or even craft-level workers, given some extra training. There was indeed a need for more generalists at all levels of skill, not just the highest.

Markets and Hierarchies

The strategies of the British companies as a whole appeared to follow a version of the 'markets and hierarchies' model (Williamson, 1975), perceiving the graduate-oriented design function as the core, and other manufacturing activities as the periphery. This meant keeping control of that which was most difficult to acquire on the market, and buying the rest in. This view is linked to that whereby each firm has a 'core competence' which it should regard as its key source of value-added (Francis, 1988), and that time spent coordinating the rest of the process would therefore be a waste of resources.

This view may be faulted on three counts. First it ignores the extent to which, as we have tried to demonstrate, *core competences and disciplines are themselves shifted through the application of new technology in products*. Second it focuses attention on a misleadingly elitist conception of human resources rather than on the product itself. What we have attempted to argue in this section is that for a more systematic control over product quality (both in design and manufacture), people with generalist skills and experience at the intermediate level of qualification (or trained up from an intermediate level) provide the best basic skill base, with which graduate specialists could interact more effectively than if left to themselves. Indeed, product quality considerations had encouraged one of the smaller high-technology firms in the British sample to bring production back in-house, having previously sub-contracted all of it.

Third, the shortage of graduates has led to a 'sellers' market' in graduate recruitment, and correspondingly high rates of turnover. These have in turn increased graduate recruitment costs. Several companies in the sample were finding it better value to train people from the shop-floor level to technician level, and then to sponsor them through university. The graduates who were produced from this internally-driven process were found to be more likely to stay with the employer. The viability of this strategy depends on talent being recognized and developed at lower levels within the firms. If a graduate-oriented core and periphery model is adopted, the possibility for this solution to high-level skill shortages is drastically reduced in the long-term. The result, ironically enough, is that the graduate-oriented firm then succumbs to the first serious wave of graduate skill shortages, whereas it would not if it had an intermediate skills base available for training up or sponsorship.

Overview

To sum up the argument thus far:

(a) British manufacturing strategies reflect a concept of dis-integration which over-emphasizes specialist skills, and under-emphasizes the importance of the product as a whole.

(b) They are reinforced in this model by a lack of the intermediate skills which could suggest a different route.

(c) This reinforcement occurs not least as the result of a traditional fear of reliance on shop-floor skills (or even technician-level skills, where this can be avoided). It was not unusual, in the British sample, to be told that 'we're still more dependent on shop-floor skills than we would like'.

(d) This lack of a generalist skill base inhibits rapid shifts of competence, when these are required. This has been the case with microelectronics where many companies are concerned, and is likely to be the case with the diffusion of optomatronics (the combination of technologies of light with mechanical and electronics technologies).

(e) This contrasts with the German case where there has been a continuing emphasis on taking control of new technological disciplines in-house and ensuring that at least some of the detailed design and assembly work in new areas is carried out by the firm's own employees.

(f) This tendency is not unconnected with the relative strength of the intermediate skill base in West German firms, maintained through sector-wide collective agreements dealing with the extent, funding and quality of training and retraining activities.

Further National Differences

German companies were less prone to functional differentiation in management — there was greater overlap between the marketing and technical functions and the training and development associated with them, although systematic liaison between engineering and marketing was seen to have increased markedly in a number of British firms. In British companies, career and organizational splits were more frequent and pervasive. Technical and project management career paths in engineering were divided at an early stage. In one British company this was seen as a means of 'keeping boffins out of harm's way'.

In Germany, even in large firms, it was more common to find technicians with relatively modest qualifications working as hardware designers. This was rare in Britain, where graduates showed a marked tendency to want graduates to work under them.

Craft-level skills in electronics saw the greatest contrast. West Germany provided twice as many electronics craftsmen via examination as Britain did. British firms were more in favour of technician-level electronics apprenticeships. This may be connected to the observation of Prais and Wagner (1983) that German electronics apprenticeship exams were more demanding. It is possible that British technical electronics apprenticeships were more comparable to the craft electronics apprenticeships in Germany. In several of the British firms, craft electronics work appeared to be confined to conceptually simple tasks. In Germany, on the other hand, half the sites investigated provided electrical and electronics worker apprenticeships, which provided the basis for work in different functions and possible further adult education for technician and engineering posts. Technical training off the job is important for supervisory promotion, unlike in the 'separate hierarchies' principle in Britain. Rather than maintaining production in its role of 'pariah', still frequently the case in Britain, the German system appears to link production with 'higher' functions.

One unexpected national difference was the practice, found in more than one large British company, of building up an 'unofficial' training budget. This represented an extreme (but apparently necessary) corollary of the voluntarist system, whereby training managers would find ways of extracting money from client departments, for example loaning apprentice labour to projects in return for a percentage of the project's success. This avoided lengthy rituals of financial justification with senior management. Such informality, while not officially sanctioned, was said nonetheless to be expected by senior management as part of the 'rules of the game'. It was not that training expenditure had to be kept low in practice, it merely had to be seen to be kept low. At least three large sites did spend between 2 and 3 per cent according to this system, while their official figures were under 1 per cent. The unofficial accumulation of training resources was facilitated by the market relation of training to other departments in the large British companies, a system less common in Germany. One of the training managers concerned saw the system as necessary on account of senior management being out of touch with technical developments and not knowing what their training response should be. Whilst not admitting this to be the case, they would give those who were better informed an (unofficially) free hand.

The German sample presented few examples of such initiative, or of such informality. There were, on the contrary, some signs of a lack of flexibility in company training strategies for non-graduate employees. Although the vocational training system in Germany has the advantage of a clear progression between the distinct stages of craft, technical and supervisory levels, none of which can normally be omitted, this apparently, in some cases at least, left little scope for technology-related further training for craft workers, if this was not linked to formal promotional training. Additionally, there was almost as little training for semi-skilled workers in German firms as there was in Britain.

We would still maintain that these weaknesses do not (as yet) significantly detract from the advantage which the intermediate skill base, with its broad apprenticeship structure, gives German firms of all sizes when coping with the demands of technological and competence change.

Conclusion

It is tempting to reiterate the relatively dismal record of British industry on training, and the extent to which West Germany, among other European countries, has evolved a system better equipped to evolve new 'production and employment concepts' (Kern and Schumann, 1987) in order to cope with rapid technological changes in products and processes, increased customer expectations and tighter competition in non-price areas such as quality and delivery. In this chapter we have given some attention to convergences in British and German practices, while emphasizing the considerable structural differences that have arisen as a result of different manufacturing and skills strategies. A number of examples were nonetheless found where results, analogous to those achieved by the national vocational system in Germany, had been achieved through the localized and sometimes covert strategies of individuals in British companies.

There is little doubt as to the areas in which British skills provision strategies need to be improved. What is more problematic is the means by which this improvement should best be achieved. In some respects, British training is torn over the appropriate course of action. Taking 'success stories' as a model, the problems of training could be left to be resolved through individual initiatives, thus following the voluntarist tradition. This approach rests on the assumption that broad-based education and awareness at senior level will percolate through into training strategies that will contrast with the neglect or narrow specialization of the past. Given that it is the voluntarist tradition itself that lies behind the present skills crisis, this may prove too risky an assumption.

Adrian Campbell and Malcolm Warner

References

CAMPBELL, A. and CURRIE, W. (1988) 'The nervous industry: Ambiguities in the labour market role of private employment agencies'. Paper presented at the annual conference on the organisation and control of the labour process, Aston University, March.

CAMPBELL, A., CURRIE, W. and WARNER, M. (1989) 'Innovation, skills and training: Microelectronics and manpower in the United Kingdom and West Germany', in HIRST P. and ZEITLIN, J. (eds), *Reversing Industrial Decline?*, Oxford, Berg, pp. 133–54.

CAMPBELL, A., SORGE, A. and WARNER, M. (1989) *Microelectronics Product Applications in Great Britain and West Germany*, London, Gower.

CAMPBELL, A. and WARNER, M. (1987) 'New technology, innovation and training: A survey of British firms', *New Technology, Work and Employment*, **1**, pp. 86–99.

COOPERS AND LYBRAND (1985) *A Challenge to Complacency*, London, MSC.

FRANCIS, A. (1988) Seminar on technology and core competences presented at Aston University, October.

HAMPDEN-TURNER, C. (1984) *Gentlemen and Tradesmen: The Values of Economic Catastrophe*, London, Routledge and Kegan Paul.

KEEP, E. (1989) 'A training scandal?' in K. SISSONS (ed.), *Personnel Management in Britain*, Oxford, Blackwell.

KERN, H. and SCHUMANN. M. (1987) 'Limits of the division of labour', *Economic and Industrial Democracy*, **8**, 2, pp. 151–70.

LANE, C. (1988) 'Industrial change in Europe: The pursuit of flexible specialisation in Britain and West Germany', *Work, Employment and Society*, **2**, pp. 141–68.

LAWRENCE, P. (1980) *Managers and Management in West Germany*, London, Croom Helm.

NORTHCOTT, J. (1986) *Microelectronics in Industry: Promise and Performance*, London, Policy Studies Institute.

POLLARD, S. (1982) *The Wasting of the British Economy*, London, Croom Helm.

PRAIS, S.J. (1981) 'Vocational qualifications of the labour force in Britain and Germany', *National Institute Economic Review*, **98**, pp. 47–59.

PRAIS, S.J. and WAGNER, K. (1983) 'Some practical aspects of human capital investment: Training standards in five occupations in Britain and Germany', *National Institute Economic Review*, **105**, pp. 46–63.

SENKER, P. and BEESLEY, M. (1966) 'The need for skills in the factory of the future', *New Technology, Work and Employment*, **1**, pp. 9–17.

SORGE, A. and WARNER, M. (1986) *Comparative Factory Organisation*, London, Gower.

SORGE, A., WARNER, M., HARTMANN, G. and NICHOLAS, I. (1983) *Microelectronics and Manpower in Britain and West Germany*, London, Gower.

WILLIAMS, K., WILLIAMS, J., HASLAM, C. and WARDLOW, A. (1989) 'Facing up to manufacturing failure', in HIRST, P. and ZEITLIN, J. (eds), *Reversing Industrial Decline?*, Oxford, Berg.

WILLIAMSON, O. (1975) *Marketing and Hierarchies*, New York, Free Press.

7 Japanese Engineers, Lifetime Employment and In-company Training: Continuity and Change in the Management of Engineering Manpower Resources

Kevin McCormick

Introduction

It has long been accepted, almost as an article of faith, that Japanese companies spend more on training their employees than do their British counterparts (Coopers and Lybrand Associates, 1985). It appeared consistent with the success of Japanese corporations in world markets for manufactured goods. Moreover, the existence of the lifetime employment system provided a ready-made explanation (IMS, 1984; Handy, 1987). It appeared self-evident that employers would invest more in employee skill development if they could be confident that they would harvest the fruits of their investment. Yet attempts to document these international differences have found that Japanese companies record lower expenditures than their British counterparts (Dore and Sako, 1987; Wersky, 1986). Here I shall examine closely the concept and practice of training under conditions of lifetime employment in order to show why differences in training effort will not be revealed by differences in training budgets (Dore and Sako, 1987:60–1). The main lesson to be learned from international comparison is not necessarily the need to spend more money but the need to re-think the nature and purpose of training in relation to business and employment strategies.

This analysis of company strategies for the graduate engineering manpower of large corporations draws on literature, surveys and interviews with personnel, training and engineering managers in fifteen Japanese companies and nine British companies in 1984. These companies ranged across the electronics, process and engineering industries. Table 7.1 illustrates the variety of Japanese companies in terms of industry, scale of activity, R&D intensity (from research-intensive electronics to public utilities) and recent financial experience (from the successful electronics companies to the ailing chemical companies).

Table 7.1 Labour force and company performance data for a sample of large Japanese companies

Industry sector/Company	(1) Capital (¥ bn) 1984	(2) Sales (¥ bn) 1984	(3) Profit (% Sales) 1984	(4) R&D (% Sales) 1984	(5) Employees[a] ('000)	(6) Recruits[a] 1984 (number)	(7) Starting salary ¥ per month[a] ('000)
Electronics							
A*	11.5	770.1	3.3	11.6	14.1	480	137
B	140.0	2648.2	3.1	7.0	75.5	880	136
C	99.9	1459.7	2.4	11.0	34.8	800	136
D	26.2	303.5	1.8	5.1	12.6	300	136
E	65.0	991.7	4.5	10.0	40.0	750	136
Process							
F	54.5	746.8	0.0	3.1	8.2	97	151
G*	43.7	355.0	-0.4	2.7	7.8	63	141
H*	77.2	658.8	0.6	3.3	5.2	55	138
I	32.9	401.2	-0.9	3.0	4.6	45	141
J	15.6	182.2	3.0	1.7	4.0	63	145
K	5.7	43.8	5.2	3.1	2.2	37	143
Steel and machinery							
L	9.5	294.8	2.7	3.6	40.0	122	145
M	101.5	1251.5	-0.5	0.9	12.7	120	146
Public utilities							
N	650	3711.8	3.3	0.8	8.0	149	143
O	129	742.1	3.4	0.9	30.1	67	144

Sources: Toyo Keizai Shinposha/Oriental Economist, *Japan Company Handbook*, 1984, Annual Reports and Company Interviews.
Note: [a]Graduate engineers * Financial data is for 1983.

Most attention to the impact of the lifetime employment system on skill development has tended to assert rather simply that there will be more training by volume without considering the way in which lifetime employment changed the nature of training philosophy and practice.

It should be clear that 'lifetime employment' does not mean 'employment for life' and 'system' does not mean that all Japanese workers operate within its terms. The concept has caused such confusion that Trevor refers to 'long-term employment' rather than 'lifetime employment' (Trevor, 1983:37). The terms are not specified in any contract for that would offend against earlier rejections of feudalism, rather they exist as a moral expectation of loyalty in exchange for benevolence. The terms and coverage have not been static for they have changed over time (Fruin, 1978:273). Currently we can say that the lifetime employment system means: (a) entry to employment directly on graduation from school or college, (b) a strong moral expectation of employment from that sole employer until retirement, (c) continual training, (d) mandatory retirement at 60, after the increase of mandatory company retirement from 55 to 60 (Inagami, 1983). Lifetime employment covers about 85 per cent of the labour force of the large companies and about 30 per cent of the total national labour force. While some British company recruitment brochures advertise opportunities for long-term careers, in Japan a sufficient proportion of the labour force has enjoyed the expectation of 'lifetime employment' to justify speaking of a 'Japanese employment system'. Moreover the small firms, which find the practice difficult, recognize lifetime employment as a norm to which they aspire.

In arguing that the 'lifetime employment system' has had a significant influence on the way in which Japanese corporations develop their graduate level engineering manpower resources, I want to advance the following propositions:

(a)   It has had a significant influence on the business strategies of the large Japanese corporations. The commitment to the principle provides a very strong stimulus to the strategies of organic growth and innovation.

(b)   It has had a significant influence on the recruitment and selection policies of companies. The system encourages the concentration on entry ports to the companies immediately after graduation, a preoccupation with potential for development rather than readily applicable skills, the use of the educational system as a filter to identify such potential, and attempts to develop long-run relations with universities as part of the recruitment process.

(c)   It has had a significant influence on the locus, content, mode, and agencies of training and employee development. The system emphasizes a preoccupation with company-specific knowledge and skills and hence a preoccupation with in-house training; it lays stress on the importance of making new recruits into company members (and hence it lays stress on organizational skills); it uses on-the-job training as the main mode of training; and it uses line managers as major agents in human resource management.

(d)   It has had a significant influence on the pay and promotion system in the large Japanese corporation. The lifetime employment system encourages the strong weight attached to seniority in the pay system and the rank promotion system.

Currently there are strong pressures which make it difficult for companies to sustain the expectations associated with the system. On the one hand, the ageing of the labour force makes seniority-based wages more expensive to bear and, on the other hand, trade frictions constrain the possibilities for continuing growth and employee promotion. As Japan has reached the technological frontiers in some areas and expanded the R&D base there are pressures for a different pattern of career development, closer in style to that obtaining in the large British companies. These are issues to which I shall return after outlining the links between lifetime employment and the training of engineers in the recent past.

Lifetime Employment, Business Strategy and In-company Training

It is becoming a conventional wisdom of the human resource development literature to argue that firms must explore the implications for their human resources of their business strategies (Von Glinow, Driver, Brousseau and Prince, 1983). It is becoming a conventional wisdom of the technological innovation literature to argue that the business strategy which ought to be followed by firms in the advanced industrial countries is to 'move up-market', adopting international best practice techniques and the promotion of industrial innovation, particularly as they lose earlier comparative advantages to follower nations (Pavitt, 1980, 1981).

In the case of British engineering and engineers the Finniston Committee of Inquiry into the Engineering Profession tried to pull these two strands together to argue that the advocated strategies of business and technological innovation implied new structures of engineering organization and that these new patterns of organization carried further implications for new skills and training among Britain's engineers (Finniston, 1980:17–39). In essence, the Committee argued that companies producing traditional products by traditional methods with traditional skills would meet increasingly severe international competition as their earlier comparative technical and commercial advantages were eroded. Therefore they argued that companies should move up-market by paying attention to the 'non-price' factors in competition, for example performance, reliability and 'general fitness for purpose'. These factors are the hallmarks of 'design' and the core of good engineering at the professional level.

The Finniston arguments were not simply for more and better engineers however, because they recognized that the engineers need to be organized in appropriate organizational structures. The emphasis was on the need to integrate and balance research, design, development and production and their linkage to the company's market strategy. Avoiding the compartmentalization of functions implies a market awareness and engineers equipped with a set of technical and organizational skills which enable them to cross organizational boundaries. Thus a narrow education and training might imply a narrow role conception and a failure to develop the appropriate organizational structures, whereas a broad education and training carries the possibilities of broader role conceptions and better integrated structures. There is the further issue of where engineers might learn these broader organizational and technical skills and develop the broad conceptions of the engineer's role. For the Finniston Committee there was no doubt that they should be learned in the workplace and that they would involve a strong commitment to continuing education (Finniston, 1980:39).

The steps in the argument are fairly clear, from business strategy to business organization to skill requirements to a policy on engineering manpower resource development strategy and practice. It is a logical flow which is even charted with arrows in the *Engineering Council Consultative Document on Training* (Engineering Council, 1988). Within the framework of capitalist economic activity it seems unexceptional that business strategy should determine human resource development strategy or that all undergraduate economists should learn that the demand for labour is a function of the demand for the product. In his account of the training of Japanese engineers within their companies, Wersky opens by 'placing the engineering formation process within the context of Japanese industry's commercial requirements and business policy' (Wersky, 1987:3). Titled *Training for Innovation*, Wersky's account emphasizes that the pattern of training follows from the innovation strategies of the large electronics companies. He shares with the Finniston Committee a common intellectual heritage in the work of the Science Policy Research Unit on technological innovation and a common didactic enthusiasm to urge British industry to adopt more business strategies based upon technical innovation, to undertake more R&D and to give higher priority to the recruitment, training and deployment of graduate engineers in the enterprise (Wersky, 1987:3; Pavitt, 1980).

While this approach correctly draws attention to the influence of business strategy on manpower development strategy, it neglects the reciprocal influence of employment strategies on business strategies. For example, it neglects the structural peculiarities of Japanese capitalism, in particular the balance of interests and stakeholders in the large Japanese corporations, which give such a strong emphasis to employment practices, and hence impetus to business strategies. Even if I do not want to turn these conventional wisdoms completely on their head by arguing that Japanese firms determined their employment practices first and that the business strategies flowed from

Table 7.2   The financial structure of the Japanese sample companies

Industry/ Company	Equity Ratio %	Major shareholders		% Foreign ownership
		% Banks and insurance companies	% Other companies	
Electronics				
A	48.7	11.4	32.9	42.6
B	28.6	14.1	n.a.	23.3
C	26.2	20.8	2.5	17.9
D	21.1	34.6	n.a.	9.8
E	33.4	23.5	16.8	24.0
Process				
F	12.9	33.6	n.a.	8.0
G	10.6	37.6	n.a.	8.5
H	15.6	27.4	n.a.	6.7
I	7.8	27.0	n.a.	2.6
J	34.2	21.9	7.0	11.3
K	51.5	14.2	51.8	7.6
Steel and machinery				
L	50.7	25.3	26.6	6.5
M	9.4	27.6	n.a.	3.9
Public utilities				
N	11.9	21.9	n.a.	5.3
O	30.3	32.9	n.a.	1.4

Source: Toyo Keizai Shinposha/Oriental Economist, *Japan Company Handbook*, 1984.

the earlier decisions, I do wish to establish the very powerful and positive feedback loop which employment practices exert on business strategies of growth and innovation.

If we start from the proposition that business enterprises are coalitions of interest groups who act as stakeholders pressing a variety of goals on the enterprises, then it is possible to see that the ownership and financial structure of the Japanese enterprise, together with the practice of lifetime employment, gives a distinctive cast to Japanese corporate capitalism (Dore, 1987). Two points stand out about the ownership and financial structure of the large Japanese corporations: first, the shares tend to be held by other companies (often business affiliates or associated companies, or banks and insurance companies) rather than individuals; and second, the companies are 'highly geared', that is, they have a high ratio of debt, typically bank loans, to equity (Table 7.2; Clark, 1979; Kiyonari and Nakamura, 1980; Abegglen and Stalk, 1985). The net effect of these features is that Japanese corporations are more insulated from shareholders than their British counterparts, and that they have more scope to consider the long-term view urged by advocates of the innovation strategy.

Now if the ties between shareholder and corporation are weaker in the Japanese case than in its British counterpart, the ties between regular employees and the corporation appear correspondingly closer because of the lifetime employment system. Lifetime employment gives a powerful stimulus to the growth objectives of Japanese corporations, to the strategies of innovation and organic growth, and the preoccupation with market share as the measure of success. Three mechanisms link lifetime employment to organic growth objectives. First, board members tend to come through the management ranks of the company as lifetime employees and strongly identify with the company (Shirai, 1983:374). By organizational socialization and current structural relations these board members are sensitive to the pressures of their middle management and regular employees (Kono, 1984). Second, under lifetime employment middle management and regular employees are keenly interested in growth in order to satisfy their aspirations for career and salary advancement within their own company. Finally, growth by acquisition is both difficult and problematic with this distinctive pattern of ownership and employment system. Table 7.2 shows for the Japanese sample survey companies, first, their low reliance on equity compared to loan finance and, second, the tendency for their shares to be held by banks or dispersed among the companies which tend to be members of the same group. The pattern of share dispersion makes acquisition difficult and, while acquisition might increase earnings per share, it does not necessarily increase the number of posts for employees. Moreover there is not only the potential problem of harmonizing another company's lifetime employees with one's own, there is a possibility that the enterprise union can be a rallying point for opposition to an attempted acquisition (Kono, 1984; Abegglen and Stalk, 1985).

Japan provides, instead, many examples of companies which have grown by diversification based on technology. For example, Casio started as a manufacturer of calculators but used its expertise in integrated circuit technology to enter the watch market with quartz digital watches, and the music markets with electronic musical instruments (Hara, 1982:21).[1]

Historically it appears that the lifetime employment system was first adopted as a solution to industrial relations problems in the 1920s (Dore, 1973; Littler, 1982). It became more widespread as an employer response to the very difficult and turbulent industrial relations problems of the early post-war years. For some companies at least, resolving labour market strategies had priority over product market strategies, partly because product market problems were less pressing, given government support, and partly because the flexed muscles of restored unionism made labour market problems particularly pressing. The synthesis of product market and labour market strategies which has come to be seen as the Japanese company model did not mature until the 1955–64 period (Okamoto, 1982:41). Japan's success in the period of postwar recovery and the later high growth period (1965–75) was largely noted for the advance in its share of world trade and the pattern of company-related, incremental innovation in the mass production industries (Hull, Hage and Azumi, 1984). To a considerable extent these innovations were developed in the process of buying-in foreign (especially US) technology, reverse engineering it, and improving it.

Kevin McCormick

Given this context of technological development, the Japanese companies did not develop the specialized R&D labs separated from production departments, with all the attendant problems of coordination, described so clearly in the British case by Burns in the 1950s (Burns and Stalker, 1966). Instead the Japanese companies put their talented engineers into production areas, whether in production R&D or in production roles either permanently or as part of rotation policy (Hull, Hage and Azumi, 1985). This pattern of emphasis on production, reverse engineering and incremental innovation is graphically described in Halberstam's comparison of Nissan v. Ford (Halberstam, 1986:263–318). The contrasts between the Japanese and US automakers in the relative proportions of engineers and accountants employed and location of a greater proportion of the Japanese engineers in the production areas have been supported in more quantitative studies too (Cole and Yakushiji, 1984).

While the absence of distractions such as aerospace or nuclear industries greatly aided the ability of mass-production industries to recruit talented engineers, the practice of lifetime employment was a crucial factor in enabling those engineers to promote incremental innovation successfully. For Aoki these innovations and productivity improvements rested critically on an organizational model characterized by horizontally-coordinated information flows and semi-autonomous and localized problem-solving. In other words, teams of talented generalists (engineers and operators) could take responsibility for the problems in hand and devise group solutions across departmental and functional boundaries (Aoki, 1986). Aoki has further argued that the lifetime employment system and the seniority wages system have fostered this capacity of work groups to share information and achieve joint understandings on mutually relevent technology; the lifetime employment system has been a device to encourage 'team-oriented learning by doing' and the seniority wage system has encouraged the acquisition of the knowledge and skills necessary for communicating effectively with others, in contrast to systems which reward specific and narrowly-defined job performance (Aoki, 1987:63–5).

Japanese employment practices and human resource development strategies appear to have served large companies well, while the main strength of Japanese industry has been in incremental innovation in the national quest to catch-up with the USA. However, some doubt how far contemporary organizational patterns and human resource development strategies will suffice as Japanese companies seek to pioneer new technologies and develop strategies for radical innovation (Hull, Hage and Azumi, 1984; Sakakibara and Westney, 1985).

Recruitment and Selection

The main implications of the lifetime employment system for the regular employees of large corporations have been to: (1) heighten the importance of recruitment at the entry posts to the company from the educational system; (2) encourage a long-term perspective on recruits so that they are selected on the basis of their potential contribution rather than their currently employable knowledge and skills; (3) favour the use of educational qualifications as indices of the capacity for learning and skill development; and (4) facilitate the development of long-term relations between the recruiters (the companies) and the providers of graduate manpower (the university professors). While the British companies operated internal labour markets for engineering manpower, they operated in external labour markets too, so their commitment to each of the above practices was considerably weaker than in the Japanese companies.

In a system emphasizing the immobility of regular employees, recruitment to the large Japanese corporations has come to focus on the graduation points from the educational system. With the enormous expansion of educational participation in the 1960s and 1970s only 5–6 per cent of the age group becomes available at the end of compulsory school-leaving at 15. Recruitment is concentrated, therefore, on the upper secondary school at 18, the five-year technical college, and the four-year university.

The main disadvantages attributed to mid-career recruitment in Japan were the lack of control over quality compared to the recruitment of a fairly standard product among new graduates, the difficulties of fitting mid-career personnel into seniority wage systems, and the potential friction with other companies over poaching. The novelty of mid-career recruitment was signalled by a declaration in one company's annual report that '... the company intends to welcome capable technical minds from other corporations and research laboratories in order to enrich the company's research and development capability'.

Large British companies attach importance to their regular recruitment from universities and colleges too, for it constitutes a regular and reliable concentration of buyers and sellers of labour in the market, but they undertake significant mid-career recruitment too. There is certainly a hierarchy of prestige in British universities and it is clear that the high academic abilities of Cambridge and Imperial College intakes, as measured by A-level results, are attractive to company recruiters as academic filters, but the prestige hierarchies are less clear-cut than in Japan and all of the British companies participated in the annual 'milk round' visits to universities and polytechnics.

Lifetime employment means that the potential for development among recruits is of far more importance than evidence of readily applicable skills. This implies acceptance by companies of a much sharper division of labour between companies and universities, with a concentration by universities on the fundamentals of engineering in the context of general education and the provision of training by companies.

The pattern of engineering education in Japanese four-year universities bears a strong resemblance to US patterns. This is not surprising given the determination by the US Occupation to democratize education through opening access and emphasizing general education for citizenship, as well as the subsequent visits of American engineering educators as advisers (Hazen, 1952).[2] There was some employer concern about vocationalism in Japan in the 1960s, leading to the creation of over 60 five-year technical colleges. The State subsequently created two more vocationally biased universities to provide more peak institutions for the technical stream. More recently Toyota created an industrial college to take only students with work experience. The point of these examples lies mainly in their claim to be unique in swimming against the overwhelming tide of Japanese higher education.

For most of the Japanese companies the main purpose of graduate recruitment, even of engineers and scientists, has been to fill the ranks of company management. Graduate scientists and engineers were expected to transfer into management posts in R&D or other functions during their forties. Although this pattern may be changing in the electronics and chemical companies the traditional pattern is still evident in the gas utility where the graduates are considered essential for the cadre of the company. The importance of potential rather than actual skills is further underlined by the stress in recruitment criteria on social acceptability and the ability to work in teams, and by the delay of allocation to first work assignment until completion of a substantial part of the training programme.

Although they offer the possibilities of a career with the company and recruitment brochures will spell out examples of careers within the company, there is much more emphasis in the British companies on the specificity of jobs on recruitment, 'Direct entry' is promoted both as offering the challenge of 'real work' after years of study and as the best means of learning. In addition to these direct approaches by companies to the graduate labour market, companies have successfully lobbied for changes in undergraduate science and engineering education towards making it more vocational and equipping graduates to make an effective contribution to companies at the commencement of their employment (Finniston, 1980).

The use of educational qualifications as a means of occupational selection in Japan meant that a fiercely competitive approach developed in the highly selective educational system of the 1920s and 1930s (Passin, 1965). The democratization of access to higher education advanced by the US Occupation in the 1940s and the educational expansion of the 1960s did not reduce the competition but translated the competition on to a much larger scale in a mass higher education system. The glittering prize of entry to the lifetime employment system remains the driving force of an educational system which produces two and a half times as many graduate engineers per head of population as Britain and which appears to draw on a higher proportion of the more academically able male students than Britain. Companies conceive of the role of Japanese universities as essentially suppliers of manpower and not as research institutions. With democratization after 1945 there has been a widespread belief that the examination system has been meritocratic (Rohlen, 1983). Confidence in the efficacy of the educational system as a talent sorting system has reinforced the tradition of the most prestigious companies recruiting at the most prestigious universities with second rank companies recruiting at second rank universities, etc. In a system where the universities have operated as talent filters, complaints are not straightforward ones about shortages by discipline or specialism but ones about shortages by university, since the university has been the guide to skill level.

The supply is fixed partly by the inertia of the traditional pecking order of universities, by the better funding, facilities and staff-student ratios of the national universities, and by the difficulties in moving resources within the system from declining to growth areas. In addition, inelasticities in supply stem from the peculiarities of the long-term supply relationships which companies seek with universities and the pivotal role of professors in allocating students to companies (Azumi, 1969).

These large companies used to operate a system of 'designated universities' but this aroused objections from both the private universities and the Ministry of Labour on the grounds of equality of opportunity. Formally at least, anyone can now apply to any company. On the other hand, invitations or 'bids' are sent to the university engineering professors who allocate students to companies: the professors will restrict the number of introductory letters that they write and such letters are accepted without question in the case of the prestigious universities. In essence, the professors share out their graduates to known companies. The advantages are clear for 'top' companies and 'top' universities, for those universities supply a standard product from a known source.

There are some disadvantages however. The homogeneous background of recruits might have served well for product innovation but may be less appropriate for invention and the new direction in R&D in Japanese companies (Sakakibara and Westney, 1985). The system is difficult for companies which seek to move into new technologies or seek to expand their intake of particular disciplines. For example, the chemical companies had well-established recruitment channels for chemical engineers but had few contacts with the electronics professors and so felt very restricted in their efforts to recruit electronics engineers to aid both their application of electronics to their existing chemical technology and their business diversification programme. Such constraints are part of the stimulus to the growth of the external recruitment of experienced engineers from other companies. Of course, companies have a range of strategies to establish new relations, for example through the provision of research grants, equipment or contacts for advice. Once contacts are made and once some recruits trickle to the company then alumni groups are used to make further contact with students directly and recruitment patterns are reinforced.

Companies in Britain complain of shortages and they have taken a range of measures to strengthen their links with universities. Yet while companies might hope that able students might be recommended to consider company X or Y, the role of the professor as intermediary is much weaker. Sponsorship of undergraduate scientists and engineers during their period of study, unknown in Japan, has grown considerably in Britain and the advantage claimed for it is that it offers companies an extended scrutiny of potential recruits so new recruits are already familiar with company operations on entry to full-time employment. Again the emphasis in the British case is on readily applicable skills.

Training and Assignments

In Britain there was a strong impression that the volume of training carried out by employers fell during the 1970s, even for engineers in manufacturing industry. For example, the Finniston Report cited the demise of the great engineering companies which had been famed for their apprenticeship schemes (Finniston, 1980:85). It saw the professional institutions and the Training Boards as unable to stimulate effective training. In our British sample there were variations by sector, industry and function; for example, there were differences between the process companies and the public utility, on the one hand, and the electronics companies on the other hand. In the former there were more formal graduate training schemes with rotation around departments. The electronics companies claimed that there had been a change towards a more effective form of training through the provision of 'direct entry' and training on the job. In addition they claimed that through vacation student work, sandwich course students, sponsored students, and training on the job for new recruits they carried a very considerable burden of training. Clearly one of the problems to disentangle is whether the differences between the British 'direct entry/training on the job' mode and the Japanese 'o-j-t' (on-the-job-training) are semantic, perceived or real.

The training programmes of the Japanese companies varied in scale (given the variations in the scale of recruitment; Table 7.1), in length (from one to two years), in content (given variations in industry and market sector), and in degree of formality. Yet some common themes emerged in the emphasis on making 'organizational members', the use of on-the-job training, and the importance attached to line managers as trainers.

Typically all recruits started on the same day, with two to four weeks of induction. The content and style of induction programmes varied, but a typical pattern included: lectures by senior management on company history, 'company spirit', and company operations; courses on communications, computer programming, and English conversation; and visits to establishments. The point about the senior management involvement was not the quality of the information imparted but their symbolic importance and visibility to the new recruits. Common entry dates and the involvement of senior management in induction were not features of the British companies.

The bulk of the subsequent training period was organised as o-j-t. In some cases this period of assignment to a senior engineer and supervisor was preceded by rotation. The engineers might go to production establishments for a month while administrative recruits went to accounts. Another variation was to include some further elements of off-the-job training. One of the process companies included a week of computer programming, quality control, and patent procedures. In each company, however, the core of training was seen in the relationships of the trainee, senior engineer and supervisor.

Although companies could produce elaborate charts mapping the career lines and training provision for company employees (often in English) they were at pains to emphasize that the core of training was through o-j-t, that this was very informal and *ad hoc*, and that there was no 'grand plan' for its conduct.

> Building group skills is very important. It is mainly done through o-j-t.
> The supervisors give the bits and pieces — there is no organized pro-
> gramme. The group leaders are not rewarded in any special way — it
> is just part of their obligation. In the Japanese working environment
> engineers seldom work alone — they are usually working in groups.
> Therefore leadership and the human skills are very necessary, and we
> tend to take it for granted that these skills will be passed from seniors
> to juniors (Engineer adviser — chemical company).

Although there may be no formal plan these comments do indicate three general principles which are crucial to the organisational socialisation of Japanese engineers through o-j-t: first, the senior-junior relationship; second, the obligations of management towards training their subordinates; and third, the importance attached to group working.

From his study of organizational socialization in a bank in the early 1970s, Rohlen drew attention to the importance of *senpai-koohai* (senior-junior) relations, a basic dyadic relation which carried the image of '"friends", one ahead and the other behind, passing along the same path of endeavour' (Rohlen, 1975:197). As an image of an ideal working relation found in the general culture it forms a strong buttress to the beneficial support which older, senior and more experienced engineers can be expected to give to younger, junior and less experienced engineers. In a society which has retained a stronger sense of hierarchy, juniors can be expected to listen. In his studies of leadership, Misumi underscores the link between the lifetime employment system and the importance of managerial responsibilities for subordinate training. 'Under the Japanese system of lifetime employment, the superior's leadership includes not only performance-oriented leadership but also educational leadership, in that the superior is supposed to provide his subordinates with training' (Misumi, 1984:531). While competences in the training of juniors were strongly featured in the evaluation of managers in the Japanese companies, the emphasis in managerial appraisal in the British companies was on task performance.

Sakakibara and Westney (1985) suggest that the weights attached to technical and performance-oriented skills relative to interpersonal skills in Japanese R&D labs are the inverse of those in US ones. Lorriman and Wersky claim that supervisors in the Japanese large electronics corporations spend up to 30 per cent of their time in training subordinates (Lorriman, 1986:575; Wersky, 1987:71). Although the basis of this estimate is not clear, its significance lies in indicating a sizeable proportion of a British training manager's belief that British line managers do not spend nearly so much effort on training (Lorriman, 1985:88). The involvement of Japanese management in training is not exhausted at the completion of the two years' training, nor is this the end of assignments and report presentations, for these feature in continuing updating and training.

The large Japanese corporations cannot take it for granted that the building of group skills is a spontaneous process; it is an enormously time-consuming affair which extends far beyond what might be considered normal working hours. New recruits live in the company dormitories. The patterns of socializing built around drinking parties and company recreation facilities are testimony to the efforts to build group solidarity (Rohlen, 1975:190–1). Recalling his experiences as a visiting engineer attached to a Japanese company, Bhasanavich noted how difficult it was to spend any time alone away from work colleagues (Bhasanavich, 1985:73).

It is tempting to accept the explanation that this is simply Japanese culture, organizing work patterns consistent with the culture of a 'group oriented' society (Nakane, 1970). However there is another aspect to this frantic socializing: the need to police conduct in a lifetime employment system. Under a lifetime employment system the company and workgroup must guard against the potential 'shirker' and 'free rider'. Citing Okuna's concept of 'mutual monitoring', Aoki suggests that effective policing is provided by the system of long-run evaluation, the payment system and ostracism for offenders (Aoki, 1987:66–7). Thus an important aspect of initial training lies in providing both the cognitive skills of interpersonal relations and the internalization of the norms of appropriate conduct, or 'right attitudes'. It is not enough to assume that the offer of lifetime employment *per se* produces a dramatic and irreversible conversion. Large Japanese companies are well aware of the problems of passivity, complacency and the 'tepid environment' which might be induced by lifetime employment (Takagi, 1985:2). Therefore Japanese companies and managements have to work very hard to secure the full terms of the *quid pro quo*.

Gregory has drawn attention to the growth of company colleges and their advanced engineering programmes. However, as indices of company investments in training, Gregory's statistics on company colleges or overseas postings can mislead as to both the form and content of that training and are better regarded as the tip of a training iceberg (Gregory, 1984:55). While the lifetime employment system carries the corollary of continuous training over the working life, the main forms of training in Japan are through on-the-job rather than off-the-job training and a good deal of the content consists of learning organizational skills and not just technical up-dating. Through company college courses equivalent to the final honours year of a British undergraduate engineering course, companies can provide an updating programme for existing staff (Gillan, 1985). In addition, self-development programmes provide an important supplement to training. For the most part these programmes are not the glamorous hi-tech of video-disc but the more prosaic texts of correspondence courses (Dore and Sako, 1987:69). For the British companies there was much more scope to use a variety of external agencies for courses and training, for example, by negotiating participation in customized courses in universities or polytechnics.

Perhaps the most impressive aspect of the training system in Japan is the way in which companies manage to elicit a high commitment to skill formation and the manner in which self-improvement is pursued as a moral crusade. It is presented as the *quid pro quo* of the moral commitment made by companies to lifetime employment. Companies take on the responsibility for developing the careers of their employees, and line managers bear heavy responsibility and involvement in the process of training their subordinates. Now it is buttressed by a lengthy tradition dating back to the very beginning of the lifetime employment system in the period 1900–18 (Hirschmeier and Yui, 1981:207). Training by o-j-t in Japan attempts to provide structured learning experiences: it includes a progression of tasks from the relatively easy to the more difficult along with experience; it links progression to internal promotion; rotation is planned so that progression involves a broadening of the range of tasks as well as a deepening of task complexity; and it is expected that close supervision and support is given by supervisors and more experienced workers. This form of training is buttressed by the emphasis on group work such as 'quality circles' or 'ability development' circles. It is the lack of structural support which suggests that all too often the British form of 'direct entry' and on-the-job training offers the shadow rather than the substance of the Japanese o-j-t.

Pay and Careers

Expectations about pay and careers reveal some of the sharpest contrasts in policies and practices for human resource development between large British and Japanese companies, although the contrasts tend to be sharper for the decentralized British electronics companies than for chemical companies. The British pay system involves constant checking to ensure starting salaries and subsequent pay are competitive with rival bidders for graduate engineers. With job evaluation as the basis for the grading structure, the newcomer is advised that individual salary progression is determined by job grade (an evaluation of the job being done) and performance rating (an annual assessment of performance by a supervisor). Company handbooks emphasize that salary is not related to age. Promotion involves a move to a new job and its associated salary and again the emphasis throughout recruitment literature and interviews is on 'the ability of the cream to rise to the top very quickly'. The company literature also emphasizes that the onus for career development is on the individual, albeit with the supportive interest of the company.

Despite all the complaints of shortages of electronic engineers, Japanese companies did not compete on starting salary. The chemical companies showed more variety and paid a somewhat higher starting salary at Y143,000 — Y146,000 per month (see Table 7.1). Japanese companies tend to pay near the industry average and the common British variations by subject and class of degree, or skilful impression of management in interview, are noticeably absent. Japanese engineering graduates do not claim any particular expertise, they are bright people available for company development over a working life. Even the Masters level graduates, so eagerly sought for the R&D labs, tend to be paid only at the level of a Bachelor with two further years' experience. If there is a small premium it tends to be justified on the grounds that they are bright people rather than that they have acquired research training, although some companies concede that the Master's course does offer further experience of project work.

The 'seniority wage system' has been dubbed the economic basis of the lifetime employment system. Relatively low and undifferentiated starting salaries have been followed by wage increases in line with length of service. Employers have been reluctant to recruit expensive, experienced recruits, instead of relatively cheap new graduates, particularly when the much-prized organizational skills tended to be organization-specific, and employees have been reluctant to abandon the prospects of enhanced rewards with continued service, particularly when increasing rewards were likely to coincide with increasing family commitments.

While seniority-based pay appealed to a culture which took age-grading seriously, there was a strong economic rationale too, as stable imported technology meant that seniority and experience were good proxies for increasing competence. More rapid technological change has weakened the economic rationale and the increase in job-related and performance elements have prompted speculation about the end of the seniority-based pay system (Magota, 1979). Marsh and Mannari (1976:129) showed how the introduction of job classification began to enhance the position of the 25-year-old graduate with three year's service relative to the 25-year-old manual worker with ten years' experience. Thus contemporary pay systems blend 'seniority wage' (i.e., based on age or length of service and educational background) with 'ability based pay' (i.e., an evaluated ability grade based on personnel appraisal of knowledge and ability; Ishida, 1986). Beyond basic pay a number of allowances for family or housing can add a further 10 per cent to pay.

A further incentive to skill acquisition comes in the form of the mid-summer and year-end bonus, additional to monthly pay, which can account for 30 per cent of annual earnings in large Japanese corporations. Although the annual negotiations with the enterprise union are intended to encourage workers' identification with overall company performance, there is also an individual element, related to performance. Supervisory ratings of performance, which can involve attitudes too, account for up to (plus or minus) 20 per cent of bonus pay in some companies.

Promotion is not only an incentive to training, it is often the occasion of training. Promotion comes through advances in job classification where the jobs are classified into ranks. The rank titles which derive from *nenko joritsu* (ranking by years of service) have a widely understood currency in Japanese society (Trevor, 1983:49). More recently the titles have become part of an ability-based management system which has been extended from blue collar to white collar staff (Inagami, 1983:16). In the Nippon Kokkan steel company after joining at entry grade, the graduate engineer becomes eligible to enter the next grade after three years. Subsequent upgrading within a rank will depend on the collection of a target number of points in annual performance reviews. Promotion across ranks, however, depends on meeting the minimum preparation period for upgrading and favourable screening by management.

The existence of maximum preparation periods does guarantee some promotion for all, up to management level, while the more ambitious can gauge their progress against the standard preparation periods. At Section Chief (*Kacho*) and above, the links between rank and office-holding become quite close, but below that level, i.e., for the first ten to fifteen years of the graduate engineer's career in the company, the Japanese system permits promotion through the ranks without a necessary assumption of higher office. There is a system in many companies through which individuals can express their preferences about job assignments, rotation and off-the-job courses, but the prime responsibility for career development rests with the company.

The Changing Context of the Lifetime Employment System

A number of pressures are leading to modifications in the system of lifetime employment and carrying implications for the systems of engineering manpower resource development operated by Japanese companies. First, the ageing labour force, trade friction and slower growth in the world economy mean the lifetime employment system is becoming both more expensive and more difficult to maintain. Therefore companies are reducing the proportion offered lifetime employment, flattening the rate of salary increases for older workers, and trying to devise alternative career routes to compensate for reduced opportunities for promotion into management (Akaoka, 1974; Kuwahara, 1986). For example, whereas the first major promotion to assistant section chief came after ten years in the high growth period, it took twelve to thirteen years in company B by the mid-1980s.

Second, the threats to competitiveness posed by increasing protectionism and the emergence of low-cost competitors among the newly-industrializing countries have encouraged the belief that Japanese corporations must redouble their innovative strategies with the aid of enhanced R&D facilities (Clark, 1984). Such efforts are evident in competition by companies to recruit more Masters graduates, in attempts to promote the role of universities in continuing education, in concern about the capacity of the system to stimulate creativity among engineers and in efforts to improve the re-education of mid-career engineers (Oshima and Yamada, 1985). However, the increase in the proportion of R&D workers is reducing the scope for rotation and flexible careers within the enterprise. In addition the premium on developing research facilities and research workers may lead to increased labour mobility and the use of external labour markets. However, the orientation of existing systems of continuing education to in-house provision through o-j-t for lifetime employees has meant that it has not supported or encouraged the mobility of R&D staff (Oshima and Yamada, 1985). This is an area in which there will be attempts to develop the collaboration of universities in continuing education.

Third, as part of their strategy to penetrate international markets despite growing protectionism, Japanese companies are becoming more overtly multi-national. Trevor described them as 'reluctant multinationals' in the past, reluctant to leave a social environment so congenial to business operations (Trevor, 1983). Now they are developing educational programmes for overseas personnel to encourage 'international mindedness' (Amaya, 1983).

Fourth, Japanese manufacturing companies are said to be engineering companies run by engineers. This thread of technological literacy permeating the large corporations is seen as a significant factor in their innovative success. It has not been an unblemished record however. Clark noted that some innovative efforts had been insensitive to markets, reflecting 'a predisposition to innovate by extending technology rather than adapting to markets' (Clark, 1984:75). Therefore it is likely that in the more constrained market opportunities of the 1990s the companies will place a greater emphasis on marketing skills.

Finally, the motivation of the younger generation is a topic which excites much concern among Japanese managers (Amaya, 1983). A willingness to engage in the rigours of the competitive educational system, a readiness to be sensitive to organizational requirements and to acquire organizational skills, and a commitment to apply those skills across widely defined tasks for long hours over a working life for one employer have been hallmarks of the moral order of a Japanese corporation. Now Japanese managers exercise themselves about *shin-jinrui* ('the newcomers') seen as a generation who do not know war or the struggles of the early post-war period, whose aspirations and values are thought alien, and whose loyalty is suspect.

Surveys of Japanese R&D workers suggest that they have two main complaints against the present operation of the lifetime employment system: first, they complain that the pace at which engineers are promoted to responsibilities commensurate with their abilities is too slow; second, they claim that the weight attached to ability and performance is too small in Japanese companies (Nakajima, 1985). Such complaints might be expected to grow as more American companies attempt to establish R&D facilities in Japan and as these companies and their personnel systems become reference points for Japanese engineers.

At present these factors do not appear to add up to a change from the lifetime employment system, rather changes in its scale and scope, and changes *within* it. Nevertheless they indicate that change is underway in the system of education and training, and they underline the need for caution against those who would borrow 'yesterday's model'.

Conclusions

Not all the Japanese companies included in this account had glowing records of success, indeed it is evident from Table 7.1 that some of the chemical and steel companies were in difficulties. Yet all the companies remained firmly committed to the concept of lifetime employment. This commitment has produced in the past some distinctive features in company strategies for the development of engineering manpower:

(i)   a sharper division of labour between education and employers as academics concentrated on a broad general education and employers provided organized training;

(ii)   a reliance on the educational system as a talent-sorting system for the production of educated manpower;

(iii)   employer recognition of the need for training if their 'permanent' labour force was to cope with business and technological change, and employee acceptance of the obligation to train and adapt as the *quid pro quo* of security;

(iv)   the conduct of training through on-the-job training with close management involvement; and

(v)   emphasis on the acquisition of 'organizational skills and knowledge'.

These features are not in themselves unique to Japan. For example, Cambridge University provides a broad engineering science course and British employers have tended to prefer the more academically able university graduate to the more vocationally equipped polytechnic sandwich course student. Moreover, some British companies have been renowned for their training schemes. The point is that these features have been so much more common in Japan that they have become a 'norm', both statistical and sociological, amongst large companies.

The 'Japanese employment system' has had a number of apparently beneficial effects for graduate engineers: the broad educational base has provided a strong foundation for subsequent learning; the mutual commitment of employer and employee to training has meant the development of a 'learning organization' in which those sent on off-the-job training have an obligation to share their learning with the work group; the homogeneity of training experiences has built a company-wide technological culture which leads to closer integration between functions such as R&D and production; the system of rotation and the lack of identification with specialisms has aided the movement of engineers to ease 'bottlenecks' and the development of new activities; finally, the emphasis on company identification and the spread of features of lifetime employment to blue collar workers has reduced the social distance between engineers and blue collar workers.

I have cautioned against treating training simply as a set of off-the-job training courses in which doubling the amount spent might double the benefits in terms of knowledge and skills, or ultimately task performance. The purpose, content and methods of training must be seen in relation to a particular economic and social system. Yet once training is seen as embedded in such a system the scope for borrowing seems more limited. Thus, even if the innovative and higher value-added strategies of Japanese companies are similar to those advocated for British companies, and even if more career development policies through internal labour markets in Britain echo lifetime employment policies, the scope for implementing these business and human resource strategies will be severely restricted if they are dependent on the peculiar financial structure of Japanese companies. Similarly, the emphasis on group work cannot simply be seen as the logical outcome of an internal labour market. Behind group work lies the influence of Japanese language and culture, where the language encouraged heavy dependence on oral communication and pre-industrial work, such as rice cultivation, required cooperative patterns of working (Smith, 1984; Hendry, 1987). Quite apart from the difficulties of borrowing out of a particular cultural context there are the problems of avoiding unwanted side-effects. The long working hours, the curbs on individual liberties and the restraints on initiative associated with lifetime employment, and the company management of careers, may appear too high a price to pay to attract increased company commitment to training. Moreover, there are signs that Japan may be moving in the direction of increased mobility between companies.

The principal lessons to be learned from international comparisons are the need to clarify the purposes of training, to make judicious selection of the 'good effects' achieved by training in other places, and to attempt to replicate those 'good effects' by means consistent with one's own culture. For the future the main needs for training discussion in Britain appear threefold.

First, there is the funding of training and the need to achieve incentives to training functionally equivalent to those of lifetime employment. If British companies are unlikely to move in the direction of lifetime employment then alternative systems of funding may have to be sought, e.g., tax concessions to companies or individuals, revised (or revived) levy-grant schemes, or training vouchers.

Second, there is the individual's stake in the organization and the need to achieve the functional equivalent of 'membership' in the Japanese company. The latter has tended to apply to employees rather than shareholders, in contrast to the British situation. If the reality and perception of a stake in the organization underlie the training efforts of companies and employees then such conditions might be stimulated in the British case more formally by industrial, democracy or, less formally, by participation schemes or by managerial redesign of non-financial rewards.

Finally, there is the commitment of line management to training, the need to apply a more critical intelligence to work organization, and to stimulate the concept of a 'learning organization'. Involving British line managers and supervisors in training raises the question of whether the current fashion for appraisal schemes might stimulate a commitment comparable to that achieved under Japanese conditions.

Acknowledgments

For considerable help and many conversations during the collection of material for this paper I am indebted to Professor Shun'ichiro Umetani (Tokyo Gaukugei University). For financial support I wish to thank the Hitachi Corporation of Japan and the Unit for Comparative Research on Industrial Relations.

Notes

1 Some contrasts could clearly be seen in the background to this research in the commitment of electronics companies in Britain and Japan to link computers and telecommunications. Fujitsu started as a telecommunications company in the 1930s which became famous in the post-war period as a computer manufacturer and now seeks to put these two aspects of its business together. While both NEC and OKI Electric were similar broad-based electronics companies seeking to promote the computer-communications link in their business strategies, the British telecommunications company STC was seeking to acquire a computer expertise through the purchase of the computer manufacturer ICL. At the same time GEC was seeking to add to its telecommunications business through the take-over of Plessey.

2 The academic streams had, however, become more general in the pre-war school system.

References

ABEGGLEN, J. and STALK, G. (1985) *Kaisha, the Japanese Corporation*, New York, Basic Books.

AKAOKA, I. (1974) 'Control of amount of employment in Japanese companies under lifetime employment', *The Kyoto University Economic Review*, April, pp. 59–78.

AMAYA, T. (1983) *Human Resource Development in Industry*, Japanese Industrial Relations Series No. 10, Tokyo, Japan Institute of Labour.

AOKI, M. (1986) 'Horizontal v. vertical information structure of the firm', *American Economic Review*, **76**, 5, pp. 971–83.

AOKI, M. (1987) 'Incentives to share knowledge and risk: An aspect of the Japanese industrial organisation', in HEDLUND, S. (ed.) *Incentives and Economic Systems: Proceedings of the Eighth Arne Ryde Symposium*, London, Croom Helm.

AZUMI, K. (1969) *Higher Education and Business Recruitment in Japan*, New York, Teachers College Press, Teachers College, Columbia University.

BHASANAVITCH, D. (1985) 'An American in Tokyo: Jumping to the Japanese beat', *IEEE Spectrum*, September, pp. 72–81.

BURNS, T. and STALKER, G. (1966) *The Management of Innovation*, London, Tavistock.

CLARK, R. (1979) *The Japanese Company*, New Haven, Yale University Press.

CLARK, R. (1984) *Aspects of Japanese Commercial Innovation*, London, The Technical Change Centre.

COLE, R.E. and YAKUSHIJI, T. (1984) *The US and Japanese Automobile Industries in Transition*, Ann Arbor, University of Michigan Centre for Japanese Studies.

COOPERS AND LYBRAND ASSOCIATES (1985) *A Challenge to Complacency: Changing Attitudes to Training*, Manpower Services Commission/National Economic Development Office.

DORE, R.P. (1973) *British Factory: Japanese Factory*, London, Allen and Unwin.

DORE, R.P. (1987) 'Late capitalism, corporatism and other -isms', in OUTWAITE, W. and MULKAY, M. (eds) *Social Theory and Social Criticism*, Oxford, Basil Blackwell.

DORE, R.P. and SAKO, M. (1987) *Vocational Education and Training in Japan*, Centre for Japanese and Comparative Industrial Studies, Imperial College.

ENGINEERING COUNCIL (1988) *Continuing Education and Training: A National System for Engineering*, (consultative document) London, The Engineering Council.

FINNISTON (1980) *Engineering Our Future: Report of the Committee of Inquiry into the Engineering Profession*, (Sir Monty Finniston, chairman) London, HMSO.

FRUIN, M. (1978) 'The Japanese company controversy', *Journal of Japanese Studies*, **4**, pp. 267–300.

GILLAN, W.J. (1985) 'Engineering education in Hitachi: Visit report', Tokyo, Science and Technology Department, British Embassy — Appendix 33 in LORRIMAN, J. (1985) *The Education and Training of Technicians and Engineers on Japan: Report on a Winston Churchill Travelling Fellowship*, Coventry, GEC Telecommunications.

GLINOW, VON, M., DRIVER, M.J., BROUSSEAU, K. and PRINCE, J.B. (1983) 'The design of a career oriented human resource system', *Academy of Management Review*, **8**, pp. 23–32.

GREGORY, G. (1984) 'Why Japan's Engineers Lead', *Management Today*, May, pp. 51–5.

HALBERSTAM, D. (1986) *The Reckoning*, New York, Avon Books.

HANDY, C. (1987) *The Making of Managers: A Report on Management Education, Training and Development in the USA, West Germany, France, Japan and the UK*, London, National Economic Development Council.

HARA, R. (1982) *Management of R&D in Japan*, Bulletin no. **87**, Tokyo, Institute of Comparative Culture, Sophia University.

HAZEN, H.L. (1952) 'The 1951 ASEE Engineering Education Mission to Japan', *Journal of Engineering Education*, June, pp. 481–8.

HENDRY, J. (1987) *Understanding Japanese Society*, London, Croom Helm.

HIRSCHMEIER, J. and YUI, T. (1981) *The Development of Japanese Business*, London, Allen and Unwin, Second Edition.

HULL, F., HAGE, J. and AZUMI, K. (1984) 'Strategies for innovation and productivity in Japan and America', *Technovation*, **2**, pp. 121–39.

IMS (1984) *Competence and Competition: Training and Education in the Federal Republic of Germany, the United States and Japan*, London, NEDO/MSC.

INAGAMI, T. (1983) *Labour-Management Communication at the Workshop Level*, Tokyo, Japan Institute of Labour.

ISHIDA, M. (1986) 'Microelectronics payments systems and personnel management in Japan', *Doshisha University Social Science Review*, **31**, pp. 1–25.

KINMONTH, E.H. (1986) 'Engineering education and its rewards in the United States and Japan', *Comparative Education Review*, **30**, 3, pp. 398–415.

KIYONARI, T. and NAKAMURA, H. (1980) 'The establishment of the big business system', in SATO, K. (ed.) *Industry and Business in Japan*, London, Croom Helm.

KONO, T. (1984) *Strategy and Structure of Japanese Enterprises*, London, Macmillan.

KUWAHARA, Y. (1986) 'The strong yen and deteriorating employment conditions', *Japan Labour Bulletin*, **26**, pp. 4–8.

LITTLER, C.R. (1982) *The Development of the Labour Process in Capitalist Societies*, London, Heinemann.

LORRIMAN, J. (1985) *The Education and Training of Technicians and Engineers in Japan: Report on a Winston Churchill Travelling Fellowship*, Coventry, GEC Telecommunications.

LORRIMAN, J. (1986) 'Ichiban — The Japanese approach to engineering education', *Electronics and Power*, August, pp. 573–7.

MAGOTA, R. (1979) 'The end of the seniority-related (Nenko) wage system', *Japanese Economic Studies*, **3**, pp. 71–129.

MARSH, R. and MANNARI, H. (1976) *Modernization and the Japanese factory*, Princeton, Princeton University Press.

McCORMICK, K.J. (1986) 'New technological and organisational developments and strategies of human resource development: The case of Japanese engineers', *Symposium on New Production Systems: Implications for Work and Training in the Factory of the Future*, CEDEFOP, EC Commission and City of Turin, 2–4 July.

MISUMI, J. (1984) 'Decision-making in Japanese groups and organisations', in WILPERT, B. and SORGE, A. (eds) *International Perspectives on Organisational Democracy*, London, John Wiley and Sons.

NAKAJIMA, A. (1985) 'Seniority system: Not for high tech ccompanies?', *Nikkei Special Report*, **1**, 2, November.

NAKANE, C. (1970) *Japanese Society*, Berkeley, University of California Press.

OKAMOTO, Y. (1982) 'The grand strategy of Japanese business', *Japanese Economic Studies*, **X**, pp. 3–56.

OKUDA, K. (1983) 'The role of engineers in Japanese industry and education', *Journal of Japanese Trade and Industry*, **5**, pp. 23–6.

OSHIMA, K. and YAMADA, K. (1985) 'Continuing education for engineers in Japan', *European Journal of Engineering Education*, **10**, 3/4, pp. 217–20.

PASSIN, H. (1965) *Society and Education in Japan*, New York, Teachers' College Press.

PAVITT, K. (ed.) (1980) *Technical Innovation and British Economic Performance*, London, Macmillan.

Kevin McCormick

PAVITT, K. (1981) 'Technology in British Industry: A suitable case for improvement', in CARTER, C. (ed.) *Industrial Policy and Innovation*, London, Heinemann.

ROHLEN, T.P. (1975) *For Harmony and Strength: Japanese White Collar Organization in Anthropological Perspective*, Berkeley, University of California.

ROHLEN, T.P. (1983) *Japan's High Schools*, Berkeley, University of California Press.

SAKAKIBARA, K. and WESTNEY, D.E. (1985) 'Comparative study of the training, careers and organisation of engineers in the computer industry in the United States and Japan', *Hitotsubashi Journal of Commerce and Management*, **20**, pp. 1–20.

SHIRAI, T. (1983) 'A supplement: Characteristics of Japanese managements and their personnel policies', in SHIRAI, T. (ed.) *Contemporary Industrial Relations in Japan*, Madison, University of Wisconsin Press.

SMITH, P.B. (1984) 'Japanese management styles: A critical review', *Occupational Psychology*, **57**, pp. 121–36.

TAKAGI, H. (1985) *The Flaw in Japanese Management*, Ann Arbor, Michigan, University Microfilm International (UMI) Research Press.

TREVOR, M. (1983) *Japan's Reluctant Multinationals: Japanese Management at Home and Abroad*, London, Frances Pinter.

WERSKY, G. (1986) 'The education and training of Japanese electronic engineers', Seminar to the Science Policy Research Unit, University of Sussex, 6 June.

WERSKY, G. (1987) *Training for Innovation: How Japanese Electronic Companies Develop their Elite Engineers*, London, General Electric Company plc.

Part 3

VET Comparisons in the European Community

8   Interactions in the Markets for Education, Training and Labour: A European Perspective on Intermediate Skills

Robert M. Lindley

Introduction

The intermediate range of skills is of particular interest in the study of how social, economic and technological factors affect the structure of employment and access to the jobs within it. The mix of education, training and work experience involved in preparing for such occupations varies quite considerably between occupations and countries. Many intermediate occupations have expanded rapidly during the post-war period, accompanied by the emergence of new occupations. As the latter crystallize out of the occupational mix they are subject to an increasing formalization of educational and training requirements. Longer-standing occupations also adapt their requirements to changing conditions.

Some intermediate occupations jostle for position between the craft and equivalent skilled non-manual occupations and the professions. Some primarily emerge on the edge of a profession where an expertise becomes separable from a wider body of professional knowledge and skill and the economic, organizational and technological environment encourages a re-jigging of the job structure. Other intermediate occupations develop primarily from lower level jobs, though they too may eventually encroach upon the traditional preserves of higher level jobs or the professions.

Examples of intermediate occupations are found particularly among such groups as supervisors, nurses and paramedics, technicians, programmers, executive secretaries and multi-skilled manual workers employed in a variety of industries but notably in engineering.

This chapter provides a European perspective on British policy questions relating to intermediate skills, drawing especially on a study of changing employment patterns in five EC countries which synthesized the available evidence both at the aggregate level and from case studies.[1] There is, however, a lack of well-rounded comparative economic analysis of the markets for education, training and labour, and of the links between them. Evidence from the five countries is used to identify the key interactions likely to affect intermediate skills, though their relative importance will differ between countries and occupations.

The chapter first examines changes in the pattern of labour demand, emphasizing qualitative aspects which affect intermediate skills. It then deals with the interactions between education, training and the labour market. Finally, it identifies four main factors which appear to have a crucial bearing on how the markets for intermediate skills will develop. These are: (i) educational crowding out, co-existing with skill shortages, (ii) the potential for substantial growth in the European intermediate skills base, (iii) the possible strains of meeting such demand for skills, likely to be felt even in countries with high quality, broadly-based VET, and (iv) pressures for greater externalization of the VET function, separating it further from the employment relationship.

The Labour Market Context

Projections of occupational employment for the UK (IER, 1989) suggest that the associate professional and technical occupations will be among the fastest employment growth areas. Similar findings emerge for a number of other European countries, though occupational projections covering the whole economy are not generally available.

Conventional economic analysis of industrial-occupational change does, however, tend to ignore changes taking place in job content within occupations and in the relationships between occupations. It omits reference to the wider conditions of employment attached to the jobs being generated and the possible connections between the occupational outcomes of organizational and technological change and the job content/contractual arrangements which are emerging. In the present context, the focus is upon job content and the remainder of this section summarizes the evidence on this issue.

In order to examine changes in job content, it is helpful to make three sets of distinctions between:

(i) function and occupation;
(ii) shifts in the way a function is organized which alter jobs sufficiently to be recorded as changes in the occupational data (as conventionally classified) and those where much significant change in job content is not captured in such data;
(iii) skills actually employed, entry requirements for a job, and qualifications held by the individual doing a job.

The functions should then represent the underlying activities rather than the way in which they are carried out via occupations. The skills should represent the abilities and experience needed to do the jobs created in the occupational hierarchy rather than the formal educational qualifications or other vocational training conditions used as minimum entry requirements or held by the 'average person' in the occupation. The most easily obtained information at national level is, however, occupation by qualification and this blurs all three distinctions made above. Of the five countries studied, only for Germany is there an analysis of function by occupation and only for the Netherlands is there an analysis (now dated) of skill content by qualification.[2]

The examination of changes in job content first looks at the 'function by occupation' and 'occupation by function' data, then highlights the main points which emerge from case-studies, and finally (at the beginning of the following section) considers the implications of 'qualification by occupation' and related data.

Function and Occupation

The evidence of the German labour force survey (Table 8.1) suggests that certain skilled trades most associated with manufacturing industries have become increasingly devoted to the setting up, adjustment, maintenance and repair of capital equipment used in production rather than with the production tasks themselves. The change has been particularly marked for electrical and mechanical engineering trades. For the more specialized skilled manufacturing trades and in mining etc., the same phenomenon can be seen, though the proportion engaged in production activities is much higher and the numbers in total (i.e., in all functions) have fallen much more significantly than is the case for the engineering trades.

For more highly-qualified technical occupations (engineers, scientists and technicians — all of which are expanding), changes in the functional distribution of work have also been substantial: the proportion engaged in production has almost halved. In addition, there have been marked reductions in the proportions involved both in planning, design, testing and research (on the face of it a rather surprising result) and in transportation and control. The functional distribution has moved towards the setting-up, adjustment and maintenance activities on the one hand and the office-based technical activities such as programming on the other hand.[3]

Amongst other white collar occupations, it is more difficult to interpret the functional evidence unambiguously, though a tendency to specialize further on the functions which previously exemplified these occupations can be seen, i.e., the reverse of the situation for blue collar workers. Thus the data suggest a concentration upon the mainstream office functions at the expense of ancillary activities which are either reduced in aggregate or transferred to more specialist functions (*Germany*:35).

The industrial classification of German employment from 1973 to 1982/83 indicates a decline in the share of total employment from 47 to 42 per cent for

Table 8.1   Occupation by function for Germany

Occupational groups and selected occupations	Year	Total employment (000s)	% engaged in[a]			
			production	regulation and maintenance	repairs	other
Agricultural trades	1973	1,967	90.6	—	—	9.4
	1982	1,386	93.4	1.0	—	5.6
Miners, quarrymen, and related workers	1973	156	87.2	—	—	12.8
	1982	127	80.4	9.9	—	9.7
Manufacturing trades	1973	9,717	61.8	7.8	13.1	17.3
	1982	8,731	52.9	14.5	18.4	14.2
— mechanics	1973	896	52.8	14.4	24.5	8.3
	1982	858	45.3	18.5	32.0	4.2
— electricians	1973	688	40.2	6.3	35.0	18.5
	1982	680	34.5	22.7	33.1	9.7
— textile and clothing trades	1973	638	76.0	2.1	12.0	9.9
	1982	397	72.8	7.3	11.4	8.5
— building trades	1973	1,257	88.4	0.8	8.1	2.7
	1982	1,013	80.2	2.0	13.2	4.6
Technical trades	1973	1,399	15.6	3.8	5.0	75.6
	1982	1,559	8.1	10.4	4.3	77.2
— engineers and scientists	1973	474	10.6	1.9	2.1	85.4
	1982	536	3.9	6.2	1.3	88.6
— technicians and technical specialists	1973	925	18.2	4.8	6.5	70.5
	1982	1,023	10.4	12.6	5.9	71.1
Service trades	1973	13,489	2.6	1.1	1.2	95.1
	1982	14,843	2.3	1.8	1.4	94.5
— entrepreneurs and managers	1973	574	13.0	—	1.7	85.3
	1982	750	6.7	1.6	2.6	89.1
All occupations	1973	27,066	31.5	3.6	5.6	59.3
	1982	26,774	24.2	6.5	7.1	62.2

Note: [a] Rows sum to 100 per cent.
Source: Vogler-Ludwig (1987), p. 36.

the *goods producing industries*; the occupational classification gives a decline from 37 to 33 per cent for production *trades*; and the functional classification yields a decline from 27 to 20 per cent for the production *function* (excluding agriculture). From this perspective, therefore, both the industrial and occupational data overstate the proportion of people employed directly in production activities and understate the decline in that proportion. However, it is worth noting that if we consider the production *context* to include the regulation, maintenance and repair functions, then the decline in the numbers employed in the production context is only from 37 to 35 per cent. Similarly if we include the more highly-qualified technical occupations alongside the production trades the decline is from 42 to 39 per cent.

The function by occupation data can also be analyzed in order to see which occupations gain at least in relative terms from the changes in production organization and technology. Table 8.2 provides a re-analysis of the

Table 8.2   Function by occupation for Germany (excluding agricultural trades)

Occupational groups and selected occupations	Year	Production %	Regulation and maintenance %	Repairs %
Miners, quarrymen,	1973	2.0	—	—
and related workers	1982	2.0	0.7	—
Manufacturing trades	1973	89.1	77.8	84.0
	1982	89.1	73.3	84.5
— mechanics	1973	7.0	13.2	14.5
	1982	7.5	9.2	14.4
— electricians	1973	4.1	4.5	15.9
	1982	4.5	8.9	11.8
— textile and	1973	7.2	1.4	5.1
clothing trades	1982	5.6	1.7	2.4
— building trades	1973	16.5	1.0	6.7
	1982	15.7	1.2	7.0
Technical trades	1973	3.2	5.5	4.6
	1982	2.4	9.4	3.5
— engineers	1973	0.8	0.9	0.7
and scientists	1982	0.4	1.9	0.4
— technicians and	1973	2.5	4.6	4.0
technical specialists	1982	2.1	7.5	3.2
Service trades	1973	5.2	15.2	10.9
	1982	6.6	15.5	11.0
All occupations above	1973	100.0	100.0	100.0
(subject to rounding in source)	1982	100.0	100.0	100.0
All occupations above (000s)	1973	6,744	974	1,516
	1982	5,185	1,726	1,901

Source: Derived from Vogler-Ludwig (1987), p. 36.

data underlying Table 8.1 in which the occupational structures of three functions are shown. Thus, 89 per cent of those engaged in the function of production in this occupational grouping within the German economy are trained in one or other skilled manufacturing trades. The German results suggest that the occupational composition of production *per se* has not in fact changed very much. It is the increasing importance of regulation, maintenance and repair at the expense of direct production activity which is the main factor. But this is then further reinforced in its effects upon occupational employment by shifts *within* the regulation and maintenance function away from mechanical engineering trades towards the electrical trades and technician trades.[4]

Case-study Evidence

Against this rough aggregate picture for Germany it is possible to consider the case-study evidence for Germany and also the other countries for whom function by occupation analyses are not directly available. It is worth stressing, however, that case studies are difficult to set into perspective. Moreover, in an international comparative context the danger of making too much out of unrepresentative cases is compounded by the danger of emphasizing the inter-country differences when in fact the intra-country differences are of equal or more significance.

The range of evidence considered by the individual country studies (chapter 3 in each) varies quite markedly and this, to a considerable degree, is due to variations in the evidence available. It also reflects the different national debates about new technology, flexibility and employment. However, all the country studies refer to the qualitative changes in job content of those industrial-occupational categories most affected by the introduction of new technology in production. The planning, control, adjustment, maintenance and repair functions have been greatly affected by the progressive reduction of employment in the production and materials handling functions. It is clear, moreover, that very real choices face management in devising occupational structures to implement even the same production technology. An analogous situation arises in the impact of information technology on office-based activities concerning general administration through to highly specialized technical work in engineering research, design and development.

Turning to the case-study evidence on changing job content, a combination of 'stylized facts and related issues' emerges rather than clear international contrasts. These are quite consistent with the analysis of more aggregate data (Lindley, 1987) and are summarized briefly below. Specific reference to a particular country will only be made where there seems to be either a marked divergence from the position being adopted or an especially strong example of the point being made.

Since this chapter is concerned particularly with intermediate skills, the qualitative evidence highlighted below will focus on those skills. However, an important aspect of occupational change is the shifting or blurring of boundaries between different groups. Intermediate skills, by their very nature, are likely to be affected by this. Reference is therefore made to such developments. Four key areas of existing or emerging intermediate skill are considered.

Occupations concerned with planning, monitoring and control — notably, managers and supervisors.   Changes in job content which will accompany the further expansion of management jobs will reflect the wider range of competence expected of managers and the need to take responsibility for a more complex process. The latter will use more capital and fewer people but with personnel engaged on more demanding tasks and involving greater autonomy. The requirement for broader expertise will affect general managers and specialists alike, with the former acquiring greater technical knowledge and the latter, more business skills.

At the intermediate level, responsibility for a greater mix of capital equipment and skilled employees will also characterize the supervisory occupations, where more emphasis will be laid upon communication with and the motivation of employees. This aspect has been ignored by some comment-ators who have expected supervisors to decline simply with the number of semi-skilled and unskilled personnel under them.

The relationship between higher and intermediate professions. This issue concerns the relationships both between long-established occupations (doctor/nurse, scientist/laboratory technician, etc.) and between relatively new occupations (software engineer/programmer, design engineer/technician/ draughtsperson, manager/data processing specialist). In many of these linked occupations, changes in product demand, labour market conditions, and vocational education are creating situations in which significant adjustments are already taking place in some countries. Relative salary costs and shortages of certain higher-level skills combined with the development of technological aids to decision-making indicate the potential for further changes (e.g., in health care) subject to institutional restraints.

In addition, in certain areas of the economy there seems to be scope for the emergence of new higher and intermediate professional groups. For example (*Italy*:45–6), the development of tourism and leisure activities need not be associated with a continuation of temporary, sometimes seasonal, low-skilled and low-paid employment. Aiming at higher quality and a wider range of service generates a demand for more professionally qualified entrepreneurs, managers and local administrators, supported by a cadre of skilled personnel. The latter may work behind the scenes or be in direct con-tact with the customer (e.g., in providing tourist/travel information, instruction in recreational pursuits, supervision of customer relations in hotel, catering and recreational establishments). The speed with which such service industries move towards the 'high value-added' end of their product market clearly determines the rate of growth of these more skilled occupations. It is also, however, determined by the rate at which appropriate new professional roles are identified and the relevant training is provided.

Other non-manual occupations. This group is dominated by clerical, sec-retarial and sales occupations. Some of these personnel are directly involved with customers in areas where attempts are being made to improve the quality of customer service. There the job content is placing greater stress on the combination of a higher level of product knowledge, inter-personal com-munication skills, keyboard skills and software knowledge needed to use the financial/sales information system, and wider commercial awareness.

In other respects, though, there seems to be some uncertainty about the net impact of organizational and technological change upon these occupations. It is generally agreed that many routine clerical tasks and the supervisory roles attached to them will be abolished with the widespread establishment and use of machine-readable data bases. The entry and interrogation of data will be organized much more efficiently but just how far supervisors, managers and other intermediate and higher professional staff will reduce their need for clerical and secretarial assistance remains to be seen. The scope for more complex analysis and presentation of data and the ability to create higher quality documentation is likely to increase the demand for certain clerical/secretarial staff. These will have higher levels of literacy and numeracy, greater knowledge of the business and its information system, and skills in the use of software for word-processing, statistical analysis and graphics.

The above developments must also be considered in the light of two further factors. First, employment in these occupations is likely to benefit from the continuing growth of the service sector, where the nature and size of many of its enterprises limit the economies of scale obtainable. Second, the quality considerations mentioned above in relation to customer service combine with efficiency arguments to create a demand for more flexible personnel. These should be able to switch from counter service to liaising with suppliers to carrying out supporting clerical and secretarial tasks. This is an emerging form of multi-skilled and multi-functional office-based occupation which receives less attention than does its manual craft counterpart (see below).

Thus, whilst the net effect of these changes upon the numbers of clerical, secretarial and sales staff is highly uncertain, the content of the average job will tend to rise quite substantially (*UK*:59).

Skilled production occupations. The fate of skilled craftsmen seems to be the crucial issue in considering the implementation of new technology. The possible consequences are: (a) abolition of the job; (b) deskilling to a large degree (e.g., to a machine-minding or materials handling function); (c) reskilling where previous knowledge is transferred to a new context requiring some retraining (e.g., transfer to maintenance from production); (d) multi-skilling, where, typically, the need for a wider craft-based competence involves the acquisition of complementary skills in electronics; and (e) upgrading to the status of technician/programmer/complex keyboard operator which exploits previous knowledge but involves substantial retraining or recruitment of new qualified staff.

The development of the multi-skilled, multi-functional, worker is highlighted in the case-study evidence for all countries (see, especially, *France*:30; *Italy*:41–2; *Netherlands*:31; *UK*:60). A worker who deploys, for example, mechanical and electronics skills and deals with production, regulation of equipment and minor repairs would fall into this category. Similar attention is paid to the specialized maintenance and repair functions employing highly-skilled craftsmen. However, the introduction of new technology generally creates far fewer such jobs than it destroys or de-skills traditional craft jobs engaged in production (*Germany*:37–42). The extent of upgrading has evidently become the litmus test of enlightened management: how the numerically controlled machine is programmed and by whom is a noteworthy example. But the evidence on the relative costs of alternative strategies, as opposed to their feasibility in terms of the technical and training requirements, is extremely limited. The emerging division of labour between skilled manual workers and more highly-qualified technical personnel at the point of technological transition is insufficiently monitored and understood at national level to allow for a satisfactory explanation of international differences.

Education, Training and the Labour Market

Qualification and Occupation

As noted at the beginning of the previous section, nationwide quantitative information on job content is extremely limited even for those occupations which have not been at the frontier of change. No country systematically collects data on the changing skill content of occupations and many do not even provide adequate data on changes in qualifications held by people employed in different occupations.

Only for the *Netherlands* (pp. 19–25) is it possible to cite a job content analysis which distinguishes content from qualification. Despite the crude nature of the data, they do provide tentative evidence for the view that changes in the overall job content of the Dutch economy during the 1970s were very small, both absolutely and relative to the increase in average qualifications. The figures also indicate a polarization in job content in favour of higher and lower levels of job content at the expense of the intermediate level (roughly equivalent to the more skilled manual and clerical work).

During a period of increasing labour surplus, the better qualified filter down the occupational hierarchy to take jobs at lower levels at the expense of those with fewer qualifications. The gap between qualifications possessed and qualifications used will widen at such times. In the Netherlands, between 1960 and 1977, those employees 'working below their level of education' increased from 7 to 26 per cent. During the 1971–7 period alone the changes in these figures were of the order of 10 percentage points in both cases. Simulations with the Dutch stock/flow model (VOSTA) of labour market and educational changes in the population actually show that the relatively high rates of unemployment amongst the less well qualified are due not to a shortage of low-skilled jobs but to a form of 'educational crowding out' (SEO, forthcoming).

The implication is that there is a smaller shortage of unskilled and semi-skilled jobs for the less able members of the workforce than appears from the unemployment statistics. The main shortage could well be for skilled manual and non-manual jobs for those in the intermediate and higher ability ranges. Note that this is expressed in terms of ability rather than qualification. A shortage of skilled jobs for able people co-exists with a shortage of those skills which are most efficiently acquired by able people. The response to the latter shortage is to limit the growth of such jobs in the development of new occupational structures which further exacerbates the former shortage.

This line of reasoning can, of course, be taken too far, especially given the nature of the data.[5] But the Dutch analysis is an effective antidote to exaggerated claims, based upon extrapolation from special cases, about the burgeoning job content of the economy as a whole and the need for educational levels to rise to keep pace with the increasing sophistication of the modern world of work.

The information on occupation and qualification for the other countries does not benefit from even the rough job content analysis available for the Netherlands. Two particular features are taken up by the German and UK studies: the importance of supply-side explanations for rising qualification rates and the evidence on polarization.

Shifts in skill content have to some extent been obscured by the waves of better educated people joining the labour market in the last two decades or so. The relationship between occupation and qualification is partly supply determined even when the occupation is very precisely defined from the demand side to take into account the full technological and organizational context of the job and the cognitive and manipulative skills required. For example, UK research suggests that roughly half of the growth in highly qualified persons (with a university degree or equivalent) between 1971 and 1981 can be attributed to the growth of those occupations where qualified people tend to be concentrated (the occupational effect) and half to the growth of qualification rates within occupations (the certification effect).[6] Assuming that the start of the period represents a good match of education to occupation, the occupational effect might be associated with changes in demand and the certification effect with changes on the 'supply-side', including the formalization of entry requirements and the 'filtering down' process. However, the UK study (p. 56) proposes that at least some of the certification effect will be due to demand-side influences reflecting genuine changes in job content. The latter require *specific* higher qualifications rather than the use of higher qualifications to screen for general ability and should also be distinguished from the activity of the professions in defending their status by increasing the educational restrictions on entry.

Turning to 'polarization', this concept refers to situations in which the impact of technological and organizational change is to reduce the employment of people in the middle of the skills range relative to both those with much less skill and those with higher level skills, for example, as in the case of skilled manual workers being replaced by operatives on the one hand and technician engineers on the other hand. Whilst the polarization in job content appears fairly clearly in the available economy-wide Dutch data, the German study emphasizes (p. 49) that, in industry, this represents the phase of *mechanization* through 'Taylorization' of the production process. Tasks are divided into less demanding components which can be done by less skilled operators working in environments created and controlled by employees requiring higher qualifications than the skilled worker. With the *automation* of production, the transformation of qualification/occupational structures then enters a second phase which dispenses with many of the less skilled jobs.

These include, for example, areas of materials handling which hitherto have been too expensive to automate compared with the costs of unskilled labour. Polarization would thus become an increasingly inappropriate metaphor. At the same time, however, it is apparently still too early to observe a reduction in polarization. This is despite the fact that the increasing educational certification of the labour force would probably distort the pattern in that direction regardless of whether or not 'certification' implied 'utilization'.

The reduction of polarization is also recognized, guardedly, as a possibility in the French study (p. 39). Here, though, the main concern is with the emergence of new intermediary occupations involving multi-skilled and multi-functional workers. The quantitative significance of this development is, however, uncertain in relation to the decline in conventional manual jobs. What characterizes the French situation is, of course, the whole nexus involving relationships between qualification, work organization, employment and socio-economic lifestyles — the *rapport salarial*. This encompasses contractual arrangements as well as job content or qualifications.

Comparisons of situations in different European labour markets provide quite consistent but not perhaps conclusive evidence for strong *potential* growth of intermediate skills during the 1990s. Whether or not this will materialize and obliterate any latent tendency towards polarization of the job structure is so far unclear.

The principal offsetting trends may arise in different sectors so that an expansion of demand for intermediate skills will take place in some industries and a polarization in others. However, the evidence for the UK suggests that polarization has not been the dominant form during the last two decades (IER, 1989). Craft occupations have been less affected than have semi-skilled operatives and other occupations requiring very little skill. Thus, even though the engineering industry's demand for intermediate and higher-level technical skills has increased, this has not been matched by a relative shift among manual workers to the least skilled groups.

Alongside the question of polarization there is also that of educational crowding out. If they were to coincide, this would present a most unfavourable position from which to promote a surge of intermediate skills growth across an economy. A VET structure built on early entry to the labour market rather than widespread upper secondary education could find it especially difficult to play an adequate facilitating role. Before considering this point further, however, it is worth returning to some basic issues of VET policy which are still not resolved.

VET and Economic Growth

International comparisons of public spending on post-compulsory education and training point not so much to the economic gains to be obtained from higher public spending but to questions of the organization and content of existing provision.[7] In particular, these concern: (a) curricula, (b) the public and private financing of different educational and training opportunities, (c) the mechanisms for supplying such opportunities, and (d) flexibility of provision.

Studies of skill shortages indicate that the poor utilization of existing skills and provision for updating or extending them is of greater significance for the growth of those industries affected than is the inadequacy of initial training of young people either in terms of the numbers being trained or the quality of their training.[8]

Research on the structure and behaviour of labour markets indicates that, whatever the inadequacies of the education system, the stance of employers on questions of recruitment, training, relative pay and other conditions of service can seriously undermine attempts by the education system to respond to the 'needs of industry'.[9]

This is not to suggest that more public spending on education and training could not have a considerable impact on the future path of the economy. It might imply, however, that the absence of additional spending is not currently a *binding* constraint upon economic growth. The reasons for this are to be found in: (a) the distribution of resources within education and training, (b) the organization of internal labour markets, and (c) the behaviour of external labour markets.

This general judgment must be qualified in three important respects: (i) it is an *ex post* assessment which ignores possible opportunity costs incurred by the economy when, for example, firms have internalized particular skill constraints by substituting alternative skills; (ii) in the qualitative sense there do appear to be significant problems — these involve the relative abilities of people undertaking different courses of VET, the adequacy of the training they receive for subsequent employment, and the efficiency with which they are used by employers once qualified; and (iii) at the disaggregate level, where concern is not so much with broad groups of educated people, like qualified scientists or engineers, but with more specialized fields, there is (as we might expect) more evidence of mismatches persisting for lack of more flexible arrangements for supplementary training or retraining.

A further caveat may also be expressed. Disappointing economic performance may not itself be due to the existence of skill constraints but, should inadequacies in complementary areas of industrial development (marketing, product strategy, R&D, etc.) be tackled, this may land the economy with a major problem with the supply of skills. On this basis, economic regeneration must take place simultaneously over a broad front with progress in one area reinforcing that in other areas.

Such an argument may be seductive to those fully committed to the human resource route to economic growth but it usually runs into scepticism among finance ministries faced with the task of allocating scarce resources. Moreover, it is not a strategy that appears to commend itself at the micro-level: British enterprises generally turn to matters of labour supply only when problems arise. With notable exceptions, the actions of British employers do not suggest that human resources have a high priority.

These are, however, very general points and it is not the aim of this paper to consider the issue of VET as a whole. The main focus is on intermediate skills.

Intermediate Skills: A British Dilemma?

The earlier discussion of developments in the structure of employment has several implications for education and training policies. First, it is essential to investigate further whether or not the emergence of a stronger intermediate skill base is indeed a prerequisite for successful economic development in the decades ahead. Second, if such a move were required, it would mean a stronger mutual reinforcement of strategies devoted to promoting economic growth generally and to improving the quality of jobs available. It would help to raise the average quality of employment opportunities, injecting into the middle of the job hierarchy a higher level of performance and reward. Third, the adoption of such an employment strategy implies the adoption of a product market strategy which shifts the organization further toward the higher value-added end of its existing market(s) or into new high value-added markets.

The education and training of those with intermediate skills lies at the conjunction of a number of debates in the field of human resources. For it is in this area of the job structure that the appropriate mix between (and meanings of) 'education' and 'training', 'general' and 'specific' training, initial and continuing training, off-the-job and on-the-job training appears to be especially debatable. This leads to corresponding disagreement about the strategies for funding and supplying different parts of the education and training cycle.

Overall, however, promoting the emergence of a larger intermediate skill base would place additional pressure on the British system of education and training at its weakest points as they affect attainment, opportunity and continuation. Britain has embraced neither mass upper-secondary education nor widely available training in intermediate skills (Table 8.3). A wariness of relying upon extended schooling to provide an appropriate mix of education and general vocational training has left it with a combination of schemes and specific training for the majority of young people. The general element of training under schemes has continually to be defended against the demands for specific relevance to the job or work experience in hand. The certification process itself is in danger of becoming too much the creature of internal rather than external labour markets and of pandering to low levels of attainment rather than promoting high levels.[10] The British system has thus encouraged a similar early entry to the labour market to that of Germany but without the provision of employer-based high quality training to accompany it.

Table 8.3   Educational enrolment of 17 year olds in OECD economies (c. 1984)[a]

	Full time education	Apprenticeship part-time, etc.	Total
Germany	51	46	97
Japan	90	0	90
United States	87	0	88
Netherlands	76	10	86
Belgium	78	8	86
Sweden	83[b]	2	85
Switzerland	27	55	82
Austria	34	44	78
Canada	76	—	76
France	65	10	75
Norway	74	1	75
Denmark	68	6	74
Italy[c]	47	23	70
Australia	46	20[d]	66
United Kingdom	30	35[e]	65
Spain	49	0	49
New Zealand	46	0	46
Portugal	38	3	41

Notes: [a] Figures are percentages of total population aged 17.
　　　　 [b] Two-year upper-secondary courses.
　　　　 [c] 1981 figures.
　　　　 [d] Mainly part-time technical education.
　　　　 [e] Including FE private and public part-time study and YTS.
Source: OECD (1987), p. 72.

The problem with the job content associated with emerging patterns of intermediate skills is that it requires a higher level of general training and a longer span of VET integrated with work experience. This makes it even less attractive for employers individually to provide the opportunities for training as part of an employment contract. The response to this may be to seek to galvanize employer collective commitment. The experience of British training in the post-war period suggest, however, that this is a lost cause. Even when statutory backing was given through the Industrial Training Boards (ITBs), the system in many industries settled for trying to persuade employers to do sufficient specific training rather than identifying primarily general training for support (Lindley, 1983). And when ITBs tried to increase the breadth and quality of training by placing the stress on general training, they were frustrated by the reactions of employers who were either reluctant to raise quality in the first place or acquiesced but then reduced quantity at a later stage.

A further aspect of intermediate skills relates to their place in the pattern of occupational mobility. At the two extremes, they may be acquired through a combination of off-the-job training and experience, essentially organized by the enterprise, or through entry to a full-time course of education followed by employment. A large variety of provision exists between these two cases. One factor which affects the provision of VET is the accessibility of the occupation via occupational mobility from above or below it (or, just 'elsewhere') in the occupational structure. Some occupations, notably technicians in manufacturing industries, have become progressively detached from their traditional craft base. Direct entry from educationally or industrially-based courses rather than promotion from craft status has come to dominate entry to these groups. A similar pattern can be observed for foremen and other industrial supervisors, except that here there are large proportions of people without any substantial technical training. The outcome is to impoverish craft trainee intakes because potential entrants are aware of the truncated opportunities for later promotion, whilst depriving the technician and supervisor levels of able, experienced entrants via the craft route.

Whilst comparative research has illuminated the differences in structure and content of vocational training in different countries, it has been less helpful in assessing the role of training in occupational mobility. The principal insight is to distinguish between 'training for present job' and 'training for future job' (or, more broadly, for present occupation and future career, respectively). It is often pointed out that a highly successful economy like that of Germany makes much of 'training for stock' when demand conditions would otherwise point to a contraction of training. This policy may be justifiable in counter-cyclical terms where demand is expected to recover or in terms of anticipating major increases in demand. But it is further believed that possession of a recognized skill, almost any skill, is of value *per se*. This is a broader argument than Finniston's favouring of an engineering culture conducive to technological progress. It is essentially concerned with the socialization and status of the labour force rather than bold advocacy of a new dominant curriculum. In spite of this, though, German companies cover most of the costs of non-school vocational education and training. The scale and resilience of the German effort is usually attributed to the power of traditional social obligation felt by employers and their happy discovery that this appears to make good economic sense. This strategy is sustained partly by a belief in the benefits of the 'hidden curriculum' involved in formal training aimed at particular skills but which is in fact of value in most jobs.

In contrast, the United States follows the Becker (1964) model relatively closely. Company expenditure on specific training is very high, however, and can itself produce situations in which general training is a profitable investment for the employer. An extension of this may also occur under the impetus to create what might be called a 'learning culture' within certain companies.[11]

It is clear that the involvement of employers within the highly stratified German system of education and training derives from a radically different style from that shown by American employers. The latter operate in the midst of a large constellation of public and private educational and training institutions where there is scope for an extraordinary range of individual strategies for developing careers and strengthening one's labour market positions. Initial vocational education and training are thus matters for the individual to sort out, on the basis of which employers aim to make further specific investments.

The notion that industry is the place for general as well as specific industrial training has had a powerful influence upon the development of British policy. The rationale for it has been to ensure relevance and this has its components of marginal and hidden curricula. The overall curricular arguments for the sort of British practice common to many production industries sit uncomfortably with both the much broader conception which underpins the German system and the very different division of responsibility characterizing the American system.

However, a shift away from relying upon the internal labour markets of organizations to foster investment in 'intermediate' human capital is likely to be required in those European countries which have successfully managed to achieve this so far. Those still struggling to make the grade should have cause to reflect on the feasibility of the strategy in the changing labour market conditions of the 1990s. Educational and training institutions would then play a larger part in providing VET and the state and individual a larger part in funding it.

Finally, another ingredient should be mentioned, given that Britain now probably has the least regulated labour market in Europe (Emerson, 1988). Deregulation of labour markets may produce gains in allocative efficiency and medium-run productivity (i.e., over the business cycle) but the effects of weakening the employment relationship are difficult to judge in the long run. It may make it more difficult for employers individually to 'seal off' their internal labour markets in ways which promote joint investment in training by reducing uncertainty and increasing commitment on both sides of the relationship. It may undermine the cohesion of collective employer commitment to 'breadth and quality' in general training. For those countries which can hardly claim the latter exists, it may weaken even the commitment to higher quality *specific* training. On the other hand, deregulation may give management the confidence to invest in the labour force because of the greater scope for deployment of personnel in line with corporate requirements.

Completion of the European Internal Market

Problems of maintaining existing employer investment in intermediate skills where it is already high and increasing it where it is relatively low may thus coincide with a period of greater 'trade' in intermediate skills. It is worth noting in this context a potentially very significant effect of the completion of the internal market.

Tax-subsidy regimes operated by European governments differ markedly. Those which directly affect the wedge between basic input costs and market prices can, in principle, be manipulated to a considerable degree in order to gain a cost advantage over a competitor. Large differentials can, however, for a variety of reasons, persist between countries — witness the differences in statutory social contributions levied on European employers and in state contributions to national spending on education and training of young people aged 16 and over. The impact of greater product market competition may well cause governments to reconsider their current practices regarding input markets, especially if given the encouragement of a liberal 'competition between regulations' approach to these matters by the Commission.

Public expenditure on education and training could become the most significant industrial subsidy to be legitimized as the Community emerges from the completion process. Accompanying this (and closely associated with the production of highly-qualified people in science and technology) will be state support for research and development. How a member country's markets for education, training and the production and exploitation of intellectual property develop in future could have very significant implications for its attractions to both foreign direct investment and domestic investment (as an alternative to overseas direct investment). Moreover, government investment of this kind in the human capital stock and the informational infrastructure of the economy may well be economically more efficient and less distorting than offering foreign and domestic firms capital subsidies via regional incentives. This area, however, requires much further theoretical and empirical research.

Completion of the European internal market will increase organizational flexibility regarding the location of different corporate functions and relationships with suppliers. This makes it necessary for each Community country to scrutinize the environment it offers to business. From the point of view of the labour market, Lindley (1989) has distinguished the 'subsidy regime', 'regulation regime' and 'human capital regime'. The first regime refers to the national and international policies governing industrial subsidies of all kinds, including employment subsidies. The second refers to the policies which regulate labour markets, for example, via constraints placed upon trade union activity, employers' hiring and firing procedures and the forms of employment contract allowed. The third refers to the mix of state funding, regulation and control of education, training and the production and exploitation of intellectual property.

Debate on the programme for completion of the internal market has now shifted to some degree from the subsidy regime to the regulation regime because of the announcement of the Commission's agenda for the 'Social Charter'. In terms of the behaviour of companies, especially those operating at international level, it appears, however, that increasing importance is being attached to the human capital regime and its associated informational infrastructure (market conditions for the generation and application of intellectual property including R&D, business information services, and related physical infrastructures, especially telecommunications). Consideration of this aspect, moreover, points to the interaction between the three regimes. Particularly significant is the subsidy regime pertaining to vocational education and training (VET).

The regulation regime covering VET is also important. The measures to promote a single labour market include the mutual recognition of qualifications and other arrangements to facilitate access to national labour markets. The Social Charter will no doubt aim to give workers rights to initial and continuing VET. But these activities are organized in very different ways by the member states. To the extent that there are 'markets' for VET, the ground rules for the explicit and implicit subsidy regimes underpinning, indeed, dominating them, will need to be given much more attention by the Community. This is because the human capital intensity of economic activity will increase in the long run and subsidies to the creation and utilization of human capital are likely to assume much greater importance in creating and maintaining European-wide product and labour markets and ensuring world-wide competitiveness of European industry.

However, the British Government is not pursuing the deregulation strategy through product market and labour market only to stop at the edge of the market for VET. Its labour market intervention has shifted from employment subsidies and job creation schemes aimed at ameliorating the effects of mass unemployment to promoting training-related schemes and raising the intensity and efficiency of job search by the unemployed (Department of Employment, 1988). This has not, though, ushered in a major increase in fiscal support for VET delivered via the employment relationship or via special schemes — the 'training and enterprise measures'. Nor has it invested markedly more in vocational education and training within the formal education system. The Government is still looking for more market leverage on what have been public VET services, either by privatizing them and hoping higher demand will materialize or by gradually creating market conditions within those services to encourage efficiency and responsiveness. Otherwise it aims to act as a catalyst for cooperation between education and industry and to demonstrate, in selective schemes, the possibilities for more innovatory VET.

Nonetheless, as the consequences of completion begin to unfold at the same time as the effects of the White Paper training measures become clearer, the British Government may be obliged to reconsider its present VET strategy — no more so than in the case of intermediate skills.

Conclusions

At present the art of European labour market comparisons is still fairly primitive. This will continue to be the case while the basic statistical tools remain crude, so that even the main shapes in the labour market landscape are none too visible (Lindley, 1987).

There is a considerable need for case studies of selected enterprises in an international comparative context, especially case studies which examine the financial, as well as the technological and organizational contexts within which employment relationships and occupational structures have evolved.

Similarly, in international comparisons of the processes of VET, whether conducted in educational institutions, training centres or at the workplace (or in a mix of these), there has been a dearth of financial analysis to accompany the studies of differences in the design and delivery of curricula and their impacts upon standards of achievement. This makes it difficult to assess the ultimate effects of these differences upon the deployment and performance of people in work.

This chapter has, nonetheless, offered four broad working hypotheses relating especially to intermediate skills. They arose out of a synthesis of evidence from several European countries. They have strong policy implications but there is a need for more conclusive research.

The first derives from the (admittedly very tentative) evidence on the relationships between occupation, job content and qualification. This suggests that there is a problem of over-qualification at the low skill end of the occupational spectrum (this is clear in the case of women) which co-exists with a more specific (and internationally variable) problem of under-qualification and skill shortages in certain intermediate occupations (notably, technicians and multi-skilled craftsmen), and amongst the more highly-qualified technological specialists, and management.

The co-existence of 'educational crowding out' and skill shortages could arise particularly in relation to intermediate skills. The phenomenon may seem paradoxical when viewed in labour market terms but the explanation is quite straightforward when interactions between the markets for education, training and labour are taken into account. It is in the intermediate range of the occupational spectrum that mismatches between the supply of and demand for skills could be most affected by the 'downward filtering' of able people because of the lack of suitable initial and continuing VET.

Second, successful European economies will extend and intensify their intermediate skills base across a wide range of production and service industries. This should raise the quality of employment overall, reduce inefficiency and inequity due to educational crowding out, and improve the performance of those in occupations above and below the intermediate skill level in the job hierarchy.

However, the potential growth in demand for intermediate skills may fail to materialize because of the difficulty of entering the virtuous circle of shifts of product strategies towards higher value-added markets and of occupational structures towards the higher skill intensity required to compete in those markets.

Third, the higher quality VET required to achieve the above will produce strains even in countries with a strong employer commitment to broadly-based training. The larger the investment required, the greater the risk of breaches in collective commitment. Despite recent policy innovations, it is doubtful whether British employers individually will have sufficient incentive to remedy this situation, or whether voluntary collective action will meet the scale of the problem and approach it sufficiently from the long-term point of view. The chances of unbalancing the training effort are also higher if an element of international mobility develops in European markets for intermediate skills, or the location of foreign direct investment is influenced by the supply conditions governing them in different countries.

Finally, in the case of the UK, there is likely to be increasing pressure to externalize more of the education and training function, despite the philosophy that 'the place for training is in industry'. This reflects the needs of an increasingly fluid or flexible labour market from both employer and employee perspectives. The creation of a much more developed market for educational and training opportunities would widen the scope for providing individuals with much greater discretion in preparing themselves for work. It would involve an increasing separation of the provision of vocational education and training from the possession of an employment contract. But it would require the wider certification of training in order to create marketable 'commodities' recognized by both employers and workers. It would also involve renegotiating the division of responsibilities currently advocated by the British Government for supplying and funding VET for intermediate skills.

Acknowledgments

I am very grateful to Paul Ryan for comments on the earlier version of this paper presented to the Manchester Seminar. The study upon which the chapter draws was funded by the Commission of the European Communities (Directorate General for Employment, Social Affairs and Education, DGV). I am grateful for helpful discussions with fellow participants: Henri Nadel and Laurent Schwab (France); Kurt Vogler-Ludwig (Germany); Bruno Contini (Italy); Tammo Oegema and Chris Van der Vegt (Netherlands); Rob Wilson and Derek Bosworth (United Kingdom); Andrew Chapman, John Morley and Klaus Kaeding (Commission DGV); and Anne Houtman (Eurostat). The views expressed in this chapter are, however, my responsibility and should not necessarily be attributed to the other participants.

Notes

1 The research project on which this chapter draws dealt with a much wider range of labour market phenomena than those relating to intermediate skills. For ease of identification, each of the country studies is cited in the text according to country, rather than author(s), with the full details given in the list of references. The section of this chapter dealing with the labour market context draws heavily on part of the comparative study (Lindley, 1987). The author would like to thank DGV for permission to use the material cited.

2 To some degree, by exploiting the most detailed level of the occupational and industrial classification it may be possible to produce a form of 'quasi-function' by occupation tabulation and a corresponding one for 'quasi-function' by

qualification. This is because at that level some occupations can be attributed roughly to functions (e.g., maintenance rather than production) even though at the more aggregate level they are combined in such a way as to cut across functions. It would be necessary to re-aggregate to preserve functional integrity; the feasibility of this depends especially upon the extent to which function is distinguished in classifying occupations at the most detailed level.

3 Disaggregated information for the functional category 'other' and for service trades are shown in the German study (p. 36). The definitions of functions in the survey do, however, make the analysis of these less straightforward than is the case for the production and related activities.

4 The results for the repair function actually suggest a decline in the employment share of electrical trades but it is not clear which other manufacturing trades compensate for this loss (Table 8.2).

5 Note, for example, that the Dutch survey also records that the numbers 'working above their level of education' fell from 36 to 21 per cent.

6 The terminology used here differs from that of the UK study (*UK*, pp. 51–8).

7 See the various NIESR studies, for example, Jarvis and Prais (1989), Prais (1989a), Steedman (1988) and Steedman and Wagner (1989).

8 See Lindley (1983) for a discussion of the part played by evidence on shortages in the development of British training policy.

9 The experience of some areas of higher education is a case in point (Lindley, 1981).

10 See Prais (1989b) for a discussion of this in a European context.

11 See Institute of Manpower Studies (1984) for a much-publicized perception of the systems adopted by the three leading economies.

References

CEC country studies cited in text:

Italy: Contini, B., Colombino, U., Treves, L. and Vitelli, M. (1987) *New Forms and New Areas of Employment Growth*: *Italy*, Brussels, Commission of the European Communities.

France: Nadel, H. and Schwab, L. (1987) *New Forms and New Areas of Employment Growth*: *France*, Brussels, Commission of the European Communities.

The Netherlands: Oegema, T. and van der Vegt, C. (1987) *New Forms and New Areas of Employment Growth*: *The Netherlands*, Brussels, Commission of the European Communities.

Germany: Vogler-Ludwig, K. (1987) *New Forms and New Areas of Employment Growth*: *Germany*, Brussels, Commission of the European Communities.

UK: Wilson, R.A. and Bosworth, D.L. (1987) *New Forms and New Areas of Employment Growth*: *United Kingdom*, Brussels, Commission of the European Communities.

Other references:

Becker, G. (1964) *Human Capital*, New York, Columbia/NBER.

Department of Employment (1988) *Employment for the 1990s*, London, HMSO.

Emerson, M. (1988) 'Regulation or deregulation of the labour market', *European Economic Review*, **32**, pp. 775–817.

Robert M. Lindley

INSTITUTE FOR EMPLOYMENT RESEARCH (1989) *Review of the Economy and Employment*, Coventry, University of Warwick.

INSTITUTE OF MANPOWER STUDIES (1984) *Competence and Competition*: *Training and Education in the Federal Republic of Germany, the United States and Japan*, London, NEDO and MSC.

JARVIS, V. and PRAIS, S.J. (1989) 'Two nations of shopkeepers: Training for retailing in France and Britain', *National Institute Economic Review*, **128**, pp. 58–74.

LINDLEY, R.M. (ed.) (1981) *Higher Education and the Labour Market*, Leverhulme Programme of Study into the Future of Higher Education, Monograph no. 1, Guildford, SRHE.

LINDLEY, R.M. (1983) 'Active Manpower Policy', in BAIN, G.S. (ed.) *Industrial Relations in Britain*: *Past Trends and Future Developments*, Oxford, Blackwell, pp. 339–60.

LINDLEY, R.M. (1987) *New Forms and New Areas of Employment Growth*: *A Comparative Study*, Brussels, Commission of the European Communities.

LINDLEY, R.M. (1989) 'Fiscal Policy, Labour Market Strategies and 1992', Conference on 'Mercato del Lavoro, Disoccupazione e Politiche di Intervento', Rome.

OECD (1987) *Structural Adjustment and Economic Performance*, Paris, OECD.

OECD (1989) *Employment Outlook*, Paris, OECD.

PRAIS, S.J. (1989a) 'Qualified manpower in engineering: Britain and other industrially advanced countries', *National Institute Economic Review*, **127**, pp. 76–83.

PRAIS, S.J. (1989b) 'How Europe would see the new British initiative for standardising vocational qualifications', *National Institute Economic Review*, **129**, pp. 52–4.

SEO (forthcoming) *VOSTA, Voorrad — Stroommodel van de Arbeidsmarkt, Amsterdam, Stichting voor Economisch Onderzoek der Universiteit van Amsterdam.*

STEEDMAN, H. (1988) 'Vocational training in France and Britain: Mechanical and electrical craftsmen', *National Institute Economic Review*, **126**, pp. 57–70.

STEEDMAN, H. and WAGNER, K. (1989) 'Productivity, machinery and skills: Clothing manufacture in Britain and Germany', *National Institute Economic Review*, **128**, pp. 40–57.

9 Interventions in Market Financing of Training in the European Community

Keith Drake

Introduction

Between 1972 and 1986, real public spending on continuing training in France grew by a factor of 2.5 and expenditures by firms by a factor of 2.3 (BIPE, 1988:37). It is a common assumption among French planners that within twenty years or so, 10 to 15 per cent of working time will be absorbed by vocational training. The future is unlikely to be very different in the former Federal Republic of Germany (hereafter Germany), in Italy or the United Kingdom. Where such a large commitment of scarce resources is at stake, the choice of financing instruments to promote both internal and external (allocative) efficiency becomes a high priority policy issue.

That this choice is far more complicated than a straight choice between prices and taxes is evident from the case of Germany. There the 1970s and 1980s witnessed a fierce debate about the financing of vocational training (Hegelheimer, 1986). It ranged over the use of a large centralized fund to equalize training costs between employers (the Edding Commission's preference), various smaller funds to deal only with shortages, the use of collectively agreed sectoral funds, and mixed systems of financing by individual firms with a variety of tax concessions. This was part of a much wider and continuing analysis of markets and planning as alternative systems of allocation and control of the education system (Timmermann, 1985).

Elsewhere, training systems are so varied that comparison is difficult. For nearly twenty years France has laid strong training obligations on firms. With only two exceptions, the British have now all but abandoned the fairly minimal statutory collective funding by sector which operated up to the early 1980s. Indeed, the British have not merely resisted centralized direction on either the French (obligation) or the Danish (central fund) model, they have developed one of the most unregulated training systems in the industrialized world. Meanwhile the Dutch have been moving in the opposite direction to the British. They have been inventing new sectoral bodies managed by the social partners and are establishing a tripartite body of unions, employers and government to set training policy — just what the British invented in their Manpower Services Commission in 1974 and finally destroyed in 1988.

It is always important to consider where we might prefer to be and how to get there. But this chapter generally eschews re-analysis of the vast range of policy options which have been examined in countries like Germany and France. Uncovering the actual practice of training finance is difficult enough. This chapter reviews some of the findings of recent research into the financing of training in member states of the European Community. It focuses on experience with different kinds of instruments for intervening in what would otherwise be a market-financed process.

Analysis of Intervention Instruments

There is a strong interest among member states in each other's experience with different kinds of intervention instruments, whether legislative, regulatory or financial. Few are disposed to leave the volume, content and distribution of vocational training entirely to unregulated market provision. The assumption of this chapter is that countries stick to relatively long-term training strategies; that they modify policies more often as they seek to implement their strategy; and that specific interventions are best understood in terms of overall struc- ture — which reflects strategy. Some structural features are formal. For example, there are member states, such as Germany, the Netherlands and Italy, where the constitution itself is a major determinant of the way in which vocational education and training can be financed. Other and no less important structural features are often informal, for instance the processes whereby firms decide whether to train or not to train, whether to 'make or buy' training, and where to buy when they purchase it on the external training market.

Financial instruments are those devices and mechanisms, such as market prices, collective funds or training taxes, which are used to raise, allocate or spend training funds. It is training policy objectives, conditioned by experi- ence, which determine the introduction, use or abandonment of the financial instruments which not only control the flows of funds but help to determine which people receive training and what sort of training that is. The test of any financial arrangement is its consequences for training volume and content — who gets what training — and for who bears the cost of producing those benefits.

An Example

Denmark experienced a decline in apprenticeships in the 1970s, which contributed to a serious loss of training opportunities for a growing population of young people. The response to this crisis was to increase the number of

Table 9.1   Intakes to youth training in Denmark 1975 and 1984

	1975		1984	
	Number	% of cohort	Number	% of cohort
Upper secondary courses etc.	23,252	31	28,750	33
Qualifying examination courses at business and technical school	4,896	7	14,904	17
Apprentice training courses	14,997	20	14,204	16
EFG-Part 2 courses	2,021	3	20,724	24
Total	45,166		78,582	
Population of 17 year olds	75,000	100	87,400	100

Source: Sorensen and Jensen (1987) Annex 1, Table 2.

training places by establishing an alternative initial training route, basic vocational training (*Erhvervsfaglig Grunduddannelse* or EFG). With EFG, apprentice training begins one year earlier with a year at a tax-financed technical or business school. The second and largely on-the-job part of the training is broadly similar to apprenticeship but just less than a year shorter. Once the first year is completed the EFG-trainee is treated contractually and financially in the same way as an apprentice.

One set of financial arrangements — initial training financed out of her/his cash flow and at her/his discretion by the employer, who also paid the apprentice a wage — was thus superseded by a new arrangement. Under this, since 1977, the employer has been fully or partially reimbursed for wages paid to any apprentices or EFG trainees from a statutory central fund financed by all private employers, the Employers' Trainee Reimbursement Scheme (*Arbedjdsgivernes Elevrefusion* or the AER). At the same time, EFG trainees receive no pay from an employer or from anyone else during the initial year of in-school basic training and general education paid for out of public funds. However, the burden of their remuneration during the next two years is shared among all private employers through the same collective fund (Koefoed, 1984; Sorensen and Jensen, 1987). Insofar as this collectivization of training costs has helped to rebuild training opportunities which were disappearing under the previous market regime, it might be said to have succeeded. It was an important innovation (Table 9.1). Training costs were redistributed between training and non-training firms. The proportion of 17 years olds starting a course of alternance training (ie. one combining school and job-based elements) was increased from 23 per cent in 1975 to 40 per cent in 1984.

However, cost-redistributing central funds can have macro-economic distribution effects and consequences for economic structure which may not be so welcome. It would be naïve to argue that training outcomes should be the only effects to be considered in the selection of financing instruments. It is necessary, for example, to consider the effects of particular financing instruments on the structure of industrial costs, on competition and on the costs and benefits facing an individual who is making a decision about training.

Table 9.2   Funding sources for continuing training in Denmark, 1976–86
(per cent of total funding)

Training supplier	Funding source	Funding shares		
		1976	1981	1986
Public authorities	General taxation	26.5	20.3	22.2
Labour Market Training Directorate, Ministry of Labour	AUD	37.6	30.9	34.7
Trade unions and employer organizations, separately and through collective agreements	Multiple; mostly members' contributions and course fees paid by employers	18.9	14.4	12.6
External training suppliers	Fees	8.5	10.8	9.6
In-house company training	Employer revenues	8.5	23.7	20.9
All		100	100	100

Source: Hedegaard (1989) Table 1.

Ideally, in addition to identifying the training and non-training consequences of a given financing instrument, it is desirable to be able to show its quantitative importance. For example, Denmark's best known financial innovations of recent years are probably the AER (1977) and the AUD (*Arbejdsmarkedets Uddannelsesfond* or Labour Market Training Fund) of 1983. The AER and AUD exemplify a national fund solution to the problem of financing adequate levels of training. But it would be false to give the impression that these central funds — which use the same administration to collect and redistribute among firms the revenue from payroll-based levies — are *the* way in which training is financed in Denmark.

The AUD finances five types of labour market training, but is heavily concentrated on three of these schemes. Out of 40,368 participants on such schemes in 1987, 38,668 were on schemes for semi-skilled workers, skilled workers and workers on retraining and vocational preparation courses (Hedegaard, 1989, Table 3.1). Excluding those programmes provided specifically for the adult unemployed, continuing training in Denmark is classified into five categories according to the source of funding (Table 9.2). Labour market training schemes financed through the AUD-fund account now for a third of continuing training's direct costs. Labour market schemes were 90 per cent financed by general taxation from 1960 to 1983 (Hedegaard, 1989:57). The introduction of the AUD fund switched the funding source to a levy or hypothecated tax paid by all workers and employers, the income from which meets total expenditure. Nevertheless, Table 9.2 also shows that in 1986 the AUD fund met a slightly smaller fraction of total continuing training costs (category 2) than had taxation plus a 10 per cent contribution from the labour market partners in 1976. Indeed, the contribution of general taxation and the AUD fund (categories 1 and 2) fell from about 64 to 57 per cent, 1976–86.

Table 9.3   Estimated public spending on youth and adult education and training in Denmark, 1986

	DKr million	
	Youth	Adult
Apprentice and EFG programmes	2,200	
Qualifying examination courses	1,100	
Courses for semi-skilled workers		1,000
Courses for skilled workers		400
All	3,300	1,400

Source: Sorensen and Jensen (1987) Annex 4, Table 3.

The last three categories — whose funds are non-statutory and more market sensitive — rose from about 36 to 43 per cent.

Thus, in Denmark, pre-existing forms of financing through general taxation or the market were supplemented rather than supplanted by the two major financing innovations, the AER and the AUD. General taxation still has to bear a large fraction of all financial costs, especially for initial training and, within that, 1.6 million DKr to finance EFG teaching (Table 9.3).

The Dominance of Market Finance?

If full-time vocational education end-on to compulsory schooling is excluded, it may be that the bulk of spending on VET in the largest member states is financed through the market. That is to say, it is financed by employers providing their own training or buying in, or by individuals paying fees or subscriptions. At the moment, the data do not always show this. For example, firms and households are estimated to have financed directly only 39 per cent of the final 1986 spend on workers' vocational training in France (BIPE, 1988:38). But French investigators, like their German and Dutch colleagues, believe that official data tend to exaggerate the importance of public funding at the expense of direct funding by both employers and households. In Germany, firms and trainees together bore 88 per cent of the full costs of the dual system in 1980–81, the Federal Institute of Labour (jointly financed by employers and employees) 2 per cent, and central and local government a mere 10 per cent (Grünewald, 1984, figure 6). By 1988 nearly 70 per cent of each age cohort was being qualified through the dual system.

Three caveats should be entered. First, a partial or entirely financial-cost accounting would probably raise the figure for German public spending on the dual system towards at least a third share in its cost. At the same time, the German practice of full cost accounting (following the Edding Commission) means that around half of all training costs borne by firms are not reflected in

Table 9.4 Education and training enrolment rates for 16 and 17 year olds, 1988

	Minimum school-leaving age	16 year olds Full time	Part time	Total	17 year olds Full time	Part time	Total
UK	16	47	37	84	32	34	66
Germany	15	69	31	100	43	49	92
France	16	78	9	87	68	10	78

Note: % of each age group in education and training, including apprenticeships, YTS and similar schemes.
Source: TA (1989), Table 8.1.

budgetary expenditures, and a large fraction of trainee costs are also non-financial. Full cost is cost defined as 'a sum of money or equivalent expended in terms of material goods or services to produce a product or service' where the product is 'the passing on of the work skills required for the job in question to the trainee' (Noll et al., 1983:9).

Second, my reluctance to combine data from different countries in one table is due to the fact that most countries find it very difficult to stabilize the definition of training within their own data systems (BIPE, 1988). There are many difficulties. For example, boundary difficulties can be problematic, between general education and training, between on-the-job training and experiential learning, between initial and continuing training. It is tempting to tabulate data on 'apprentices' across, say, Germany, the Netherlands, the United Kingdom and Denmark. However, the same word — 'apprentice' — is used for very different activities and attainments from country to country. An apprenticeship in the Netherlands is now likely to average about two and a half years, against three to four years in Denmark, so there is a serious risk of producing more misinformation than illumination. The training statisticians are still struggling to produce useable comparative training data for the member states, without writing for each country in each table a short explanatory essay on the nature of the training.

Third, it is necessary to clarify what is meant by the shorthand 'market financing'. Radical differences between training systems have to be recognized. In France, there is a strong preference to carry out a very large fraction of initial training in full-time vocational institutions, whereas the Germans have an equally strong preference for part-time vocational schooling (Table 9.4). In France, unsurprisingly, a larger proportion of post-compulsory vocational education and training is tax-financed and a smaller proportion market-financed than is the case in Germany. The effect of such structural features on the degree of reliance on taxes or prices is not even limited to initial VET. The baseline for CET (continuing education and training) is initial education and training. In some member states a large part of CET has to compensate for deficiencies of initial education and training. An extreme case is Portugal. Over 80 per cent of the people have no more than six years of schooling. A large part of CET needs to be devoted to remedial secondary education for adults, delivered through the education system. This is financed by Portugese taxes and supplemented by those of other member states — the European Social Fund, whose contribution in 1987 reached 1 per cent of Portugal's Gross National Product (de Sousa, 1989:56). Even a large industrialized member state like the United Kingdom has this need for compensatory CET because of the inadequacies of its initial education and training relative to countries like France and Germany (Table 9.4).

Whereas structural idiosyncracies influence the relative shares of tax and market financing from country to country, the extent and nature of market financing is further clouded by the ambiguities which are caused by interventions themselves. It is probably true that, once people have left full-time VET, the market is either *the* most important or *almost* the most important means of financing subsequent training. But what does that mean? The distinction between public and market financing is not always a sharp one. In relation to continuing training in France, José Rose (1984:4) has remarked that 'the funds channelled by the 1971 laws may be seen as public as a result of their compulsory fiscal nature, or private in terms of their methods of allocation'. In Denmark the AUD is a public, statutory intervention in the process of allocating the resources of employers and of employees to training. Parliament annually decides the overall income and expenditure for the AUD. But target groups, volume, content and control of training are to a substantial degree still managed by the labour market partners, as was the case before 1983 (Hedegaard, 1989:58).

Though the distinction between public and private is often blurred in practice, market or non-tax financing, though less visible than legal enactments, remains a potent force. It is sometimes said that training within firms has little to do with market forces. In certain cases this may be true in the sense that an enterprise manages to operate a strong internal labour market, with long-term investment in training as a major component and with corporate benefit. But such training is exclusively financed from sales of the firm's products, its nature is sensitive to those product markets, and there may be very little influence on company training from public interventions. Far more often, however, company training is very sensitive to the external market for ready-made skills and the external market for skill-making, as well as to skill requirements feeding back from its product markets. The mere fact that in a given country only one-fifth of enterprise training is bought on the external training market is not evidence that the other four-fifths are either impervious to market forces or not being privately financed. Any firm's training, including the decision to train or not to train, is subject to the imperatives of that firm's strategy in its business environment. Market forces are market forces, whether they are direct or indirect.

For example, the argument about poaching in the United Kingdom is cast largely in terms of market phenomena: firms who poach skilled workers from other employers instead of training up their own employees put pressure on internal pay structures, which in turn discourages poached firms from investing in the training of those employees who are potentially most mobile on the external labour market. In the end, however indirect the connections, market financing encompasses all those modes of financing training which do not depend on tax money and are subject to the horizontality of market relations, rather than the top-down power relations which characterize interventions from 'above'. The more powerful the interventions, the less responsible are enterprises, households and intermediate organizations for training activities and outcomes.

Modes of Intervention

Interventions either bend or replace market financing of training. They can be located along a spectrum of four financing modes, the market-reliant, the market-regulating, the market-supplementing and the market-displacing. The *market-reliant* mode is the minimalist mode with respect to interventions. The only training that is supplied is that which is paid for out of non-tax funds, and legislative intervention is limited to that which is necessary to enforce contracts and maintain the efficiency of markets. The *market-regulatory* mode merely extends this legislative framework to produce more heavily regulated occupational markets and perhaps greater regulation of suppliers of training. The *market-supplementing* mode characteristically adds in tax revenues to subsidize either the supply of or demand for training. The signalling system of the particular market is still employed, but there is considerable interference with signals. Finally, the *market-displacing* mode is the mode of bureaucratic rather than market financing of training. The raising and allocation of funds is not as decentralized as it is in the market modes, and the bureaucracy (typically through manpower planning) replaces the market as the information system for matching needs to resources. Tax funds of one sort or another replace funds volunteered by firms, other organizations and households. This is the financing mode for a command economy of training; but, as in any command economy, market forces are not entirely absent.

Taken as a whole, the practice of national training systems enables us to position them towards one or other end of this spectrum. But every member state operates a mixed economy of training: all modes co-exist in any particular country. One way of analyzing the rather confusing practice of these mixed economies is to examine the characteristics and use of specific financing instruments. These instruments are very important operators within the market-regulating, supplementing and displacing modes. They can be conveniently classified into (i) legal instruments, (ii) those used to raise money, and (iii) instruments for allocating or spending money.

Legal Instruments

Legal interventions often affect the operation of the external labour market and especially the hiring practices of employers. For example, German firms quite often find it attractive to take on apprentices. But law and regulation prescribe that they can do so only if they hire a *Meister* to train the apprentices. So there is an incentive for firms to train up staff to *Meister* level or to hire a *Meister*. Legal intervention can boost demand for training. It can also change costs and benefits to training firms and to individuals. Legislation in France and certain German *Länder* gives workers training rights, and in both France and Germany pay is frequently related to qualification by law. The recent change in the legal status of Dutch apprentices from employees to trainees has made them much cheaper for enterprises to take on and increased the share of the full cost of apprenticeship which is borne by the apprentice.

But legal interventions with financial consequences take many forms. In all member states except for Belgium, Ireland, the United Kingdom and Denmark, membership of Chambers of Commerce is compulsory for all enterprises. The scale of Chamber involvement in local training activity, including Chamber training initiatives, is vastly different 'between the private and public law systems' (Platt, 1989). Platt contrasted the Paris and London Chambers. The first is compulsory for 250,000 members, with an annual income of £150 million, running thirty educational establishments and providing training for 8,000 full-time and over 25,000 part-time students a year. The second is voluntary, Britain's largest, with an annual income of £3.5 million and a training effort which, though growing, is quite negligible by Parisian standards.

Raising Money

Research into the financing of training provides many instances of apparent shifts in the balance of fund-raising between public borrowing, general and hypothecated taxation and direct spending from the cash flow of enterprises and households. However, the limited accuracy and coverage of financing data in almost all member states does not permit anyone to be definitive about the net trend of substitutions. In a given country, is it from taxes to prices or vice versa? It is easier to be sure about specific experiments than about the overall picture. A great deal of training is financed by enterprises, or suppliers of training to other people, offering a product, charging a price and using the sales revenue. The starkest alternative is to raise money by public borrowing or taxation and use it to provide training at zero money prices.

Public borrowing. In some countries, such as Denmark, Ireland and Belgium, the level of public borrowing as a percentage of gross domestic product reached a level in the 1970s where governments felt impelled to reverse the trend. Although public borrowing had been used to finance all types of public spending, and not specifically to finance training, the determination to reduce borrowing clearly pushed governments towards alternative intervention instruments. There was more use of general taxation to finance fire-fighting programmes than to provide training for young or adult unemployed. But otherwise governments resorted to dedicated taxes or increased and compulsory employee and employer contributions towards economy-wide training costs, administered through a central fund. The same impulsion sometimes led to renewed reliance on the funding of training services through the market.

General taxation. It is difficult to disentangle the role of general taxation in mixed systems of VET financing. Emergency programmes which are tax-financed are easy enough to identify. The problem comes with highly mixed mainstream vocational training, where elements like vocational schools are totally financed out of general taxation, there are special subsidies to promote certain programmes within an enterprise-financed component, and there are tax concessions all over the place (DES, 1988).

No better example exists than the German dual system, characterized by Hegelheimer (1986:78) as a 'varied system with diverse types of mixed private sector and public sector financing'. In the early 1980s the dual system took under 50 per cent of the age cohort straight from compulsory schooling in a given year but this proportion amounted to 65 to 70 per cent of the same cohort who eventually completed training. One of the great advantages of Uwe Grünewald's cohort approach to the analysis of VET financing (1984:1–14) is that it throws into sharp relief the interplay between public and enterprise financing. Of the 1979 school leavers who eventually completed training in the dual system, 68 per cent had proceeded directly from Secondary Level 1 to apprenticeship, where their off-site training was paid for by the *Länder* and their in-plant training and remuneration by the enterprises. The remaining 32 per cent had attended other courses before taking up in-firm training, mostly in vocational schools but about 3 per cent completing Secondary Level 2. All these had their pre-apprenticeship schooling paid for publicly, except the few (under 1 per cent) who went on courses provided by the Federal Institute of Labour and financed jointly from employers and employees.

The three financing partners of the dual system are: (i) those private and public sector employers who offer training, (ii) trainees or their parents, (iii) the public authorities. There are three kinds of public authority. The Federal government uses its taxes for promotion measures, especially in aid of those who find if difficult to enter the dual system, and to subsidize group training workshops. The *Länder* pay the running costs of vocational schools and for some promotion measures. Communes (administrative districts) provide some education and training establishments.

Since the contribution of public money to the full cost of the dual system remains relatively subsidiary (10 to 15 per cent), it was an essentially market-financed system which coped (between 1979 and 1983) with strains from the vagaries of the business cycle and of the demographic bulge, as Table 9.5 indicates. There was some queuing in the publicly-financed vocational schools, because, especially in 1981, firms did cut back somewhat on new training places and did not comfortably exceed the 1979 offer of new training contracts until 1983. But the role of tax-financed vocational schools was to give the largely market-financed in-firm training system time to cope. By 1987 the number of training places available exceeded the number of registered applicants, although there were serious supply/demand imbalances in certain sectors (CEDEFOP, 1988:28).

The dual system is primarily a market system. In financing terms, it has shifted slightly from the market-regulating towards the market-supplementing mode. The strains on the system from the mid-1970s to the mid-1980s illustrate the importance of co-determination and tripartism in regulating and managing the evolution of the system. There was a shortfall in company financing of training places. The eventual resilience of apprentice intakes was not due to a threat of Federal intervention in the form of a fire-fighting levy on firms under the 1976 Training Promotion Act. Even before the 1980 ruling by the Constitutional Court that the Training Promotion Act was unconstitutional, the Federal government declined to use this instrument for exceptional intervention. Yet the conditions to justify this almost certainly existed in the autumn of 1980, when the number of training places offered by employers fell by 8 per cent. There was always widespread agreement between unions, employers and political parties on the complete inadequacy of the instrument to meet the problem. By the early 1980s, annual Federal and *Länder* subsidies to the dual system had increased so much that in total they far exceeded the amount which could have been produced had it been legal to levy annually at the Act's rate of 0.025 per cent on the payroll of firms having twenty or more employees.

Hypothecated taxes and fund levies. Hypothecated taxes shade off into compulsory training fund levies. Some are clearly hypothecated taxes, for example the *taxe d'apprentissage* in France and the Youth Employment Levy in Ireland. Others produce a fund-managed revenue, such as the employer and employee contributions to Germany's Federal Institute for Labour or the far more important levies on private employers and then on private and public employers and on employees for the AER and AUD in Denmark. Nothing illustrates better the variety of response to a crisis in the provision for youth training than comparison of Ireland with Germany. The Irish response depended heavily on the introduction of the Youth Employment Levy and major use of the European Social Fund, married to general taxation. In the Federal Republic general taxation by central and local government started to play a larger, but still subsidiary, role. No new dedicated tax was used, nor was there much help from the Social Fund.

In the Netherlands, as in Denmark and the United Kingdom, the apprenticeship system suffered a serious decline in spite of injections of public funds.

Table 9.5 Trainees in the West German dual system 1977–87, and pupils in full-time school-based training, 1979–83

Year	Trainees in millions	% increase or decrease per annum	New training contracts	% increase or decrease per annum	New training contracts as % of 16 year olds	PVYs BVYs and full-time pupils[a] ('000)	% increase or decrease per annum
1977	1.397				55.1		
1978	1.517				61.4		
1979	1.645	+8.4	640.3	+6.4	62.1	446.7	+6.0
1980	1.716	+4.3	650.0	+1.5	61.9	461.5	+3.3
1981	1.677	−2.3	605.6	−6.8	58.7	493.0	+6.8
1982	1.676	−0.1	631.4	+4.2	61.6	526.2	+6.7
1983	1.722	+2.7	677.7	+7.3	68.9	537.6	+2.2
1984	1.800				73.9		
1985	1.831				77.7		
1986	1.805				85.5		
1987	1.739				84.7		
Growth, 1979–83 (%)		+4.7		+5.8			+20.3

Notes: [a] PVYs and BVYs refer to those in the Pre-Vocational and the Basic Vocational Training Year, full-time pupils to those in vocational schools.
Sources: Münch (1982) Table 13; Grünewald (1984) Table 1; Federal Ministry of Education and Science (1988) p. 52

The situation in the Netherlands is complex, changing and therefore difficult to establish clearly. But at least thirty-eight sectoral collective agreements and twenty-two company-wide collective agreements together applied to 1,800,000 employees by 1984 (Kraayvanger, Hövels and van Onna 1989:28). Nearly all these agreements included youth and continuing training, and many covered rights to paid educational leave. In 1984, twenty-nine of the thirty-eight sectoral collective agreements provided for training and development funds under bipartite control, financed by a payroll levy ranging from a few hundredths of one per cent to about 1.5 per cent. The Ministry of Social Affairs and Employment also contributes tax money to such funds and so subsidizes apprentice training (*ibid.*:30–31).

In the Netherlands these new collective funds were intended to double the number of apprentices, and in the metal, electrical engineering and some other sectors they quite rapidly did so. In 1985 there were in total around 35,000 in apprenticeships averaging about two and a half years, whereas there are now approximately 80,000. Many of the employers are now committed to increase training, and the metal and electrical engineering industry contribution to its training and development fund has increased annually from 0.2 per cent under the 1983 collective agreement to 0.9 per cent in 1987 (*ibid.*:40). The relationship between training financed through these collective funds and public spending on training is not easy to clarify. A 1987 survey of sectoral training programmes found that, of sectoral training organizations' revenue, 40 per cent came from course fees, 30 per cent from firms' contributions, almost 25 per cent in government subsidies, and 5 per cent from other sources. Amongst much else, it was not known what proportion of course fees was paid by firms and what by participants themselves (*ibid.*:39).

In practice there is a wide range of collective fund solutions. They start from the nation-wide statutory funds which both levy for their revenues and make grants to training firms (AUD and AER); pass to collectively-agreed sectoral versions with some tax support, as in this Netherlands example, and end with collectively-agreed sectoral or regional funds, without tax support, with very limited operations and purposes.

In the last group are the four collective agreement funds and the Chamber levies in Germany. Some German Chambers do have a training levy, but it is largely confined to financing special Chamber activities, like the maintenance of training workshops open to all member firms. Such a levy is merely a variation on the usual Chamber dues. In Germany some trade unions strongly favour a collectively-bargained vocational training policy, including those funds paid for by employers who are party to the collective agreement. They aim to influence the quality of in-plant training (micro-level) and the regional and national vocational training market (macro-level). However, the four existing funds — for the construction industry, horticulture and landscape gardening, stonemasonry and stone carving, and roofing and tiling — do not go as far as refunding to the levied firms the total costs of vocational training. Employer contributions are used chiefly to meet expenses incurred by firms for supra-firm training centres, especially during the first year of apprenticeship (Grünewald, 1984:18; Hegelheimer, 1986:50–54). Characteristically, Hegelheimer regards the chief advantages of such collectively-agreed funds to be: (i) the guaranteeing of training places is established by contract; (ii) the system does not bear the marks of a centrally planned economy, the partners to the agreement being independent of the state; and (iii) that, though there may be some equalization of the cost burden between firms, the decision whether or not to provide training facilities remains with the firms.

However, Hegelheimer also argues that collectively-agreed funds do not escape many of the problems of statutory central training funds. First, training levies for either type of fund have to be referenced to some yardstick which is relatively neutral with respect to the business cycle, but in practice use of payroll is difficult to avoid. Second, if payroll is the basis of levy calculation, it produces systematic distortion between capital-intensive and labour-intensive firms within the sector and a similar distortion between capital-intensive and labour-intensive branches of industry covered by different collective agreements on training funds. Arguably, the degree of distortion of competition will be greater with collectively-agreed funds than with a single national fund. Finally, a widespread use of collectively-agreed funds would produce differences in training for the same occupation in different geographical areas or branches of industry, thus limiting the mobility of labour geographically and between branches of industry — this in a country which insists on a high degree of uniformity of occupational and training regulations.

Allocation and Spending

Some studies, for example on Belgium (Leroy, 1984; 1988), show that once public funds have been raised, a large part may be transferred more or less out of central government control. So the intervention mechanisms at the level of allocation and expenditure become decisive for who gets training. In Belgium a dynamic labour market institution, the National Employment Office (ONEM), has played an increasingly active role in the continuing training of both the unemployed and the employed. In 1980 no less than 50 per cent of that Office's training expenditures took the form of transfer payments to households. Of course, transfers and related maintenance expenditures always tend to account for a rather high proportion of public spending. This reflects in the fact that financial compensation for the time cost of training tends to be a large part of the total (money plus time) costs.

In France the total public spending on continuing training in 1986 reached almost FF 70,000 million (i.e., roughly £7 billion; BIPE, 1988:32). Over 50 per cent of this spend went on allied costs such as trainee pay and exemptions from social security charges as well as connected activities such as training administration, trainee transport, accommodation and meals. The core funding of the training activity (direct costs, including pay of trainees) is reckoned to have been nearer to FF 30,000 million.

Control slippage. There are two points to be made here. First, when public funding becomes decentralized at the level of expenditure, control may slip. The original intervention objectives may not be so closely followed. Regional and/or cultural differences within one country can mean that the same legal provision, governed by public policy and a national scheme, has quite different outcomes for who receives training and what kind of training that is. For example, Leroy (1988) shows that since 1980 ONEM traineeships in the Flemish Community were more than twice as numerous as in the French Community. The Flemish Community had 50 per cent of the unemployed but 70 per cent of the traineeships. But the average spend per traineeship in the French Community was 2.5 times that in the Flemish. In this way one training scheme for the unemployed had two quite different sets of training and financial outcomes.

Of course, the training of the unemployed has to run largely on public money, whereas enterprise training operates in a market, and there are occupational training markets dominated quantitatively by the professions and their suppliers. But the control problem is quite a general one when public money is being allocated to regions or organizations. Some of the organizations demonstrate agency capture, especially where the employers come to dominate what is technically an organization run by the social partners — for example the Training Insurance Funds in France (Méhaut, *et al.*, 1982).

In France, following decentralization in 1983, the state transferred very wide-ranging powers over continuing vocational training, including responsibilities for apprenticeship, to Regional Councils. These Councils prepare a programme of schemes to be financed and then receive funds from the Regional Vocational Training and Apprenticeship Fund whose resources come from the decentralization appropriation which the State distributes among the Regions and the revenue from the tax on vehicle registration cards (BIPE, 1988:4). In addition to state financing of training through a raft of agencies like the Vocational Training and Social Advancement Fund and through the Regional Councils, French enterprises spend on training roughly double their legal obligation of 1.2 per cent of the payroll, including the use of joint agencies for the purpose of individual training leave and mutual societies approved for the purpose of vocational training by alternance. Funds come from European Community programmes. Further, as BIPE (1988:6) adds wanly, 'funds, for which there are few statistics, also come from Départements, Communes and households'. A big, complex and increasingly devolved system of interventions like that in France, is not easy to monitor for effectiveness, defined as the gearing of outcomes to objectives. As BIPE notes (1988:8), 'there are major shortcomings in existing measurement systems as regards the evaluation of the information genetrated by the continuing training system'.

The market components in a training system with mixed financing do have the benefit of feedback. The quality of that feedback can be quite seriously impaired when the time price paid by the buyer of VET is not 'received' by the seller, as it would be if the effective price was simply a single dimension, unsubsidized money price. Nevertheless, and particularly in the case of trends, the market feedback system is valuable for matching wants and resources. Despite extremely different training structures and cultural preconceptions, and despite devolution of decision-making to localities or social partners, German and French investigators (e.g., Tessaring, 1985; Paul, 1985) tend to express essentially similar reservations about the capacity of intervention systems to overcome the information problem of non-market allocation. After reviewing German experience of making and using manpower-requirements projections, Tessaring (1985:67) concluded that

> neither education nor labour-market changes occur independently, and they cannot be predicted without regard to political, social, financial and economic developments, which also need to be explained and projected. As long as this cannot be done (and it is doubtful whether this could ever be achieved), even medium-term projections will be subject to major error.

Flexibility. The second point concerns the inflexibility of some intervention instruments compared with that of their market counterparts. In 1987 nearly five million workers — which in France includes civil servants — took part in training schemes, and this is close on 25 per cent of the working population. Indeed, in the overall figures for all state expenditure on vocational training, trainee pay accounts for just under 45 per cent and the cost of courses for almost 55 per cent (BIPE, 1988:39). The difference between the state and enterprise figures for trainee pay may not be meaningful because of aggregation and comparability problems.[1] But the essential point is the massive size of this component in training expenditures in either case. Understandably, rates paid to trainees on public schemes tend to be standardized and are unlikely to reflect either occupational or regional variations. If a scheme is to elicit the targeted participation in high wage occupations or regions it will often be necessary to fix the standard rate above what is required in other occupations and regions. Since this item accounts for around two-fifths of total training expenditures the relative lack of flexibility in the state schemes may significantly reduce the number of people who can be trained with a given amount of money, relative to the number when trainee pay is more sensitively related to market variations.

It is a feature of the essentially market-financed and resilient dual system in Germany that trainee pay differs as greatly as gross cost according to occupation, and even within an occupation according to size of firm and, to a lesser extent, by region (Noll *et al.*, 1983; Grünewald, 1984; Hegelheimer, 1986). The difference between sectors is even larger for net costs than for total costs, and the variance between sectors is at its smallest in the case of trainee remuneration (Table 9.6). In a comparison of sectors, the costs are largely determined

Table 9.6 Average total costs, income generated by trainees, net costs and trainee remuneration per trainee for all training occupations by training sectors, West Germany, 1980

Training sector	Total costs (DM)	Income (DM)	Income as % of total costs	Net costs (DM)	Net costs as % of total costs	Trainee remuneration (DM)	Trainee remuneration as % of total costs
All occupations	17,043	6,754	40	10,289	60	5,954	35
Industry and commerce	19,442	6,995	36	12,447	64	6,782	35
Small crafts/trades	14,513	6,564	45	7,949	55	5,107	35
Professions	17,512	6,236	36	11,276	64	5,802	33
Public service	23,689	3,733	16	19,956	84	7,333	31
Agriculture	13,825	10,181	74	3,644	26	6,125	44

Notes: The data derive from a survey of 2,141 firms with trainees in the 45 most
heavily-frequented occupations requiring formal initial training. Around 75 per cent of
all trainees train for these occupations.
Source: Noll *et al.* (1983), Table 1.

by the revenues resulting from the trainees' contribution to production. As a percentage of gross costs this income ranges from 16 per cent in the public service to 74 per cent in agriculture.

Except for agriculture (44 per cent), the share of trainee remuneration in total costs always lies within the 31–35 per cent range. The flexibility of this single cost item, trainee pay, was illustrated by Noll and her colleagues when they showed that in the 1972–80 period net costs per trainee per year rose, on average, by 135 per cent in nominal and 33 per cent in real, terms. But, with the exception of the agricultural sector, all other sectors recorded a significantly lower growth of trainee remuneration than the growth of total and net costs. On average, the share of trainee remuneration fell in all sectors from 43 to 35 per cent. It was possible to have a decline in the cost of trainee remuneration which compensated for a pronounced increase in expenditure on training staff.

Reflections

There is, of course, no pure market. The Coase agenda is not to analyze market failure alone but to treat market and non-market failure symmetrically by comparing how well direct government provision and market provision work in practice. But any VET market needs a strong frame of regulation and property rights in order for it to exist at all. All that is feasible is to compare one corrective intervention with another within an ever-changing context which is already replete with public interventions. More acceptable is the spirit of the Coase agenda, that government interventions have a pathology no less common than if different from, the pathology of the market. Dertouzos and his colleagues (1989) have recently revealed the causes of America's industrial decline. Among these causes, and figuring large, were the short time horizons of managers and investors, poor schooling, lack of training at work and the way in which business and government, workers and bosses behave like adversaries rather than partners. This contrasts sharply with the 'shared fate' system of Japanese industrial relations (Morita, 1988:153). However, such macro-pathology comes in waves and is difficult to substantiate above the level of Delphic opinion. It may be better to avoid such issues and to concentrate on a few specifics from recent studies and on the questions which they provoke.

Market Failure?

There are some good non-externality grounds for regulating, supplementing and, in some cases, displacing the market as the means to finance training (Drake, 1983:42–51). Training for the unemployed must run on public money. It is arguable that there are other well-defined groups of people who are no less disadvantaged by the existing distributions of income and values. To leave their vocational education and training entirely to what they could buy on the open market is socially unacceptable. Deficiencies in the way that both training and labour markets actually operate also justify at least corrective interventions. But the kernel of the case for fundamental, market-displacing or market-supplementing public interventions in training markets is *not* that existing markets seriously undersupply vocational education and training because of these various imperfections.

The kernel of the undersupply argument is that even a society of perfect markets, in which all individuals had identical incomes and values, would still suffer from a less than optimal supply of training unless an omniscient government intervened to correct market failures. The proposition is that many forms of VET, for example Becker's completely general training, may be quasi-collective goods. They may yield benefits which spill over spatially, inter-sectorally and into the whole quality of life. This is not the place to address the important and intricate subject of the extent and nature of external effects from VET. But recent studies have thrown up a number of relevant points.

First, the evidence from France and Germany is that enterprises tend to increase investment in what they regard as 'their' areas of training quite as rapidly as governments do. In France, since 1977 the statutory contribution rate for continuing training has been at 1.2 per cent. But the percentage of the wage bill paid by enterprises has climbed from 1.35 per cent in 1972 to 2.34 per cent in 1986. Existing data show considerable inter-sectoral variation, with the outlay in some sectors running at up to 7 per cent of payroll. Although the growth in the rate of investment seems to be tailing off in firms with less than fifty employees, it continues to grow in medium-sized and large firms. There is a growing size gap since training outlay seems to grow with enterprise size, from slightly over 1.1 per cent for firms with ten to nineteen employees to almost 4 per cent for firms with at least 2,000 employees (BIPE, 1988:46). Moreover, enterprise investment has been outgrowing public investment in continuing training since the mid-1980s.

The French investigators' conclusions concerning existing data are that they not only exaggerate state funding but under-represent enterprise expenditures (by excluding everything except the training expenditures on the employers' tax declaration.) At the same time the data are held to under-represent spending by training suppliers operating chiefly with private funding (BIPE, 1988:39). This last undermeasurement fits with the universal scepticism about the 1.2 per cent which existing data show to be the entire share of French households in total annual training expenditure.

Nor is France alone in recognizing severe undermeasurement of human capital formation. Research in Heidelberg suggests that in German firms 50 per cent of continuing training actually appears in budget heads which have no obvious relation to training. German participation data show three in four individuals self-financing their continuing training. Maybe they do. On the other hand, some German employers pay fees gross and recover them from the Federal Institute of Labour; and most individuals surveyed in 1985 claimed to receive their training on schemes. It could be that they were ignoring some training by firms, just as the firms' training accounts do. Whatever the truth, there is a strong feeling among French and German researchers that investment in vocational skills and knowledge is being underestimated; and that it is probably the effort of enterprises and of households which is being systematically under-recorded. If there is undersupply, it could be less severe than the data suggest. The market could be financing more VET than is realized. Given the general superiority of public over private data systems, this seems to be the direction in which the error lies.

Second, countries where there is a strong current in favour of tripartism (social partners plus government) are nevertheless experimenting also with 'more market'. This is happening not only in Denmark; the Netherlands is also a case in point. On the one hand the Dutch are setting up their tripartite commission on national training policy and have a raft of sectoral funds managed by the social partners. Simultaneously, the Dutch government is withdrawing from both the financing and administration of much CET by five different routes. These are privatization; replacing open-ended by capped public budgets; enabling vocational training schools to bid for contracts and then manage their own finances; restricting publicly-financed part-time general secondary and pre-university education to subjects relevant to subsequent training; and increasing the personal financial contribution from trainees in line with the principle of consumer-paid services (Kraayvanger, Hövels and van Onna, 1989:68). Appropriately, one recent study focuses on 'training policy between market forces and regulation' (Hövels, Geurts and Van Wel, 1989). Government and market failure can co-exist, so it is not surprising that a shift away from market-supplementation co-exists with a shift towards increased market-regulation through collective agreements.

Third, the data reveal nothing of the strategic value of some investments. Administrative or market data — on what training costs to provide or was sold for — can be very deceiving as to the value of training unless we can believe that price is a reasonably accurate measure of value. Many managers and workers do not believe that. Most boards of directors believe that the value of the firm's assets is not reflected in the share price. Workers believe that the value of their labour is not reflected in their wage.

Unsurprisingly, system-wide studies encourage analysis of systemic interventions and of structural innovations. They draw attention to legislation, taxation and social security regulations. But this can lead to an underestimation of the importance of idiosyncratic interventions which lead to a new conception of the strategic role of training in business development. Western Europe has had sharp lessons in competitiveness from IBM mainframes, the Sony Walkman and Panasonic televisions. But IBM did not owe its climb to ascendency in mainframes to technological innovation or product leadership — those laurels belonged to other firms. It achieved commercial pre-eminence by becoming a completely marketing-orientated organization, where training was a key factor in implementation (Watson, 1963). Outside the great innovating firms, the role of training in commercial innovation is not always appreciated. Its value is certainly not captured by the data.

Japan's competitive success may be ascribed to its concentration on increased productivity by means of high rates of saving, investment and R&D; heavy investment in human resources by companies; and maintaining a demanding educational system. Continuing quality control and product flexibility requires a large education and training capacity to keep shifting people from lower to higher value-added market sectors. Maybe the profit-sensitive American and British companies too quickly abandon sectors which Japanese companies are making the subject of a fierce export drive and price cutting. To counter-attack successfully would require comparable resources and a willingness to use them to invest in market share at the expense of present profit (Scott, 1989:17; Morita, 1988:203–25). Of course, as Morishima points out (1982:175–6), in a group-oriented society with a total command of modern technology, the complete subordination of educational institutions, especially universities, to the needs of big business 'can easily release a menacing productive energy.'

Nevertheless, the personal reality behind the competitive success is leaders who put quality before price and enterprise training near the top of their own list of essential ingredients (Watson, 1963; Morita, 1988). At present there is no way of telling whether the training investments of French and German firms have the strategic significance and productivity in competitiveness — commercial value — that training has in IBM, Sony and Panasonic. The study of the financing of training is still the study of the financing of inputs or, at best, of an activity, not of commercial value-added.

Perhaps the problem is mis-specified anyway as undersupply of *training*?

There is some danger that the relative (if skewed) abundance of data on expenditures will lead people into the blind alley already overpopulated with City economists and British businessmen. These are the people who appear to think that money prices are the dominant criterion in economic decisions. City economists seem to think that price is the most, rather than the least important factor in international competitiveness. Businessmen talk as if firms and consumers buy largely on price. Both groups show a fine disregard for the overwhelming evidence that everyone does not buy the cheapest currency, car or meal.

Similarly with training. There is a powerful argument that financial cost data are the last data which should be collected. The priority question is what is being learned as a result of — or without any assistance from — training. It is necessary to know what is being learned, by whom and with what effects. Then is the time to set about indentifying the financial and non-financial costs of that learning; and of training insofar as other-person-organized planning, resourcing and management of the learning process is the way in which learning is best promoted.

At present, it is extremely unclear from most studies as to what is really being costed. Until that becomes more certain the users of such studies inevitably make assumptions derived not from the studies but from their own cultural and work experience. The first question is whether there is an undersupply of work-related learning. The second question concerns the extent to which any undersupply is best remedied by training.

Conclusion

In the end, public policy on training is about risk management. Governments set the legal and regulatory framework within which employers and individuals, in search of increased productivity or higher incomes, invest in skills. Governments can reduce investor risk by boosting employer demand for skills, subsidizing the supply of training, mandating corporate revenues, or collectivizing investment costs over a tax area, an industry sector or all employers and employees.

However, adequacy of training is a function not merely of quantity, but also of training quality and distribution. Even those European training systems which rely heavily on market-regulating and market-supplementing interventions leave a large discretion to employers and to individuals in deciding the nature of training. But these same regimes are predisposed to minimize risk by giving a strong steer in favour of broad-based initial vocational education and training. Much of the skill and knowledge content of their initial training is either transferable or provides a foundation upon which to add whatever specific skills the market and competitiveness require. In determining the volume, quality and distribution of training, no member state relies as heavily on the market as the United Kingdom. No country is as relaxed as the United Kingdom about both market failure and management failure.

Acknowledgments

The author gratefully acknowledges helpful comments and suggestions made by the editor, Uwe Grünewald and Ben Hövels.

Notes

1   If the unemployed and first job seekers are netted out of French figures on continuing training, then the remainder, the workers in jobs, accounted in 1986 for FF 65,000 million and transfers for pay and social security charge exemptions were a substantial item. Conceptually, BIPE (1988:14) prefers to define vocational training as 'an organised and evaluated transfer of knowledge to people who, on admission to this training, are considered to be workers, i.e., looking for or occupying a job, which explains why the term "workers' vocational training" is used.' Their basic education can be defined as 'all training aimed at non-workers whose studies have not been interupted' (*ibid*.:15). In practice this kind of definition is difficult to apply because financial data are not arranged within such boundaries. Overall growth is not in doubt since one worker in eight attended a continuing training scheme in 1974 and almost one in four in 1986. Nor were these all employees, since the working population includes the unemployed, some 30 per cent of whom attended publicly-financed training schemes. However, the French figures for continuing training include 220,000 apprentices, over 450,000 more on training schemes for young people aged under 26, who left school and looked for a job and, more surprisingly, over 500,000 young people on job placement programmes, 'the data for which, although not strictly speaking vocational training, are generally included in continuing training statistics' (BIPE, 1988:33). Most countries have similar data problems in practice, and anyway 80 per cent of the French people in training so defined were workers in jobs. It is just inter-country comparison which becomes extremely difficult under such conditions.

References

BIPE (1988) *The Financing of Continuing Vocational Training*, Bureau d'Informations et de Prévisions Economiques, Berlin, CEDEFOP, December.
CEDEFOP (1988) 'International comparisons — Problems, possibilities and limits', *Vocational Training*, **3**, pp. 18–30.
DE SOUSA, S. (1989) *Financing Continuing Vocational Training in Portugal*, Berlin, CEDEFOP.
DEPARTMENT OF EDUCATION AND SCIENCE/PICKUP (1988) *Tax Concessions for Training:*

A Review of Current Allowances in the United Kingdom and Eight Other Major Industrial Nations, London, HMSO.

DERTOUZOS, M., LESTER, R., SOLOW, R., et al. (1989) *Made in America*, Cambridge, MA., MIT Press.

DRAKE, K. (1983) *Financing Adult Education and Training*, Monograph 21, University of Manchester Department of Adult and Higher Education.

FEDERAL MINISTRY OF EDUCATION AND SCIENCE (1988) *Basic and Structural Data 1988/89*, Bonn.

GRÜNEWALD, U. (1984) *Financing and Promotion of Vocational Training in the Federal Republic of Germany*, Berlin, CEDEFOP.

HEDEGAARD, B. (1989) *The Financing of Continuing Training in Denmark*, Berlin, CEDEFOP.

HEGELHEIMER, A. (1986) *Financing of Vocational Training*, Mannheim, German Foundation for International Development.

HÖVELS, B., GEURTS, J. and VAN WEL, J. (1989) *Opleidingsbeleid tussen market en sturing* (Training policy between market forces and regulation), The Hague, OSA.

KOEFOED, E. (1984) *The Funding System for Vocational Education and Training in Denmark*, Berlin, CEDEFOP.

KRAAYVANGER, G., HÖVELS, B. and VAN ONNA, B. (1989) *The Financing of Adult Vocational Education in the Netherlands,* Institute for Social and Behavioural Studies, Berlin, CEDEFOP.

LEROY, R. (1984) *Funding of Vocational Training in Belgium,* Berlin, CEDEFOP.

LEROY, R. (1988) *La formation continue en Belgique*, Berlin, CEDEFOP.

MÉHAUT, P. et al. (1982) *Syndicats, Patronats et Formation*: *Les Fonds d'Assurance Formation de Salaries*, Nancy, Presses Universitaires de Nancy.

MORISHIMA, M. (1982) *Why Has Japan 'Succeeded'?* Cambridge, Cambridge University Press.

MORITA, A. (1988) *Made in Japan*, London, Fontana.

MÜNCH, J. (1982) *Vocational Training in the Federal Republic of Germany,* Berlin, CEDEFOP.

NOLL, I. BEICHT, U., BOU, G., MALCHER, W. and WIEDERHOLD-FRITZ, S. (1983) *The net cost of firm-based vocational training in the Federal Republic of Germany*, German original, Federal Institute for Vocational Training, Berlin, CEDEFOP.

PAUL, J.J. (1985) 'Forecasting skilled manpower needs in France: Concepts and methods' in YOUDI, R.V. and HINCHLIFFE, K. (eds) *Forecasting Skilled Manpower Needs*, Paris, UNESCO/IIEP.

PLATT, A. (1989) 'The UK's great disadvantage', *Financial Times*, November 7, p. 19.

ROSE, J. (1984) *Funding of Basic and Continuing Vocational Training: Trends in France during the Seventies*, Berlin, CEDEFOP.

SCOTT, B.R. (1989) 'Competitiveness: Self-help for a worsening problem', *Harvard Business Review*, **89**, 4, pp. 115–21.

SORENSEN, J.H. and JENSEN, G. (1987) *The Role of the Social Partners in Youth and Adult Vocational Education and Training: Denmark*, Berlin, CEDEFOP.

TA (1989) *Training in Britain: A Study of Funding, Activity and Attitudes*, Main Report, Department of Employment Training Agency, London, HMSO.

TESSARING, M. (1985) 'An evaluation of labour-market and educational forecasts in the Federal Republic of Germany' in YOUDI, R.V. and HINCHLIFFE, K. (eds) *Forecasting Skilled Manpower Needs*, Paris, UNESCO/IIEP.

Keith Drake

TIMMERMANN, D. (1985) *Educational markets or educational planning: A critical analysis incorporating two alternative systems of allocation and control and their implications for the educational system*, Mannheim, German Foundation for International Development.
WATSON, T.J. JR. (1963) *A Business and Its Beliefs: The Ideas That Helped Build IBM*, New York, McGraw Hill.

Part Four

VET and Labour Market Structure

10   Institutional Structures and the Provision of Intermediate Level Skills: Lessons from Canada and Hong Kong

David N. Ashton, Malcolm J. Maguire and Johnny Sung

Introduction

The aim of this chapter is to examine the delivery of intermediate level skills in Canada and Hong Kong with a view to establishing what lessons, if any, their experience may have for Britain. These two societies have traditionally relied on the market for solutions, although in the last two decades they have adopted different strategies in attempting to address the problem of intermediate level skills shortages. However, the strategies adopted involve different understandings of the nature of skills and so before embarking on a description of the routes followed we start with a brief discussion of the concept of skill.

The concept of skill and its function in the learning process has received relatively little attention in the academic literature although the processes involved in skill acquisition are starting to be investigated more systematically in the field of psychology. In educational circles there is still a clear distinction between the study of education, with its emphasis on personal development, and training, with its focus on the acquisition of specific skills or manual dexterity. Indeed, the Oxford dictionary defines skill as 'expertness, practised ability, facility in doing something, dexterity'; the emphasis being on practice or repetition and dexterity.

In order to move beyond such a narrow and restrictive conceptualization we distinguish three different ways in which the concept of skill has been used. The first and most commonly used is skill as manual dexterity or practised ability, which we refer to as routinized skills; the second is skill as the application of expertise or a body of theoretical knowledge, which we refer to as applied skills; and the third is skill as the ability to solve abstract conceptual problems, which we refer to as conceptual skills.

The idea of skills as practised ability for achieving concrete results is associated with the development of modern industry. The attempts of manufacturers to break down the tasks involved in the production process to their most elementary forms resulted in the highly specialized and fragmented division of labour we associate with mass production. It involved the training of the operative in a small number of elementary tasks at which they rapidly became proficient. Once acquired, the efficiency came from the fact that the action was performed in the same manner time and time again. For this reason we describe these skills as being routinized. They are typically, but not exclusively, found in the labour-intensive large batch and mass production industries.

The second type of skills are those which may also rely on manual dexterity but where their application relies on the internalization of a body of theoretical knowledge and its usage in variable contexts. It is for this reason that we refer to them as applied skills. The fact that they are applied in variable contexts from a given body of knowledge gives them another distinctive quality in that they are transferable across a range of jobs. Unlike the routinized skills, these skills are not tied to a specific technology but are constantly evolving with developments in theoretical understanding and in the techniques utilized in the practice of such skills. They are typically found in the various branches of construction, engineering, medicine and other professions, although they are by no means confined to such occupations.

The third type of skills are those involved in resolving problems at a conceptual level. They are the problem-solving skills which focus on the manipulation of abstract symbols, requiring the marshalling of evidence and the ability to think through a problem and to work out solutions to problems created by new situations and combinations of events.[1] Such skills are usually found in managerial, administrative and scientific occupations, but again are by no means confined to them.

Although these three types of skill are associated with different occupational groupings, they are conceptually distinct in that they can be combined in variable proportions in any one occupation. For example, Baran (1985) reports that the new type of highly-skilled clerical worker to be found in some insurance companies combined keyboard (routinized) skills with conceptual skills as their 'daily activity is centred around the comprehension and manipulation of abstract symbols'. Similarly, some craft occupations involve both conceptual and routinized skills. When we posit a relationship between a particular type of skill and a given occupation we are merely suggesting that a particular skill is dominant in that occupation.[2]

In addition to the types of skill we must also make a distinction between the various institutional forms through which skills can be transmitted. These distinctions are more well known and so need less elaboration. Within the educational system they refer to forms of general (academic) education as opposed to vocational education. Within the labour market the two major institutional forms are occupational labour markets and firms' internal training systems.

Educational institutions have traditionally been used to transmit both abstract, problem-solving skills and applied skills. General education, and especially higher education, is usually seen as the main agency for transmitting conceptual skills, the abstract, problem-solving skills which the acquisition of a degree is believed to confer, although there is no inherent reason why A-level learning experiences should not develop such skills. Moreover, given recent changes in the technological and organizational basis of industry, a great deal of accumulating evidence suggests that these skills are now required for jobs at the intermediate skill level (Ashton, Maguire and Spilsbury, 1990). The costs of producing such skills are notoriously difficult to recoup because of their character as 'public goods', that is goods in which all may share without diminishing the quantity available to others.[3] In policy terms the widespread provision of such skills has, so far, only been made available through further and higher education. The use of the educational system to transmit elementary applied skills in the form of vocational education has long been a feature of most industrial societies. In Britain this has been through incorporating vocational education into a predominantly 'academic' curriculum, while in other societies the vocational curriculum is more central. Here again, the costs of producing such skills are difficult to recoup because of their character as public goods.

Within the labour market, occupational labour markets are often associated with the transmission of applied skills, precisely because of their character as public goods. Such occupational markets can be unstable and require considerable institutional support if they are to function effectively (Marsden, 1986). Because of the transferable character of these skills, if training is left to a small number of employing organizations, these employers stand to carry the cost of training for the industry or occupation as a whole. Competitors who do not incur the costs of training can poach trained labour through the offer of higher wages precisely because of their lower costs. Thus, to ensure a continuous supply of skilled labour, the institutions which support occupational labour markets function to share the cost of training in transferable skills among the various parties involved. These institutions usually take the form of a regulatory body external to the firm, which functions to oversee and organize the funding of the training and to ensure that standards of performance are met. From the point of view of the firm, the employer loses control over the organization and structuring of the internal labour market as such workers come with a given set of skills which the employer then utilizes. This results in internal labour markets in which the hierarchical ordering of skill acquisition or progression are difficult to develop.

As labour market institutions for the provision of training, firms' activities or training systems take on a number of different forms. In some instances they may be confined to the provision of the routinized skills which are essential for the process of production. In other instances training may be provided as one component of an occupational labour market, while in others the focus may be on the provision of conceptual skills, often in the form of management training. Clearly some firms combine elements of all three. An alternative strategy is for companies to abandon any attempt to integrate training with occupational labour markets, by taking full control over their training activities and creating an internal labour market which, through the provision of job ladders or clusters, provides recognized avenues of promotion. These alternative strategies are not entirely a matter of choice, as whether a firm develops an internal labour market or integrates its training activities with occupational labour markets will depend on the characteristics of the national system of relations between the firms and the educational and training and industrial relations systems (Maurice, Sellier and Silvestre, 1986).

We now turn to the relationship between the types of skill identified above and the forms of institutional provision through which they are delivered. The first point to make here is that there is no one-to-one correspondence between the two. Theoretically we could specify a large number of possible relationships. In practice, however, routinized skills tend to be provided by employers because of their specificity in relation to the production process. There would be little economic or pedagogic value in public educational institutions providing specific task-related skills unless they form part of a more general applied type of transferable skill, as few school leavers would ever use them. Similarly, conceptual skills tend to be delivered through institutions of higher education because of their general transferable character and also because of the belief that such skills have a pedagogic importance in ensuring personal development. The greatest variability tends to occur in respect of the provision of applied skills, where, as we have already seen, they can be delivered through public educational institutions, occupational labour markets or firms' internal training provision. As the craft variants of such skills tend to form the core of intermediate level skills, they will be the focus of the rest of the paper.

The Canadian Experience

Although it is now characterized as a resource-based economy, Canada did develop a strong manufacturing base in the late nineteenth century. In 1900 it was estimated to be the seventh largest manufacturing country in the world (Laxer, 1989:11). The skilled labour required for this industry was largely made available by the waves of immigrants that constantly flowed into the country, primarily from Europe. Indeed, throughout the nineteenth century the supply of labour exceeded the demand and much labour drifted south to the USA. This set a pattern which was to continue throughout much of the twentieth century, whereby there was a reliance on immigrants to provide skilled labour for the country's industries.

The fact that Canada could rely on its immigration policy as a means of meeting the demand for skilled labour meant there were no strong internal pressures created for the development of forms of institutional provision to ensure a continuous supply of skilled labour internally. In addition, during the course of the twentieth century, the development of the primary industries and the growing domination of the manufacturing base by foreign capital (Laxer, 1989) restricted the growth in demand for skilled labour from the manufacturing sector. Thus there was little internal impetus for the creation of the sort of strong institutional structures which would have ensured a continuing supply of skilled workers from each new generation of young people.

European immigrants brought with them a knowledge of the apprenticeship system but this system was never established on a widespread scale (Weiermair, 1984). Moreover, trade unions, faced with the constant influx of immigrant labour, had little incentive to develop the apprenticeship system as a means of controlling the supply of and price of skilled labour. Elements of the British and European apprenticeship system did develop, especially in the manufacturing provinces of Ontario and Quebec, and later in Alberta, but it never achieved the same degree of importance that it achieved in the UK, either as a mechanism for ensuring the supply of intermediate level skills (Ashton, 1988) or as a means of ensuring, from the workers' point of view, a relatively high level of income and status in the labour market.

Where it has developed, the apprenticeship system has, not surprisingly, taken on a somewhat different institutional form to that found in Britain. Moreover, the form of provision also differs from one province to another and in the absence of strong support from either the employers or unions the provincial government, as in the case of Alberta, has had to play a prominent role. In Alberta it is a requirement that, in order to practise a designated trade, a person has to have completed an apprenticeship. Where trades are so designated the provincial government has established a board, usually consisting of major employers and employee representatives, to oversee the establishment and development of the curriculum and to determine the time taken to pursue the apprenticeship and the standards of achievement that have to be met. In 1987, out of a total labour force of just over one million, 3,788 completed apprenticeships. The trades with the most apprentices were in the construction industry (carpenters, electricians, plumbers), auto mechanics, beauticians and cooks. With only a very small manufacturing base and an economy reliant on the resource industries and the service sector, the dominance of the construction trades is to be expected. However, this example shows that where there is an internal demand for transferable applied skills, the provincial government has had to act and provide the requisite institutional framework.

Given that the apprenticeship system is variable in its existence across provinces and is fragmentary in its coverage of occupations within those provinces where it does exist, how do employers satisfy their demand for skilled labour? The answer, as one would expect in the absence of strong institutional supports for an occupational labour market (Marsden, 1986), is that they establish their own internal labour markets (Ashton, 1988). This means that, after being recruited, new employees enter the lower levels of the organization, where they may be given the opportunity to move up to more highly skilled jobs. This provides the employer with a period of months or years during which time the behaviour and potential of the employee, as well as those with skills acquired outside the organization, can be assessed.

Where the apprenticeship system has been established, as in Alberta, it has been incorporated into the firm's internal labour market in a way which is alien to the system in Britain. In Alberta, before people are accepted as apprentices they often have to complete a probationary period within the firm to establish their credibility. Thus, typically, the apprentices in Alberta are much older than their counterparts in Britain. The average age of an apprentice in Alberta is 24 and the majority are married.

In Canada as a whole, the absence of a strong tradition of industrial training by industry meant that there were persistent pressures on the educational system to include vocational education and training in the school curriculum. In the nineteenth century the publicly supported schools incorporated such subjects as penmanship, accounting and surveying into the curriculum. Despite later attempts by some school officials to adhere to a more classical curriculum, the incorporation of vocational subjects persisted throughout the twentieth century (Gaskell, 1989). The result is a high school curriculum which looks like the 'smörgasbord' or 'cafeteria' model described in the USA, where students select their courses from a variety of options, which includes both academic subjects (maths, science, English and social studies) and vocational subjects (carpentry, electronics, marketing, accountancy, etc.). There, the educational system has traditionally taken on some of the responsibility for preparing young people for the acquisition of intermediate level skills.

The Canadian system of training for intermediate level skills is not without its problems. While the educational system can provide a basic level of competence, in the absence of a supply of skilled immigrant labour the firm has to provide its own firm-specific training. Even where the apprenticeship system provides a crude occupational labour market, the relevant forms of certification are only valid within a single province.[4] This also means that the country has been heavily dependent on attracting skilled labour from other societies; a policy which has made Canadian industry vulnerable to political changes both at home and abroad which may affect the supply of skilled labour. At home the rise of nationalism led to demands for Canadians to be given priority for skilled jobs and calls to limit immigration. Abroad, it rested on the prospect of a continuous supply of skilled labour in other European societies. In the 1960s and 1970s, changes in both these spheres led to reductions in the flow of immigrants and hence in the supply of skilled labour. This coincided with a growing awareness of the need for Canada to upskill its labour force to meet the needs of technological change and the expansion of the information-based industries.

During the post-World War II period it became increasingly obvious that Canada required a more effective means of ensuring that it had an adequate supply of skilled labour at the intermediate and higher skilled levels. The economy was fast becoming one of the most highly developed service-based economies of the Western world. Indeed, by 1987 seven out of ten Canadians worked in the service sector (Gower, 1988). In 1986 only 16.4 per cent of the labour force was employed in manufacturing (Krahn, 1989). The small-scale apprenticeship system was providing skilled labour for the manufacturing and construction industries. Elsewhere, however, employers did not have the institutional structures with which to enhance the flow of skilled workers to the service sector. However, the educational system had a tradition of supplying high school and college graduates with a combination of academic and vocational skills.

The political response was to expand the educational system, especially through the provision of higher education (Porter *et al.*, 1982). The result was that by 1986, 22.4 per cent of the adult Canadian population possessed some post-secondary educational credential (Krahn, 1989b). This expansion of educational provision has also been associated with an increase in the period of time young people stay on within education to complete their high school graduation at the age of 18. In 1986–7, 90 per cent of 14 to 17-year-old Canadians were enrolled in an elementary or secondary school (Krahn, 1988). Studies of young people's attitude towards school reveal a high level of commitment on the part of Canadians to the educational system (Gaskell, 1989). They are keen to stay at school. This commitment has been reinforced by the recruitment policies of employers, who are increasingly demanding high school graduation as a condition of entry to the 'good' jobs.

In general terms the political response to the problem of the skills shortage has been to rely primarily on the educational system to enhance the supply of conceptual and elementary applied skills. The emphasis has been on preparing young people and young adults with a broad basic education which includes both academic and vocational skills. While the skills acquired through vocational education may or may not be directly used in their eventual employment,[5] they do, together with more academic training, provide young people with competences in general problem-solving skills. This has been supplemented in provinces such as Alberta by an attempt by the government to develop the institutional supports necessary for a limited number of occupational labour markets to develop.

Associated with the growth in participation in education has been a second, and perhaps unintended, feature of the Canadian system of preparation for work, namely the incorporation of paid work experience with ongoing education. This has occurred in two ways. First, further and secondary education has been extended in such a way that it accommodates to students' needs for the income from part-time work experience, as well as the desire of some of those in full-time employment to further their education. For example, college and university terms have been designed in such a way that they provide for an extended period of paid work experience in the summer vacation, while short summer courses enable those who wish to take up paid work for longer to maintain their educational progression.

Second, there has been a growing propensity on the part of Canadian youth to move back and forth between education and paid work until they are 'settled' in an occupation. This has recently been vividly illustrated by the results of a longitudinal study of high school and college graduates in three Canadian cities, which found that 68 per cent of high school students and 62 per cent of university students had held a paying job in the course of their previous year's education (Krahn 1989a). For those in Canadian secondary and higher education, experience of paid work is the norm. A second and distinctive finding of this research was the high proportion of young people who, on leaving full-time education, either continued on in education after high school or university on a part-time basis, changed programmes or schools, or dropped out of education for a period of time only to return later. In short, the picture that is painted of the preparation for work is one of a blurring of the distinction between educational experience and work experience. What emerges is a picture of a continuous and almost parallel process of movement through both the educational system and the labour market as young people seek to establish themselves in a career and as employers seek to recruit the products of such a system into their internal labour markets.[6]

In such a system the role of the Federal Government's training programmes are marginalized. The enhanced skill levels of those eventually leaving the educational system provide employers with recruits capable of rapidly acquiring the intermediate and higher level skills. Where necessary these are supplemented by the actions of Provincial Governments in providing the institutional framework necessary to ensure the supply of applied skills. Federal Government training schemes, such as the Canada Jobs Strategy, then focus primarily on establishing provision for groups for which mainstream provision has failed, such as, high school dropouts, and native Canadians or for groups for whom it was never intended to cater, such as women who are returning to the labour market. Significantly, Federal Government intervention is also targeted at students and provides subsidies to employers to encourage them to recruit students for short-term summer jobs. Given the high level of general education and inculcation of problem-solving abilities, there has been little need for the Federal Government to intervene in an attempt to restructure the basic provision of training as has occurred in Britain.[7]

The Hong Kong Experience

Although a latecomer to the ranks of the industrial nations, Hong Kong is often seen as an outstanding example of what can be achieved by the free play of market forces. With few exploitable natural resources it has achieved rates of economic growth higher than those of the Western industrial societies and now has a level of GDP per capita that is the second highest in Asia after Japan (*Financial Times*, 29 June 1989).

As recently, as 1931 Hong Kong had a population of only 880,000, which rose to 1.6 million at the outbreak of World War but was reduced to 600,000 in 1946. However, immigration from China and economic growth increased the population to 2.5 million by the end of 1955 and to over 5 million by the 1980s. In 1987 it had a labour force of 2.7 million. The early growth of the post-war economy was based on the manufacture of clothing and textiles in the 1950s and subsequently plastics and electronic goods in the 1960s.

In the 1970s the economic situation facing Hong Kong started to change significantly. On the one hand, Hong Kong's relative advantages in manufacturing were gradually eroded. This was due mainly to continuous increases in land and labour costs (although manufacturing still employs 40 per cent of the labour force). Countries like Korea and Taiwan were gaining ground rapidly. On the other hand, the first 'oil shocks' gave rise to protectionism in the main export markets, namely the USA and the EC. All this signified that the days of low-cost high-volume production were numbered. Industrial diversification, and in particular the growth of financial and business services, was seen as the answer by both government officials and business leaders.

Since the early 1970s this change in direction has been reflected in a significant proportion of low labour cost manufacturing being relocated to the Chinese mainland, where Hong Kong entrepreneurs now employ two million workers. It has also been reflected in attempts to upgrade products and to move into new, more sophisticated markets. However, one of the major changes associated with it has been the growth of business and financial services and the subsequent emergence of Hong Kong as a major international financial centre.[8]

Changes of this magnitude inevitably have very important implications for the structure of education and training. The Hong Kong system of education and training, like that of Canada, has some of its origins in the British experience, but, unlike in Canada, the Hong Kong system has been directly influenced by post-war developments in Britain. The educational system is partly modelled on the British system of primary and secondary education. Six years of primary education is followed first by junior secondary education, after which young people are free to leave school at the age of 15, and then by senior secondary education. Secondary schools are of three types, grammar, technical and pre-vocational. In the British tradition, the emphasis in the grammar schools is on the academic curriculum, whereas the technical schools are meant to have a stronger practical component, as they were in Britain. However, the distinction between the two is narrowing as many grammar schools now include practical subjects in their curriculum. The pre-vocational schools are distinguished by the fact that almost half the curriculum is devoted to practical subjects. In practice the system is dominated by the academic grammar schools which comprise 390 of the 425 schools in the public system, with technical (twenty-two in number) and pre-vocational schools (thirteen in number) providing a small alternative sector (Cheng, 1986).

The main difference between the Hong Kong and British systems is the deliberate attempt to separate both the organization and funding of mainstream technical education, especially that technical education which is geared towards the training of craft workers and technicians, from that of academic education. Vocational training, and the technical colleges and training centres which deliver it, are under the separate control of the Vocational Training Council (VTC). These institutions are totally devoted to the provision of technical and vocational education and do not provide any 'academic' courses. This has important implications for the effectiveness of provision and for enhancing the availability of intermediate level skills. Professional and technologist training is generally left to the polytechnics and universities, although the VTC does attempt to influence it through the Management Development Centre and the Engineering Graduate Training Scheme.

Apart from the provision made by government, traditionally, relatively little training has been conducted by employers on a formal basis in Hong Kong (Ng, 1987).[9] In the manufacturing sector, the typical firm has been and remains relatively small; for example, in 1980, 92 per cent of establishments employed fewer than fifty people (Lin and Ho, 1982). In these circumstances training was a question of learning by doing. In the words of the Director the VTC, 'In the early era of industrialisation, organised industrial training generally was non-existent, except in a few of the larger concerns and government departments' (Knight, 1987).[10] In part, this was no doubt a consequence of the labour intensity and low skill content of the jobs in the industries on which Hong Kong's early success as an industrial producer was built. However, even with such industries, skill shortages were apparent and in the 1960s the government appointed the Industrial Training Advisory Committee (ITAC) to identify training and related problems and make recommendations. The work of this body laid the foundations for the government's response to the training problems encountered in the attempt to diversify the economy and upgrade the skills of the labour force that took place in the aftermath of the 'oil shocks'.

The reaction was to upgrade both the general level of education and, in particular, the level of technical education. Vocational education and training became an integral part of Hong Kong's new economic policy (Hong Kong Government, 1979). In 1982 the Vocational Training Council was created under the direction of Horace Knight to oversee all aspects of manpower policy, including industrial training. There followed a concerted attempt to improve the general level of education and to increase opportunities for higher education, or, in the terms used above, to increase the supply of conceptual skills. However, the main thrust of the policy, given the large manufacturing base, was to create a new infrastructure which would ensure an outflow of young people trained in transferable occupational skills.

The Advisory Committee (1965–72) had identified a number of problems in the delivery of intermediate and operative level skills. Among these were the following: the lack of reliable information on future manpower demands;

the lack of accepted standards or criteria for measuring the skills required for the principal jobs in all industries; a lack of technical education and training facilities; unwillingness on the part of employers to undertake training and the need for effective coordination of the training effort (Knight, 1987). By the end of the 1960s Hong Kong had a technical and educational infrastructure which was typical of that found in developing countries; 'an infrastructure for training generals but not soldiers or even NCOs. As the findings of the first manpower surveys conducted by the ITAC indicate clearly, the infrastructure was totally at odds with the needs of industry and inadequate for meeting the needs of Hong Kong's industries for craftsmen and technicians' (Knight, 1987). Steps were taken to remedy these deficiencies with the establishment of the Hong Kong Training Council in 1973 and intensified with the establishment of the VTC in 1982.

The main thrust of the policy was to identify the future demand of employers for intermediate level skills in particular, and to set up a series of technical institutes and training centres capable of producing sufficient numbers of trained (young) workers to meet that demand. Apprenticeship training was regulated by the 1976 Apprenticeship Ordinance, which required employers to enter into a contract of apprenticeship when engaging a person aged 14 to 18 in a designated trade. In 1987 this system produced 4,900 apprenticeship agreements. Technical institutes, of which there are now eight in operation, represent the main thrust of the strategy, providing a total of 12,600 full-time places (5,600 craft and 7,000 technician), 32,000 part-time day places and 32,000 part-time evening places. These institutes are financed by the VTC and only provide vocational training. This means that, unlike the case in British technical colleges, the heads of such organizations are not torn between the demands of some students for academic courses leading to higher education, and the demands of employers for technically competent workers. The principals of technical institutes are unambiguously concerned with meeting the needs of the local labour market. Morever, they are guided in that task by the outcome of the biannual manpower surveys. The institutes provide, in a well-resourced environment, the theoretical off-the-job training required for technician and craft courses leading to BTEC and similar qualifications.

The main responsibility for industrial training lies with the nineteen Training Boards and seven General Committees. The training boards, which are similar in principle, if not in operation, to those established in Britain under the 1964 Industrial Training Act, cover specific manufacturing industries, such as clothing, electronics and plastics, and service industries such as transport, wholesale and retail distribution, hotels and banking. The majority of members are usually prominent employers, together with representatives of workers, educationalists and government officials. They rely for their direction on a strong input from employers informed by the permanent staff and the results of the bi-annual manpower survey. The general committees cover training areas which affect more than one sector of the economy, such as management training, apprenticeship and trade testing and precision tool training. Each of the training boards is responsible for determining the manpower estimates for their sector and for making recommendations on how training needs should be met (VTC, 1988). Manpower needs are estimated through the use of a biannual manpower survey which focuses on two areas: the existing employment structure and future manpower requirements. Practical training for the industry or sector in both craft and routinized skills is delivered through a series of training centres, of which sixteen were in operation in 1988, in such areas as plastics, electronics, hotels, etc.

Apart from that for two of the Training Boards, all the money for running the system of training comes from government revenues. The exceptions are the two earliest boards, those responsible for construction and clothing, which finance their activities from a general levy. The income from the levies cover the building, equipping and maintenance of the training centres. Problems of devising suitable levies for the other industries led the government to step in to fund the later boards.

There is little doubt that the Hong Kong government has achieved considerable success in devising a set of institutional structures capable of enhancing the delivery of the intermediate level skills necessary for it to compete with its rivals among the new industrial countries. The separation between academic education and training is almost complete and this, together with the development of the training boards and their associated courses and training centres has enabled the system to respond rapidly and accurately to the needs of the labour market.[11] As in the Canadian case, the system is not without problems. Ng (1987) argues that there is a danger that the theoretical training provided by the technical institutes is biased towards Western practices and is providing a general training in occupational skills geared to the needs of the public service and large-scale monopolies rather than the small businesses which make up such a large part of the economy. This suggests that there may be room for further improvement in the system. Moreover, Hong Kong still has a training problem in that it is losing many of the workers with intermediate and higher level skills because of the 'brain drain', but the establishment of the training infrastructure has made a major impact on the relationship between education and industry. It has established a series of pathways from school to work leading to the acquisition of transferable occupational skills. In addition, it has taken the ideas contained in the British proposals for Industrial Training Boards and used them to underwrite the costs of creating occupational labour markets for intermediate level skills.

Lessons from the Canadian and Hong Kong Experiences

At first sight it may appear that the histories and present circumstances of the two societies are such that they can have little to offer Britain. Canada is a mature advanced industrial society, while Hong Kong is a new industrial society still in the early stages of industrialization. In addition, there are numerous cultural differences which could be cited. However, there are also compelling reasons why we should pay attention to their experiences. Both faced the need to come to terms with new forms of global competition, and, in response, both societies, like Britain, are attempting to upgrade the quality of their labour forces at the level of intermediate and higher skills. In response to this challenge they have adopted different measures. From a theoretical stand-point they provide fascinating examples of the implications of choosing one route rather than another. A further reason for studying them with regard to the problem of intermediate level skills is that both have been influenced by the British tradition and in this respect are closer to Britain than many of Britain's partners in Europe.

The position of Britain in relation to these case studies is that, after a long experience of support for the delivery of applied (craft) skills, first through the establishment of the apprenticeship system and later in the attempts to pro-vide institutional support for occupational labour markets through the Indus-trial Training Boards, public support for this approach to the problem is being withdrawn. This means leaving the provision of training in the hands of individuals and employers, who are expected to fund the full cost of training. The only exceptions are the costs of the Youth Training Scheme and Employ-ment Training. Yet neither of these schemes is exclusively devoted to training. Both have dual functions, providing some training but also acting as a measure to relieve unemployment. Increasingly, Britain is moving to a position where the full cost of training is to be carried by either individuals or employers. The decentralized delivery of the two main national programmes, should they con-tinue in their present form, is unlikely to alter this scenario. As the problem of youth unemployment has receded in the more affluent parts of the country, the marginal foothold which YTS has secured in the labour market has been revealed, as employers have opted out in favour of a policy of direct recruit-ment to jobs which often offer little or no training. Meanwhile the scheme continues to perform the function of reducing the level of unemployment in the depressed regions. The administration of such schemes by employer-dominated TECs will not change their fundamental character or address the problem of skill shortages at the level of intermediate skills.

The Canadian experience offers one alternative, which is for the govern-ment to rebuild the institutional supports necessary for providing intermediate craft skills for those industries which still rely on the transferable skills pro-vided through occupational labour markets. For the majority of firms and industries, however, this strategy may be inappropriate. For them, instead of relying on these old mechanisms, the emphasis could shift in the direction of enhancing the provision of general conceptual problem-solving skills through the establishment of a broad-based curriculum which included both academic and vocational courses for all pupils. This would require a number of changes, on the part of both government policy and the attitude of the working class towards education.

Government policy could encourage the expansion of educational provision and the incorporation of vocational education centrally into the curriculum. To be effective this policy would require changes in the examination system, and especially in the age at which educational certification is achieved. In particular, it would mean ending certification at the age of 16 in order to encourage youths to stay on at school and develop the problem-solving skills required by employers recruiting for jobs demanding intermediate level skills. It would also require changes in areas outside the direct control of the government, notably in the attitudes of the working class towards education. When compared with Canadian society, it is clear that the distrust of education and the low value placed on it by many working-class families are products of the British class structure.[12] Moreover, as we move towards an economy with a high knowledge base component, such a cultural heritage is likely to provide a major obstacle to economic growth, unless action is taken to counteract it. It may be that the introduction of a more relevant curriculum could act as a catalyst in bringing about a change in the attitude of working-class youth.

Given the speed of industrial and commercial change and the difficulties of predicting future skill requirements in advanced industrial societies, this policy would have the advantage, as has been evident in the Canadian experience, of producing a labour force that is adaptable and willing to move between educational institutions and the labour market to acquire the necessary skills. It could then be left for the employers to adapt the products of an extended educational experience to their firm-specific skill needs and the demands of the internal labour market. Indeed, as the institutional structures associated with the apprenticeship system diminish in significance, firms will have greater freedom to develop internal labour markets similar to those which characterize Canadian and American organizations. Such a strategy would mean that as resources are devoted to building a strong base of conceptual problem-solving skills among those entering the labour force, government schemes could then be left to focus on the needs of specific groups rather than attempting the dual function they perform in Britain.

The Hong Kong experience offers an equally interesting alternative strategy. It suggests the possibility of rebuilding the institutional supports to sustain and carry the cost of maintaining the occupational and industry-specific training necessary to deliver the requisite skills. It would mean developing effective instruments for identifying, as far as possible, the current and short-term demand for intermediate level skills. The bi-annual surveys and their input into the Hong Kong training boards have shown how this can be achieved. Institutional provision could then be directed at ensuring a sufficient supply of people with appropriate skills to meet the demand. Here again, important lessons can be learnt from Hong Kong. If this route were to be taken, then the task is to build up a set of institutional structures which can transmit those skills in an efficient manner. In rebuilding these structures the Hong Kong experience suggests that two conditions should be met. One is the need to develop a system of Training Boards in which the bureaucratic administration is minimized and employers and workers' representatives occupy dominant positions. Additionally, the Boards should control the provision of all aspects of the training and have a substantial influence over the provision of the theoretical component of training. This means ensuring that technical training is provided in institutes which are exclusively devoted to the transmission of technical information and so do not have to balance the demands for technical training against those of an academic education. In practice the training authorities would be handed financial control over technical education.

The second lesson is that training measures should be kept separate from those designed to alleviate unemployment. In the same way that the technical institutes in Hong Kong respond quickly and unambiguously to the signals from the labour market, because they are exclusively devoted to the function of providing training, so too does the rest of the training system. By contrast, in Britain, the development of training schemes which have the dual function means that such schemes cannot focus exclusively on either function. As a result measures may enhance one function, while hindering the other. Events in Hong Kong have shown that the development of institutional structures for the exclusive transmission of intermediate level skills can deliver a rapid increase in such occupational and industry-specific skills. If, however, the delivery and transmission of those skills is hindered by budgetary and temporal restrictions, imposed because such schemes also have to cater for large numbers of the unemployed, then this is bound to affect the process of training adversely.

One final lesson from Hong Kong is that centralized delivery of occupational and industrial intermediate level skills can work under different systems of funding, in this case from both central government funding and the levy system. Moreover, in the absence of a high level of general education to provide the problem-solving skills necessary for effective job-specific training at this level in internal labour markets, such centralized delivery may be essential. Because of its small geographical size, delivery through one central location is an obvious strategy for Hong Kong. In Britain, with the geographical dispersion of its industry, such a highly centralized system would require modification. In this respect the local TECs, under the supervision of a central agency, could provide for effective delivery at the local level. The proviso is, of course, that such bodies should be exclusively concerned with the administration of training.

Conclusion

In this brief chapter we have sought to outline two contrasting solutions to the problem of delivering intermediate level skills. We are not advocating the wholesale adoption of one or the other. Differences in political arrangements, class structure and cultural heritage would preclude that. Rather, we offer them as contrasting models with which to inform the debate in Britain on the direction in which policy could move. The Canadian model points to the possibility of moving towards the eradication of the distinction between academic education and vocational training and creating a system for the delivery of high level problem-solving skills to the mass of the population. This would be supplemented by the rebuilding of institutional support for those areas where occupational labour markets remain the most effective way to resolve the problem of supplying applied skills. However, the main policy thrust would be to provide a broad base of conceptual skills, thereby leaving industry and the individual with considerable autonomy with regard to how those skills are developed. An alternative is to maintain, or accept the maintenance of, a rigid division between general education and training and rebuild a series of institutional structures that will ensure the effective delivery of occupationally-specific skills.

In this article we have not advocated one or the other. Indeed the two should not be seen as mutually exclusive. However, we would point out that, at the moment, Britain appears to be dismantling the structures previously developed to deliver intermediate level skills without replacing them with any meaningful alternatives. As the Training Boards lose their powers, the only institutional structures left are the TECs, whose powers are confined to delivering schemes which, as presently constituted, are somewhat marginal to the task of securing an adequate supply of intermediate level skills. Similarly, if the division within the educational system between academic and vocational education is maintained and post-16 participation rates in education remain low, then the prospects of the educational system delivering the kind of problem-solving abilities which employers require as a basis on which to teach firm-specific intermediate level skills is not good. We hope this chapter has shown that there is no shortage of ideas on how these problems may be overcome.

Acknowledgments

The authors wish to thank Paul Ryan for his critical comments on an earlier draft of this chapter. His remarks have greatly improved the presentation of our ideas.

Notes

1 Marquand (1989) provides the discussion of the significance of problem-solving skills in enhancing the individual's ability to learn which informs this section of the chapter.
2 Although the occupations with which the three types of skills are associated are hierarchically ordered in the labour market, this does not necessarily mean that

the skill types are also hierarchically ordered. The relationship between these three types of skill is more complex than that implied by a simple hierarchical ordering. Routinized skills were created by the decomposition of the craft variant of applied skills but in this process new skills of manual dexterity were developed. This implies that applied skills are more complex, involving the use of abstract theories and hypothesis formation to test possible modes of action. But this greater complexity is also a feature of conceptual skills. The major difference between applied and conceptual skills is that the latter are used independently of any given theoretical body of knowledge.

3 For a discussion of the problems of evaluating the financial and economic returns to different types of skill, see Ashton, Green and Hoskins (1989).

4 Discussion between some of the provinces is currently under way to resolve this problem.

5 For a discussion of the relationship between the experience of vocational education and labour market destinations, see Gaskell (1985).

6 In this process, the rigid distinction we have adopted on the basis of the European experience between intermediate and advanced higher level skills is also blurred.

7 We are not arguing that Canada has solved all the problems of training provision. What it does have is an effective, publicly-funded infrastructure. There remains a problem of training attributable primarily to the reluctance of individual firms to invest in training.

8 Another major change in the economy has been the growing involvement with Communist China associated with which has been a massive increase in trade between the two economies, increasing by 1,105 per cent since 1979.

9 Ng argues that the acceptance of public responsibility for industrial training, in addition to their previous provision of technical education, was in part a response to the recommendations of a panel of OECD educational advisers who visited Hong Kong in 1982 (Ng, 1987).

10 Much of the account presented here of the Hong Kong system of training is based on the paper by Knight (1987).

11 There are some exceptions, for example, during 1988 the doubling in the number of hotels being constructed led to demands for hotel workers which could not have been foreseen and which could not be met from the output of the training centres.

12 This is discussed more extensively in Ashton and Lowe (1990).

References

ASHTON, D.N. (1988) 'Sources of variation in labour market segmentation: A comparison of youth labour markets in Canada and Britain', *Work, Employment and Society*, 2, pp. 1–24.

ASHTON, D.N., GREEN, F. and HOSKINS, M. (1989) *An Overview of the Evaluation of the Net Benefits of Training*, Sheffield Department of Employment, Training Agency.

ASHTON, D.N. and LOWE, G.S. (eds) (1990) *Making Their Way: Education, Training and the Labour Market in Canada and Britain*, Milton Keynes, Open University Press.

ASHTON, D.N., MAGUIRE, M.J. and SPILSBURY, M. (1990) *Restructuring the Labour Market: The Implications for Youth*, London, Macmillan.

BARAN, B. (1985) 'Office automation and women's work: The technological transformation of the insurance industry' in CASTELLS, M. (ed.) *High Technology, Space and Society*, Sage, London.

CHENG, J.Y.S. (1986) *Hong Kong in Transition*, Hong Kong, Oxford University Press.

GASKELL, J. (1985) 'Explorations in vocationalism: Through the eyes of high school students', in MASON, G. (ed.) *Transitions to Work*, Winnipeg, Institute for Social and Economic Research.

GASKELL, J. (1989) 'Education as preparation for work in Canada: Structure, policy and student response', mimeo, Department of Social and Educational Studies, University of British Columbia.

GOWER, D. (1988) 'Annual update on labour force trends', *Canadian Social Trends*, Summer, pp. 17–20.

HONG KONG GOVERNMENT (1979) *Report of the Advisory Committee on Diversification*, Hong Kong, Government Printer.

KNIGHT, H.R. (1987) 'Technical education and industrial training — The Hong Kong experience', Internal Working Paper, Hong Kong, Vocational Training Council.

KRAHN, H. (1988) 'A Study of the Transition from School to Work in Three Canadian Cities: Research Design, Response Rates and Descriptive Results', Population Research Laboratory, University of Alberta, Canada.

KRAHN, H. (1989A) 'The School to Work Transition in Canada: New Risks and Uncertainties', Paper presented to the First International Symposium on Status Passages and Social Risks in the Life Course, University of Bremen.

KRAHN, H. (1989) 'The changing Canadian labour market', in ASHTON, D.N. and LOWE, G.S. (eds) (1990) *Making Their Way: Education, Training and the Labour Market in Canada and Britain*, Milton Keynes, Open University Press.

LAXER, G. (1989) *Open for Business: The Roots of Foreign Ownership in Canada*, Toronto, Oxford University Press.

LIN, T.B. and HO, Y.P. (1982) 'The past experience, present constraints and future course of industrial diversification in Hong Kong', in CHENG, J.Y.S. (ed.) *Hong Kong in the 1980s*, Hong Kong, Summerson Eastern Publishers.

MARQUAND, J. (1989) *The Sources of Economic Growth: Learning and Change in the Information Age*, Brighton, Harvester.

MARSDEN, D. (1986) *The End of Economic Man?* Brighton, Wheatsheaf.

MAURICE, M., SELLIER, F. and SILVESTRE, J.J. (1986) *The Social Foundations of Industrial Power: A Comparison of France and Germany*, London, MIT Press.

NG, SEK-HONG (1987) 'Training problems and challenges in a newly industrialising economy: The case of Hong Kong, *International Labour Review*, **26**, pp. 467–78.

PORTER, J., PORTER, M. and BLISHEN, B.R. (1982) *Stations and Callings: Making it Through the School System*, Toronto, Methuen.

VTC (Vocational Training Council) (1988) *Annual Report 1987/8*, Hong Kong, VTC.

WEIERMAIR, K. (1984) *Apprenticeship Training in Canada: A Theoretical and Empirical Analysis*, Ottowa, Discussion Paper No. 250, Economic Council of Canada.

11 Initial Training, Labour Market Structure and Public Policy: Intermediate Skills in British and German Industry

David Marsden and Paul Ryan

Introduction

The comparative merits of vocational preparation in Britain and Germany have been widely discussed in recent years, to the overwhelming credit of Germany.[1] The influence of German practice can be seen in such British policies as the core curriculum in schools, the lowering of pay for young trainees and the creation of Training and Enterprise Councils.

The possibility of effective learning from the experiences of other countries is often questioned. Those who see vocational preparation as part and parcel of national institutions and culture emphasize the futility of grafting one dimension, such as a training practice, onto the institutional life of another country (Maurice, Sellier and Silvestre, 1984, 1986; Piore, 1987). Recent British policy borrowing from Germany is particularly open to criticism on this score (chapter 1 above).

The scope for international comparisons is therefore restricted. In the first place, they require sufficient institutional and cultural similarity between the countries to make them meaningful. Second, they must consider the institutions in which particular training practices are embedded. Finally, they serve not so much to reveal solutions to specific problems as to help understand the conditions for and constraints upon their solution.

We argue that the scope for international policy learning is relatively high in the Anglo-German context. The two countries have shared a pronounced role for occupational labour markets and a preference for the workplace over the schoolroom as the primary locus of vocational preparation for industrial skills. At the same time, the limits to Anglo-German comparability are clear and increasing. Collective organization — particularly that of employers — and public regulation of markets are both much more important in Germany than in Britain and the latter difference has increased sharply since 1979.

Turning to the second requirement, the training outcome in which we are interested involves intermediate skills in industry. Craft and technician skills remain prominent shortage areas even at a time of slack economic activity, with adverse effects upon productivity levels and the trade balance in industry (Sentance and Williams, 1989). The policy upon which we focus is the development of workplace-based training, encouraged by low trainee pay and payroll costs. Finally, the institutional constraints which we emphasize involve the structure and regulation of labour markets.

A key ingredient in the success of German methods has been low apprentice remuneration, which reacts favourably on employers' training costs and, consequently, their willingness to offer training places (Jones, 1985; Wiederhold-Fritz, 1986; Streeck, 1989). The British government has accepted the argument and urged the deregulation of labour markets and the reduction of trainee pay and labour costs in this country. The results have, however, been unimpressive (Marsden and Ryan, 1990; Garonna and Ryan, 1991). We argue that low trainee pay and payroll costs cannot be generalized by deregulation, in unionized industrial workplaces at least. Such conditions require instead an explicit link to occupational labour markets and apprenticeship training, which both employer practice and public policy have eroded in recent years.

Our analysis draws upon a research project on youth pay, employment and training in EC economies,[2] supplemented by secondary sources. Its scope is limited. We do not attempt the full comparative institutional history of the two countries for which there is a great need. In particular, we reach only tentative conclusions on the role of pay structure and training finance relative to other salient features — such as employer organization, product mix and the qualifications of trainers — in generating divergent training outcomes in Britain and Germany.[3] Finally, we focus on industrial skills at craft and technician level, in occupations which are still, in both countries, occupied overwhelmingly by males.

The links between vocational training, labour marker structure and youth relative pay are discussed next, with reference to four large EC economies as they stood at the end of the 1970s. The comparative attributes of British and German institutions and their evolution in the post-war period are then considered, leading to an assessment of youth training policy in Britain.

Market Structure, Training and Youth Pay in Large EC Economies

The distinction between occupational and internal labour markets is central to this discussion. *Occupational markets* encourage the mobility of qualified workers amongst employers and work best with a system of standardized vocational qualifications. Workers seek security not from any particular employer but from the wider labour market, in association with certified skill and knowledge. In the UK, examples are found in manual crafts in building and engineering, in clerical work in big cities and in the professions.

Internal markets are organized around particular workplaces or employers. Jobs above entry level are generally filled by internal promotion; skills are learned as part of employment and qualifications are of secondary or no importance. Workers gain security through claims upon particular employers rather than through possession of externally recognized skills. British examples include production work in most process industries and much administrative work, particularly in the public sector.[4]

A third category is of increasing importance in Britain: secondary labour markets, in which workers enjoy little or no job security and in which both skill requirements and pay are low. Examples include much casual employment in service occupations.

The preceding characterization of internal and occupational structures involves ideal types. In practice, mixed forms are common. Thus internal and occupational structures often function side by side, as in much of the process and extraction industries in Britain, with maintenance and catering skills acquired from occupational markets, production skills by internal promotion and cleaning ones from secondary markets (Gallie, 1978; Marsden, 1982). Moreover, occupational and internal structures often overlap. Although professional scientists and engineers can use their qualifications to change employers within occupational markets, in Britain most still base their careers around the internal markets provided by particular employers (Mace, 1979; Creedy and Whitfield, 1986).

The importance of occupational and internal structures differs between countries. Internal structures are more pronounced in French and Italian than in German and British industry, as indicated, *inter alia*, by the growth of pay and occupational status with age and seniority (Marsden, 1990). On such criteria Britain and Germany share a relatively high ratio of occupational to internal features.[5]

Training systems are associated with labour market structure. Occupational markets require the development and certification of skills on a basis wider than the needs, resources and inclinations of individual employers. Internal markets, by contrast, involve more informal and limited training, provided largely at the workplace but geared to immediate job requirements. Vocational preparation in secondary schooling may then be developed to compensate for the deficiencies of training in internal markets.

In practice, training for industrial skills in both Britain and Germany, has relied upon employer provision under apprenticeship.[6] (Certification may be external, internal or even automatic, as in traditional British time-serving). In France and Italy, apprenticeship has played a minor role in industrial training, remaining confined mostly to the artisanal sector. Vocational education functions in Germany and Britain as a part-time complement to workplace training under apprenticeship, whereas in France it is a full-time alternative to apprenticeship for 14–18 year olds (Table 11.1; Combes, 1988; Steedman, 1988).

The association of apprenticeship with occupational markets appears

Table 11.1   Attributes of youth manual employment and training in industry in large EC economies 1978 (cols 3–7 are percentages)

(1) Country	(2) Dominant Market Structure	(3) Share of apprentices in manual employment	(4) Youth pay relative to adult pay males app excl	(5) app incl	(6) females app excl	(7) app incl
France	ILM	0.4	76	(76)	86	(86)
Italy	ILM	1.3	85	(85)	90	(90)
FR Germany	OLM	5.1	77	(46)	83	(79)
UK	OLM	4.2	(69)	62	(66)	66

Note: All estimates refer to all industrial establishments employing 10 or more persons; figures in parentheses are authors' estimates; pay is gross hourly earnings (or pro-rated monthly allowances, for German apprentices).
Source: Eurostat, *Survey of Earnings in Industry*, 1978 and *Labour Cost Survey*, 1978; details in Marsden and Ryan (1988, 1991).

paradoxical, given the incentives to employers to provide only narrow, firm-specific training, which hampers worker mobility (Ryan, 1984a). School-based preparation, with its inherent orientation towards broad transferable skills, appears in this respect to be more suited to occupational markets — and indeed dominates training for many non-manual occupations. However, whatever the reasons, for intermediate industrial skills apprenticeship has been more closely associated with occupational structures, as in Britain and Germany, and schooling with internal ones, as in France (Steedman, 1988; Marsden and Germe, 1991). Britain and Germany thus show long-standing similarities in training for intermediate industrial skills, linked to occupational labour markets.[7]

The relative pay of young workers and trainees is an important link between labour market structure and workplace training. In occupational markets, the access of young workers to apprenticeship is favoured by low allowances or pay rates, under 'wage for age' schedules or reduced trainee rates. Internal markets, however, typically permit no reduction in pay in entry level jobs for youths or trainees. Any young people who secure employment receive pay close to or the same as that of adult workers in the same job.[8]

A correspondence between youth relative pay and labour market structure is also visible in practice. Youth relative pay has long been markedly higher in France and Italy than in Germany and Britain (Table 11.1). In 1978, the last year for which comparable statistics were collected, manual male youth pay (apprentices included) amounted to 77 and 85 per cent of that of adults in France and Italy respectively, but only 46 and 62 per cent in Germany and the UK respectively. The difference between the two pairs of countries is marked, with Germany and Britain showing more pronounced occupational markets and lower youth relative pay.[9]

The difference between youth relative pay in Britain and Germany is also substantial and previous comparisons limited to the two countries have not surprisingly depicted Britain as a country of high youth and trainee pay (Jones, 1985). However, the more striking contrast is that between Britain and Germany, on the one hand, and France and Italy, on the other, as high and low youth pay categories respectively.[10] That dichotomy has, if anything, intensified during the 1980s with the moderate decline in youth relative pay in Britain (Marsden and Ryan, 1990; Garonna and Ryan, 1991).

Explanations of Links between Pay Structure and Institutions

These associations between market structure, training methods and youth relative pay can be interpreted from either a technical or an institutional standpoint. Human capital theory would interpret apprenticeship as training for skills which are both costly and transferable across a wide range of employers. Under such conditions, it makes economic sense for the ex-apprentice, as the seller of the resulting skill in an occupational market, to pay for its development by accepting low earnings during the training period. Similarly, as internal markets tend to provide only informal, inexpensive and employer-specific training, there is little economic reason for trainees to earn below the rate for the job for which they are being trained. The gap in youth pay between occupational and internal markets can thus be interpreted in terms of the cost and specificity of the skills produced (Becker, 1964; Doeringer and Piore, 1971; Siebert, 1985).

An explanation in terms of technology and competitive forces alone faces two difficulties. First, the importance of occupational relative to internal structures varies across firms, sectors and countries which use basically similar technologies and should therefore, *ceteris paribus*, show similar institutional attributes. Second, the cost and specificity of training is itself influenced by institutions. Occupational structures encourage — and usually require — costly and transferable training; internal ones, cheaper and more specific training.

An alternative interpretation looks towards industrial relations and personnel practice and emphasizes the legitimacy of pay differentials in the eyes of workers. Two issues may be distinguished: norms of fair payment and the prevention of substitution (Ryan, 1984a).

On the normative side, low pay for trainees may offend experienced workers by violating the norm of equal pay for equal work. Trainees are indeed unlikely to be as productive as experienced workers at a given job but, unless their status is clearly differentiated from that of regular workers, they are likely to be considered to be 'doing the job'. Differences between the status of trainee and experienced workers in internal markets are not general sufficient to legitimate low pay for trainees, let alone young workers in general. However, when apprenticeship is clearly and legitimately distinguished from employment, apprentices can be viewed more as students than as workers and low trainee compensation need not violate norms of fair pay.

Second, there is the threat of cheap trainee labour, encouraging employers to substitute young workers for adults. Although trainees may in some occupations be only poor substitutes for experienced adults, technology often permits trainees to perform at least some of the less complex tasks of skilled jobs. The acceptability of low youth pay to adult union members depends then upon effective institutional restraint on 'job substitution' by employers (Ryan, 1987, 1989). Apprenticeship can provide such safeguards, whether because of employer respect for skill and training or because of external regulation by some mixture of government, employer associations and trade unions. As such restraints are weak and absent, respectively, in internal markets, experienced workers are reluctant to accept special rates for trainees or young workers.

The importance of trainee rates in occupational markets contrasts with their rarity in internal ones, reflecting primarily the contrasting ability of the two structures to legitimate such payment rules, reinforced by underlying differences in the cost and specificity of skills themselves.

Institutional Development in Britain and Germany

Although the preceding section classed Britain and Germany together in the 'occupational' category, the two economies show both internal structures interwoven with occupational ones and a secular increase in the relative importance of internal structures. Occupational and internal structures combine less harmoniously, however, in Britain than in Germany.

The Growth of Internal Markets

The development of internal markets in large German companies has been encouraged not only by the general employer interest in retaining and motivating employees, but also by the specifically German influence of Works Councils, present at all large establishments as part of codetermination in industry.

Several attributes point to the importance of internal structures in German industry (Ahner, 1978; Keller, 1981). Large firms encourage long service amongst their skilled workers and Works Councils resist redundancies. The result is a turnover rate little different from that of their French counterparts (Marsden, 1990, Table 1). Large employers usually offer employment to all of their graduating apprentices, most of whom prefer in turn to continue in the internal market rather than to seek their fortunes in the external one (Casey, 1986). Works Councils have been criticized for acquiescing in the orientation of further training to the interests of individual employers, at the expense of employees' potential mobility in the external labour market.

Internalization appears to have increased in Germany in recent decades. The marked post-war expansion of job security at plant level has since 1974 been rolled back only partially in pursuit of increased numerical flexibility.[11] More recently, large industrial firms have responded to information technology with flexible specialization, promoting universal skill development as well as employee loyalty (Streeck, 1985; Lane, 1988). Such developments suggest some convergence between occupational and internal structures in German industry.

Internal structures have also increased in Britain, but in an uneven manner. Many of the sectors where occupational markets had been most pronounced, notably engineering and shipbuilding, have gone into decline, serious and terminal respectively. Even there, internal structures developed slowly from the late 1950s, notably in the form of increased job security, as employers moved away from earlier unrestricted 'hire and fire' practices.[12]

In contrast to Germany, the burgeoning large corporation has increasingly replaced the employers' association as the locus of pay bargaining in Britain. This development, promoted both by tight labour markets and piece-work bargaining in the immediate post-war period and by the Donovan Commission and associated managerial reforms after 1965, has, if anything, intensified in the 1980s. Large employers have sought to determine pay at company and plant level, and have favoured internal promotion, job evaluation, company training schemes, flexibility agreements and other attributes of the internal rather than the occupational market.[13]

The growth of internal structures in British industry has, however, remained uneven and incomplete. Flexible specialization and skill-rich internal markets remain the exception (Lane, 1988). Moreover, an important attribute of occupational markets remains largely intact in established plants: occupational immobility amongst adults. While internal markets permit employees to gain skills as they progress up job ladders, occupational markets restrict them, unless they acquire further external qualifications, to the stratum for which they were initially trained.

Internal upgrading is common in new and foreign-owned plants, but elsewhere it is still widely blocked by informal demarcation. Less than 1 per cent of semi-skilled manual workers were upgraded to skilled jobs in 1983–4 in Britain (Marsden, 1990, Table 1).[14] The flexibility agreements which might be expected to encourage mobility generally do so *between* skilled occupations rather than *into* them (GBNEDO, 1986; Marsden and Thompson, 1990). The long-term drift towards internal markets in the UK has yet to generalize internal lines of promotion between occupational strata.

Although comparable data are not readily available, internal upgrading appears to be more extensive in Germany, facilitated by the apprenticeship qualifications held by the great majority of German industrial workers, which entitle them to seek occupational advancement by acquiring further

David Marsden and Paul Ryan

qualifications along a hierarchy which runs from *Facharbeiter* through *Meister* into technician and professional qualifications. Although few go the whole way, many go part of the way and occupational upgrading is moderately extensive in large German plants (Hofbauer, Konig and Nagel, 1973), reflecting the more successful blending of internal and occupational structures in German industry (Sorge and Warner, 1980).

Youth Training and Employment

Industrial training has mirrored labour market structure in both Britain and Germany in the post-war period. The historical importance of apprenticeship has reflected in each the importance of occupational markets. At the same time, the growth of internal markets has modified apprenticeship in both countries and contributed to its undermining in Britain.

Germany.   German apprenticeship is remarkable in several respects: breadth of coverage, transparency, coherence, joint regulation, and resilience in adversity.[15]

Its coverage is almost universal amongst early school-leavers. The vast majority of people aged less than 18 who are active at workplaces function as apprentices. Initial training for intermediate industrial skills is conducted almost wholly through apprenticeship. The number of apprentice places offered by German industry has been affected only moderately by economic cycles and has increased significantly during the last twenty-five years (Table 11.2). [16]

The broad coverage of German apprenticeship reflects primarily its popularity with young people. Although it is sometimes taken to be mandatory for 15–18 year olds who have left school, in fact only part-time further education is actually compulsory.[17] The fact that only a small and declining minority of early school-leavers (6 per cent in 1979; Münch and Jung, 1980:142) enters ordinary employment — some of whom would have chosen apprenticeship had it been available to them — testifies to its appeal to youth.

The contracts and remuneration of young German workers are regulated in transparent fashion. The pay of young workers is differentiated more by trainee status than by age. Apprenticeship contracts are sharply distinguished in both legal and industrial practice from employment contracts. German apprentices receive low incomes relative to their British counterparts (Jones, 1985) while, by contrast, young *employees* are paid relatively highly in Germany (Table 11.1, cols 4–7).

Youth pay structures have also been relatively stable over time. Apprentice allowances vary greatly by sector, depending on a range of bargaining and labour market factors (Beicht and Wiederhold, 1985; Beiht and Holzschuh, 1990; Casey, 1990).[18] They have risen relative to adult rates, notably during the industrial unrest of the early 1970s (Table 11.3; Müller-Jentsch and Sperling,

258

Table 11.2   Apprentice numbers and employment shares in British and Germany industry, 1964–86

Year	Numbers (1964 = 100)		Shares (%)[a]	
	GB[b]	FRG[c]	GB[b]	FRG[c]
1964	100	100	3.0	4.5
1974	58	90	2.0	4.1
1979	65	101	2.2	4.7
1983	43	107	1.9	5.4
1986	26	119	1.2	6.0

Notes: [a] As a percentage of apprentices plus (other) employees.
   [b] Manufacturing only; excludes an unknown number of places converted to YTS after 1982.
   [c] Industry and commerce (roughly, large firms); for Germany the denominator for apprentice shares (employment in industry, commerce and transportation plus apprentices in industrial occupations) results in underestimation of shares as it includes employment both in transportation and in artisan firms in those sectors.
Sources: *Employment Gazette*, September 1980 and subsequent issues; Statistiches Bundesamt, *Statistiches Jahrbuch*, various issues.

Table 11.3   Pay/allowances of apprentices as percentage of that of skilled workers in metalworking (engineering) sector: negotiated rates, Britain and FR Germany

Year	GB[a]	FRG[b]	Difference
1951	38.9	23.1	15.8
1965	46.6	28.2	18.4
1980	67.5	33.6	33.9
1989	72.5	35.2	37.3

Notes: [a] Basic time rate of 17–18 year old apprentices and skilled workers, fitting trades; for 1951, Manchester and Birmingham district rates; for 1989, average of rates for modules 1 and 2, excluding YTS subsidies.
   [b] Average allowances of years 2–3 apprentices and average monthly basic rates of *Facharbeither*, Nordrhein-Westfalia.
Sources: GB Department of Employment, *Time Rate of Wages and Hours of Work*, various years; IGM, collective agreements (Ryan, 1991a).

1978).[19] Unofficial apprentice strikes in 1972–3, aimed at both higher pay and better training, led to increased apprentice incomes in metalworking (Schmidt, 1973; Reuling, 1974). However, in metalworking at least, relative apprentice incomes have otherwise been stable for long periods (Ryan, 1991a). Moreover, the relative pay of young *employees* hardly changed between 1966 and 1978, two years for which comparable data are available (Table 11.4).

On the procedural side, apprenticeship is subject to an elaborate system of tripartite regulation, operating at national (BIBB), regional (*Länder*), local (Chamber of Commerce) and plant (Works Council) levels (Streeck *et al.*, 1987). Trade unions participate in decisions at all levels, including Chambers of Commerce. Quality control involves both processes and outcomes. The curricula, instruction and examinations provided for apprentices, as well as the

David Marsden and Paul Ryan

Table 11.4 Youth relative pay in large EC economies, manual occupations in industry, 1966–78

Country	Males			Females		
	1966[a]	1978[a]	Change	1966[a]	1978[a]	Change
France	71.9	75.7	5.3%	77.9	86.1	10.5%
Italy	77.0	84.8	10.1%	84.4	89.9	6.5%
FRG	77.1	76.9	–0.3%	81.8	83.3	1.8%
GB[b]	51.2	61.6	20.3%	66.4	65.8	–0.9%

Notes: [a] Average gross hourly earnings of manual employees aged less than 21 as a percentage of those of employees aged 21 or over of the same gender; apprentices excluded for all countries except GB.
[b] Distinction between young and adult females drawn at 18 years of age.
Source: Eurostat and GB Dept of Employment (Marsden, 1985, Table 2).

qualifications of those who instruct them, are regulated and inspected by public authority. Employers whose trainees do not perform adequately in examinations are required and assisted to make appropriate improvements.

Low apprentice allowances encourage employers to provide training places. Guarantees of training quality in turn induce unions to accept low incomes for young workers to a degree rarely found elsewhere, particularly outside apprenticeship.[20] At the same time, employers have responded to wider social and educational goals, in terms of the content of training and the intake of apprentices. The result is a 'low pay, high quality, high volume' training system.

Apprenticeship also buttresses occupational structures in German labour markets. By requiring broad, transferable qualifications, it impedes tendencies for workplace training to be dominated by the requirements of individual employers. The reform of apprenticeship curricula, reducing the number of recognized occupations and increasing the range of skills provided in each, has strengthened its contribution in this respect.

The leading deficiency of German apprenticeship of relevance to this discussion is the uneven quality, the narrowness and specificity of training, as well as the extensive use of apprentice labour for production, in much of the artisan (roughly, small business) sector. These defects partly reflect the difficulty of regulating training in small enterprises, partly the strength of employer interests within regulatory structures, and partly internal labour markets.

Internal markets foster a status differentiation between scarce, high cost apprenticeships in large industrial firms, which select the most qualified school-leavers, and abundant, low cost apprenticeships in small firms, to which the less qualified young entrants must turn. The former usually feed directly into skilled employment with the sponsoring company; the latter often feed via the external labour market into subcraft industrial employment in large companies in an entirely different occupation from that learned as an apprentice (Ahner, 1978). The result is a heterogeneous, almost dualistic, system which reflects the coexistence of occupational and internal structures in the labour market.

Nor has German apprenticeship proved an arena of harmonious joint regulation. Conflict proved extensive in the 1970s over the desire of trade unions and the SPD to increase the time spent by young people in vocational education at the expense of workplace training and to extend public regulation from the quality to the quantity of employer provision. The early 1980s saw widespread concern over the adequacy of apprenticeship to deal with the coincidence of a baby boom youth cohort and slack economic activity.

Such conflicts and concerns have largely subsided. The set of recognized skills has recently been regrouped in order to promote still broader training, particularly in industry. The gap in both quantity and quality between industrial and artisanal training has narrowed during the 1980s. German apprenticeship has been consolidated into a coherent and still improving system of quasi-universal youth training.

Britain.   Youth institutions in Britain contrast sharply with those in Germany. Taking transparency first, the status and incomes of apprenticed and non-apprenticed youth have all but converged in Britain. Although contracts of apprenticeship and service are still distinguished at law, the two have for most purposes become legally equivalent.[21] British apprentices receive wages rather than training allowances, underlining their essentially employee status.

Moreover, youth pay is structured in Britain by age more than by trainee status. Not only is the pay of apprentices much higher, relative to that of both young workers and adults in the same occupation, than in Germany; the pay of *non-apprenticed* youth is also lower relative to that of adults in the UK than in Germany (Table 11.1, cols 4–7). Age lacks, however, the logic and legitimatory potential of trainee status as a basis for pay differentiation.

Low differentiation between the pay of apprenticed and other young British employees reflects the generality of wage-for-age schedules in youth employment, applying to apprenticed and non-apprenticed youth alike, along with the payment of similar rates to each. Adult rates are commonly attained in ordinary youth employment at age 18, but in some agreements as late as age 20; starting pay for 16 year olds typically lies between 40 and 70 per cent of the adult rate (IDS, 1987).

Similar provisions apply to young employees in German collective agreements (Münch and Jung, 1980:92–3). However, German and British practice differ in two ways. In Germany, adult rates are usually attained by 18 years of age and the great majority of 15–17-year-old school-leavers function on the much lower apprentice allowances.

Youth pay structures have also been much less stable in Britain. The pay of apprentices rose relative to that of skilled adults so much more rapidly

Table 11.5   Training of craftworkers in British engineering by age, 1972–6

		Age group (years)		
		< 25	25–44	> 44
Initial training	Apprenticeship	98%	84%	69%
(one or more)	Armed forces	0	18	25
	Dilution (upgrading)	2	6	9
Further-education	Any [a]	91%	54%	16%
qualifications	None	9	46	84

Notes: [a] Primarily City and Guilds certificates.
Source: Venning et al. (1980), Tables 5.7, 5.9.

during the post-war period in British than in German industry that the difference between the two relativities more than doubled (at broadly comparable stages of training; Table 11.3).[22] Similarly, the relative pay of young male manual employees increased more rapidly between 1966 and 1978 in Britain than in any other leading EC economy, in contrast to its stability in Germany (Table 11.4; Marsden and Ryan, 1991).

The volume of apprentice activity has also been unstable. Apprentice numbers have been falling in British industry since the mid-1960s, with an acceleration after 1979, again in contrast to the significant rise in Germany (Table 11.2). During the same period the quality of training rose strongly, if un-evenly, and by the early 1980s certification in British industry usually reflected skills comparable to those required in Germany (Prais and Wagner, 1983). The proportion of skilled workers who had undertaken apprenticeship or possessed any formal qualifications both rose rapidly during the period (Table 11.5).[23]

Interpretation.   The instability of British apprenticeship has therefore involved increases in relative pay and training quality and falls in volume. These linked developments reflect the opacity and weakness of youth institutions in Britain. In particular, it is arguable that the absence of a clear demarcation along German lines between apprenticeship and youth employment has contributed to increases in relative pay for all young workers, not just apprentices.

The history of that process has not been told but an outline is visible. Although relative apprentice pay was at least as low in Britain until the early 1950s as it is in Germany nowadays, training quality was also poor (Table 11.3; Lee, 1979; Ryan, 1986), as reflected in the scarcity of formal qualifications amongst skilled metalworkers trained before 1940 (Table 11.5). Such a 'low pay, low quality, high volume' system lacked legitimacy in the eyes of trade unions and apprentices alike. The result was a bargaining effort to raise both youth relative pay and training quality, with pay in the lead.

The role of apprentices appears to have been crucial. As in Germany, apprentices proved willing to strike in pursuit of higher pay and better training and to do so without official sanction and outside disputes procedure if neces-sary. However, apprentice strikes were not confined in Britain to a single upheaval but were distributed episodically across the years 1937–64, resulting in a series of increases in relative pay, whose cumulative effect is reflected in Table 11.3 (Ryan, 1987).

The concentration of apprentice unrest in a much narrower timespan in Germany, despite relative incomes which remained much lower than in Britain, suggests a greater legitimacy for low incomes (in association with higher training quality and returns to skill) amongst German than amongst British apprentices and trade unionists (Schober, 1983). (The lower national strike rate in Germany may also contribute to the difference in apprentice militancy.)

The increase in training quality in Britain came at a late stage in the upward drift in relative pay, particularly after 1963 as the newly created Training Boards (ITBs) required employers to meet quality criteria in order to receive refunds of their training levies. However, as quality improvement proceeded independently of trainee pay, it proved a mixed blessing for the institution of apprenticeship. Higher training quality meant higher training costs for employers and, in the absence of adequate cost redistribution by the ITB levy-grant system, lower apprentice intakes — unless trainee relative pay was to be cut or public subsidy increased (Lindley, 1975).

Institutional and cultural factors militated against lower trainee pay and public subsidies. The ITB's terms of reference did not allow the linking of improved training quality to lower apprentice pay. In metalworking, the roles of the (Engineering) ITB, on the one hand, and the employer and trade union federations (EEF and CSEU), on the other, remained divorced. The former dealt with training content and structure, the latter with apprentice pay, age and recruitment (Marsh, Hackmann and Miller, 1981:168–72). Trainee pay was negotiated separately, with little regard to training considerations.

Although apprentice allowances are negotiated collectively in Germany as well, German employers have insisted on linking trainee income with training provision and unions have broadly accepted the argument (Wiederhold-Fritz, 1986). As the bargaining parties could have similarly linked the issues in Britain, the difference between the two countries may be taken as evidence of a lower priority given to skills and training amongst both employers and unions in Britain.

Nor were subsidies to employer training costs readily adopted instead. British practice and politics had long opposed an active public role in industrial training (Sheldrake and Vickerstaffe, 1987). The Training Boards were intended to correct rather than to replace the market and received no public subsidy beyond their administrative costs. When public subsidies to apprenticeship intakes were eventually introduced in the mid-1970s, it was only as a temporary antidote to a cyclical crisis in recruitment (Lindley, 1983).

Consequently, instead of a 'low pay, high quality, high volume' training system along German lines, the UK moved towards a 'high pay, high quality, low volume' one. Such a development suited the interests of those who secured an apprenticeship — they received both better training and higher pay than had their predecessors. However, as the training costs borne by employers increased strongly — to between £9,000 and £15,000 per capita in metalworking by 1984 (Jones, 1986) — low volume was assured. Apprentice numbers went into secular decline soon after the start of ITB operations. The EITB set its seal on the process when in 1984 it formally abandoned its long-standing efforts to increase the intake of craft apprentices.[24]

The spread of internal labour markets affected apprenticeship in Britain as well. The importance of job security to skilled workers (GB NEDO, 1977) joined rising training costs in inducing large employers to avoid apprentice intakes beyond their own prospective needs for skilled labour. Metalworking employers successfully pressed their Training Board in the 1980s to permit training curricula to be tailored more to the needs of individual firms.[25] More generally, in the absence of incentives to preserve apprenticeship, employers increasingly avoided the broad occupational training which it promoted in favour of training geared to their own requirements.

Finally, although the joint regulation of apprenticeship in Britain has never matched that in Germany, it nevertheless received statutory support between 1964 and 1988. The Training Boards were themselves tripartite bodies. When their powers were curtailed in 1973, tripartism was elevated to national scope with the creation of the Manpower Services Commission (MSC; Lindley, 1983). The demise of the MSC in 1988 has, however, underlined the fact that unions have never won the enduring rights to joint regulation of training, particularly at national and workplace levels, which are central to German practice.

Overview. The consolidation of apprenticeship in Germany and its erosion in the UK reflect other factors, in addition to relative pay and labour costs. However, the relevance of financial considerations to the absolute decline of apprentice activity in Britain is underlined by the fact that other, oft cited causes of low training by British companies — notably the lack of interest in skill and the weakness of collective organization — were arguably no stronger a deterrent in 1990 than they had been in 1964. They may well contribute to persistently low levels of training in Britain relative to Germany but their apparent constancy rules them out as causes of the relative decline in apprenticeship in Britain.

The question arises then: could Britain have found — or might it yet find — an institutional foundation for low trainee pay and labour costs? We argue that a sharp distinction along German lines between apprentices and other young workers, linked explicitly to joint regulation of training quality, might have made low apprentice incomes acceptable to both trade unions and apprentices in the UK, thereby fostering apprenticeship itself. The argument is not just an historical conjecture of particular relevance to the policy debates of the late 1940s and early 1960s. It is a live issue for contemporary training policy.

The Youth Training Scheme

The decline of apprenticeship in Britain would not be a matter for regret if apprenticeship were to be replaced by an equivalent or superior training system. The Government holds that such is already the case: in its view, lower pay for young trainees and high quality initial training have already been achieved by the deregulation of labour markets and the 'resounding success' of the Youth Training Scheme (YTS; GB DE, 1988a, 1988b).

A range of deregulatory policies has been adopted since 1979 — including low trainee allowances, fixed term contracts, reduced social security entitlement, training subsidies and the removal of statutory wage minima — with the announced goal of pricing young workers into jobs and training. The tendency for deregulation, as applied to youth, to encourage the growth of low paid, low quality youth employment has been discussed elsewhere (Marsden and Ryan, 1990; Garonna and Ryan, 1991). We concentrate here on the leading training initiative, YTS, and assess its claims as a superior alternative to apprenticeship.

In 1990 YTS was reconstituted as (New) Youth Training and its delivery decentralized to the emerging Training and Enterprise Councils (TECs). This discussion refers primarily to YTS as it operated in its two-year form (YTS2) during 1986–90 — and may be expected in key respects to continue to operate in the early 1990s.[26]

Content of YTS. Viewed as a training scheme, YTS seeks to universalize youth training by lowering youth pay and training costs, in particular in the many non-craft occupations in which formal training was previously absent. The announced principles of the scheme certainly correspond more to those of occupational than of internal markets. It promotes universal initial training with both foundation and occupational content, leading to recognized credentials. Young school-leavers function on two-year contracts which are in most cases formally distinct from employment contracts, receiving allowances pitched at around one-third of pay rates in regular youth employment. It is delivered by Managing Agents, who may or may not subcontract out work experience, and who receive a public subsidy which covers trainee allowances and some direct training costs.

The formal specification of YTS training involves minimum quality standards. At least one-fifth of the trainee's time is to be spent in off-the-job instruction. The work experience which constitutes the remainder is to involve a structured programme of learning experiences. Trainees are to receive a training agreement, specifying the variety of training and work experience with which they will be provided and the certificate of achievement of formal qualifications to be obtained *en route*, and to record their activities in individual log books. The Training Standards Advisory Services (TSAS) monitors training quality and can recommend the withholding of Approved Training

Organisation (ATO) status, and with it the right to activity in YTS, from sponsors of substandard schemes. Courses are provided for YTS supervisors and trainers who need help to bring their efforts up to par.

In a parallel development, the National Council for Vocational Qualifications (NCVQ) is developing a national system of vocational qualifications (NVQ) to which YTS sponsors are to be required to train (Thompson, 1989). Those qualifications could, when fully developed, provide both a yardstick against which to evaluate the efforts of YTS providers and a prop for occupational markets in general.

On the procedural side, YTS was developed in consultation with, and received the approval of, employer and trade union representatives on the MSC. All individual YTS schemes had until 1988 to be approved both by appropriate union officials at the workplace and by the local MSC Area Manpower Committee, on which trade unions were represented.

The Government had until recently shown a commitment to YTS which, in terms of funding and longevity, far exceeded that to any other of the host of employment and training schemes. By 1987/8, more than a billion pounds were being spent yearly on the three-fifths of 16 to 17 year old school-leavers who entered the scheme (GB TA, 1989:15).

The separation of training contracts from employment contracts; the low allowances and fixed-term contracts for trainees; the sequence of foundation and occupational training; the training agreements, the monitoring of training quality and the certification of trainee achievements; the training of trainers; the involvement of unions at all levels; the high degree of 'market penetration' — such attributes might suggest that YTS provides not simply a surrogate for apprenticeship but rather a superior, German-style 'low pay, high quality, high volume' variant.

There is an element of truth in such a view. Most of the young people active on YTS receive only the standard training allowance, pitched at around one-third of average 16 to 17 year old pay and, as that is paid by government, sponsoring employers incur no payroll costs for their trainees. Many YTS schemes, particularly those sponsored by large firms, local authorities, charities and ITBs, have provided high quality training. Apprenticeship for construction, engineering and electrical crafts has been widely converted to YTS without loss of quality. The 1983 training agreement in electrical contracting provided an exceptional instance of the YTS-induced recasting of craft training in a 'low pay, high quality, higher volume' mould (IDS, 1983). Systematic training has been introduced into many service occupations in which it was previously unknown.

Failings of YTS. However, the similarities between YTS and apprenticeship, particularly its German variant, are both incomplete and hollow: incomplete, in the limited coverage achieved by YTS, and in the scheme's indifference to educational objectives; hollow, in that quality control has remained a matter of form rather than content. The potential of YTS and NVQ as vehicles for occupational training consequently remains largely unrealized.[27]

The first failing of YTS involves its ambition to universalize youth training. It is true that the clear majority of early school-leavers who have entered YTS in recent years represent an advance on their predecessors, who went mostly into jobs without training. However, attrition rates on YTS are extraordinarily high: only one-fifth of those leaving the scheme in 1988 had completed their contracts (GB TA, 1989:16). Consequently, fewer 16–17 year olds function as YTS trainees than as ordinary employees. The proportion on YTS showed signs of falling after 1987 in the face of economic recovery, strenuous marketing notwithstanding.[28] Thus, in contrast to the small minority of young Germans who prefer employment to apprenticeship or, having started an apprenticeship, fail to complete it, a majority of Britons, when given the choice, prefer ordinary jobs to YTS.

An important source of low youth interest in YTS is training quality. Quality is not easy to measure or assess. However, fieldwork conducted in a town in the South of England by a team from Essex University suggests a distribution of training quality with a thick lower tail and a low mean. The Essex group found widespread tendencies for off-the-job training to lack either educational content or relevance to work experience; and for work experience to be provided by small employers lacking interest in YTS training objectives and to comprise either inactivity or hard repetitive work — the 'noddy' and 'dogsbody' jobs of trainee terminology, respectively. The 'training entrepreneurs' who flourished under YTS had even undermined existing training standards in some craft occupations.

Although the Essex research did not quantify the incidence of low and high quality training, more than half the traineeships in their survey appear to have involved poor quality. 'Only a few genuine traditional craft and clerical placements had any semblance of a supervised training programme'. The share of low quality training appeared to have increased during the scheme's first five years (Lee, Marsden, Rickman and Duncombe, 1990a:69; Lee *et al.*, 1988, 1990b; Lee, 1990).[29]

National statistics also suggest quality problems. Although the proportion of YTS trainees who acquire a recognized qualification (as opposed to simply a certificate of completion) has risen, it was still only 29 per cent in 1987/8 (GB TA, 1989, Table 2) and even that limited count included many qualifications of dubious worth (chapter 5, above; Dore, 1987, chapter 2; Jones, 1988; Steedman and Wagner, 1989; Jarvis and Prais, 1989; Prais, 1989).[30]

Similarly 'job substitution' — of YTS trainees for regular employees — is estimated to account for four out of every five places, reflecting the dominance of trainee time by work experience in jobs with low training requirements (Begg, Blake, Deakin and Pratten, 1990, Table 6.3). Substitution usually implies low training quality: in the absence of YTS most young people would be mainstream employees rather than apprentices or trainees.[31]

Finally, not only is the turnover rate amongst young trainees high; low quality in work experience and training tops the lists of complaints amongst those who leave the scheme (GB DE, 1986; GB TA, 1988). The weak earnings benefits from participation in YTS — which may even be negative (Main and Shelly, 1988) — are also consistent with a low average quality of training.

Causes of low quality. The proliferation of poor training under YTS does not reflect the scheme's proclaimed objectives, which have always involved uniformly high quality. It results first from the dominance of the employment over the training objectives of the scheme; second, from the need for YTS to adapt to existing labour market institutions and practices in order to achieve its numerical targets; and, third, from the lack of the resources, the mechanisms and ultimately the political will to achieve quality standards.

The priority of places over training quality has been embodied in the enduring 'Christmas guarantee' of a place for all unemployed early school-leavers. Employer goodwill was required to meet that target at short notice in both 1982–83 and 1985–86. Quality control became, as a result, not costly and difficult, but also (from the government standpoint) undesirable, in that it would kill off the many low quality places which were essential to meeting the scheme's dominant employment objectives (Keep, 1986; Ryan, 1984b).

Second, notwithstanding its stated orientation towards marketable skills, the operations of YTS correspond more to the requirements of internal than of occupational labour markets. Young people look to YTS mostly for a route to employment within the sponsoring enterprise. Large employers use it widely to screen young people for employment, limiting training content to the needs of internal markets. Thus only around one in every ten ex-trainees uses skills learned and certified on YTS to gain employment through the external labour market. The success of YTS is widely appraised publicly in terms of rates of transition to employment within the sponsoring organization, during as well as after the traineeship.

Consequently, both sponsors and trainees often show no interest in using YTS for occupational training. In this respect, the downgrading of YTS occupational ideals 'goes with the grain' of much of the contemporary British labour market (Raffe, 1987, 1988b, 1990a; Sako and Dore, 1986; Lee et al., 1988, 1990b). The scheme goes with the grain in another sense. Its promotion of short-term work experience placements in small enterprises interested in cheap, insecure labour dovetails with the growth of secondary, casual employment in the 1980s (Lee et al., 1990a; Brosnan and Wilkinson, 1988). YTS entry is still predominantly less able, underqualified and ethnic minority, promoting a vicious circle of low expectations and low achievements (Raffe, 1987).

Third, training quality depends upon the resources and mechanisms available. Resource constraints have remained problematic throughout. YTS has indeed eliminated trainee payroll costs and made it possible for sponsors to profit from the scheme when training for occupations with short training periods and low non-wage training costs. However, as training for intermediate industrial skills can last three years and involve high non-wage training costs, employers who use YTS to conduct it must still dig deep into their pockets (Jones, 1986).

The flat-rate funding of YTS places which prevailed until recently had two implications. Given the variability of training costs across occupations, training provision was slanted away from costly intermediate skills towards low cost, low level ones, for which training needs are limited, work experience is necessarily dominated by productive activity and job substitution extensive. Low quality was thus built into the occupational mix promoted by YTS. Roughly three-quarters of trainees receive their work experience in the service sector, usually in low-level occupations (GB MSC, 1988:59, 62). (The 1990 decision to vary funding according to an occupation's training costs should however reduce this bias.)

The second implication applies within occupations and reflects the incentives to sponsors to reduce training quality in order to increase short-term profits. Some Managing Agents who would otherwise have favoured better training have been forced to cut quality through competition for limited funds and work experience placements (Lee *et al.*, 1990a). Low quality results unless such dilution can be prevented by linking funding to the attainment of standards. Otherwise not even lavish funding would produce acceptable training — YTS would simply become a more expensive subsidy to youth labour.

The problem is that contractual and administrative mechanisms of quality assurance are costly and unpopular with the Government. Although plans were laid in 1982–83 and 1985–86 to give legal force to YTS training contracts, in practice the MSC has provided trainees only with a legally unenforceable training agreement.[32] It has relied instead upon administrative controls. The quality of training is monitored and access to further funds made dependent on satisfactory performance, relying since 1986 upon three mechanisms: Managing Agent responsibility for work experience subcontractors, ATO status requirements for Managing Agents, and their inspection by TSAS (GB MSC, 1987a).

The first mechanism is illogical. Effective control of the quality of work experience is not to be expected of the many entrepreneurial Managing Agents, who share with subcontractors an interest in profiting from YTS and who can do so by accepting the wholesale use of trainees for productive work and charging their subcontractors for the services of trainees.

The effects of requiring ATO status and TSAS inspection are less readily discerned in the absence of recent independent fieldwork. Other evidence is, however, less than reassuring. Despite evidence of widespread low quality on one year YTS, only a handful of Managing Agents were denied ATO status under YTS2.[33] Some dubious candidates amongst its early recipients obtained ATO status just by stating what they knew the MSC wanted to hear — in some cases, simply copying out the MSC's own model schemes (Lee *et al.*, 1990a). In any case, the most entrenched quality problems lie lower down, in the army of work experience subcontractors who remain exempt from any ATO-type requirement for, e.g., the presence of qualified trainers.[34]

Nor do the reports of the TSAS inspectorate inspire confidence. Its criteria of good training practice are job-specific when they are not vague. TSAS has adopted low inspection rates, depicting quality problems in YTS as ones of information rather than control, with sponsors eager to train but needing advice on how to do it. Although TSAS points to problems of trainer quality, workplace supervision and training records in YTS, it describes the scheme as a broadly homogeneous whole rather than one with a large dispersion of training quality (GB TA TSAS, 1990).

TSAS' presentation of training quality in YTS contradicts that by the Essex team. While quality may well have improved since 1987, when the Essex research ended, the paucity of details and the absence of statistics in TSAS' report, combined with the poverty of its qualitative judgments, induces serious doubt concerning its assessment of quality in YTS. Placed alongside the evidence discussed above, the TSAS picture invites interpretation as a case of 'his master's voice' speaking through a dependent creature.[35]

Quality control has lately begun to turn from processes to outcomes. Trainees and their sponsors are encouraged to train towards NVQs and funding is to be geared partly to their achievement by trainees. A requirement that all trainees prepare for established qualifications could do much for training quality and occupational markets more generally. However, such a requirement has yet to be adopted; even if it were, the problem of low grade qualifications would still have to be addressed.

Finally, quality control has been constrained at the root by the Thatcher Governments' free market, deregulatory enthusiasm. YTS does indeed involve a formal apparatus for regulating training and it is remarkable that *laissez-faire* Governments should have spent so heavily on, and intervened so extensively in, initial training. That interventionism owes much to the semi-autonomous status and activism of the Manpower Services Commission (allied to the Government's political interest in action on youth unemployment and training). But the same deregulatory orientation has hamstrung the desire, well represented in the higher echelons of the MSC, to develop either a convincing regulatory framework for YTS or a superior replacement for the scheme itself (Davis, 1986; Keep, 1986).[36] The Government has instead encouraged lower youth pay, let employers get on with it and relied on market forces to generate results. Given serious market failure in the skill context, the lopsided results of such a policy come as no surprise.

The free market orientation has weakened YTS on the procedural side as well. Lack of a convincing commitment by the Government to quality in YTS has deprived TUC leaders of any effective reply to criticism by trade unionists of substitution and exploitation in YTS. TUC support for YTS has consequently been largely defensive, depicting it as the lesser of two evils and urging the undesirability of leaving young workers with nothing at all (Ryan, 1991b).

The already low legitimacy of YTS within the union movement suffered a further setback in 1988 when the Government ended TUC participation in the public regulation of training, absorbing the MSC into the Department of Employment as the Training Agency. It was the longstanding dispute over funding, quality and substitution in training programmes which led to the end of tripartite regulation, though the immediate context was adult rather than youth training.

Whether or not the end of tripartism as operated in the 1980s hurts the unions themselves, the loss of the MSC has damaged the beleagured cause of occupational training by removing its leading advocate within government. The legitimacy of YTS within the union movement has sunk further, worsening the scheme's limited ability to improve training for intermediate industrial skills.

YTS and Apprenticeship: Overview

YTS resembles German apprenticeship in both its formal design and some aspects of its operations — notably low trainee pay and labour costs, the dispersion in training quality and the adaptation of occupational training to internal labour markets. However, the similarities end there. The formal design of German apprenticeship is largely realized in practice; that of YTS is not. The legitimation of low trainee pay through high quality training is extensive and rare respectively. Low quality is curbed in German apprenticeship by requirements for qualified instruction, vocational education, linkage to established training schedules, the acquisition of craft-level qualifications and the involvement of trade unions. The analogous arrangements for YTS are mostly empty; low quality remains the scheme's Achilles' heel.

Therefore, to pair YTS and German apprenticeship, let alone to present YTS (and NVQ) as the more desirable methods of training and qualification — as their enthusiasts are prone to do — is to beggar belief.[37] Such claims carried no weight with German banks when instituting a two-year course of initial occupational training for their UK operations. Seeking to replicate in this country the outcomes of the dual system, they explicitly avoided YTS, despite the financial assistance which it offered, as they found it an inadequate vehicle for the skills and knowledge which they sought.[38]

Little comfort can be derived, therefore, from the rise of YTS in considering the decline of apprenticeship in Britain. YTS has absorbed much and undermined some of what remained of 'high pay, high quality, low volume' apprenticeship training. It has developed a 'low pay, low quality, high volume' segment but there are unfortunately few instances of the 'low pay, high quality, high volume' occupational training which the scheme is supposed to universalize.

Conclusions

Accepting international evidence pointing to the shortcomings of the country's vocational preparation, the British government has sought to remedy its defects by deregulation and subsidization of youth training at the workplace. Relying on the workplace as the locus of training certainly conforms to traditional practice. Given that, the government's interest in lower trainee pay is appropriate, with or without public subsidy.

However, two conditions for the success of such a strategy are suggested by the preceding analysis. Both require institutional development in order to legitimate low trainee pay in the eyes of young people, adult workers and trade unions.

The first is the protection of occupational structures in the labour market, including apprenticeship — in content if not in name. The low trainee allowances which might encourage employers to improve training are consistent with occupational markets and apprenticeship training rather than with internal markets and job training. Although apprenticeship has been improved by requiring training to standards in place of time-serving (GB DE, 1981), current policies, in favouring the replacement of apprenticeship by YTS, undermine a key institutional vehicle for the achievement of lower trainee pay.

The second condition is the joint regulation of training. Guaranteed quality itself goes a long way to ensure that trainee services will not be abused at the workplace. The involvement of employee representatives in the regulation of training adds strength to any guarantee and contributes to the legitimation of training arrangements. Again, current policies have moved emphatically in the opposite direction.

It is difficult to conceive of vocational preparation of adequate quantity and quality in the key plants of British industry, which remain highly unionized, without an externally regulated system of occupational training along apprenticeship lines. The Government appears to understand this, at least to the extent that YTS, NVQ and the TECs formally adopt many of the attributes of such a system. However, the conformity of current training policy to institutional requirements is largely limited to form only. Deregulation has meant hollow institutions.

The Occupational Route

Two broad alternatives can be discerned, both of which recognize institutional realities in the labour market. The first would insert content into the shell provided by present policies. Occupational structures would be fostered and apprenticeship generalized, with serious educational content and subject to joint regulation. Such a policy could still build upon influential occupational structures, notably an industrial work organization structured more towards occupational than internal markets; an apprenticeship system, however decimated; and public schemes for youth training and qualification which formally espouse occupational objectives and which might yet be upgraded towards real occupational training.[39]

The importance of meeting the two conditions outlined above depends then upon the role of financial factors — notably trainee pay and labour costs — in determining training provision by employers. Lower trainee pay is neither necessary nor sufficient for improvement here: not necessary, because public subsidy could at least formally achieve similar effects; not sufficient, because collective organization and funding would probably also be required to coax enough training places out of employers. But financial factors are crucially important. As the chief influence capable of explaining the decline in apprenticeship during the last quarter century, they remain essential to any proposals for its resurrection.

Such a course faces questions of both feasibility and desirability. Proposals for apprenticeship and joint regulation evoke fears of restrictive practices, which are consistent with the greater importance of occupational elements in both union structure and industrial work organization in Britain than in Germany. The role of occupational structures in restraining internal upgrading in British industry has already been noted. However, to attribute such practices simply to craft restrictiveness is to overlook the contribution of managerial inaction to their continuance. Moreover, few trade unionists would wish to move back to time-serving, from training to standards and multiskilling has already become widespread in craft training.

The role of apprenticeship in sustaining craft practices has been widely exaggerated (Lee, 1979). Trade unions have called in the last decade for the extension as well as the defence of apprenticeship standards in training. The term 'apprenticeship' can even make a useful contribution to the legitimation of training institutions amongst industrial workers.

Other obstacles are more serious. Many British industrial employers are either wedded to product-cum-manufacturing strategies involving low skill requirements or are unaware of their true skill requirements. They have also fought long and hard against the external regulation of workplace training.[40] Regulation is costly and difficult to enforce, particularly in non-union workplaces. Training will be inclined towards narrowness and specificity as long as it is based primarily upon the workplace. Craftworkers have demonstrated their aversion to the risks involved in occupational labour markets under conditions of industrial decline by opting for less skilled work in more stable sectors (GB NEDO, 1977). Such difficulties create interest in other approaches, particularly ones which do not depend on employer provision.

The Internal Route

An alternative strategy looks to French, Swedish and (to some extent) Japanese training practices rather than to those of Germany. It accepts as given the growth of internal markets and job-oriented training and expands upper secondary schooling, whether academic or vocational in content, as an alternative (Dore, 1987; Sako and Dore, 1988; Raffe, 1990b). Young people would then be expected to leave school at age 18 rather than 16, taking with them craft-level qualifications rather than lower level academic ones or none at all.

Occupational structures and individual access to portable skills could still be fostered, but it would be by public provision and finance rather than by prodding employers to provide suitable training. A hierarchy of qualifications with strong educational content would be needed to provide individuals with routes around the mobility bars which still characterize most of British industry. Employers, faced with a more skilled and demanding workforce, would be pressed to take skills more seriously than at present.

An 'internal' strategy would gain by marginalizing the two conditions outlined above for the reduction of trainee pay. As vocational preparation would no longer be based primarily around the workplace, low trainee pay would be unnecessary as well as undesirable. Employers will finance subsequent job-specific training. Joint regulation might still contribute to industrial due process and employee involvement but it would be tangential to vocational preparation.

This alternative strategy would have to face difficulties in its turn. There is, first, the well-known resistance of national politics and educational practice to broadening 'A levels' into a *baccalaureate* or towards vocational education. Second, even where it has been established, vocational education finds it difficult to keep up with the best practice at the workplace. Third, the transition from school to work would be more uneven than under apprenticeship, showing higher rates of both unemployment and occupational downgrading amongst young people.[41] Finally, a fiscally restrictive government would hardly favour the increase in public expenditure necessary to fund full-time education for all 16–18 year olds.

Which of the two strategies is chosen certainly matters. We see merit in occupational structures and apprenticeship training, not least for the quantity and quality of youth employment and training which they can provide under effective regulation. But it would be better to choose one or the other strategy and pursue it consistently, recognizing the institutional realities of the labour market, than to plough on blind to them.

Acknowledgments

We thank the Joseph Rowntree Memorial Trust for financial support; the Department of Employment and the Training Agency for access to unpublished data; and Martin Baethge, Gerhard Bosch, William Brown, John Cassels, Alain d'Iribarne, Ronald Dore, Bernard Elbaum, David Finegold David Lee, Robert Lindley, S.J. Prais, Brian Napier, David Raffe, Peter

Senker, W.S. Siebert, Rita Stockmann, Hilary Steedman, Wolfgang Streeck and Rudolf Welzmuller for comments, criticism and suggestions.

Notes

1   Prais (1981, 1985), Prais and Wagner (1983, 1985, 1988), Steedman and Wagner (1987, 1989); Hayes, Anderson and Fonda (1984), Russell and Parkes (1984), Russell (1989); Dougherty (1987); Raggatt (1988); Lee (1990); Campbell and Warner (1989) and chapter 6, above. The entity referred to here is the former West Germany.

2   This chapter discusses in more detail many of the issues covered in Marsden and Ryan (1990). Other results are presented in Marsden and Ryan (1986, 1988, 1989a, 1989b, 1991).

3   For example, the centrality of the *Meister* to the success of skill utilization and training in Germany is emphasized by Flower and Russell (1982), Russell and Parkes (1984), Prais and Wagner (1988), Russell (1989) and Rose (chapter 3, above); that of employer organization and joint regulation by Streeck, Hilbert, van Kevelaer, Maier and Weber (1987).

4   The occupational/internal distinction is similar to those between 'guild' and 'manorial', 'craft' and 'enterprise' structures, 'market' and 'organization' jobs, and 'contract' and 'status' bases for worker security (Kerr, 1954; Doeringer and Piore, 1971; Dore, 1987, chapter 2; Streeck, 1987). See also Marsden (1986, chapter 8) and Creedy and Whitfield (1988).

5   Studies of social effects in work organization have emphasized the differences between France and Germany and the (partial) similarities between Britain and Germany (e.g., Maurice, Sellier and Silvestre, 1984, 1986; Sorge and Warner, 1980).

6   Given the lack of a clear boundary between apprenticeship and other forms of training, we define apprenticeship functionally, as any system of vocational preparation which depends primarily upon workplace-based provision by employers and which teaches a wide range of occupational skills and knowledge in one continuous training period. In Britain, much historical 'apprenticeship' failed to meet the quality criterion (Ryan, 1986), whereas many contemporary traineeships could do so easily. The predominance of apprenticeship training for industrial skills applies to males rather than to females in both Britain and West Germany.

7   A different grouping of the four countries results when they are classified by the educational content of contemporary training. France then joins West Germany in imposing an educational purpose upon initial training, while Britain and Italy share a propensity to leave initial training to economic forces, largely untouched by wider educational objectives (Campinos-Dubernet and Grando, 1988).

8   The 'rate for the job' payment rules which typify internal markets outside Japan do not, however, imply full parity of earnings between young and adult employees. To the extent that job level and pay increase with experience and seniority, youth earnings will fall short of those of adults in internal markets, even though young people must generally be paid the same if they fill particular jobs.

9   National differences in youth pay remain sharp even if the focus is narrowed to apprentices, who in Italian industry received until recently 95 per cent of the normal adult rate (Mariani, 1986). The position of French apprentices, who receive

between 30 and 75 per cent of the national minimum wage (Marsden 1985, Table 4) is, however, close to that of their German counterparts.

10   The situation for females is similar, except that youth relative pay is higher in all countries than for males and West Germany lies closer to France and Italy. Differences in the age and skill composition of the youth labour force account for only a small part of differences in youth relative pay (Marsden and Ryan, 1991).

11   Streeck (1987), Sengenberger (1981), Sengenberger and Kohler, (1987), Buttler (1987), Bosch and Sengenberger (1989).

12   Dore (1973); Mackay *et al.* (1971); Alexander and Jenkins (1970); Leeson (1973); Gospel (1991). The growth of subcontracting in construction represents a trend in the opposite direction.

13   Brown (1981), chapter 2; Millward and Stevens (1986), chapters 8, 9; GB NEDO (1986); Brown and Nolan (1988), Marginson, Edwards, Martin, Purcell and Sisson (1988).

14   Although managerial estimates suggest higher rates of upgrading, with as many as 12 per cent of skilled manual vacancies filled internally (Millward and Stevens, 1986, Table 8.4), the estimate may refer not to vacancies recently filled by internal promotion but to jobs which *could* be so filled when vacant, if management wished.

15   This characterization of German apprenticeship draws upon Krais (1979), Taylor (1981), Prais and Wagner (1983, 1988), Schober (1983), Noll *et al.* (1983), Clement (1985), Casey (1986, 1990), Wiederhold-Fritz (1986), Streeck *et al.* (1987), Dougherty (1987), Mason and Russell (1987), Raggatt (1988), Schober and Wadensjo (1991).

16   The low cyclicality of German apprentice intakes reflects a variety of economic and political factors, as well as offsetting tendencies towards pro-cyclicality amongst large employers and counter-cyclicality amongst small ones (Casey, 1986, 1990).

17   A year of full-time vocational schooling may be substituted for the requirement for part-time further education to age 18 (Prais, 1989).

18   For example, apprentice allowances were raised sharply in construction in the 1970s in order to attract more and better candidates to the industry (Streeck *et al.*, 1987, chapter 5).

19   The data in Table 11.3 indicate at most broad tendencies, given that they involve collectively negotiated rates rather than hourly payroll costs and that they refer to metalworking in two *Länder* rather than to German industry as a whole.

20   The Netherlands constitutes an exception, combining long duration wage for age scales with short duration apprenticeships (Marsden and Ryan, 1991).

21   Thus an employment contract is defined at law as either a contract of service or a contract of apprenticeship, which means that apprentices share the statutory rights of employees, with the principal exception of provision for redundancy at the end of apprenticeship (Employment Protection (Consolidation) Act 1978, s.153 (1); Hepple and O'Higgins 1981, chapter 12).

22   Increases in apprentice rates in Britain during the post-war period have been discussed by Wells (1983), Jones (1985) and Ryan (1986).

23   The data in Table 11.5, based on self-reporting with evidence of selection bias, probably overstate the increase in qualifications over time. Craft qualification in British industry still differs from that in Germany in its lack of external assessment, practical testing and coordination of theoretical and practical learning (Prais and Wagner, 1983; Prais, 1985; Steedman, 1988).

24 Daly, Hitchens and Wagner (1985), p. 60.

25 Such attributes lead Raffe (1990a) to classify contemporary apprenticeship as the main component of a 'sponsorship' sector geared to recruitment and training for internal labour markets. While the influence of internal markets on apprenticeship in modern Britain is undoubted, such a classification conceals the enduring strength of its occupational orientation, given the transferable skills which it develops and which many skilled workers rely upon to change employers in both metalworking and construction.

26 The rules and practices of YTS are outlined in GB MSC (1987a), GB TA (1989) and Jones (1988).

27 Evaluation of YTS is complicated by the size and heterogeneity of YTS, the difficulty of measuring training quality, and the propagandist orientation of official documents.

28 GB TA (1989), Table 1; Cassels (1990), p. 33. 'To maintain adequate levels of recruitment some [YTS providers] have adopted aggressive marketing strategies which include high quality advertising copy ...' (GB TA TSAS, 1990, para 41).

29 The Essex evidence refers primarily to one-year YTS during 1983–86. More recent evidence points in the same direction. Managing Agents in Liverpool and Devon commonly treated trainees as products to be sold, for what they would bring in, to employers offering work experience, with wider training concerns being lost in the process (Chandler and Wallace, 1989).

30 A statistic more favoured in official presentation of YTS — that 54 per cent of trainees entering their second year on YTS had gained a vocational qualification during their first year (*Employment Gazette*, 1988, p. 352) — is less than impressive given high drop-out rates and low quality qualifications.

31 The rate of substitution appears to have risen strongly during the life of the scheme. Similarly based studies estimated substitution rates of one-third at the outset and one-half in 1985–86, though more narrowly based studies have suggested lower rates (Deakin and Pratten, 1988; Jones, 1988).

32 The feasibility of enforcing training quality by legal means is dubious, however, given the cost of writing and enforcing contracts for an activity as heterogeneous as training.

33 Only 2 per cent of applicants for ATO status were rejected, though low quality providers are likely to be overrepresented amongst the one quarter of 1985 Managing Agents who withdrew under two year YTS (Jones, 1988). Lax assessment for ATO status is also indicated by the decision to grant it to providers of a related adult training scheme (ET) upon submission of a three month 'development plan' without any operational requirements at all (*Independent*, 11 September 1990).

34 Of providers of work experience in 1987/88, 52 per cent stated that they incurred no additional supervision costs for YTS trainees and only 2 per cent had actually hired additional staff (whether qualified or not) for such purposes (GB MSC, 1988:61).

35 '[Inspectors are] impressed by the commitment of scheme staff and the motivation and enthusiasm of young people participating in YTS ... [YTS2] offers a balanced mix of training and work experience which enhances employability and helps increasing numbers of young people to secure a foothold on the employment ladder ... employers have been alerted to the need for more comprehensive training' and, most revealing of all, 'among [inspectors] there is a concensus that YTS is

a significant improvement on what has gone before' (GB TA TSAS, 1990, paras 28–33). Such claims, impoverished in both form and content, contrast sharply with assessments of schooling quality by the (relatively independent) HMI schools inspectorate.

36 The distinction between MSC and Government inclinations is less than sharp, given that the Government found joint regulation valuable for launching its schemes and that many MSC officials, particularly after the 1982 change of leadership in both MSC and the Department of Employment, shared the Government's deregulatory and commercial values.

37 For example, a private training consultant has claimed that 'in the training industry we confidently expect our often-quoted German partners to start using our work-based training and assessment techniques, once they realise how much better they are than the rather hidebound methods currently favoured in the *Fachhochschulen*' (letter, *Financial Times*, 3 May 1989). Similar claims have been made at international conferences by representatives of Government, MSC and NCVQ.

38 *Financial Times*, 8 November 1988.

39 Proposals for the reform of VET in Britain advanced by Finegold and Soskice (1988), *inter alia*, include the revitalization of apprenticeship.

40 Chapter 6, above; Rainbird and Grant (1985); Lee (1990).

41 Marsden and Germe (1991); Garonna and Ryan (1991).

References

AHNER, D. (1978) *Arbeitsmarkt und Lonhstruktur*, Tübingen, J.C.B. Mohr.

ALEXANDER, K.J.W. and JENKINS, C.L. (1970) *Fairfields: a Study of Industrial Change*, London, Allen Lane.

ASHTON, D.N. and BROWN, P. (eds) (1988) *Education and Economic Life*, London, Falmer Press.

ASHTON, D.N., MAGUIRE, M.J. and SPILLSBURY, M. (1988) 'The changing structure of the youth labour market', Report to ESRC, University of Leicester.

BAIN, G.S. (ed.) (1983) *Industrial Relations in Great Britain*, Oxford, Basil Blackwell.

BECKER, G.S. (1964) *Human Capital*, New York, NBER.

BEGG, I.G., BLAKE, A.P., DEAKIN, B.M. and PRATTEN, C.F. (1990), YTS and the Labour Market, Final Report to Employment Department Training Agency; Department of Applied Economics, University of Cambridge.

BEICHT, U. and HOLZSCHUH, J. (1990) *Die Ausbildungsvergütungen in der Bundesrepublik Deutschland: Zeitreihenuntersuchung auf der Grundlage tariflicher Vergütungen von 1976 bis 1988*, Bonn, Bundesinstitut für Berfusbildung.

BEICHT, U. and WIEDERHOLD, S. (1985) 'Entwicklung der Ausbildungsvergütungen von 1976 bis 1984', report, Bonn, Bundesinstitut für Berufsbildung.

BOSCH, G. and SENGENBERGER, W. (1989) 'Employment policy, the state and the unions in the Federal Republic of Germany', in ROSENBERG, S. (ed.) *The State and the Labour Market*, New York, Plenum.

BROSNAN, P. and WILKINSON, F. (1988) 'A national minimum wage and economic efficiency', *Contributions to Political Economy*, 7, pp. 1–48.

BROWN, W. (ed.) (1981) *The Changing Contours of British Industrial Relations*, Oxford, Basil Blackwell.

BROWN, W. and NOLAN, P. (1988) 'Wages and labour productivity: The contribution of industrial relations research to the understanding of pay determination', *British Journal of Industrial Relations*, **26**, pp. 339–62.

BUTTLER, F. (1987) 'Labour market flexibility by deregulation: The case of the Federal Republic of Germany', *Labour and Society*, **12**, pp. 19–36.

CAMPBELL, A. and WARNER, M. (1989) 'Training practices and product strategy in high technology enterprises', *Computer-Aided Manufacturing Systems*, **2**, pp. 38–48.

CAMPINOS-DUBERNET, M. and GRANDO, J-M. (1988) 'Formation professionnelle ouvrière: Trois modeles Europèens', *Formation Emploi*, **22**, pp. 5–29.

CASEY, B. (1986) 'The dual apprenticeship system and the recruitment and retention of young persons in West Germany', *British Journal of Industrial Relations*, **24**, pp. 63–82.

CASEY, B. (1990) *Recent Developments in West Germany's Apprenticeship Training System*, London, Policy Studies Institute.

CASSELS, J. (1990) *Britain's Real Skill Shortage*, London, Policy Studies Institute.

CHANDLER, J. and WALLACE, C. (1990) 'Some alternatives in youth training: franchise and corporatist models', in GLEESON (ed.) (1990).

CLEMENT, W. (1985) 'Is the dual system responsible for the low unemployment of young workers in the Federal Republic of Germany?', *European Journal of Education*, **20**, pp. 203–19.

COMBES, M-C. (1988) 'L'apprentissage en France', Working Paper number 33, CEREQ, Paris.

CREEDY, J. and WHITFIELD, K. (1986) 'Earnings and job mobility: Professional chemists in Britain', *Journal of Economic Studies*, **13**, pp. 23–37.

CREEDY, J. and WHITFIELD, K. (1988) 'The economic analysis of internal labour markets', *Bulletin of Economic Research*, **40**, pp. 247–69.

DALY, A., HITCHENS, D. and WAGNER, K. (1985) 'Productivity, machinery and skills in a sample of British and German manufacturing plants', *National Institute Economic Review*, **111**, pp. 48–61.

DAVIS, N. (1986) 'Training for change', in Hart, P.E. (ed.) *Unemployment and Labour Market Policies*, Aldershot, Gower.

DEAKIN, B. and PRATTEN, C.F. (1987) 'Economic effects of YTS', *Employment Gazette*, **95**, pp. 491–7.

DOERINGER, P.B. and PIORE, M.J. (1971) *Internal Labour Markets and Manpower Analysis*, Lexington, MA, D.C. Heath.

DORE, R. (1973) *British Factory — Japanese Factory*, Berkeley, University of California Press.

DORE, R. (1987) *Taking Japan Seriously: A Confucian Perspective on Leading Economic Issues*, Stanford, Stanford University Press.

DOUGHERTY, C. (1987) 'The German dual system: A heretical view', *European Journal of Education*, **22**, pp. 195–9.

FINEGOLD, D. and SOSKICE, D. (1988) 'The failure of training in Britain; Analysis and prescription', *Oxford Review of Economic Policy*, **4**, 3, pp. 21–53.

FLOWER, F. and RUSSELL, D. (1982) 'The industrial tutor in the Federal Republic of Germany', mimeo, Further Education Staff College, Blagdon.

GALLIE, D. (1978) *In Search of the New Working Class*, Cambridge, Cambridge University Press.

GARONNA, P. and RYAN, P. (1986) 'Youth labour, industrial relations and deregulation in advanced economies', *Economia e Lavoro*, **20**, 4, pp. 3–19.

GARONNA, P. and RYAN, P. (1991) 'The regulation and deregulation of youth economic activity', in RYAN, P., GARONNA, P. and EDWARDS, R.C. (eds) *The Problem of Youth: The Regulation of Youth Employment and Training in Advanced Economies*, London, Macmillan.

GB DEPARTMENT OF EMPLOYMENT (DE) (1981) *A New Training Initiative: a Programme for Action*, Cmnd 8455, London, HMSO.

GB DEPARTMENT OF EMPLOYMENT (DE) (1986) 'Why some young people reject YTS', *Employment Gazette*, July, pp. 271–3.

GB DEPARTMENT OF EMPLOYMENT (DE) (1988a) *Training for Employment*, Cm 316, London, HMSO.

GB DEPARTMENT OF EMPLOYMENT (DE) (1988b) *Employment for the 1990s*, Cm 540, London, HMSO.

GB MANPOWER SERVICES COMMISSION (MSC) (1987a) *Annual Report 1986/1987*, Sheffield, MSC.

GB MANPOWER SERVICES COMMISSION (MSC) (1987b) 'Transition from school to work', *Labour Market Quarterly Report*, September, pp. 7–9.

GB MANPOWER SERVICES COMMISSION (MSC) (1988) Survey of YTS Providers, final report to MSC, mimeographed, Sheffield, MSC.

GB NATIONAL ECONOMIC DEVELOPMENT OFFICE (NEDO) (1977) *Engineering Craftsmen — Shortages and Related Problems*, London, NEDO.

GB NATIONAL ECONOMIC DEVELOPMENT OFFICE (1986) *Changing Working Patterns*, London, NEDO.

GB DEPARTMENT OF EMPLOYMENT, TRAINING AGENCY (TA) (1988) 'Youth Training Scheme (YTS)', *Labour Market Quarterly Report*, October, pp. 14–16.

GB TA (TRAINING AGENCY) — (1989) *YTS Progress Report 1987/88*, Sheffield, Training Agency.

GB TRAINING AGENCY, TRAINING STANDARDS ADVISORY SERVICE (TA, TSAS) (1990) *Review of Activity, 1 April 1988 to 30 September 1989*, Sheffield, Training Agency.

GLEESON, D. (1990) *Training and Its Alternatives*, Milton Keynes, Open University Press.

GOSPEL, H. (1991) *Markets, Firms and the Management of Labour in Modern Britain*, forthcoming, Cambridge, Cambridge University Press.

HAYES, C., ANDERSON, A. and FONDA, N. (1984) Competence and Competition, Report to NEDC and MSC, Institute for Manpower Studies, University of Sussex.

HEPPLE, B.A. and O'HIGGINS, P. (1981) *Employment Law*, 4th ed., London, Sweet and Maxwell.

HOFBAUER, H., KÖNIG, P. and NAGEL, E. (1973) *Betriebszugehörigkeitsdaure bei männlichen deutschen Arbeitnehmern*, Mitteilungen aus der Institut für Arbeitsmarkt und Berufsforschung, Nürnberg, IAB.

INCOMES DATA SERVICES (IDS) (1983) Report 383, London, IDS.

INCOMES DATA SERVICES (IDS) (1987) Young workers' pay, Study 383, London, IDS.

JARVIS, V. and PRAIS, S. (1989) 'Two nations of shopkeepers: Training for retailing in Britain and France', *National Institute Economic Review*, **128**, pp. 58–74.

JONES, I.S. (1985) 'Skill formation and pay relativities', in WORSWICK (ed.) *Education and Economic Performance*, Aldershot, Gower.

JONES, I.S. (1986) 'Apprentice training costs in British manufacturing establishments: Some new evidence', *British Journal of Industrial Relations*, **24**, pp. 333–62.

JONES, I.S. (1988) 'An evalutation of YTS, *Oxford Review of Economic Policy*, **4**, pp. 54–71.

JUNANKAR, P.N. (ed.) (1987) *From School to Unemployment? The Labour Market for Young People*, London, Macmillan.

KEEP, E. (1986) 'Designing the stable door: A study of how the Youth Training Scheme was planned', Warwick Paper in Industrial Relations number 8, Industrial Relations Research Unit, University of Warwick.

KELLER, B. (1981) *Interne Arbeitsmärkte und Arbeitsmarktstruktur*, Tübingen, J.C.B. Mohr.

KERR, C. (1954) 'The Balkanization of labour markets', in BAKKE, E.W. (ed.) *Labour Mobility and Economic Opportunity*, Cambridge, MA, MIT.

KRAIS, B. (1979) *Relationships between Education and Employment and their Impact on Education and Labour Market Policies*, Berlin, CEDEFOP.

LANE, C. (1988) 'Industrial change in Europe: The pursuit of flexible specialisation in Britain and West Germany', *Work, Employment and Society*, **2**, pp. 141–68.

LEE, D. (1979) 'Craft unions and the force of tradition: The case of apprenticeship', *British Journal of Industrial Relations*, **17**, pp. 34–49.

LEE, D. (1990) 'Poor work and poor institutions', in BROWN, P. and SCASE, R. (eds) *Poor Work*, London, Macmillan.

LEE, D., MARSDEN, D., HARDEY, M., RICKMAN, P. and MASTERS, K. (1988) 'Youth training, life chances and orientations to work: A case study of the Youth Training Scheme', in ASHTON, D.N. and BROWN, P. (eds) *Education and Economic Life*, London, Falmer Press.

LEE, D., MARSDEN, D., RICKMAN, P. and DUNCOMBE, J. (1990a) *Scheming for Youth: a Study of YTS in the Enterprise Culture*, Open University Press, Milton Keynes.

LEE, D., MARSDEN, D., RICKMAN, P. and DUNCOMBE, J. (1990b) 'Surrogate employment, surrogate labour markets and the development of training policies in the 1980s', in WALLACE, M. and CROSS, M. (eds) *Youth in Transition: The Sociology of Youth and Youth Policy*, London, Falmer Press.

LEESON, R.A. (1973) *Strike: A Live History, 1887–1971*, George Allen and Unwin, London.

LINDLEY, R.M. (1975) 'The demand for apprentice recruits by the engineering industry', *Scottish Journal of Political Economy*, **22**, 1, pp. 1–24.

LINDLEY, R. (1983) 'Active manpower policy', in BAIN, G.S. (ed.) *Industrial Relations in Great Britain*, Oxford, Basil Blackwell.

MACKAY, D.I., BODDY, D., BRACK, J., DIACK, J.A. and JONES, N. (1971) *Labour Markets under Different Employment Conditions*, London, George Allen and Unwin.

MACE, J. (1979) 'Internal labour markets for engineers in British industry', *British Journal of Industrial Relations*, **17**, pp. 50–63.

MAIN, B.G.M. and SHELLY, M.A. (1988) 'Does it pay young people to go on YTS?' in RAFFE (1988a) *Education and the Youth Market*, London, Falmer Press.

MARGINSON, P., EDWARDS, P.K., MARTIN, R., PURCELL, J. and SISSON, K. (1988) *Beyond the Workplace*, Oxford, Basil Blackwell.

MARIANI, I.F. (1986) 'Youth pay and employers' recruiting practices: The Italian experience', *Social Europe*, Supplement on Youth Pay and Employers' Recruitment Practices for Young People in the Community , pp. 135–43.

MARSDEN, D.W. (1982) 'Career structures and training in internal labour markets in Britain and West Germany', *Manpower Studies*, **4**, pp. 10–18.

MARSDEN, D.W. (1985) 'Youth pay in Britain compared with France and FR Germany since 1966', *British Journal of Industrial Relations*, **23**, pp. 399–414.

David Marsden and Paul Ryan

MARSDEN, D.W. (1986) *The End of Economic Man? Custom and Competition in the Labour Market*, Brighton, Wheatsheaf.

MARSDEN, D.W. (1990) 'Institutions and labour mobility: Occupational and internal labour markets in Britain, France, Italy and West Germany', in BRUNETTA, R. and DELL' ARRINGA, C. (eds) *Markets, Institutions and Cooperation: Labour Relations and Economic Performance*, London, Macmillan.

MARSDEN, D.W. and GERME, J-F. (1991) 'Young people and entry paths to long-term jobs in France and Great Britain', RYAN, P., GARONNA, P. and EDWARDS, R.C. (eds) *The Problem of Youth: The Regulation of Youth Employment and Training in Advanced Economies*, London, Macmillan.

MARSDEN, D.W. and RYAN, P. (1986) 'Where do young workers work? Youth employment by industry in various European economies', *British Journal of Industrial Relations*, **24**, pp. 83–102.

MARSDEN, D.W. and RYAN, P. (1988) 'Youth labour market structures and the quality of youth employment in major EEC economies', report to the Joseph Rowntree Memorial Trust, York.

MARSDEN, D.W. and RYAN, P. (1989a) 'Employment and training of young workers: Have the government misunderstood the labour market?', in *Education and Training UK 1989*, Newbury, Policy Journals.

MARSDEN, D.W. and RYAN, P. (1989b) 'Statistical tests for the universality of youth employment mechanisms in segmented labour markets', *International Review of Applied Economics*, **3**, pp. 148–169.

MARSDEN, D.W. and RYAN, P. (1990) 'Institutional aspects of youth employment and training policy in Britain', *British Journal of Industrial Relations*, **28**, pp. 351–69.

MARSDEN, D.W. and RYAN, P. (1991) 'Pay structures and youth employment in six European economies', RYAN, P., GARONNA, P. and EDWARDS, R.C. (eds) *The Problem of Youth: The Regulation of Youth Employment and Training in Advanced Economies*, London, Macmillan.

MARSDEN, D.W. and THOMPSON, M. (1990) 'Flexibility agreements in Britain and their significance in the increase in productivity in British manufacturing since 1980', *Work, Employment and Society*, **4**, pp. 83–104.

MARSH, A., HACKMANN, M. and MILLER, D. (1981) *Workplace Relations in the Engineering Industry in the UK and the Federal Republic of Germany*, London, Anglo-German Foundation.

MASON, C. and RUSSELL, R. (1987) 'Why does the corporatist state regard vocational education and training as an issue?', working paper 2250, Further Education Staff College, Blagdon.

MAURICE, M., SELLIER, F. and SILVESTRE, J-J. (1984) 'The search for a societal effect in the production of company hierarchy: A comparison of France and Germany', in OSTERMAN, P. (ed.) *Internal Labor Markets*, Cambridge, MA, MIT.

MAURICE, M., SELLIER, F. and SILVESTRE, J-J. (1986) *The Social Foundations of Industrial Power*, Cambridge, MA, MIT.

MILLWARD, N. and STEVENS, M. (1986) *British Workplace Industrial Relations 1980–1984*, Aldershot, Gower.

MÜLLER-JENTSCH, W. and SPERLING, H-J. (1978) 'Economic development, labour conflicts and the industrial relations system in West Germany', in CROUCH, C. and PIZZORNO, A. (eds). *The Resurgence of Class Conflict in Western Europe*, volume 1, London, Macmillan.

MÜNCH, J. and JUNG, E. (1980) *The Material and Social Standing of Young People during the Transition from School to Work in the Federal Republic of Germany*, Berlin, CEDEFOP.

NOLL, I., BEICHT, U., BÖLL, G., MALCHER, W. and WIEDERHOLD-FRITZ, S. (1983) 'The net cost of firm-based vocational training in the Federal Republic of Germany', mimeo, Berlin, CEDEFOP.

OSTERMAN, P. (ed.) (1984) *Internal Labor Markets*, Cambridge, MA, MIT.

PIORE, M. (1987) 'Historical perspectives and the interpretation of unemployment', *Journal of Economic Literature*, **25**, pp. 1834–50.

PRAIS, S.J. (1981) *Productivity and Industrial Structure*, Cambridge, Cambridge University Press.

PRAIS, S.J. (1981) 'Vocational qualifications of the labour force in Britain and Germany', *National Institute Economic Review*, **98**, pp. 47–59.

PRAIS, S.J. (1985) 'What can we learn from the German system of education and vocational training?', in WORSWICK, G.D.N. (ed.) *Educcation and Economic Performance*, Aldershot, Gower.

PRAIS, S.J. (1989) 'How Europe would see the new British initiative for standardising vocational qualifications', *National Institute Economic Review*, **129**, pp. 52–4.

PRAIS, S.J. and WAGNER, K. (1983) 'Some practical aspects of human capital investment: Training standards in five occupations in Britain and Germany', *National Institute Economic Review*, **105**, pp. 46–65.

PRAIS, S.J. and WAGNER, K. (1985) 'Schooling standards in England and Germany: Some summary comparisons bearing on economic performance', *National Institute Economic Review*, **112**, pp. 53–76.

PRAIS, S.J. and WAGNER, K. (1988) 'Productivity and management: The training of foremen in Britain and Germany', *National Institute Economic Review*, **123**, pp. 34–47.

RAFFE, D. (1987) 'The context of the Youth Training Scheme: An analysis of its strategy and development', *British Journal of Education and Work*, **1**, 1, pp. 1–32.

RAFFE, D. (ed.) (1988a) *Education and the Youth Labour Market*, London, Falmer Press.

RAFFE, D. (1988b) 'Going with the grain: youth training in transition', in BROWN, S. and WAKE, R. (eds) *Education in Transition: What Role for Research*, Edinburgh, Scottish Council for Research in Education.

RAFFE, D. (1990a) 'The transition from YTS to work: Content, context and the external labour market', in WALLACE, M. and CROSS, M. (eds) *Youth in Transition: The Sociology of Youth and Youth Policy*, London, Falmer Press.

RAFFE, D. (1990b) 'Beyond the mixed model: Social research and the case for the reform of 16–18s education in Britain', mimeo, Centre for Educational Sociology, University of Edinburgh.

RAGGATT, P. (1988) 'Quality control in the dual system of West Germany', *Oxford Review of Education*, **14**, pp. 163–86.

RAINBIRD, H. and GRANT, W. (1985) 'Employers, associations and training policy', Institute for Employment Research, University of Warwick, Coventy.

REUBENS, B.G. (ed.) (1983) *Youth at Work: An International Survey*, Totowa, NJ, Rowman and Allanheld.

REULING, J. (1974) 'Zur situation der jugendlichen in der ausbildung', *Kritisches Jarhrbuch '74*, Frankfurt, Fischer Verlag.

ROSENBERG, S. (ed.) (1989) *The State and the Labour Market*, New York, Plenum.

RUSSELL, R. (1989) 'Vocational training in West Germany and the culture of mastery', Working Paper 2556, Further Education Staff College, Blagdon.

RUSSELL, R. and PARKES, D. (1984) 'Career development in the Federal Republic', mimeo, Further Education Staff College, Blagdon.

RYAN, P. (1984a) 'Job training, employment practices and the large enterprise: The case of costly transferable skills', in OSTERMAN, P. (ed.) *Internal Labor Markets*, Cambridge, MA, MIT.

RYAN, P. (1984b) 'The New Training Initiative after two years', *Lloyds Bank Review*, **152**, pp. 41–45.

RYAN, P. (1986) 'Apprentices, employment and industrial disputes in engineering in the 1920s', paper presented to Workshop on Child Labour and Apprenticeship, University of Essex, May.

RYAN, P. (1987) 'Trade unionism and the pay of young workers', in JUNANKAR, P.N. (ed.) *From School to Unemployment? The Labour Market for Young People*, London, Macmillan.

RYAN, P. (1989) 'Youth interventions, job substitution and trade union policy in Great Britain, 1976–86', in ROSENBERG, S. (ed.) *The State and the Labour Market*, New York, Plenum.

RYAN, P. (1990a) 'Job training, individual opportunity and low pay', in BOWEN, A. and MAYHEW, K. (eds) *Improving Incentives for the Low Paid*, London, Macmillan.

RYAN, P. (1991a) 'The post-war evolution of relative apprentice pay in metalworking in Britain and West Germany', mimeo, King's College, Cambridge.

RYAN, P. (1991b) 'Trade union policies towards the Youth Training Scheme in Great Britain: the arguments', in RYAN, P., GARONNA P. and EDWARDS, R.C. (eds) *The Problem of Youth: The Regulation of Youth Employment and Training in Advanced Economies*, London, Macmillan.

RYAN, P., GARONNA, P. and EDWARDS, R.C. (eds) (1991) *The Problem of Youth: The Regulation of Youth Employment and Training in Advanced Economies*, London, Macmillan.

SAKO, M. and DORE, R. (1986) 'How the Youth Training Scheme helps employers', *Employment Gazette*, **94**, pp. 195–204.

SAKO, M. and DORE, R. — (1988) 'Teaching or testing: the role of the state in Japan', *Oxford Review of Economic Policy*, **4**, 3, pp. 72–81.

SCHMIDT, E. (1973) 'Spontane streiks 1972/3', in JACOBI, O., MÜLLER-JENTSCH, W. and SCHMIDT, E. (eds) *Gewerkschaften und Klassenkampf, Kritisches Jarhrbuch '73*, Frankfurt, Fischer Verlag.

SCHOBER, K. (1983) 'Youth employment in West Germany', in REUBENS, B.G. (ed.) *Youth at Work: An International Survey*, Totowa, NJ, Rowman and Allanheld.

SCHOBER, K. and WADENSJÖ, E. (1991) 'Contrasting forms of youth training and employment in Sweden and West Germany', in RYAN, P., GARONNA, P. and EDWARDS, R.C. (eds) *The Problem of Youth: The Regulation of Youth Employment and Training in Advanced Economies*, London, Macmillan.

SENGENBERGER, W. (1981) 'Labour market segmentation and the business cycle', in WILKINSON, F. (ed.) *Dynamics of Labour Market Segmentation*, London, Academic Press.

SENGENBERGER, W. and KOHLER, C. (1987) 'Policies of workforce reduction and labour market structures in the American and German automobile industry', in TARLING, R. (ed.) *Labour Market Flexibility*, London, Academic Press.

SENTANCE, A. and WILLIAMS, N. (1989) 'Skill shortages: A major problem for British industry?' *CBI Economic Situation Report*, March, pp. 21–4.

SHELDRAKE, J. and VICKERSTAFFE, S. (1987) *The History of Industrial Training in Britain*, Aldershot, Avebury.

SIEBERT, W.S. (1985) 'Developments in the economics of human capital', in CARLINE, D., PISSARIDES, C., SIEBERT, W.S. and SLOANE, P., *Labour Economics*, London, Longman.

SORGE, A. and WARNER, M. (1980) 'Training, manufacturing organisation and workplace relations in Great Britain and West Germany', *British Journal of Industrial Relations*, 18, pp. 318–33.

STEEDMAN, H. (1988) 'Vocational training in France and Britain: mechanical and engineering craftsmen', *National Institute Economic Review*, 126, pp. 57–70.

STEEDMAN, H. and WAGNER, K. (1987) 'A second look at productivity, machinery and skills in Britain and Germany', *National Institute Economic Review*, 122, pp. 84–95.

STEEDMAN, H. and WAGNER, K. (1989) 'Productivity, machinery and skills: Clothing manufacture in Britain and Germany', *National Institute Economic Review*, 128, pp. 40–57.

STREECK, W. (1985) *Industrial Relations and Industrial Change in the Motor Industry — An International View*, Industrial Relations Research Unit, University of Warwick, Coventry.

STREECK, W. (1987) 'The uncertainties of management and the management of uncertainty', *Work, Employment and Society*, 1, pp. 281–308.

STREECK, W. (1989) 'Skills and the limits of neo-liberalism; The enterprise of the future as a place of learning', *Work, Employment and Society*, 3, pp. 89–104.

STREECK, W., HILBERT, J., VAN KEVELAER, K-H., MAIER, F. and WEBER, H. (1987) *The Role of the Social Partners in Vocational Training and Further Training in the Federal Republic of Germany*, Berlin, CEDEFOP.

TAYLOR, M.E. (1981) *Education and Work in the Federal Republic of Germany*, London, Anglo-German Foundation.

THOMPSON, P.J. (1989) 'NVQs — What they mean', *Employment Gazette*, 97, pp. 14–16.

VENNING, M., FRITH, O. and GRIMBLEY, C. (1980) *The Craftsman in Engineering*, Watford, Engineering Industry Training Board.

WALLACE, M. and CROSS, M. (eds) (1990) *Youth in Transition: The Sociology of Youth and Youth Policy*, London, Falmer Press.

WELLS, W. (1983) 'The relative pay and employment of young people', Research Paper number 42, London, Department of Employment.

WIEDERHOLD-FRITZ, S. (1986) 'Is there a relationship between the cost of in-company vocational training and the offer of training places in the Federal Republic of Germany?', *Social Europe*, Supplement on Youth Pay and Employers' Recruitment Practices for Young People in the Community, pp. 39–48.

WORSWICK, G.D.N. (ed.) (1985) *Education and Economic Performance*, Aldershot, Gower.

Author Index

Abegglen, J. 164, 165
Ahner, D. 256, 261
Akaoka, I. 175
Alexander, K.J.W. 83, 276
Amaya, T. 176
Anderson, A. 275
Anderson, M. 64
Antal, A.B. 90
Aoki, M. 166, 172
Ashton, David N. 11, 14, 18, 57, 233–49
Atkinson, M. 103
Axelrod, R. 105
Azumi, K. 165, 166, 169

Baran, B 234
Barnett, C. 93
Becker, G.S. 199, 224, 255
Beesley, M. 150
Begg, I. 267
Beicht, U. 258
Bell, C. 61, 63, 64
Bennett, R. 56
Bhasanavich, D. 172
Blake, A. 267
Bolton, E. 39
Booth, S. 64
Bosch, G. 276
Braybrooke, D. 72
Brosnan, P. 268
Brousseau, K. 162
Brown, A. 64
Brown, G.F. 25
Brown, W. 276

Bruno, S. 75, 96
Burnhill, P. 61, 63
Burns, T. 166
Buttler, F. 276

Calmfors, L. 14
Campinos-Dubernet, M. 24, 275
Campbell, Adrian 7–8, 17, 102, 146–57, 275
Campbell, T.D. 64
Casey, B. 256, 258, 276
Cassels, J, 277
Chandler, J. 277
Cheng, J.Y.S. 241
Clark, R. 164, 176
Clegg, C. 24, 34
Clement, W. 276
Cole, R.E. 166
Coleman, W. 103
Combes, M.-C. 253
Cooke, P. 107
Courtenay, G. 51, 54, 57, 63
Creedy, J. 253, 275
Currie, W. 152, 154

Daly, A. 24, 142, 277
Davies, S.W. 142
Davis, N. 270
Deakin, B. 267, 277
Dehnboster, P. 77
Deloitte, Haskins & Sells, 89
Dertouzos, M. 223
Dickenson, H. 81

Diepold, P. 110
Doeringer, P.B. 255, 275
Dore, R. 24, 35, 42, 94, 159, 164, 165,
    173, 267, 268, 274, 245, 276
Dougberty, C. 275, 276
Drake, Keith 10, 14, 18, 207–28, 224
Driffill, J. 14
Driver, M.J. 162
Duncombe, J. 267
Durkheim, E. 48
Dutton, P. 74

Edwards, P.K. 276
Elbaum, B. 12
Emerson, M. 200
Erben, M. 81
Evans, K. 39

Fairley, John 52, 63, 64
Finegold, David 6–7, 17, 18, 34–5, 43,
    47, 63, 71, 89, 90, 93–114, 278
Finniston, Sir Monty 162–3, 168, 170
Fisher, A. 37
Flower, F. 275
Fonda, N. 38, 94, 97, 275
Ford, B. 32
Francis, A. 154
Freeman, G.P. 73
Fruin, M. 161

Gallie, D. 253
Garnett, N. 25
Garonna, P. 252, 265
Gaskell, J. 238, 239, 249
Germe, J-F. 254, 278
Geurts, J. 225
Gillan, W.J. 173
Gospel, H. 276
Gower, D. 239
Grando, J-M. 24, 275
Grant, N. 48
Grant, W. 278
Gray, J. 48
Green, F. 249
Gregory, G. 172
Grünewald, Uwe 211, 216, 218, 220, 222,
    228

Hackman, M. 263
Hage, J. 165, 166
Halberstam, D. 166
Hamilton, S.F. 81
Hampden-Turner, C. 150
Handy, C. 159
Hara, R. 165
Hartmann, G. 150
Haslam, C. 153
Hayes, C. 38, 94, 97, 275
Hazen, H.L. 168
Hedegaard, B. 210, 213
Hegelbeimer, A. 207, 216, 220, 222
Hendry, J. 178
Hepple, B.A. 276
Hilbert, J. 275
Hirschmeier, J. 173
Hirst, P. 94, 106
Hitchens, D. 142, 277
Ho. Y.P. 242
Hofbauer, H. 258
Hoskins, M. 249
Hövels, Ben 219, 225, 228
Howieson, Cathy 61, 63
Hull, F. 165, 166
Humes, W. 56
Hyman, R. 107

Inagami, T. 161, 175
Ishida, M. 174

Jarvis, Valerie 7, 13, 15, 17, 18, 24, 31,
    119–44, 205, 267
Jenkins, C.L. 276
Jensen, G. 209, 211
Jensen, M. 113
Jones, I.S. 75, 252, 255, 258, 264, 267,
    269, 276, 277
Jung, E. 258, 261

Katzenstein, P. 94, 110
Keep, Ewart 4–5, 169, 23–43, 58, 64, 71,
    73, 147, 152, 251, 268, 270
Keller, B. 256
Kern, H. 157
Kiyonari, T. 164
Knight, Horace 242, 243, 249
Koefoed, E. 209
Kohler, C. 276

König, P. 258
Kono, T. 165
Kraayvanger, G. 219, 225
Krahn, H. 239
Kraise, B. 276
Kushner, S. 27
Kuwahara, Y. 175

Lane, C. 152, 257
Lauglo, J. 19
Lawler, G. 25, 37
Lawrence, P. 80, 149
Laxer, G. 236, 237
Lazonick, W. 12
Leborgne, D. 106
Lee, D. 64, 262, 267, 268, 269, 273, 275, 278
Leeson, R.A. 276
Leroy, R. 220, 221
Lillis, K. 19
Lin, T.B. 242
Lindbloom, C.E. 72
Lindley, Robert M. 9–10, 14, 17, 18, 185–205, 263
Lipieta, A. 106
Littler, C.R. 165
Lorenz, E. 114
Lorriman, J. 172
Lowe, G.S. 249

Mace, J. 253
Mack, Donald 52, 63, 64
Mackay, D.I. 276
Maclure, S. 37
Magaziner, I. 94, 97, 98, 107, 113, 114
Magota, R. 174
Maguire, Malcolm J. 11, 14, 18, 233–49
Maier, F. 275
Maier, H.E. 24
Main. B.G.M. 61, 268
Mannari, H. 174
Mansell, J. 36
March, J.G. 72
Marginson, P. 276
Marquand, Judith 70, 75, 96, 248
Marry, C. 94
Marsden, David W. 11, 13, 14, 15, 18, 24, 33, 235, 237, 251–78
March, A. 263

Marsh, R. 174
Martin, R. 276
Mason, C. 276
Maurice, M. 17, 24, 47, 94, 236, 251, 275
May, E.R. 72
Mayhew, K. 43, 71
McCormick, Kevin 8–9, 17, 24, 35, 159–79
McFarland, L. 18
MaKinsey and Co. 24
McLean, I. 105
McPherson, Andrew 48, 49, 51, 54, 56, 57, 58, 61, 63
Mehaut, P. 38, 221
Miller, D. 263
Millward, N. 276
Misumi, J. 171
Moore, C. 64
Moore, A. 25
Moorhouse, H.F. 100
Morishima, M. 226
Morita, A. 224, 226
Müller-Jentsch, W. 258
Münch, J. 218, 258, 261

Nagle, E. 258
Nakajima, A. 177
Nakamura, H. 164
Nakane, C. 172
Neave, G. 51, 58
Neustadt, R.E. 72
Ng, Sek-Hong 242, 244, 249
Nicholas, I. 150
Nickell, S. 19
Nolan, P. 276
Noll, I. 89, 212, 222, 223, 276
Northcott, J. 148

Oakeshott, M. 76
Oeschslin, J.J. 36, 37
O'Higgins, P. 276
Okamoto, Y. 165
Oliver, N. 15
Oshima, K. 176

Page, Edward 72, 89
Parkes, D. 275
Patinkin, M. 94, 97, 98, 107, 114
Paul, J.J. 222

Pavitt, K. 162, 163
Peacock, A.T. 71
Pell, C. 38, 39
Pellegrin, J. 73
Perry, P.J.C. 25
Pickard, J. 36
Piore, M.J. 94, 97, 106, 251, 255, 275
Platt, A. 215
Pointing, D. 25
Pole, C. 81
Porter, J. 239
Prais, S.J. 1–2, 7, 13, 15, 17, 18, 24, 31, 79, 119–44, 147, 156, 205, 262, 267, 275, 276
Pratten, C.F. 16, 267, 277
Pressman, J. 83
Prince, J.B. 162
Purcell, J. 276

Raab, Charles 48, 49, 56, 57, 58, 63
Raffe, David 5, 12–13, 14, 47–65, 71, 75, 76, 113, 268, 274, 277
Raggatt, P. 275, 276
Rainbird, 43, 108, 278
Rau, E. 77
Read, A.R. 25
Reich, R. 113
Reissert, B. 75
Reuling, J. 259
Rickman, P. 267
Rigg, M. 80
Ripper, C. 144
Rist, R.C. 79
Rohlen, T.P. 168, 171, 172
Rose, Richard 5–6, 15, 24, 63, 68–90, 108, 275
Ross, D. 49
Russell, R. 144, 275, 276
Ryan, Paul 3, 11, 13, 14, 15, 18, 24, 33, 63, 113, 204, 248, 251–78

Sabel, C. 94, 97, 106
Sachs, J. 75
Sakakibara, K. 166, 169, 172
Sako, M. 24, 35, 159, 173, 268, 274
Sardoni, C. 96
Sayer, A. 98, 107
Schmid, G. 75

Schmidt, E. 259
Schmitter, P. 106
Schober, K. 263, 276
Schoenfeldt, E. 77
Schuman, M. 157
Scott, B.R. 226
Sellier, F. 17, 24, 236, 251, 275
Sengenberger, W. 276
Senker, P. 113, 150
Sentance, A. 252
Sheldrake, J. 25–6, 263
Shelly, M. 61, 268
Shepherd, R. 29
Shirai, T. 165
Siebert, W.S. 255
Silvestre, J-J. 17, 24, 33, 236, 251, 275
Simon, H.A. 69, 72
Sisson, K. 43, 276
Smith, A.D. 142
Smith, P.B. 178
Solow, R. 68
Sorensen, J.H. 209, 211
Sorge, A. 1, 17, 24, 32, 146, 147, 150, 152, 153, 258, 275
Soskice, D. 34–5, 47, 71, 75, 90, 94, 96, 100, 109, 113, 278
Sousa, S. de 213
Sperling, H-J. 258
Spiers, B-G. 24
Spilsbury, M. 235
Spours, K. 54, 55, 56, 62, 63
Stalk, G. 164, 165
Stalker, G. 166
Steedman, Hilary 2, 24, 31, 33, 142, 205, 253, 254, 267, 275, 276
Stevens, M. 276
Streeck, W. 33, 34, 37, 43, 106, 107, 112, 252, 257, 259, 275, 276
Sung, Johnny 11, 14, 18, 233–49

Takagi, H. 172
Taylor, M.E. 77, 276
Tessaring, M. 86, 222
Thompson, P.J. 257
Thurow, L. 96
Timmermann, D. 207
Tomes, N. 52, 57
Trevor, M. 15, 161, 175, 176
Turner, R. 54

van Kevelaer, K-H. 275
van Onna, B. 219, 225
van Wel, J. 225
Varlaam, C. 52, 81
Venning, M. 262
Vickerstaffe, S. 25–6, 263
Vogler-Ludwig, K. 188–9, 204
von Glinow, M. 162

Wadensjö, E. 276
Wagner, Karin 2, 7, 13, 15, 17, 18, 24, 31,
    33, 79, 119–44, 156, 205, 262, 267, 275,
    276, 277
Walford, G. 50
Wallace, M. 277
Walton, R. 94, 98, 107
Wardlow, A. 153
Warner, Malcolm, 1, 7–8, 17, 24, 32, 102,
    146–57, 258, 275
Watkins, G. 24
Watson, T.J. 226
Watts, A.G. 39
Weber, H. 275
Weiermair, K. 237
Weir, A.D. 55, 64

Wersky, G. 159, 163, 172
Westney, D.E. 166, 169, 172
White, M. 15, 113
Whitfield, K. 253
Wiederhold-Fritz, S. 252, 258, 263, 276
Wiener, M. 93
Wildavsky, A. 71, 83
Wilkinson, B. 15
Wilkinson, F. 268
Williams, K. 153
Williams, N. 252
Williamson, B. 77
Williamson, O. 154
Willms, D. 61
Wilson, T. 28, 29
Windolf, P. 24
Wiseman, J. 71
Worswick, G.D.N. 24

Yakushiji, T. 166
Yamada, K. 176
Yui, T. 173.

Zeitlin, J. 94, 106
Zysman, J. 94, 101, 103

Subject Index

A levels 143, 167, 235, 274
  compared with Germany 79, 82, 84, 87
  compared with Highers 50, 54–5, 64
Abitur 79, 82, 87, 143
Action Plan (SED) 5, 52, 55–7, 59, 62–4
adult training 28–9, 156, 211, 216, 271, 277
advertising 114, 132
AER (*Arbedjdsgivernes Elevrefusion*), Denmark 209–11, 217, 219
aerospace industries 148, 150, 166
age 26, 39, 198, 246, 253, 258, 262
  apprentices 238, 243, 253, 254, 258, 261, 263
  Canada 238, 239
  Denmark 208–11
  German dual system 211, 216, 218, 258, 260–1
  Hong Kong 241, 243
  hotel workers 133, 143
  Japan 161, 162, 167, 173, 174, 175
  percentage of labour force 79
  and qualifications 85–8
  retirement 161
  salary 173, 174, 254, 260–1, 276
  school-leavers 50–1, 111, 167, 212, 241, 258, 274
  Scottish schools 48, 50, 54–5
  YTS 266, 267
agriculture 52, 188, 223
Alberta 237–8, 239
Anglo-German Foundation for Research in Industrial Societies 25, 89

applied skills 11, 233–6, 239, 240, 245, 249
apprentices and apprenticeships 3, 85, 105, 198, 245–6, 275, 278
  age 238, 243, 253, 254, 258, 261, 263
  Canada 11, 237–9
  Denmark 208–9, 211, 212
  engineering 152, 153, 156–7, 170
  France 35, 212, 221, 228, 253, 254, 275–6
  German dual system 77, 80, 111
  Germany 12–13, 36, 82, 110, 212, 215–17, 220, 253–67, 271–3, 276
  Hong Kong 243
  hotels 129, 131–4, 136–7, 143
  internal labour market 272–4, 277
  Italy 253, 254
  Netherlands 212, 215, 219, 276
  occupational labour market 253–4, 272–3
  pay 1, 252–6, 258–61, 263
  Scotland 52, 63
  strikes 262–3
  tax (France) 35
  YTS 15, 265, 266, 267, 271
Approved Training Organisation (ATO) 265–6, 269, 270, 277
assessment 61, 62, 173
  Germany 82, 276, 277
  hotel staff 133, 136–40, 144
attitudes 3, 8, 15, 99, 147
  class 93–4, 245–6
  employers 15, 28–31

government to VET 32–7
  Japan 172, 175
AUD (*Arbejdsmarkedets
  Uddannelsesfond*) of Denmark 210–11,
  213, 217, 219
Australia 41, 97, 198
Austria 120, 198

baccalauréate 274
banks 15, 164, 165, 171, 243
BEC 82
Belgium 198, 220–1, 215
Benelux countries 19
Berlin hotels 121, 122, 123
Berufsbildung system (Germany) 77–9,
  83, 87
blockage 6, 69, 74–6, 88
British Steel 26
BTEC 87, 127, 128, 133–7, 140, 144, 243
budgeting 70, 102, 156, 159
building trade 188–9, 252
  see also construction

Canada 4, 41, 77, 198, 233, 236–40,
  244–6, 248–9
  compared with Hong Kong 11, 14,
    244–7
Canada Jobs Strategy 240
Casio (Japanese company) 165
Cassels, John (director-general of
  NEDO) 32
Caterbase 128, 138, 139
catering 52, 119, 191
  in hotels 121–2, 138–9, 143
CBI (Confederation of British Industry)
  25, 26, 29, 30, 84
Certificate of Sixth Year Studies
  (Scotland) 51
certification 7, 13, 194, 238, 246, 253, 262
  YTS 266, 267
CGLI 53
Chambers of Commerce (EC) 144, 215,
  259
chemical companies 159, 169, 173, 177
chemical engineers 102, 168, 169, 174
China 240, 249
City and Guilds 82, 262
  hotel staff 134–9, 144
city technology colleges 58

class, social 11, 61, 93–4, 113, 245–6, 247
clerical work 31, 110, 185, 191–3, 234,
  252
clothing and textiles 2, 31, 119, 188–9
  Hong Kong 241, 243, 244
Coca Cola 97
collective bargaining 33, 108
colleges 58, 84, 121
  Canada 239, 240
  Germany 80, 110, 111
  Hong Kong 242, 243
  hotel staff 121, 133, 136, 138, 139, 140
  Japan 161, 167, 168, 172, 173, 177
  Scotland 50–2, 64
Commission of European Communities
  9
competence shift 150–1, 152
computers 98, 152, 179
  hotels 125–6, 131–2
conceptual skills 11, 233–6, 242, 245–8
construction industry 3, 52, 188–9, 234,
  252, 266, 277
  Canada 237, 239
  Germany 120, 219
  Hong Kong 244
continuing education and training (CET)
  212–13, 225
Coopers and Lybrand Report (1985) 153,
  159
Corning Glass 98
correspondence courses 173
costs 2–3, 15, 110, 112, 235, 245, 255–6
  apprentices 260
  automation 195
  Danish training 209–10
  European training 200, 215–16, 226,
    227
  French training 220
  further education (to school-leavers)
    94–6, 102
  German training 14, 78, 89, 211–12,
    220, 222–3, 252
  hotel equipment 124–5, 126, 143–4
  HSE (high skill equilibrium) 89, 96–9,
    101, 104–6
  international transportation 109, 113
  publishing 114
  of training to employers 11, 263–4
  US training 41

youth training 265, 268–9, 272–3
crowding out 9, 185, 193, 195, 203
CSEs 79, 81, 82, 143
CSEU 263
culture 6–7, 94, 113, 221, 245, 247
  effect on comparative research 14–15,
    17, 19, 41, 47, 61, 69, 73
  effect on training policy 75–6, 199, 251
  Japan 9, 171–2, 174, 178
curricula 111, 196, 235, 241, 245–6, 251,
  264
  Canada 237, 238, 245
  Germany 259, 260
  for jobs 199–200, 203
  Scotland 52–3, 54, 55–6, 61, 62–3, 64

degrees 51, 82, 86–7, 153, 194, 235
  hotel staff 127, 128
demarcations 107, 152, 262
Denmark 120, 198
  financing training 10, 207–11, 213, 215,
    217, 225
  youth training 208–11
Department of Education and Science
  50, 56, 79
  see also White Papers
design 8, 187, 190
  engineering 151–6, 162–3
Donovan Commission 257
drop out rate (YTS) 277
dual system 69–70, 74, 111
  Germany 31, 35, 37, 69–70, 77–80, 83,
    89, 215–18, 222, 271
  engineering 147
  funding 211

economic growth 68–9, 71, 79, 109, 113,
  162, 196–7
Economic and Social Research Council
  (ESRC) 63
Edding Commission 207, 211
Education for the Industrial Society
  Project 55
EEF 263
EFG (*Erhvervsfaglig Grunduddannelse*)
  of Denmark 209, 211
Egan, Sir John (Chairman of Jaguar) 26
EIS (Educational Institute of Scotland)
  64

electrical engineering 148, 156, 205, 219
  Germany 187–9
electronics 8–10, 147–57, 170
  Hong Kong 241, 243, 244
  Japan 159, 160, 164, 168–9, 172–4,
    179
Electronics Industry (NEDO Report) 24
Emilia Romagna 94, 106
employers' associations 105, 106, 110,
  111
  funding training 210
  pay for trainees 252, 256, 257
  Scotland 57
Employers' Trainee Reimbursement
  Scheme (Denmark) *see* AER
Engineerinc Council 163
Engineering Graduate Training Scheme
  242
Engineering ITB 29, 263–4
engineers and engineering 4, 28–9, 106,
  162–3, 185, 234, 252, 262
  apprenticeships 152, 153, 156–7,
    170
  Germany 146–57, 187–9, 190, 195,
    199, 257
  Japan 8–9, 159, 161, 163, 166–78
  on-the-job training 171, 172–3
  pay 173–5
  qualifications 139, 153, 154, 156, 252,
    262
  Scotland 51
  youth training 51, 266
European Centre for the Development
  of Vocational Training (CEDEFOP)
  10, 41, 84
European Community (EC) 9–10, 71, 73,
  241
  comparative research 4, 5, 19, 41, 42,
    60–1
  single market 10, 42, 200–2
  training finance 14, 207–28
  training policy 58, 200–3
  youth pay 252–6, 260, 262
European Social Fund 213, 217
examinations 85, 168, 211, 246
  Germany 78–82, 89, 120, 156, 259, 260
  hotel staff 120, 133, 136–8, 140, 143,
    144
exports 69, 106, 108–10, 111

Facharbeiter 258, 259
Fashschule diploma 127, 143
Fawlty Towers 132, 143
Federal Institute of Labour (Germany)
 211, 216, 217, 225
fees, funding training 210, 211, 219
financing of training 10, 89, 100–1
 EC 207–28
 Germany 14–16
 youth 81
 see also funding for training; public
 funding
Finniston Committee 162–3, 168, 170,
 199
flexibility 18, 140–1, 190, 192, 196,
 222–3, 257
 engineering workforce (Germany) 152,
 157
Ford Motor Company 28–9, 30, 166
Forsyth, Michael (Scottish Education
 Minister) 49
France 18, 31, 35–7, 69, 198, 212–13,
 256, 273–4
 apprenticeships 221, 228, 253–4,
 275–6
 comparative research 1–2, 4, 17, 24,
 42, 77, 88
 funding training 10, 207–8, 211, 213,
 217, 220–2, 224–6, 228
 job changes 192, 195
 pay for youth 254–5, 260, 276
 retraining 38
 right to training 35–6, 215
 taxes for funding 35, 36, 212, 217, 221
 youth training 26
Frankfurt 121, 123, 142
Fujitsu 179
funding of training 13–14, 178, 199–201,
 204, 235, 245, 274
 Canada 249
 Denmark 209–11, 213–14, 225
 EC 207–8, 215–17, 219–20
 France 10, 207–8, 211, 213,
 217, 220–2, 224–6, 228
 Germany 10, 14, 199–200, 207, 211,
 217, 219–20, 224–6
 Hong Kong 242, 244, 247
 ITBs 11
 Scotland 57

 youth 60, 84, 266, 269, 273
 see also financing of training; public
 funding
fungibility 6, 69, 74–5, 76
further education 96, 258, 262
 Scotland 50, 62
 see also higher education

GCSEs 50, 62, 134
GEC 179
gender 51–2, 79, 120, 142, 252, 254
 pay 260, 276
Germany 18–19, 101, 113, 192, 207–8,
 251, 256–8, 273, 277
 apprenticeships 12–13, 215, 220,
 253–64, 266–7, 271–273, 276
 comparative research 1–2, 4, 16–17,
 24, 42
 dual system 31, 35, 37, 69–70, 77–80,
 83, 89, 111, 215–18, 222, 271
 electronics 9–10
 employers' training 28, 33–4, 197
 engineering 146–57, 187–9, 190, 195,
 199, 257
 examinations 78–82, 89, 120, 156, 259,
 260
 exports 100
 funding training 10, 14, 199–200, 207,
 211, 217, 219–20, 224–6
 hotels 7, 13, 15, 119–44
 labour force survey 187–9, 205
 legislation retraining 36
 Meister 6, 80–2, 87, 90, 113, 215, 258,
 275
 metalworking 7–8, 119, 259
 post-compulsory education 198, 212
 qualifications 2, 5–6, 78–83, 86–90,
 194
 schools 18, 213
 trainee pay 11–12, 222–3, 252, 254–5,
 260–2, 266, 276
 youth training 26
Gill, Ken (MSF trade union) 26
graduates 8, 167, 170
 electronics 147, 150, 152–7
 Japan 8, 159, 161, 163, 168–9, 173–5,
 176–7
 pay 173–5
grants for UK training 263

HCIMA (hotel staff) 127
higher education 9, 41, 235, 236, 243
  Canada 239, 240
  Japan 168
  Scotland 50
  see also further education
Higher National Units (Highers)
  Scotland 50–1, 54–5, 64
Highlands and Islands Development
  Board (HIDB) 53, 60
Highlands and Islands Enterprise (HIE)
  50, 53, 59, 60
high-skill equilibrium (HSE) 6–7, 93,
  94–8, 99–112
HNC (Scotland) 53, 82, 127, 128
HND (Scotland) 53, 82, 127, 128, 143
Holland, Geoffrey (director MSC) 32
Hong Kong 11, 14, 42, 233, 240–4,
246–7, 249
Hotelfachmann course (Germany) 134, 136
Hotelmeister 127
hotels 2, 119–44
  equipment 124–6, 143–4
  Germany 7, 13, 15, 119–44
  Hong Kong 243, 244, 249
  Italy 191
  qualifications of staff 7, 15, 121, 125,
    127–9, 131–41, 143
  quality of training 132–7
  size and staffing 120–4, 135
  youth employment (Scotland) 52
housekeeper 121, 123, 126, 129–30, 131,
142
  qualifications 127, 140
  training 134, 136–7, 139
Hughes initiative 53, 56, 64

IBM 226
ICL 179
immigrants 236–7, 238, 240
incentives 93–4, 178, 201, 215, 237, 254,
264
  HSE 99, 102, 107, 110–12, 113
  Japan 175
  managers 101, 102, 111, 112
  policymakers 96
  YTS 269
industrial relations 17, 41, 94, 108, 110,
112, 236, 258

  Japan 165, 224
  pay differentials 255
  Scotland 47, 49
  Sweden 37
  training systems 33, 35
Industrial Service Centre (Italy) 106
Industrial Training Act (1964) 243
Industrial Training Advisory Committee
  (ITAC) 242, 243
Industrial Training Boards (ITBs) 11, 38,
  170, 198, 244–8, 263–4, 266
  Engineering 29, 263–4
  Scotland 52, 57, 58
Industry Department for Scotland 54
inflation 3, 18, 69, 95, 97
information-processing 148, 149, 151
in-house training 8, 210
  Japan 159, 161, 162
  see also on-the-job training
innovation 7–8, 93, 101, 152
  HSE 107–10, 112, 113
  Japan 162, 163, 166, 169
Institute of Manpower Studies 205
internal labour market 10–11, 33, 178,
  196–7, 252–3, 275
  apprentices 254–6, 258–61, 264,
    272–4, 277
  Canada 236–8, 240, 246
  Europe 199–202, 213
  France 254
  Germany 256–8, 258–61, 264
  HSE 102, 111
  Italy 254
  Japan 167
  training 234–8, 247
  YTS 265, 268, 271
interventions 217, 220
  EC 221, 222–4, 226
  funding of training 213–14, 215
Ireland 24, 73, 77, 215, 217
Italy 24, 73, 94, 106, 198, 207
  financing training 208
  labour market 191, 192, 253, 254
  youth pay 254–5, 260, 275, 276

Jaguar Cars 26
Japan 4, 13, 19, 28, 34–5, 88, 113, 240
  comparative research 15, 17, 41, 42
  engineers 159–79

exports 69, 110
finance 101
industrial relations 165, 224
job rotation 8, 102, 166, 170, 173, 176, 178
labour market 273–4, 275
lifetime employment 8–9, 77, 159, 161–2, 164–8, 171–8
post-compulsory education 198
productivity 15, 226
schools 9, 18, 111, 161
steel industry 114, 160, 164, 175, 177
Jenkins, Clive 26
job content 186–95, 203
job ladders 236, 257
job security 8, 105, 177, 253, 257, 264
   see also lifetime employment

Keynesians 72, 75
Korea 109, 114, 241

labour forces 69, 79
   age 79, 162, 175
   qualifications 1, 5–6, 70, 82–9
   Japan 160–2, 175, 177
   see also labour market
labour market 10–12, 33, 39, 71–2, 105, 224
   Belgium 220
   Denmark 210
   Europe 185–93, 193–204, 213–15
   external 9, 33, 102, 111, 167, 179, 196–7, 213–15
   Germany 222
   Japan 165, 167, 168, 176
   Scotland 51–2, 54, 57, 61, 62
   youth 57, 61, 75–6
   see also internal labour market;
      occupational labour market
Labour Market Training Fund
   (Denmark) *see* AUD
Lang, Ian (Scottish Education Minister)
   64
LDCs 19
Lead Industry Bodies (LIBs) 55, 56, 57, 58
LENS (Local Employer Networks) 38
LEST (Laboratoire d'Economie et de
   Sociologie du Travail),

Aix-en-Provence 17, 19, 24
leveraged buyouts (LBOs) 100, 113
Lifetime employment (Japan) 8–9, 77, 159, 161–2, 164–8, 171–8
line managers 170, 172, 173, 179
literacy 135, 192
local education authorities 50, 53, 84
Local Enterprise Companies (LECs) 53, 59, 62
local government 106, 211, 217
Local Government Audit Commission 71
low-skill equilibrium (LSE) 84, 94–7
loyalty 13, 161, 176, 257
Lucas 25, 26

management 6, 23, 29, 81, 93, 95, 97, 99–102, 104–5, 107–9, 111–12, 190–1, 234
   engineering 146, 152–3, 155–6, 159, 162, 165
   hotels 7, 121, 125, 127, 129, 131–3, 140, 143–4
   incentives 101, 102, 111, 112
   Japan 159, 162, 165, 168, 170–2, 175–7
   pay 143–4
   training 16, 17–18, 112, 113, 133, 134, 146, 226
Management Development Centre 242
Managing Agents (YTS) 265, 269, 277
Manchester Seminar (1989) 4, 11, 63, 204
Manpower Services Commission (MSC) 36, 37, 38, 40, 208, 264, 278
   comparative research 25–7, 28
   Competence and Competition 29–30, 32, 38, 49
   reports 26, 29–30, 32, 38, 49
   Scotland 50, 59, 64
   TA 56, 58
   YTS 266, 269, 270, 271
manufacturing 97–8, 150, 170, 176, 199
   Canada 236–7, 239
   gender of employees 142
   Germany 7, 119, 120, 124, 187–9, 259
   Hong Kong 241, 242, 243
Manufacturing Science Finance (MSF) 26
mass production 98, 165, 166, 234
mathematics 64, 79, 135, 140, 141, 238

mechanical engineering 148–52, 155, 187–9
Meister (German trainer) 6, 80–2, 87, 90, 113, 215, 258, 275
metalworking 2, 7–8, 119, 259, 276, 277
  qualifications of employees 262–4
Michelin guides 122, 124
microelectronics 102, 146, 148, 149–51, 155
'Milk round' 167
mining 97, 187–9
Ministry of Social Affairs and Employment (Netherlands) 219
Mittlere Reife (German exam) 79
mobility of labour 176, 198–9, 204, 220, 254, 257
motivation 93, 94–5, 108, 112, 113, 190–1
  Japan 8–9, 176
myths
  in comparative research 5, 12–13, 16
  of Scottish education 48–9, 55, 56–7, 63

NAFE 51, 54, 58
National Awards (Scotvec) 53, 59, 64
National Certificate (Scotvec) 51, 52–6, 59, 62, 64
National Council for Vocational Qualifications (NCVQ) 31, 53–6, 59, 84, 266, 278
  hotels 139, 141, 144
National Economic Development Office (NEDO) 24, 25, 27, 29–30, 32
National Institute for Economic and Social Research (NIESR) 2, 3, 7, 18, 24, 26–7, 31, 33, 119, 205
National Training Task Force 59
National Vocational Qualifications (NVQs) 12, 53, 59, 62, 139, 141
  YTS 266, 267, 270, 271, 272
NEC 179
Netherlands 120, 192, 198, 205
  apprentices 215, 217, 276
  funding training 10, 207–8, 211, 219, 225
  qualifications 9, 193–4
new technology 8, 101–2, 108, 110, 166, 190, 192

engineering 154, 155
New Training Initiative (1981) 30
New Zealand 41, 198
Nicholson, Sir Brian (chairman MSC) 36, 37, 84
Nippon Kokkan 175
Nissan 166
Non-Statutory Training Organisations (NSTOs) 34, 42, 52
Norway 198
numeracy 55, 135, 192
nursing 82, 185, 191

O grades (Scotland) 50–1
O levels 50, 79, 81, 82, 85, 87, 134
occupational labour market 234–8, 245, 252, 275
  apprentices 253–6, 258–61, 272–3, 277
  Canada 236–8, 245, 248
  Germany 251–4, 256–8, 258–61
  Hong Kong 244
  YTS 265–6, 268, 270
OKI Electric 179
ONC 87, 153
ONEM (National Employment Office of Belgium) 220–1
on-the-job training 87, 197, 212
  German dual system 77, 80
  Japan 8, 162, 170–3, 176, 177
  see also in-house training
opting out, schools 49, 58
Organization for Economic Cooperation and Development (OECD) 69, 71, 73, 249

paid educational leave 36, 219
Panasonic 226
pay 14, 33, 81, 153, 196, 215, 253, 257
  French trainees 220, 222
  German trainees 11–12, 222–3, 260–4
  hotels 143–4
  Japan 8, 162, 167, 172, 173–5
  trainees (and apprentices) 11–12, 220, 222–3, 251–6, 258–66, 270–6
  see also salaries; wages
payroll levy
  France 36, 221
  Germany 219–20

plastics 241, 243, 244
Plessey 179
plumbers 52, 102, 237
poaching 6, 104–5, 112, 167, 214, 235
polarization of skills 9, 193–5
policymakers 6, 58–9, 93, 95–6, 103, 106, 107, 110–12, 153
  comparative research 5, 16, 18, 23–5, 27, 28, 30, 38, 40–3
  design of VET 32–7
  prospective evaluation 68–9, 71–3, 75–9
  youth training 72–3, 83–5
polytechnics 167, 173, 177, 242
Portugal 198, 213
post-compulsory education in Scotland 55, 62–3
practised ability 233–4, 236, 244, 249
prices 207–8, 212, 215, 226
  hotels 124, 142–3
Private Industry Councils (PICs) 25, 40
process industry 159, 160, 164, 170, 171
Proctor and Gamble 97
productivity 2, 3, 7, 16, 18, 107, 200, 252
  HSE 96, 98, 99, 102
  Japan 15, 226
  labour per guest-night 122–4, 139
  quality of training 132–7
  service sector 119–41
programmers 185, 191, 192
promotion 3, 80, 101, 199
  internal labour market 236, 253, 257
  Japan 162, 173, 175, 176
public funding of training 70, 195–6, 215–16, 224
  Belgium 229, 221
  Denmark 210, 211
  EC 201, 207, 213, 215–16
  France 10, 207–8, 211, 213, 220, 221
  Germany 216–17
  Netherlands 219

qualifications 2, 61, 70, 102–3, 107, 110, 252, 253
  EC 9, 60, 84–5, 202
  engineering 139, 153, 154, 156, 252, 262
  Germany 1, 5–7, 77–83, 86–8, 90, 257–8, 260, 276

hotels 7, 15, 121, 125, 127–9, 131–41, 143
  Japan 167, 168
  and rewards 94, 96, 215
  school-leavers 78, 79, 85, 274
  Scotland 57
  for various jobs 186–7, 193–5, 203, 205
  YTS 265–6, 267, 270, 271, 273, 277

receptionists 121, 123, 125, 129, 131–2, 142
  qualifications 7, 127, 140
  training 134–7, 138–9
recruitment 8, 24, 34, 112, 192, 196
  apprentices 263, 277
  Canada 239, 240
  electronic engineers 146, 147, 149, 150, 152–4
  engineers 9, 160, 166
  hotel staff 130, 141
  Japan 160, 161, 166–70, 174
redundancy 24, 34, 107, 108, 256
Regional Councils (France) 221
Regional Vocational Training and Apprenticeship Fund (France) 221
research and development (R&D) 113, 163, 187, 190, 196, 201
  investment 99–100, 101, 106
  Japan 159–60, 162, 166–9, 172, 174, 176–9, 226
restaurants 109
  in hotels 122, 123, 128, 134, 137, 138
retail sector 2, 31, 109, 150, 191–2, 243
  training 82, 120, 128
retirement 161
retraining 33, 34, 38, 108, 114, 192, 196, 210
  enginering 150–2, 155
reverse engineering 165–6
risk of investment in ET 96–7, 101, 105, 227
ROSLA 58
rotation of jobs 102, 170
  Japan 8, 102, 166, 170, 173, 176, 178

salaries 94, 191
  Japan 160, 165, 175
  see also pay; wages

sandwich courses 170, 177
Scandinavia 19, 35
school-leavers 69, 94, 236
   age 50–1, 111, 167, 212, 241, 258, 274
   Canada 239
   Germany 80, 212, 216, 258, 260, 261
   Hong Kong 241
   hotels 134, 138, 141, 143
   Japan 167
   qualifications 78, 79, 85–8
   Scotland 51, 64
   YTS 265, 266, 267, 268
schools and schooling 3, 10, 11, 18, 77,
   93, 211
   Canada 238–9
   Germany 218
   Hong Kong 241
   Japan 9, 18, 111, 161
   Scotland 49, 50, 52–5, 61, 64
   TVEI 84
   see also school-leavers; secondary
      education
Schools Council Industry Project 55
Scotland 4, 5, 13, 47–65
Scottish CBI 53
Scottish Development Agency (SDA) 53,
   60
Scottish Education Department (SED)
   50, 58
   Action Plan 5, 52, 55–7, 59, 62–4
Scottish Enterprise (SE) 50, 53, 59, 60,
   64
Scottish Vocational Education Council
   (Scotvec) 51, 59
   NC modules 51, 52–3, 56, 64
Scottish Vocational Qualifications
   (SVQs) 53, 59, 64
Scottish Young People's Survey 63
secondary education 4, 84, 253
   Canada 239, 240
   Hong Kong 241
   Netherlands 225
   Portugal 213
   Scotland 50, 61
   upper 11, 18, 195, 197–8, 209, 274
secretaries 185, 191–2
   see also clerical work
Secretary of State for Scotland 50, 53, 58
service sector 2, 7, 203, 253

Canada 237, 239
Germany 188–9, 205
Hong Kong 243
Italy 191
youth training 266, 269
see also hotels
shipbuilding 24, 257
Simon, Herbert A. 68
Singapore 109, 114
Single European Act 74
Social Charter 201, 202
social partnership 37, 40, 225
social scientists 17, 69, 70–1, 73, 74, 75
Sony Walkman 226
Spain 198
Standard grades (Scotland) 50–1, 62, 64
status
   apprentices 215, 237, 260, 261
   in electronics 149
   financial sector 150
   in hotels 130, 140
   labour force 199, 253, 255
   Meister 81
   occupation 19
   qualification 102, 140
   retailing sector 150
   Scottish ET 57, 59, 60
   trainees 255, 258
   unions 108
STC 179
steel industry 113–14
   Japan 160, 164, 175, 177
strikes 97, 262–3
subsidies
   Canada 240
   Netherlands 219
   training in Europe 200–2
   UK training 227, 263, 265, 269, 272,
      273
   YTS 137, 138, 141
supervisors 7, 185, 190–1, 199, 266
   Japan 170–2, 173
   training 147, 179
Sweden 4, 34, 35, 37, 77, 97, 111, 198
   labour market 74, 76, 88, 104, 273–4
   unemployment 68–9
Swedish National Labour Market Board
   25
Switzerland 111, 120, 198

Taiwan 241
take-overs 8, 100–1, 113, 179
taxation 96
　concessions for training 178, 200, 207
　Denmark 209–11
　EC funding 207–8, 213, 214, 215–17,
　　227
　France 35, 36, 212, 217, 221
　funding training 219, 221, 226, 227
　Germany 216–17
　Netherlands 219
　Portugal 213
technical trades 187, 188–9
Technical and Vocational Education
　Initiative (TVEI) 4, 49, 84
　Scotland 54, 58, 62, 63, 64
telecommunications 109, 179, 201
textile trade *see* clothing and textiles
Thatcher, Mrs. Margaret 76, 84, 270
Toyota 168
trade unions 78, 106–8, 110, 112, 113,
　201
　apprentices 273
　Canada 237
　Denmark 210
　Germany 34, 217, 219, 259, 260–1,
　　263–4
　hotels 121, 137
　Japan 165
　low trainee pay 256, 260, 263–4, 272
　Netherlands 207
　policymaking 25, 26, 28, 32, 35, 37–9
　Scotland 57, 64
　Sweden 34
　YTS 266, 270–1
Training Agency (TA) 70, 74, 80, 82, 89,
　271
　Scotland 50, 53, 56, 58, 59, 60
training boards (Hong Kong) 243, 244,
　246–7
　see also Industrial Training Boards
Training and Enterprise Councils
　(TECs) 82, 140, 245, 247–8, 265
　policymaking 25, 34, 42, 251, 272
　Scotland 53, 58
　Wales 62
Training Insurance Funds (France) 221
Training Promotion Act (1976)
　(Germany) 217

Training Standards Advisory Services
　(TSAS) 265, 269, 270
transportation costs 109, 113
turnover of staff 129–30, 154, 256,
　268

unemployment 71–3, 79, 103, 202
　Belgium 220, 221
　Denmark 210
　France 228
　Germany 77
　Netherlands 193
　school-leavers 50
　Scotland 50, 60
　Sweden 68–9
　training 27, 31, 103, 216, 224, 247
　youth 27, 31, 60, 72–3, 75, 82
　YTS 245, 268, 270, 274
United States of America 69, 94, 100,
　107, 236, 238, 241
　comparative research 4, 18, 41, 77
　engineering 167–8
　and Japan 165, 166, 172
　PICs 25, 40
　post-compulsory education 198
　steel industry 113–14
　training 10, 33, 199–200
universities 113, 194
　Canada 239, 240
　Hong Kong 242
　Japan 161, 167–9, 173, 176, 226
　milk round 167
　qualifications 79, 88
　Scotland 50–1
　see also degrees
upgrading 31, 257–8, 276
upper-secondary education 11, 18, 195,
　197–8, 209, 274
utilities 109, 170
　Japan 159, 160, 164, 168

Vocational Training Council (VTC)
　(Hong Kong) 242, 243, 244
Vocational Training and Social
　Advancement Fund (France) 221
Volkswagen 110
VOSTA (Netherlands) 193
vouchers for training 178

wages 3, 88, 95, 97, 98, 104, 108, 109, 124, 226, 235, 265
  apprentices (Denmark) 209
  see also pay; salaries
Wales 47, 49, 121
  education 50, 51, 53, 54, 56, 62, 63
White Papers 29, 73, 202
  Employment for the 1990s 26, 33–4, 39, 40, 42, 83
women returners 240
work experience 4, 198, 277
  Canada 239, 240
  Germany 80, 82
  YTS 265, 267–70
Works Councils 256, 259

Youth Cohort Study 63
Youth Employment Levy (Ireland) 217

Youth Training Scheme (YTS) 15, 28, 35, 74, 85, 212, 265–72, 277
  and apprentices 12, 13, 259
  content 265–6
  drop outs 80
  employers 30–1
  failings 266–8
  funding 245
  hotels 128, 129, 137, 138, 141
  low quality 268–71
  low trainee pay 16
  MSC report 26
  numbers 198
  Scotland 50–1, 58, 61, 62, 64
  unemployment 80, 245, 268, 270, 274
youth unemployment 72–3, 74, 75, 82
  Scotland 60–61
  training policy 27, 31, 79–80
  YTS 80, 245, 268, 270, 274